Lao-tzu and the Tao-te-ching

Lao-tzu and the Tao-te-ching

Edited by
Livia Kohn and Michael Lafargue

State University of New York Press

Cover Art: Ink painting "Lao-tzu Writing the *Tao-te-ching*", Clifton Karhu, Kyoto. Painted specifically for this volume, property of Livia Kohn.

Chapter 1 "The Origins of the Legend of Lao Tan" by A. C. Graham first appeared in *Studies in Chinese Philosophy and Philosophical Literature*, published by the Institute of East Asian Philosophies, Singapore, 1986, and reprinted in a volume with the same title by SUNY Press in 1990. Reprinted here courtesy of Judy and Dawn Graham.

Chapter 3 "Lao-tzu in Six Dynasties Taoist Sculpture" by Yoshiko Kamitsuka contains a figure entitled "The Venerable Lord of Tu Ch'ung-?" which is a reproduction of a statue of the god Lao-tzu owned by Tokyo University of Fine Arts and Music. Used with permission. This chapter also contains a figure entitled "The Sovereign Venerable Lord of Yao Po-to," which is a reproduction of a statue of Yao Po-to, Yao District Museum, plate number 62, *Chugoku shodo zenshu*, volume 2, Wei, Jin, Nanbeichao. Used with permission.

Chapter 8 "The Thought of the Tao-te-ching" by Benjamin Schwartz originally appeared as "Lao-tzu and the ineffable Tao" from Schartz' *The World of Thought in Ancient China*. Reprinted with permission of the publishers from THE WORLD OF THOUGHT IN ANCIENT CHINA by Benjamin Schwartz, Cambridge, Mass.: Harvard University Press, Copyright © 1985 by The President and Fellows of Harvard College.

Published by

State University of New York Press, Albany

© 1998 State University of New York

For information, address the State University of New York Press,

State University Plaza, Albany, NY 12246

Production by M. R. Mulholland

Marketing by Nancy Farrell

Library of Congress Cataloging-in-Publication Data

Lao-tzu and the Tao-te-ching / edited by Livia Kohn and Michael
    LaFargue,
        p. cm.
    Includes bibliographical references and index.
    ISBN 0–7914–3599–7 (alk. paper). — ISBN 0–7914–3600–4 (pbk. :
alk. paper)
    1. Lao-tzu. Tao te ching. 2. Lao-tzu. 3. Taoism. I. Kohn,
Livia, 1956– . II. LaFargue, Michael.
B1900.L35L3755   1998
299'.51482—dc21   97–7857
                                                          CIP

10 9 8 7 6 5 4 3 2 1

Contents

Tables and Figures

Permissions

Cover Art: Ink painting "Lao-tzu Writing the *Tao-te-ching*", by Clifton Karhu, Kyoto. Painted specifically for this volume, property of Livia Kohn.

A. C. Graham, "The Origins of the Legend of Lao Tan" is reprinted from *Studies in Chinese Philosophy and Philosophical Literature*, published by the Institute of East Asian Philosophies, Singapore, 1986, and reprinted in a volume with the same title by State University of New York Press in 1990. Used by permission of the Press and the courtesy of Judy and Dawn Graham.

Benjamin Schwartz, "The Thought of the *Tao-te-ching*" is a slightly abbreviated reprint of pages 194-215 of *The World of Thought in Ancient China*, copyright Harvard University Press. Used by permission of the Press and with the author's revised ending.

Yoshiko Kamitsuka, Figure 1, "The Venerable Lord of Tu Ch'ung-?" shows an object that is currently the property of the Tokyo University of Fine Arts and Music. Photographed and reprinted with permission.

Yoshiko Kamitsuka, Figure 2, "The Sovereign Venerable Lord of Yao Po-to," shows a stele currently the property of the Yao District Museum and photographed in *Chūgoku shodō zenshū* (Tokyo: Heibonsha, 1986), 2:62. Used with permission.

Preface

The idea of this book arose when the two editors first met at a lecture organized by Boston University's Institute for Philosophy and Religion. Finding our differing perspectives and areas of expertise in regard to Lao-tzu and the *Tao-te-ching* highly complementary, we decided to put them to good use and create an integrated volume that focused equally on the text and the thinker and provided helpful guidance for teachers and students alike.

Inquiring among specialists in the field, we selected a number of relevant topics and asked scholars to contribute. Our foremost thanks at this time therefore go to our authors, who have been serious in their efforts and unstinting in their support, replying promptly to the many queries and agreeing cheerfully to necessary editorial changes. Whether writing completely new articles, rewriting existing work, allowing the translation of a previous piece, or permitting its republication, all contributors gave freely of their time and effort to make this volume possible.

We are also grateful to Harvard University Press for granting permission to reprint from Benjanmin Schwartz's *The World of Thought in Ancient China*, and to Henry Rosemont and Judy Graham for graciously allowing the renewed publication of A. C. Graham's "The Origins of the Legend of Lao Tan."

In organizing the volume and writing the introduction, moreover, we were fortunate to have the help of friends and colleagues. First and foremost, Clifton Karhu agreed to create the delightful ink painting that graces the cover. Next, Yoshiko Kamitsuka provided information on recent manuscript finds, Liu Xiaogan and Gerd Waedow informed us about the Xi'an conference, Gary Arbuckle distributed new translations of related texts over the Internet, and Russell Kirkland sent us a list of *Tao-te-ching* translations—while at the same time numerous scholars, by speaking and writing about the *Tao-te-ching*, contributed to our account of current research and created a relevant environment for this volume.

We are further indebted to our home institutions, Boston University and University of Massachusetts, Boston, for providing a fruitful and stimulating atmosphere of research. Last, and certainly not least, we would like to extend our heartfelt thanks to James Miller, who spent many hardworking hours in proofreading, editing, and xeroxing the manuscript.

A brief note on transcription. The method adopted here is the Wade-Giles system, with few exceptions, such as *yuan* and *hsuan*. Since in these cases diacritics are not necessary to avoid mispronunciation, we have opted for more simplicity. In addition, we have changed the simple *i* to *yi* because it is less confusing to English readers.

Editors' Introduction

Livia Kohn and Michael LaFargue

> Lao-tzu cultivated Tao and its virtue. He taught that one should efface oneself and be without fame in the world. He lived under the Chou dynasty. After a long time he realized that the dynasty was declining. He decided to leave. When he reached the western frontier, Yin Hsi, the guardian of the pass, said : "You want to withdraw forever. Please write down your thoughts for me." Thereupon Lao-tzu wrote a book in two sections dealing with the Tao and its virtue [the *Tao-te-ching*]. It had more than five thousand words. The he left, and nobody knows what became of him.
>
> —(*Shih-chi*, ch. 63)

Thus runs Ssu-ma Ch'ien's description of Lao-tzu writing the *Tao-te-ching*, a text so closely associated with him that it has been called the *Lao-tzu* for much of Chinese history. The old man, wise and retiring, feels the situation in his land decline and decides to leave. At the western border, a customs officer stops them, then asks about his teachings, upon which Lao-tzu writes down his ideas in a book, the which came to about five thousand words, and was arranged in two volumes and eighty-one sections. In fact, the exact character count varies among editions between 5,748, 5,722, 5,630, 5,386, and 5,610 words (Giles 1914, 70), and the order of the two volumes—the part on the Tao (Way) and that on the Te (Virtue)—were reversed in a manuscript found in 1973 at Ma-wang-tui, where it had been buried with the Marchioness of Tai in 168 B.C.E. But the eighty-one sections have remained constant, with only little variation in order and cut-off points, even though their formal definition, with headings, was only added by commentators of the early Common Era.

Both the *Tao-te-ching* and the figure of Lao-tzu have been a source of fascination for the Chinese imagination and, more recently, for the

1

imagination of people in the West and all over the world. The current volume too follows this fascination, describing the development of the Lao-tzu legend and of *Tao-te-ching* interpretation in China and the West, and presenting modern attempts at translating and interpreting the *Tao-te-ching* in the light of recent academic standards.

Several of the accounts given here may come as a surprise to Western fans of Taoism and the *Tao-te-ching*. The associations Westerners have with Taoism most often derive from popular presentations such as Fritjof Capra's *Tao of Physics* (1991), Benjamin Hoff's *The Tao of Pooh* (1982), or another of the almost one hundred books now in print beginning with "The Tao of . . . ." The image one gets from such books seems shaped to a large degree by feelings of alienation from Western culture, and in this light the teaching of the *Tao-te-ching* is construed as a simple inversion of some prominent elements of the modern sociocultural scene.

Those alienated from Western intellectualism, for example, find in the *Tao-te-ching* a rejection of analytical reason and an emphasis on following unreflective spontaneous impulse. Others, hampered by the moral strictures of conventional society, see in it a liberating radical criticism that undermines all social conventions and value judgments, a rejection of civilization in the name of a return to nature. Similarly, for Westerners alienated from government, the *Tao-te-ching* represents a populist anarchist's dream—a liberation from all government power and forms of elitism. For those, moreover, dissatisfied with authoritarian church Christianity, the text contains a substitute religionless religion or philosophy, an individual mysticism focused on an impersonal Tao, which each person can have access to within herself, the very opposite of organized religion. In short, what we basically have in the *Tao-te-ching* is a radical romantic rejection of modern social values and constrictions, the individualism of Jean-Jacques Rousseau two millennia earlier.

While this westernized vision of Taoism has become widely familiar in our society, many readers are unaware that it represents only one of the most recent examples of a continuous line of *Tao-te-ching* interpretations. From the beginning around 250 B.C.E. and over the last two millennia, the text has undergone numerous reinterpretations, each of which has reshaped its message to fit the needs and dreams of a new generation. Modern Western visions of the text and its ideas are thus widely different from the reinterpretations that many earlier Tao devotees in China have provided and which are described in this volume. One will find here, for example, that the most common and influential Taoism in traditional China was in fact that nemesis of most Western Taoists—an organized religion: a hierarchy of priests headed by a pope-like Celestial Master; a deified Lao-tzu coming from heaven to give divine revelations to the church's founder and worshiped in Taoist temple ritual as a god with the title Highest Venerable Lord; the *Tao-te-ching* used as a magical chant to secure supernatural blessings, and used also (the final insult!) as the source of a detailed list of rules to be followed by all members of the Taoist church. Those turned off by this may want to take refuge in the still common view that this, after all, is just "religious Taoism," which as everyone knows is merely a corruption of original and pure "philosophical Taoism." Yet even here one will be amazed to find that venerated philosophical Taoists in China were usually not the reclusive dropouts they are made out to be but members of the educated and elitist upper classes, who saw Taoist teachings as a foundation for the monarchical rule of an emperor and a guide to paternalist governmental policy, not as an inspiration to social withdrawal.

Thus, in traditional China each generation fascinated by Lao-tzu and the *Tao-te-ching* has reshaped the vision of thinker and text in accord with its own needs and dreams. Focusing entirely on ancient China, the contributions in the first half of this volume discuss these in historical studies, unmasking the polemical moves that contributed to the first Lao-tzu biography, showing his evolution to devotional deity of the Tao, and discussing the varying concepts associated with the text in early and later commentaries. As both Lao-tzu legends and *Tao-te-ching* interpretations are of central importance in traditional Chinese culture, these articles trace the cultural contexts and forces that were responsible for their development and multiplicity. The second half of the book, parts III and IV, then describes Western approaches to the text, looking both at the various ways its ideas have been interpreted and at the methodological issues involved in understanding and translating it. The studies trace the work from its first reception in the nineteenth century to contemporary scholarship, place its ideas both in a general Western and highly up-to-date Chinese context, study possibilities of recovering its original meaning, and critically examine some of its most frequently used English translations.

Taken together, the collection is intended to serve as an introductory survey of current scholarship on Lao-tzu and the *Tao-te-ching*, both historical and hermeneutic, that covers the ancient Chinese and Taoist traditions as much as the contemporary scholarly and philosophical.

Historical Unfolding

The *Tao-te-ching* first emerged in a period of Chinese history called the Warring States (479–221 B.C.E.). Although formally a single kingdom, the central power of the royal house of Chou was failing, and about sixteen bigger and smaller states engaged in an all-out fight for supremacy and territorial expansion. There was no one single political ideology at the time; instead, a large number of informally organized groups, the so-called hundred schools, gathered around respected teachers and traveled about to various states to advocate their moral and political teachings as solutions to the problems of the time (see Hsu 1965). The *Tao-te-ching*'s teachings of moderation, simplicity, and tranquility were thus intended as a remedy for a society deeply troubled by war and collapsing order.

Also a time of transition between a predominantly oral tradition and the growing book culture of the elite, the period saw the first philosophical compilations, representing the traditions of various schools. Rather than the product of a single author, these works were collections of material assembled over several generations—a factor that accounts for the disjointed nature of much of the writings, including also the *Tao-te-ching* (see Mair 1990). In addition, the biographies of most thinkers remain rather hazy, so that little reliable information is found about them and legends abound, those around Lao-tzu gathering particular strength.

The Warring States period came to an end in 221 B.C.E. when the western state of Ch'in defeated its competitors and united China under the first imperial dynasty. A strict military dictatorship, Ch'in rule was unpopular and short-lived. However, it created a unified empire, so that the succeeding Han dynasty (206 B.C.E.–220 C.E.) under its 400-year rule could consolidate a unified Chinese culture and political structure. Thinkers then competed for influence at the court of a single emperor and often joined together for greater political influence. As a result, Confucianism, increasingly a recruiting and training ground for government administrators, merged with traditional cosmology and adopted certain Taoist teachings. Similarly, the teaching of the *Tao-te-ching*, by then closely associated with Lao-tzu, was merged with traditional yin-yang cosmology (the teaching of the Yellow Emperor) and certain Confucian administrative ideas into the philosophy of Huang-Lao.

Huang-Lao followers believed in the intimate link between cosmology, personal cultivation, and good government. Unlike Confucians and Legalists who favored a more active regulation of society, they wanted to instruct rulers in self-cultivation that would align them with the cosmic powers and allow them to rule through nonaction, that is, by staying in the background while steering the natural flow of events with inner purity and ritual activities. They venerated the *Tao-te-ching* as an inspiration for personal purity, which would sensitize them to the cosmic flow and allow them a life of personal peace and social stability. To this end, they memorized and recited the text on a daily basis and honored its author as a sage.

The Han dynasty also saw a great development in book culture, especially after paper was invented in the first century C.E. Thus, writing, collecting, and studying books became a preoccupation of the elite, now aptly described as literati. The *Tao-te-ching* in this environment was read and recited, and received major new interpretations in commentaries, notably that of Ho-shang-kung, which reflected the thinking of Huang-Lao. At the same time Lao-tzu, credited with the text's wondrous teaching, was more closely associated with the powers of the Tao and began to receive veneration as a god.

The gradual disintegration of the Han dynasty in the second century C.E. went hand in hand with the emergence of the first religious Taoist movements, the Celestial Masters and Great Peace. Their members, hoping for a millenarian revival of the world, honored Lao-tzu as a divine manifestation of the Tao, who would appear to selected mediums and dispense instructions and revelations. The *Tao-te-ching* in this context became a sacred text, the mere chanting of which could grant long life and magical powers.

After the fall of the Han, the text rose to new prominence among the literati, especially those deprived of political office who devoted themselves to intellectual and aesthetic pursuits. Known as devotees of Pure Conversation (*ch'ing-t'an*) and Profound Learning (*hsuan-hsueh*), they wrote commentaries to many Taoist texts. Among them Wang Pi's interpretation of the *Tao-te-ching* is outstanding, providing an interpretation that, although not without political concerns, focused largely on what Western philosophers call metaphysical questions. Both his understanding and edition of the *Tao-te-ching* became standard later on.

In the following three centuries (317–589 C.E.), China was divided into a northern, Hun-ruled state and a southern Chinese dynasty, both wreaked by instabilities and frequent changes in rulership. The political insecurities together with the increased influx of Buddhism caused a major rise in Taoist activity, both religious and philosophical. New commentaries to the *Tao-te-ching* appeared, and Lao-tzu became a popular savior god, depicted prominently in religious art. While religion in the north was largely state-sponsored and Lao-tzu venerated for his gift of social peace, the south saw the rise of several new Taoist schools, each using text and god in a different way. Highest Clarity (Shang-ch'ing), for example, first founded through a revelation to the medium Yang Hsi in 364, was highly individual and aimed at conveying the practitioner into the realms of the immortals. Lao-tzu here was a god residing in the body whose vision increased the adept's immortal powers, while the *Tao-te-ching* was a magical mantra that bestowed access to heaven. Numinous Treasure (Ling-pao), on the other hand, begun by Ko Ch'ao-fu in the 390s, was a more communal form of Taoism which heavily integrated Buddhist ideas and practices. Lao-tzu here, like the Mahāyāna Buddha, was a symbol of the universe, whose powers were both prayed to and visualized in meditation. The southern Celestial Masters, finally, continued the Han vision of the god Laozi, venerating him as their central key deity, the world's creator and savior of humankind.

The T'ang dynasty, ruling the reunified empire for the next three centuries (618–906 C.E.), inherited and continued the medieval mixture of Buddho-Taoist thought and devotional practice, giving rise to new heights of *Tao-te-ching* interpretation in the school of Twofold Mystery (Ch'ung-hsuan) and raising Lao-tzu to the position of senior state-protecting deity. The succeeding Sung dynasty (960–1260), on the other hand, saw a reduction of Lao-tzu worship on the devotional level and a strong revival of Confucianism philosophically. Joining ancient Confucian moral values with the soteriological ideas of Taoism and Buddhism, the Neo-Confucian synthesis grew intellectually while denigrating the more popular practice of the organized religions. In this environment, commentaries to the *Tao-te-ching*, both philological and philosophical, abounded, reading it technically in the light of Taoist inner alchemy and morally in relation to Neo-Confucian doctrine.

Rising to state orthodoxy under the following dynasties (Yuan, 1260–1368; Ming, 1368–1644; and Ch'ing, 1644–1911), Neo-Confucianism increasingly included Taoist ideas and practices while keeping popular cults at a safe distance—an overall attitude inherited also by the Chinese communists when they came to power in 1949. Until very recently, popular religious Taoism was therefore not classed a proper religion but persecuted as "feudalistic, shamanistic, and superstitious." Taoist thought as represented by the *Tao-te-ching*, on the contrary, was tolerated and is just coming back to the foreground as a possible worldview to fill the vacuum in Chinese ideology left by the demise of communism. A conference in Xi'an in the fall of 1995 points vigorously in this direction.

In the West, the *Tao-te-ching* was first translated into French in the early nineteenth century C.E., with English renditions following in the 1860s. Soon a critical note about its authorship crept into the overall appreciation of the text, following an ancient Chinese tradition of textual criticism. Even as early as the third century, the text *Lao-tzu* was considered a forgery, a later work that had little to do with the actual ideas of the sage Lao-tzu, who—it was then believed—had been divinely inspired and indeed lived around the time of Confucius. About Ts'ui Hao (381–450), for example, a medieval statesman of north China, the dynastic history says:

> He was not fond of the writings of Lao-tzu and Chuang-tzu. Whenever he read either of them, he did not get through many pages

before he threw the book aside and cried out: "These willful and false statements, altogether out of keeping with human nature, were certainly never made by Lao-tzu!" (*Wei-shu* 35; Giles 1914, 77)

A more common argument against the authenticity of the *Tao-te-ching* as Lao-tzu's original work was the fact that none of the contemporaneous Confucian writers mentioned it. Typically people would say, "If this book was written by Lao-tzu, which would make it anterior to Mencius, how is it that Mencius, who would necessarily have denounced it, never mentioned it?" (Giles 1914, 77).

This position, already solidly established among textual critics in traditional China, came to the fore in the text's Western reception around the turn of the century, at which time the *Tao-te-ching* had already seen a number of translations: into French in parts by J. P. Abel-Rémusat in 1823, and complete by Stanislas Julien in 1842; into English by Chalmers in 1868; and into German by Victor von Strauss in 1870 (Seidel 1969, 8n2). Especially Herbert A. Giles in his essay "Lao Tzu and the *Tao te ching*," whose title we gratefully imitate in this volume, responds to James Legge by presenting a list of eighteen arguments why the *Tao-te-ching* could not possibly be a work of the sixth century: it was not mentioned in early histories or philosophers; ideas associated with Lao-tzu in the *Chuang-tzu* and *Han-fei-tzu* had little to do with the text; and even in Han-dynasty sources, statements made by Lao-tzu were usually not found in the text associated with his name (Giles 1914).

The argument has proven sound and laid the foundation for an academic tradition that divided the study of the text from that of its alleged author, analyzing its sayings and textual patterns, studying its commentaries, and producing ever greater numbers of translations, while leaving the sage aside as a semilegendary and ultimately unimportant figure. In fact, while both text and author had their distinct histories, they also went together in praise and decline and are intimately related in the very mystique that surrounds the biography and the obscurity of the text's origins. This volume therefore puts the two back together again, presenting the sage's legends together with the text's linguistic, philosophical, and interpretative dimensions.

Lao-tzu and the *Tao-te-ching* in China

The first source that connects the thinker and the text is Ssu-ma Ch'ien's *Shih-chi* (Records of the Historian), dated to 90 B.C.E. Admitting uncertainty and referring to several figures who might have been Lao-tzu, he focuses predominantly on an archivist at the royal Chou court by the name of Lao Tan. A contemporary of Confucius, Lao Tan lectured the latter in the rites and recommended that he give up all pride and desires. Later, finding the dynasty declining, Lao Tan emigrated across the pass to the west and transmitted his teaching on the Tao and its virtue.

A. C. Graham, analyzing this first biography of Lao-tzu, locates its source among originally Confucian stories, which were written to provide Confucius with a respected archivist as teacher and show his unwavering eagerness to learn. Following this, several polemical moves led to the composite legend of Lao-tzu. First, the sage was linked to the growing *Tao-te-ching* collection around 250 B.C.E., which elevated him to a senior "Taoist" thinker. Next, after the Ch'in rise in 256, he was identified with the Grand Astrologer Tan of Chou, who in 374 had predicted its supremacy—an identification that recommended Taoist advisers to the Ch'in ruler. It also established a claim of extended longevity for Lao-tzu, useful in view of the First Emperor's immortality aspirations (see Yü 1964). The story about Lao-tzu's departure for the west was then added to explain why the Old Master, although long-lived, was no longer around to advise the Ch'in emperor in person. Under the Han, finally, when the Taoists' link with the toppled Ch'in became a liability, Lao-tzu was not given up but resettled, his birthplace now near the Han rulers' place of origin in P'ei (southern Ho-nan) and his descendants of the Li clan loyal subjects to the house of Han.

Taking up where A. C. Graham leaves off, Livia Kohn's study of "The Lao-tzu Myth" gives a historical account of the process, from the Han through the Six Dynasties (200 B.C.E. to 600 C.E.), by which the figure of Lao-tzu became an immortal and divine personage venerated among both literati and peasants. Lao-tzu was adopted by various groups as an ideal representative and unifying symbol. First, practitioners of immortality stylized him as a superior magician who had achieved eternal life through wisdom and the practice of longevity techniques. Second, the elite at the imperial court divinized him as an embodiment of the transcendent Tao, a supernatural emperor who ruled the cosmos in perfect harmony and served as the source of great peace for the Chinese empire. Third, the millenaristic cults of the second century found in him the savior of the masses and inspired messiah, who appeared to their leaders in trance to dispense instructions and revelations. Finally, under the growing influence of Buddhism, the divine Lao-tzu assembled a full hagiography, being born of the virgin Jade Maiden of Mystery and Wonder, descending to create the world and support its development under the great Chinese culture heroes, and appearing in India as the Buddha to teach the values of Chinese civilization to the Indian "barbarians."

This divinized Lao-tzu of the middle ages is further evident in statues, as described by Yoshiko Kamitsuka. Found mainly in northern China under the Wei dynasty (386–534 C.E.), they are indicative of the wide popularity and complex interaction of Taoism and Buddhism, with Taoism opening the way for the early Chinese appropriation of Buddhism, and Buddhism supplying numerous doctrines and practices for Taoism—including the very idea of making statues of gods. Often Lao-tzu and the Buddha, bodhisattvas and immortals appear on the same object, jointly placed on open mountain sides to serve as mediators between heaven and earth. Prayers found in inscriptions, moreover, beg Lao-tzu and the other gods to bring good fortune to the living and help the ancestors on their journey through the otherworld. They express hopes for personal prosperity, ancestral happiness, social harmony, imperial well-being, and peace in the world—showing not only the all-inclusive powers attributed to the god but also the continued political concerns of Buddho-Taoist followers.

While the figure of Lao-tzu was divinized and venerated, the text of the *Tao-te-ching* was recited and interpreted. Discussing the two earliest and most influential commentaries of the text, by Ho-shang-kung and Wang Pi, Alan Chan places the former in the context of Huang-Lao thought, showing how it connects ideas about self-cultivation and nourishing life with cosmological speculation about *ch'i*-energy, and also with a political philosophy centered on the sage king. He then shows how the commentary by Wang Pi represents a reaction against this cosmological thought from the viewpoint of a sophisticated intellectual with philosophical or metaphysical leanings. Highly valued by the literati, Wang Pi's commentary established both the standard edition of the text and the mainstream interpretation of its ideas.

The interpretive tradition continues with numerous works written in later dynasties. As Isabelle Robinet's analysis of about thirty commentaries shows, the *Tao-te-ching* under the T'ang, Sung, and Yuan dynasties was interpreted both philologically and philosophically, scholars collecting glosses and repunctuating the text to find new meanings. In terms of general outlook, Taoist, Buddhist, and Confucian tendencies can be distinguished: Taoists read the text as a manual for self-cultivation, nourishing life, or the practice of inner alchemy; Buddhists found philosophical statements about emptiness and nonbeing in its verses; and Confucians saw state-supporting virtues and advice for self-improvement contained in its lines.

The study of the Chinese tradition concludes with a second contribution by Livia Kohn that focuses on the ritual and liturgical uses of the *Tao-te-ching*. It was applied as a source of codified guidelines and rules for the faithful, a magical chant to bring benefits to believers, and as a manual of meditation instruction. In addition, the *Tao-te-ching* was used in rituals undertaken to communicate with the immortals and became one of the key texts to be transmitted at Taoist ordination.

From the first traces of the Lao-tzu legend to Neo-Confucian commentaries and Taoist ritual, the multiplicity of interpretations and visions of both text and thinker document their richness and importance in traditional Chinese culture. Highly controversial and multifaceted from the beginning, both man and book unfolded gradually and to ever higher ranges of sophistication and cultural complexity. It is no wonder, then, that the Western reception of the text has also been complex and led to manifold speculations and renditions.

The *Tao-te-ching* in the West

The *Tao-te-ching* made its Western debut in the late eighteenth century and has been vigorously used and adapted ever since. As Julia Hardy describes it, in every generation the dominant concerns of Western readers have determined their understanding and interpretation of the text. Thus the first interpreters, as Christian missionaries, were preoccupied with questions about similarities and differences to Christian doctrine. Later came discussions of religion versus philosophy, of whether the ideas of the *Tao-te-ching* represented a rational and this-worldly philosophy or a quasi-religious mysticism centered on a world-transcending absolute. Finally, Westerners found in the text solutions to modern problems, adapting the text to their own cultural environment. While such reception led occasionally to "Orientalist" interpretations of the *Tao-te-ching* that were shaped more by the needs and dreams of interpreters than by the text itself, they also contributed to its Western adaptation, continuing the very same processes that had made the book so important in traditional China. The kind of alternative religion developed by this type of interpretation may even have much to offer in the context of America's problems today, "bad scholarship" ultimately leading to "good religion."

The multivalence of *Tao-te-ching* visions becomes clear in the work of Benjamin Schwartz, reprinted here from his *The World of Thought in Ancient China* (1985). The *Tao-te-ching* can be read as a religious, political, military, or naturalistic treatise, dealing with psychology, the natural world, or society. And even if one decides on one particular reading, contradictions abound. Thus, while there is an obvious relation of the "ineffable Tao" to the absolute of mystics, it is not clear whether the Tao is immanent or transcendent. While there also seems to be a naturalistic philosophy in the text that could be linked with modern Western science, it yet shows a high concern for government policy and advice on human activity. Similarly, the text contains both a strong rejection of all value-judgments and clear preferences for one member of the opposite pairs that it poses (softness over hardness, femininity over masculinity, etc.). Sorting out these various positions and their interrelation, Schwartz illuminates the complexity of *Tao-te-ching* thought as seen by Western scholars.

In modern China, on the other hand, the text's complexity is taken in stride and streamlined to offer a practical philosophy one can hold on to in one's daily life. Foremost here are the value of naturalness (*tzu-jan*) and its practical application in nonaction (*wu-wei*). Focusing on these two concepts, Liu Xiaogan demonstrates how the *Tao-te-ching* can still be relevant for people in China today, especially now when the traditional values of Confucianism have been badly battered and communism is not a valid alternative any more. Such a practical relevance of the text does not have to ignore its history either. Aware of the vast cultural gap that separates us from the world in which the *Tao-te-ching* was originally composed, Liu does not simply read preconceived ideas into the text but presents a historical analysis of several passages on naturalness and nonaction. Only after that does he point out ways of applying the two concepts today, showing how a "natural" life could improve people's lot so that they can make valid decisions that encourage modernity and change but do not force life along through abrupt transitions. Thus in accordance with naturalness, people can live in a harmony that grows from the inside and is not imposed by domineering governments.

Focusing away from the various philosophical readings of the *Tao-te-ching*, critical Western scholarship is also looking back at the text itself. William Baxter, in a linguistic analysis, shows how the rhyme structure and the rhetorical characteristics of the text, such as rhythm, repetition of words, and the use of paradoxes, go back to a period of about 350 B.C.E., being similar to certain patterns found in the *Shih-ching* (Book of Odes) and the *Ch'u-tz'u* (Songs of Ch'u), but neither consonant with nor contemporaneous with them. He documents the importance of recovering the actual words of the text and not losing sight of the root from which the philosophy ultimately stems.

A similar concern with the text is found in Michael LaFargue's work on historical hermeneutics, the attempt to recover the original meaning of the text in its sociocultural context through careful analysis of its sayings and proverbs as understood in the society of the time. Unlike Isabelle Robinet, who takes the inherent polysemy of the text for granted, LaFargue does not believe that the *Tao-te-ching* is originally or by nature polysemic. It had some definite meaning for its original authors and audience, and only became polysemic when it was read outside of its original context, in the light of alien assumptions and concerns. The fact that this definite message cannot be directly conveyed in straightforward speech is due to the limitations of language, not to the vagueness and indeterminate character of the meaning itself. At the same time, a traditional "scriptural" reading of the *Tao-te-ching*, which uses it to reconfirm previously held views, does not constitute an "illegitimate misuse" of the text. Scriptural reading is just one kind of reading, different from a reading informed by historical research. These two ways of reading have different aims, which must be kept separate. The original meaning of the *Tao-te-ching*, then, can be elucidated by studying its proverb-like aphorisms, seen no longer as statements of general laws or philosophical first principles, but as sayings with specific meanings relevant to the ancient Chinese.

The position of the Western scholar as determined by training in linguistic, hermeneutic, and historical disciplines becomes highly relevant when it comes to translating the *Tao-te-ching*. As Michael LaFargue and Julian Pas show in the last chapter of the volume, there are serious problems anyone encounters in rendering this difficult classic into English. Beginning with questions of edition—should one use the transmitted version of Wang Pi or the earlier Ma-wang-tui manuscript?—any translator has to deal with details of the language: the use of "loan characters" in ancient Chinese, the wide range of meaning of some words, and the vagaries of the syntax of an uninflected language. Once the edition is settled and the meaning of the words clarified, further decisions have to be made: How literal should one be? How much should one paraphrase? Should one translate for anyone, taking the text out of its historical context? Or should one prepare a rendition that requires background knowledge about ancient China? Should one pay more attention to getting ideas across or try to stick as closely to the style of the original as possible? Every translator deals with these problems differently, which partly accounts for the sometimes startling discrepancies among *Tao-te-ching* translations. Clarifying the issues and comparing seventeen of the most influential English translations (with detailed samples), the contribution provides a guideline for nonspecialist readers on how to select a suitable *Tao-te-ching* translation.

Current Trends

Neither study nor translation or interpretation of the *Tao-te-ching* are anywhere near complete. The text continues to furnish scholars with new materials, there still appear several new translations every year (e.g.,

Möller 1995), and its meaning is seen in ever new relevance both in the West and in China. One clear indication of the Chinese revival of Lao-tzu's thought is a conference held in Xi'an, October 23-27, 1995, which focused entirely on the text and had the title "Lao-tzu— Interpretation and Impact" (Hoster and Waedow 1995, 156). Sponsored by the Chinese Academy of Social Sciences, Beijing, and the provincial government of Shensi in cooperation with the German Konrad-Adenauer-Foundation and the academic journal *Monumenta Serica*, it assembled sixty-five scholars from China and Germany to speak about nothing but the *Tao-te-ching*, its inherent ideas and potential for stimulating social change today. The expressed purpose of the meeting, aside from improving current understanding of the ancient text, was to "offer a perspective to the younger Chinese generation in its search for a meaningful way of life in a society that is increasingly characterized by a capitalist strife for profit, social hardship, self-alienation, and insecure future for the individual" (Hoster and Waedow 1995, 156). The ancient *Tao-te-ching*, in a mode closely resembling its uses in the West, is thus called upon to support China in her search for a new cultural identity and a way to modernization, providing contemporary inspiration on the basis of ancient tradition.

Following various addresses of welcome and presidential greetings, about forty presentations were given, nine of them by German scholars, who often focused on the text's reception in Western thought (e.g., "Lao-tzu Reception in the Thought of Martin Heidegger"). The remainder were by Chinese scholars, who in some cases dealt with general or programmatic points ("Suggestions for a History of Lao-tzu Studies") or with the overall metaphysical interpretation of the text ("The World of the Tao in Lao-tzu's Thought"). Many of them also concentrated on bringing out the relevance of the book in contemporary China. Topics here included "The Meaning of Lao-tzu's Philosophy Today," "Ethical Thinking in *Lao-tzu*," "Taoist Thought and Social Change," "Lao-tzu's Reflections about the Dignity of Human Life," and "The Importance of Taoist Thought for the Modern Transformation of Chinese Culture" (Hoster and Waedow 1995, 157).

In addition, six Chinese presentations specifically discussed naturalness and nonaction, as also treated by Liu Xiaogan in this volume, reflecting the contemporary importance of these concepts. Overall, so the reports, the discussion was engaged yet disciplined and wishes were expressed for an increased exchange with Western thinkers and *Tao-te-ching* interpreters. Despite an overall emphasis on the philosophical doctrines of the book, moreover, the devotional aspect was not entirely neglected, so that on the last day of the meeting participants had the opportunity to visit Lou-kuan-t'ai, the Taoist monastery in the Chung-nan mountains where, according to the legend, Lao-tzu transmitted the *Tao-te-ching* to the border guard Yin Hsi (Hoster and Waedow 1995, 158).

A similar trend of keeping the text's message alive was also seen at the Ninth International Congress in Chinese Philosophy, held in Boston in August 1995, where six presentations focused on the book. Ellen-Marie Chen spoke about the "Key Metaphysical Idea in Taoism" and compared it to ancient Greek thought, finding that the *Tao-te-ching* emphasizes nonbeing and change, where the Greeks focus on being and stability. Similarly, Taoist thought is immanent, where Western thinking strives for transcendence; the mind is seen as an obstacle in China but features as the key means to realization in Greece. Overall, these differences reflect a shift away from the feminine matrix to masculine predominance in the West, a shift that had not yet taken place in the *Tao-te-ching*, which consequently "is perhaps the world's oldest functioning feminist metaphysics" (Chen 1995).

Also a comparative approach was taken by Wang Qingjie in his work on the term *heng* or "constancy." Expressing a vision of the Tao as in constant flux, like water, the term is linked with ideas of return (*fan*) and permanence (*chiu*), and compares to the ancient Greek understanding of constant motion, relating it further to concepts like *logos*, *physis*, Heidegger's *Ereignis*, and Derrida's *différance* (Wang 1995). Similarly applying Western analysis to Taoist philosophical method, Xiao Jinfu described the aim of Taoist thought as transcending the limitations of the visible world and attain the universe's origin. To reach this aim, Taoist thinkers move from relativism to dialectics, recognizing the interdependence of opposites and using this recognition as a basis to equalize and transcend them. Reaching a point where only Tao as Tao or Tao as not-Tao remain, they move beyond all limitations of conscious knowledge. This process of ancient Chinese thought as manifested in the *Tao-te-ching*, according to Wang, can help Western philosophy to reach new positions (Wang 1995).

Moving further in the same direction, Cristal Nuang related Lao-tzu's dialectical methodology of confronting opposites to Derrida's deconstructionist hermeneutics. She documented the text's high awareness of the hermeneutic process, which in all cases works through a dialectic relation between the interpreting subject and the interpreted object, moving to ever new understandings of meaning. The *Tao-te-ching* in particular proceeds in continuous hermeneutic circles to ever subtler ranges of deconstruction, always raising the awareness of the interpreting subject in relation to the interpreted object (Nuang 1995). In addition, there were two presentations specifically on naturalness and nonaction in contemporary society, emphasizing the need to adapt to the ongoing flux of natural processes without giving up scientific knowledge and technology (Liu 1995; Zhang 1995).

Taken together, the two conferences with their many contributions on the *Tao-te-ching* and its thought show the increased relevance of the text in the modern world. It plays a key role in scholarship as it helps to elucidate fundamental similarities and differences between ancient Chinese and Western modes of thought. It is also highly relevant to formulating a new Chinese awareness of subjectivity, dignity, and human rights, thus participating actively in the new philosophical climate in mainland China (see Li, Hargett, and Ames 1995). However abstruse and difficult the text itself, its message, in historically researched form or modern interpretation, continues to provide inspiration for thought and practical living.

New Studies

Academic analysis of the text outside of philosophy, too, has not ceased. A recent Western study by John Emerson, for example, proposes a detailed analysis of the various layers that make up the *Tao-te-ching*, distinguishing four strata: an early layer that focuses on themes of mother, child, chaos, namelessness, and return, and that is more introverted and "mystical" in nature; a medium layer that retains the return theme without the mother/child image and adds paradox sequences of reversal, focusing more on abstract, intellectual aguments; an added layer—the odd one out—that deals with endurance, longevity, and promises of success; and a later layer that is more outward and politically oriented, "the locus of the sly political devices that gave Laozi a bad name with the Confucians" (Emerson 1995, 8).

Another recent work, by the Japanese scholar Mukai Tetsuo that picks up on an earlier study by Wang Ming (1984), looks at the relation of the *Tao-te-ching* to the *Liu-t'ao* or "Six Tactics," a pre-Han military treatise ascribed to the founding saint of the Chou dynasty and military genius T'ai-kung Wang (see Allan 1972). It was thought a later reconstitution until a manuscript was found in 1972 at Lin-yi (Shan-tung) that could be dated to the second century B.C.E. Not only rather close to a number of passages in various pre-Han philosophers, the work shows a close connection to the *Tao-te-ching* and can be ranked among its immediate precursors, thus placing it in a more political and military context rather removed from metaphysics and mysticism (Mukai 1994).

The dating of the *Tao-te-ching*, apparently settled on at about 250 B.C.E., too, has come under new scrutiny, both from linguistic studies and from new manuscript finds. Liu Xiaogan in particular argues that after a long period of grave doubts about their authenticity and reliability, Chinese scholars are recovering trust in traditional sources. In a recent book he writes extensively in favor of an early date of the *Chuang-tzu*, which, he says, was complete in much of its present form before unification in 221 B.C.E. (Liu 1994a). Along the same lines, and supported by extensive comparisons of rhymes in the *Tao-te-ching* with those in the *Shih-ching* (Book of Songs), he argues for an early date of the text, placing it around the lifetime of Confucius (551–479 B.C.E.). He thereby rehabilitates the ancient story of the *Shih-chi*, so strongly criticized by A. C. Graham.

Unresolvable by mere textual analysis, the fires of this debate are further stoked by archaeology. Opening a tomb of the southern Ch'u culture in Ching-men township (Hu-pei) in August 1993, the local archaeological team unearthed 804 bamboo slips containing roughly 16,000 characters of text. The materials, dated to the mid–Warring States period or fourth century B.C.E., are as yet unpublished but said to contain parts of five ancient philosophical works, including the *Tao-te-ching*. First claimed an entirely new version of the book, shorter and written in dialogue format (*Chung-kuo wen-wu pao*, March 19, 1995), the so-called "Bamboo Lao-tzu" was later recognized as yet another variant of the Ma-wang-tui manuscripts already translated. It was buried together with other philosophical works, which were indeed written in dialogue (*Chung-kuo wen-wu pao*, August 20, 1995). Still, even without shocking surprises, the discovery of this bamboo manuscript throws new light on the origins and antiquity of the text, making it clear that it existed well before 250 B.C.E. There is no telling what this and future archaeological finds will yet uncover to revise and extend our knowledge of the ancient classic.

Along slightly different lines, the tradition of the *Tao-te-ching* in China receives further elucidation by the study of related later works, some of which are discussed avidly on Internet forums. An example here is Gary Arbuckle's presentation and partial translation of the "Sixteen Canons," a manuscript discovered in Ma-wang-tui. "Holding on to the female," an obscure phrase in the *Tao-te-ching* is thus clarified to mean following the guidance of the Empress who calculates cosmic tendencies by examining the proportion of disastrous male influence—expressed in "arrogance, excess, love of strife, and plotting in secret"—and beneficent female influence, described as being "compliant and good, respectful and frugal, humble and restrained" (Internet communication, 1995).

Texts in the Taoist canon are another source for the increased interpretation of the *Tao-te-ching*. To give just one example, the late T'ang *Ch'ing-ching-ching* (Scripture of Purity and Tranquility) is notable for its combination of *Tao-te-ching* ideas with the practice of religious Taoist meditations and the structure of the Buddhist *Heart Sūtra*, a collection of essential ("heart") passages and spells from a longer scripture used for inspiration, meditation,, and ritual (Nattier 1992, 175). Not only an adaptation of the *Tao-te-ching* in a completely different religious environment, the text later became the central scripture of the monastic school of Complete Perfection (Ch'üan-chen), where it is recited daily to the present day. The text has two recently English translations (Kohn 1993, 24–29; Wong 1992) and is increasingly studied, for instance by Mitamura Keiko in a critical examination of its earliest commentary by the later T'ang Taoist Tu Kuang-t'ing (Mitamura 1994).

Last but not least, the god Lao-tzu has moved back into the scholarly limelight. In China he features prominently in the recently published series on "Taoism and Chinese Culture" (Zhu 1992, 5–15; Li 1993, 19–41), and has even merited a detailed journalistic account of his myths and history (Wang 1991). In the West, after the pathbreaking work of Anna Seidel on his divinization under the Han (1969) and Florian Reiter's translation of his illustrated Yuan-dynasty hagiography (1990), he plays an important role in Kristofer Schipper's work (1994) and has a lengthy entry in the *Encyclopedia of Religion* (Boltz 1987).

All this shows that, as over the millennia so today, Lao-tzu and the *Tao-te-ching* play a continuous role in Chinese culture, being ever newly appropriated and reinterpreted. In all cases, the text and its author have never stood alone but were presented in the changing light of the ages, interpreted by new readers, and connected with various contemporaneous contexts. The ancient legend of the text's transmission for this reason has never lost its relevance but continues to demonstrate in a mythological way that the sage never stands alone and formulates his ideas only in active cultural context and for the sake of a specific audience. Just as Yin Hsi thus extracted the *Tao-te-ching* from the emigrating Lao-tzu, so hundreds of generations have distilled their particular vision of the world from its words, and are still doing so. Reception and interpretation are therfore as much part of the work as its words and sentences and must not be relegated to an inferior position.

References

Allan, Sarah. 1972. "The Identities of T'ai-kung-wang in Chou and Han Literature." *Monumenta Serica* 29: 57–99.

Boltz, Judith M. 1987. "Lao-tzu." In *Encyclopedia of Religion*, ed. Mircea Eliade, 8: 454–59. New York: Macmillan.

Capra, Fritjof. 1991 [1975]. *The Tao of Physics: An Exploration of the Parallels between Modern Physics and Eastern Mysticism* Boston: Shambhala.

Chen, Ellen Marie. 1995. "Towards a Metaphysical Key in Taoism: A Comparative Study on Greek and Taoist Metaphysics." Paper presented at the 9th International Congress in Chinese Philosophy, Boston.

Emerson, John. 1995. "A Stratification of Lao Tzu." *Journal of Chinese Religions* 23: 1–28.

Giles, Herbert A. 1914. "Lao-tzu and the Tao-te-ching." In *Adversaria Sinica*, ed. Herbert A. Giles, 58–78. Shanghai: Kelly & Walsh.

Hoff, Benjamin. 1982. *The Tao of Pooh*. New York: Dutton.

Hoster, Barbara, and Gerd Waedow. 1995. "Internationale Konferenz in Xi'an: Laozi — Interpretation und Wirkung." *China Heute* 14.6: 156–58.

Hsu Cho-yun. 1965. *Ancient China in Transition: An Analysis of Social Mobility, 722–222 B.C.*. Stanford, Calif.: Stanford University Press.

Kohn, Livia. 1993. *The Taoist Experience: An Anthology*. Albany: State University of New York Press.

Li Longqi, Henry Rosemont, and Roger T. Ames. 1995. "Chinese Philosophy: A Philosophical Essay on the `State-of-the-Art'." *Journal of Asian Studies* 54: 727–58.

Liu Xiaogan. 1994a. *Classifying the Zhuangzi Chapters*. Ann Arbor: University of Michigan, Center for Chinese Studies, Monographs, no. 65.

———. 1994b. "Lao-tzu tsao-ch'i shuo-shih hsin-ch'eng." *Tao-chia wen-hua yenchiu* 4: 419–37.

———. 1995. "Naturalness, the Core Value of Taoism." Paper presented at the 9th International Congress in Chinese Philosophy, Boston.

Mair, Victor. 1990. "*[The] File [on the Cosmic] Track [and Individual] Dough[tiness]*: Introduction and Notes for a Translation of the Ma-wang-tui Manuscripts of the *Lao-tzu [Old Master]*. *Sino-Platonic Papers*. Philadelphia: Department of Oriental Studies, University of Pennsylvania.

Mitamura Keiko. 1994. "Taijō rōkun setsu chō seishōkyō chu ni tsuite." In *Dōkyō bunka e no tembō*, ed. Doōyō bunka kenkyūkai, 80–98. Tokyo: Hirakawa.

Möller, Hans-Georg. 1995. *Laotse: Tao Te King. Nach den Seidentexten von Mawangdui*. Frankfurt: Fischer.

Mukai Tetsuō. 1994. "Rikutō no kisoteki kenkyū." *Tōhōshūkyō* 83: 32–51.

Nattier, Jan. 1992. "The Heart Sutra: A Chinese Apocryphal Text?" *Journal of the International Association of Buddhist Studies* 15.2: 153–223.

Nuang, Cristal. 1995. "Lao-Zi, his Dialectical Interpretation of Logos and the De-constructing Model of Understanding." Paper presented at the 9th International Congress in Chinese Philosophy, Boston.

Reiter, Florian C., ed. 1990. *Leben und Wirken Lao-Tzu's in Schrift und Bild. Lao-chün pa-shih-i-hua t'u-shuo*. Würzburg, Germany: Königshausen & Neumann.

Schipper, Kristofer. 1994. *The Taoist Body*. Translated by Karen C. Duval. Berkeley: University of California Press.

Seidel, Anna. 1969. *La divinisation de Lao-tseu dans le Taoisme des Han*. Paris: École Françise d'Extrême-Orient. Reprinted 1992.

Wang Ming. 1984. "Lun Lao-tzu ping-shu." In *Tao-chia ho tao-chiao ssu-hsiang yen-chiu*, ed. Wang Ming, 27–36. Ch'ung-ch'ing, PRC: Chong-kuo she-hui k'o-hsueh ch'u-pan-she.

Wang Qingjie. 1995. "Heng Tao—A New Vision of Tao." Paper presented at the 9th International Congress in Chinese Philosophy, Boston.

Wong, Eva. 1992. *Cultivating Stillness: A Taoist Manual for Transforming Body and Mind*. Boston: Shambhala.

Xiao Jinfu. 1995. "The Modern Significance of Taoist Academic Style." Paper presented at the 9th International Congress in Chinese Philosophy, Boston.

Yü Ying-shih. 1964. "Life and Immortality in the Mind of Han China." *Harvard Journal of Asiatic Studies* 25: 80–122.

Zhang Bingnan. 1995. "Man Emulates Nature: The Modern Significance of an Ancient Philosophical Thesis." Paper presented at the 9th International Congress in Chinese Philosophy, Boston.

Part 1

Ancient Myths

1

The Origins of the Legend of Lao Tan

A. C. Graham

Editor's Introduction

The philosopher Lao-tzu is first known from his biography in Ssu-ma Ch'ien's Shih-chi (Records of the Historian), dated to 104 B.C.E., which focuses on an ancient figure called Lao Tan.[1] The account here runs as follows:

Lao-tzu was a man of Ch'ü-jen village of Lai District of Hu Province in Ch'u. Surname: Li. Personal name: Erh. Style: Tan. He was a historiographer in charge of the archives of Chou.

Confucius once traveled to Chou because he wished to ask Lao-tzu about the rites. Lao-tzu said: "The sages you speak about have long withered along with their bones. Also, when a gentleman attains proper timeliness, he rides in a carriage; when his time has not come, he wanders about with the wind. I have heard that a good merchant fills his storehouses but appears to have nothing; a true gentleman is overflowing with virtue but looks as if he was a fool. Give up your prideful airs and your manifold desires, get rid of your stiff deportment and your lacscivious thoughts. All these do you no good at all. I have nothing else to tell you."

Confucius left and later told his disciples, "Birds, I know, can fly; fish, I know, can swim; animals, I know, can run. For the running one can make a net; for the swimming one can make a line; for the flying one can make an arrow. But when it comes to the dragon, I have no means of knowing how it rides the wind and the clouds and ascends into heaven. Today I have seen Lao-tzu who really is like unto a dragon."

Lao-tzu cultivated the Tao and its Virtue. He taught that one should efface oneself and be without fame in the world. After he had lived in Chou for a long time, he perceived the Chou was in decline, so departed. When

23

he reached the passes, the keeper of the pass, Yin Hsi, said: "We shall be seeing no more of you. I insist that you write a book for us." Lao-tzu wrote them a book in two parts, discussing the ideas of the Way and of Virtue in some 5,000 words, and departed. No one knows where he ended his life.

Some sources speak of one Lao-lai-tzu who also came from Ch'u. He authored a work in fifteen sections, which speaks of the practical uses of the Taoist school. He also was a contemporary of Confucius.

It seems that Lao-tzu lived at least 160 years, some say at least 200 years, as a result of cultivating the Way and nurturing longevity.

One hundred twenty-nine years after the death of Confucius [479 B.C.E.], the historiographers record that Tan, Grand Historiographer of Chou, visited Duke Hsien of Ch'in and said: "At first Ch'in was joined with Chou. Having been joined 500 years, they parted. After having been parted seventy years, a hegemon and king will arise here." Some say Tan was Lao-tzu, some say not. No one in our time knows whether or not it is so.

Lao-tzu's son had the personal name Tsung. Tsung was a general of Wei, enfiefed in Tuan-kan. Tsung's son was Chu, Chu's son Kung. Kung's great-great-grandson was Chia. Chia held office under Emperor Wen of Han [179–157 B.C.E.] and Chia's son Chieh became tutor of Ang, Prince of Chiao-hsi, and so settled in Ch'i.

The following essay by A. C. Graham investigates each item of information offered in the above biography as to its earliest source, finding that Lao-tzu's name, birthplace, genealogy, and emigration appear here for the first time. Only the incident about Confucius is older and thus serves as the starting point of the entire legend, with a connection to the Tao-te-ching and the Grand Historiographer Tan added later.[2]

A modern reader approaches the legend of Lao Tan with certain questions in mind. Is he a historical person? If so, when did he live? What is his relation to the book *Lao-tzu*? Since we have little evidence other than frankly fictitious dialogues in *Chuang-tzu*, inquiry usually starts from the biography by Ssu-ma Ch'ien, that puzzling litter of odds and ends—particulars of name, place and office, two events (the visit of Confucius, the journey to the west), two tentative identifications, a genealogy of descendants—which Arthur Waley described as amounting to "a confession that for the writing of such a biography no materials existed at all" (Waley 1934, 108).

Preoccupation with this source tends to distract attention from a guiding thread which can be traced throughout the older traditions. From its origins in the fourth century B.C.E., the nucleus of the legend, and its only constant element, is the meeting of Lao Tan with Confucius. There may be advantages then in approaching familiar problems from another direction, asking different questions. How did the legend of Lao Tan originate and develop? Was he known from the beginning as the author of the *Lao-tzu*, as the founder of Taoism, even as a Taoist at all? What philosophical and political interests have shaped the story in the different stages of its growth?

Lao Tan in Early Sources

Down to the time of Ssu-ma Ch'ien (145–90 B.C.E.), Lao Tan is never called Li Erh or said to come from Ch'u. A few references in the "Outer" and "Mixed Chapters" of the *Chuang-tzu*[3] and the *Lü-shih ch'un-ch'iu* to a Taoist philosopher Kuan-yin ("Keeper of the Pass"), presumably the official to whom, according to Ssu-ma Ch'ien, Lao-tzu presented his book before his departure, suggest that the story of the journey to the west was already current by 240 B.C.E.[4] However, there are no direct allusions to the story, and a reference to Lao Tan's funeral in the "Inner Chapters" (8/3/14) shows that it does not belong to the oldest stratum of the legend. On the other hand, the meeting with Confucius is attested at every stage, although developed treatments, Taoist or Confucian, are of uncertain date. *Chuang-tzu* has no less than seven dialogues with Confucius, all in the "Outer Chapters."[5]

In this cycle, Lao Tan, with ineffable condescension, instructs the humble sage in the Taoist message. In one episode, Lao Tan is a retired archivist in Chou, and Confucius first visits him to deposit the "Twelve Classics" (*Chuang-tzu* 35/13/46); in another, Confucius in old age comes to P'ei to inquire about the Way (38/14/44). The "Outer Chapters" are quite heterogeneous, and their materials may come from any time between the fourth and the second centuries B.C.E. But in two of the episodes, it has long been noticed that there is evidence of Han-dynasty origins in their references to the "Twelve Classics," traditionally understood as the six *ching* (classics) plus the six *wei* (Han-dynasty apocrypha). Even the enumeration "Six Classics" is unattested before the Han. Moreover, the depositing of the classics suggests the Ch'in burning of the books [in 213 B.C.E.], and P'ei was the ancestral home of the Han.[6]

A similar problem arises with the Confucian *Tseng-tzu-wen* (Questions of Tseng-tzu), in which Confucius four times quotes Lao Tan as a teacher from whom he learned about funeral rites. In this source, there are no historical or biographical details, but one notices with interest that as in *Chuang-tzu* Lao Tan is a senior who address the Master by his personal name Ch'iu. As for its date, its inclusion in the *Li-chi* (Book of Rites) is evidence only that it is not later than the last century B.C.E., and the recent editor of the *Li-chi* Wang Meng-ou can add only that its use of Kung-yang learning suggests that it belongs to the Han (Wang 1960, 243).

Also Confucian, or at any rate not specifically Taoist, are an isolated dialogue in the *Shuo-yuan* (Garden of Stories)[7] and Ssu-ma Ch'ien's previous account of Lao Tan's meeting with Confucius, occasioned by the Master's journey to Chou to inquire about the rites (*Shih-chi* 47.1909). Both these episodes reappear in the *K'ung-tzu chia-yü* (K'ung Family Annals), which in its present form dates from the third century C.E.[8]

The Teacher of Confucius

In *Chuang-tzu* and elsewhere Lao Tan does, of course, talk to others besides Confucius. But in these dialogues, which have little or no narrative setting, he is merely one of many interchangeable spokesmen of Taoism. What distinguishes the dialogues with Confucius from the rest is not merely that they are especially numerous, but that throughout the Taoist, Confucian, and eclectic sources, the meeting itself is something more than a prop for imaginary dialogues. It rather is an *event*, the one thing everybody knows about Lao Tan. The very first mention of it is an indirect one, in the story in the "Inner Chapters" about the man with a chopped foot who studied under Confucius (13/5/29). Talking about Confucius afterwards with Lao Tan, he remarks: "Why does he make all that fuss about having learned from you?"[9] Similarly, when Tzu-kung goes to see Lao Tan, it is after hearing the Master's enthusiastic report of his own visit (*Chuang-tzu* 39/14/60–74). When Yang Tzu-chü travels to call on Lao Tan it is at P'ei, the place (otherwise unmentioned in *Chuang-tzu*) of the meeting with Confucius (77/27/26; 38/14/44).

There are also a couple of points, on which the dialogues with Confucius seem to serve as models for others in the *Chuang-tzu*. We have noticed that, both there and in the *Tseng-tzu-wen*, Lao Tan addresses Confucius as Ch'iu. Use of personal name is not a usual Taoist gesture of irreverence (Chuang-tzu's other great butt, the sophist Hui Shih, is never called Shih except by himself in 94/33/81), and of course in the Confucian document is not irreverence at all. But there are three dialogues in *Chuang-tzu*, one of them in the "Inner Chapters," in which Confucius is addressed or mentioned as Ch'iu by others than Lao Tan, as though they were following his example.[10] Again, the use of Ch'iu is only the most obvious symptom of the tone of authority assumed by Lao Tan toward

Confucius, at its most extreme in the aggressive personal criticisms of the *Shih-chi* biography.[11] But we find the same brutal directness in his conversation in *Chuang-tzu* with Shih-ch'eng Ch'i (35/13/53–60), with Nan-jung Ch'u (62/23/23–42), and with Yang Tzu-chü (76/27/25–30).

Before he came to be recognized as founder of the Taoist school, what could give Lao Tan the right to assume this tone? What else but that even Confucians acknowledge that he talked down to their own Master, so he can say what he likes to anybody?

Apart from the allusion in the "Inner Chapters," acceptable as written by Chuang-tzu himself in the late fourth century B.C.E., the earliest firmly datable reference to the meeting is the "Tang-jan" (Infections) section of the *Lü-shih ch'un-ch'iu* (ca. 240 B.C.E.), which has, "Confucius learned from Lao Tan, Meng Su, and K'uei Ching-shu" (2.4a; Hsü 2.16a). The two other teachers mentioned are otherwise unknown. Since the theme of this essay is the importance of being influenced by the right teacher and it extols the Confucians and Mohists with their successive generations of teachers and disciples, the implication is certainly not that Lao Tan converted Confucius to Taoism. The tradition assumed must be the Confucian one, of Lao Tan as a teacher of the rites. This is certainly the case in the Confucian *Han-shih wai-chuan* (Outer Transmission of the Songs of Han; ca. 150 B.C.E.), where Tzu-hsia illustrates the importance of learning by listing the teachers of eleven sages.[12] The last item in the series is "Confucius learned from Lao Tan." Here it is interesting that, with a choice of three names in the *Lü-shih ch'un-ch'iu*, a Confucian should pick Lao Tan.

The Origins of the Story

How did the story originate? As Taoist propaganda against Confucianism or as a Confucian moral tale of the Master's willingness to submit himself to an insignificant teacher of the rites, of which Taoists later took advantage?

We are so habituated to thinking of Lao Tan as the founder of Taoism that it takes an effort of the imagination to consider the second possibility, yet there is nothing inherently improbable about it. It was accepted practice for Taoists to borrow the spokesmen of their enemies, even Confucius himself. Nothing could be more natural than to play this trick with a teacher acknowledged by Confucians to have been entitled to address their founder condescendingly by his personal name. The writing of the text *Lao-tzu* in his name would consolidate his status as a Taoist sage.

Then, by the second century B.C.E., when the Taoist school took shape among the Six Schools (including also Legalists, Cosmologists, Mohists, and Sophists) as the strongest rival of the Confucians, in urgent need of providing itself retrospectively with a founder, Lao Tan would present himself as a very suitable candidate. On this hypothesis, it would hardly matter whether the obscure instructor in the rites was a historical person or a Confucian invention to point the lesson that even the greatest must be willing to learn. The importance of Lao Tan would begin with this transformation by Taoist legend.

We have seen that the first firmly datable reference to the meeting is in a Taoist source, the "Inner Chapters" of *Chuang-tzu* (there not recorded as a theme of Taoist legend but as a known event mentioned in passing), and the next in the eclectic *Lü-shih ch'un-ch'iu*, which implies the Confucian rather than the Taoist tradition. We cannot therefore decide the issue by comparing the dates of sources. But there is other evidence, and all of it points to the Confucian origin of the story.

1. In the first place, there is the general shape of the recorded lives of Confucius and Lao Tan. The story of Confucius is a rich and varied legend with a firm historical nucleus. A minor incident in it, attested rather late, is his study of the rites under a certain Lao Tan, not identified as a Taoist. The documented story of Lao Tan before 100 B.C.E. consists, as far as solid narrative is concerned, of *nothing but* the visit of Confucius. Is there not something odd about the supposed founder of a philosophical school whose recorded life amounts to nothing but a peripheral incident in the legend of his great rival?

2. If the story was originally Confucian, Taoists would have an easily comprehensible motive for borrowing Lao Tan as a spokesman of their own. But if Lao Tan was from the first a Taoist, what possible motive could Confucians have to put themselves at a disadvantage by acknowledging him as their Master's teacher? The Lao Tan episode is very unlike, for example, the tales of encounters with hermits in Book 18 of the *Lun-yü* (Analects). Confucius does not offer himself as a disciple to the madman of Ch'u. When the two hermits he meets ploughing speak to him in the tone which Lao Tan assumes in *Chuang-tzu*, he firmly condemns their withdrawal from the world, as does Tzu-lu when he meets the old hermit with the basket (*Lun-yü* 18.5–7).

3. Both in *Chuang-tzu* and in the *Tseng-tzu-wen*, Lao Tan addresses Confucius as Ch'iu. Why would Confucians reproduce this detail from a Taoist tale, in which its function would be to humiliate their Master? Only as long as Confucians knew the story as an unchallenged part of their own tradition, not yet exploited by their enemies, would it seem harmless to have the Master's reverend teacher address him by his personal name.

4. The Taoist narrator has an ax to grind, the Confucian has none. Let us concede for a moment that there could be Confucians foolish

enough to accept a Taoist yarn that the Master listened humbly to sermons from Lao Tan. Then surely they would counter-attack by insisting
that the sermons were not Taoist, that Lao Tan taught benevolence, righteousness, the values of a Confucian gentleman. Why should they reduce
Lao Tan to a mere instructor in the minutiae of the funeral rites?

5. In *Chuang-tzu*, Lao Tan is keeper of archives in the dying court of
Chou. This dry-as-dust occupation is an odd one for a Taoist (one thinks
of Chuang-tzu as a carefree fisherman by the river), and in the *Shih-chi*
biography one has a sharp sense of incongruity when the archivist expresses the truly Taoist thought, "The men you talk about have already
rotted with their bones, only their words survive." Is this archivist of
Chou intelligible except as a Confucian hero? Quite apart from their
scorn of written tradition, Taoists care nothing for the Chou. The "Inner
Chapters" of *Chuang-tzu* never mention King Wen, King Wu, the Duke
of Chou, the Chou dynasty itself. In the rest of the book there is only a
single instance of one of the founders of Chou figuring as a speaking
character in a story, in the tale of King Wen and the old man of Tsang
(56/21/47–57), which implies however that the Chou should not have
conquered the empire by force.

6. Before Ssu-ma Ch'ien, Lao Tan has no surname, he is simply Old
Tan. This is quite suitable to a person in Confucian legend revered as a
guardian of ancient tradition, as documented in the *Lun-yü*: "In transmitting and refusing to innovate, and faithfully caring for antiquity, I
venture to compare myself with our Lao P'eng" (7.1).[13] But why would
Taoists forget or fail to invent a surname for the man they came to regard
as their founder?[14]

7. There is a marked reluctance in the older literature to use the form
"Lao-tzu." *Chuang-tzu* uses it throughout an episode only once (35/13/
53–60), uses it in four more episodes after introduction as Lao Tan,[15] but
otherwise uses Lao Tan alone. The *Lü-shih ch'un-ch'iu* uses Lao Tan, not
Lao-tzu, although it uses Chuang-tzu, not Chuang Chou. It might be
suggested that the respectful suffix *tzu* is added to surnames, and since
Lao Tan has no surname the practice of adding it to *lao* "old" took time to
develop. But this does not explain why the sage is nearly always introduced as Lao Tan even when afterwards called Lao-tzu, a practice also
exemplified in the *Shuo-yuan* (20.10a). Confucius and Hui Shih are called
K'ung-tzu and Hui-tzu throughout whole episodes in *Chuang-tzu* without ever being introduced as K'ung Ch'iu and Hui Shih. There is however a parallel in Keng-sang Ch'u, who is introduced in the sentence
"Among the disciples of Lao Tan there was a Keng-sang Ch'u" (61/23/1),
and from then on called "Keng-sang-tzu." It would seem that there is no
point in mentioning Lao-tzu unless one ensures at the start that the

reader identifies him as Lao Tan, the "Old Tan" who taught Confucius, the single event from which all his authority derives.

8. We admit that the earliest authority which mentions Lao Tan is Taoist, the "Inner Chapters" of *Chuang-tzu*. But it is notable that the "Inner Chapters" display throughout an obsession with characters in the legend of Confucius, and exploit as spokesmen of Taoism Confucius himself, his disciples, Ch'ü Po-yü whom he met in Wei, Chieh Yü the madman of Ch'u. Making his first appearance in extant literature in such company, there is some presumption that Lao Tan already had a place in the life of Confucius, but none at all that he was a Taoist. Nor does it seem that Chuang-tzu thinks him especially important. He is credited with only one extended Taoist discourse (20/7/11–15), but there are no less than three ascribed to the madman of Ch'u (2/1/27, 12/4/86–90, 20/7/4–7). We have already noticed that the mutilated criminal who studies under Confucius appeals to Lao Tan as a man under whom Confucius himself studied, a fact mentioned obliquely as though it were common knowledge.

There remains one more reference to Lao Tan, at the end of chapter 3:

> When Lao Tan died, Ch'in Shih went to mourn him, wailed three times and came out.
>
> A disciple said, "Were you not the master's friend?"
>
> "I was."
>
> "Then is it allowable to mourn him like this?"
>
> "It is. Previously I thought he was the man, but now he is not." (8/3/14–16)[16]

Ch'in Shih goes on to criticize the exaggerated mourning of the disciples, which proves that they have not been taught to accept death. This is a strange way for Chuang-tzu to be talking about the founder of his own philosophy, especially since reconciliation with death is his greatest theme.

Who is this Lao Tan? Surely only the man who instructed Confucius in funeral rites.

Lao Tan and the *Lao-tzu*

When does Lao Tan first appear as a teacher with a philosophy of his own? The first clear evidence is in listings of philosophers from the middle of the third century B.C.E. For example, Hsün-tzu (ca. 230 B.C.E.)

has, "Lao-tzu had some insight into bowing down, none into stretching out" (64/17/51).[17] And the *Lü-shih ch'un-ch'iu* says, "Lao Tan valued yielding" (17.7; Hsü 17.30a).

Both these sources credit Lao Tan with the theory of government based on a strategy of yielding in order to conquer, which we find in the book *Lao-tzu*, later called the *Tao-te-ching*. Hsün-tzu clearly distinguishes it from Chuang-tzu's philosophy of withdrawal into private life and trust in the spontaneity which is from Heaven rather than in the obedience to fixed principles which characterizes man. "Laoist" and "Chuangist" schools are still distinguished in chapter 33 of *Chuang-tzu*, which may be as late as the second century B.C.E.,[18] and did not merge as "Taoists" until Ssu-ma T'an (died 110 B.C.E.) classified the "Six Schools." Lao Tan in the "Inner Chapters" was already expressing thoughts which would later be called Taoist, but when did he start to be a "Laoist"?

There is no tradition of philosophy of yielding taught by Lao Tan which does not derive from *Lao-tzu* itself, a book for the date of which the quotations from *Hsün-tzu* and *Lü-shih ch'un-ch'iu* just offered are the earliest external evidence. In most of *Chuang-tzu*, including the seven dialogues with Confucius in the "Outer Chapters," Lao Tan is teaching "Chuangism." Where we do find Lao Tan approaching the thought of *Lao-tzu*, in dialogues in the "Mixed Chapters" with Nan-jung Ch'u and with Yang Tzu-chü, he also echoes the book verbally.[19] Nor is there any tradition of quoting dicta of Lao Tan missing from *Lao-tzu*, in marked contrast with the case of Confucius, a high proportion of whose sayings quoted in pre-Han literature do not appear in the *Lun-yü*. Except when he is a speaker in anecdote, the formula "Lao Tan said . . ." almost always introduces a quotation from the text of *Lao-tzu* more or less as we have it. (Witness the almost negligible collection of quotations without parallels in the extant text assembled in the end of Ma 1956.)

It would seem then that Lao Tan first emerges as an independent philosopher with the ascription to him of the book no later than about 250 B.C.E., either by the author or—if we think of the book as older but previously neglected—by some publisher. The motive for using the name of Lao Tan would be the same as Chuang-tzu's, to claim the authority of the man who talked down to Confucius. However, although the name of Lao Tan might impress philosophers, by 250 B.C.E. propaganda for *Lao-tzu* would also have to take into account a power hostile to all the schools, the state of Ch'in, which would by 221 B.C.E. reunite the empire and in 213 B.C.E. burn the books.

Now, there is a stratum in the Lao Tan legend which connects him with Ch'in. In *Chuang-tzu* there is just one biographical detail which is independent of the meeting with Confucius. It states: "Yang Tzu-chü went south to P'ei. Lao Tan traveled west to Ch'in" (76/27/25). We have already noticed that the Yang Tzu-chü episode is dependent on the text *Lao-tzu*. We have no reason to assume therefore that this element in the legend is earlier than the circulation of the book. It connects with the identification by some of the Chou archivist Lao Tan (*t'nam or *tam) with a certain Grand Historiographer Tan (*tam) of Chou, which is mentioned by Ssu-ma Ch'ien:

> One hundred twenty-nine years after the death of Confucius, the historiographers record that Tan, Grand Historiographer of Chou, visited Duke Hsien of Ch'in and said: "At first Ch'in was joined with Chou. Having been joined 500 years, they parted. After having been parted seventy years, a hegemon and king will arise here."
>
> Some say Tan was Lao-tzu, some say not. No one in our time know whether or not it is so. (*Shih-chi* 63.2142)]

This second Tan is known only by the single incident of his visit to Ch'in, but his prediction of the victory of the state seemed so important to Ssu-ma Ch'ien that he recorded it no less than four times (*Shih-chi* 4.159, 5.201, 28.1364, 63.2142). The prediction was not forged retrospectively, for in its different versions the commentators on the *Shih-chi* fail to fit it neatly to later historical events. In the state of Ch'in it must have been a treasured memory.

Let us imagine the position of admirers of *Lao-tzu* who wish to win tolerance, if not patronage, from a state so hostile to philosophers. It would be a magnificent strategy to identify Lao Tan with the Grand Historiographer who prophesied the ascendancy of Ch'in over Chou. The only difficulty would be the long interval between the death of Confucius and the visit to Ch'in, estimated by Ssu-ma Ch'ien at 129 years. Chronologically, Ssu-ma Ch'ien finds the identification dubious but not impossible. He says,

> It seems that Lao-tzu lived at least 160 years, some say at least 200 years, as a result of cultivating the Way and nurturing longevity. (63.2142)

Clearly the identification must always have assumed that Lao Tan was a cultivator of long life. It will be objected perhaps that Taoist legend scorns chronology. But even the stories in *Chuang-tzu* have a solid chronological framework for persons on public record, with very few anachronisms (see Huang Fang-kang in Ku 1963, 4.369–77). Confucius is always firmly placed in the historical sequence, and as for the visit to Ch'in of the Grand Historiographer Tan, all the four accounts in the *Shih-chi* specify the date. This is natural since a prophesy is impressive only if one knows when it was made. In the annals of Chou the date is the third year of King Lieh (374 B.C.E.), in those of Ch'in the eleventh year of Duke Hsien (also 374 B.C.E.). While here it is slightly miscalculated as 129 years after the death of Confucius, which was in 479 B.C.E., in the treatise on sacrifices it is estimated as forty-eight years after an event itself undated.

Those who made the identification must always have seen the implication drawn by Ssu-ma Ch'ien, that Lao Tan lived 200 years or so. Might not a propagandist for *Lao-tzu* hesitate to risk such a tall story? Not perhaps if the ruler he is trying to convince is the King of Ch'in, China's First Emperor and first great aspirant to physical immortality. Whoever first saw the advantages of identifying the author of the text *Lao-tzu* with a man who put the Ch'in in his debt might also discover positive advantages in the implication that Lao Tan lived beyond the normal span of human life.

Lao Tan's Journey to the West

Let us pursue this line of speculation. The King of Ch'in is to be presented with a book which as a work of philosophy he would dismiss with contempt were it not that its author is supposedly that revered prophet who came to Ch'in in 374 B.C.E. to predict its ascendancy over Chou, and who also, as it now appears, had arts to defeat death. A question would surely occur to him: "Why is not Lao Tan still here in Ch'in to advise me about the government of the state?" He would have an answer in the only story which, apart from the meeting with Confucius, Ssu-ma Ch'ien tells about Lao Tan:

> After he had lived in Chou for a long time he perceived the Chou was in decline, so departed. When he reached the passes, the keeper of the pass, Yin Hsi,[20] said: "We shall be seeing no more of you. I insist that you write a book for us."
>
> Lao-tzu wrote them a book in two parts, discussing the ideas of the Way and of Virtue in some 5,000 words, and departed. No one knows where he ended his life. (*Shih-chi* 63.2141)]

Lao Tan, despairing of the Chou, departs for the west. He arrives at the passes of Ch'in (which Ssu-ma Ch'ien, writing under the Han, prefers not to name). He writes the book *Lao-tzu* as a present to the kingdom of

Ch'in and proceeds on his journey. Perhaps he is still alive somewhere in the far west. The problem of disposing of the body, as in a murder story, has been neatly solved.

The bibliography of the *Han-shu* (History of the Han Dynasty) records a book ascribed to the keeper of the pass, *Kuan-yin-tzu*, no longer extant. Assuming the identity of Kuan-yin with the keeper of the pass, which is by no means universally accepted (see Kuo 1962, 150), the appearance of his name in the *Lü-shih ch'un-ch'iu* (9.4, 17.8) confirms that the story of the journey to the west was already current by 240 B.C.E. We have clear evidence that Kuan-yin was supposed to have lived not long before or after 374 B.C.E. in two series of philosophers in chronological order in the "Pu-erh" (Nondualism) section of the *Lü-shih ch'un-ch'iu* (17.7, Hsü 17.30a–31a) and the "T'ien-hsia" (The World) chapter of *Chuang-tzu* (91/33/16–69).

Comparison between them shows an interesting discrepancy in the case of Lao Tan. The *Lü-shih ch'un-ch'iu* series starts with the names Lao Tan, Confucius, Mo-tzu (late fifth century B.C.E.). Then comes Kuan-yin, followed by philosophers who when datable belong to the fourth century (T'ien P'ien, Yang Chu, Sun Pin). The *Chuang-tzu* sequence has five thinkers of pairs of thinkers running from Mo-tzu down to Chuang-tzu. Kuan-yin and Lao Tan occupy the fourth place, immediately before Chuang-tzu, who according to Ssu-ma Ch'ien lived in the time of King Hui of Liang (370–319 B.C.E.) and King Hsüan of Ch'i (319–301 B.C.E.).

The presence of Kuan-yin and his placing early in the fourth century B.C.E. suggest that in both lists Lao Tan is identified with the Grand Historiographer. This would imply crediting him with a life of some 200 years, allowing considerable latitude in assigning him his place in a line of shorter-lived philosophers. The *Lü-shih ch'un-ch'iu* puts him at the head of the list, before his junior Confucius. But it was at the very end of his life, or at any rate his life in China, that he wrote *Lao-tzu* on Kuan-yin's invitation, so the *Chuang-tzu* series (which in any case does not reach back to Confucius) puts him side by side with Kuan-yin in the early fourth century B.C.E.

The *Shih-chi* Biography

We now at last arrive at the stage where studies of Lao Tan generally begin, Ssu-ma Ch'ien's biography. The first point which attracts attention is that the visit of Confucius is still the nucleus of the Lao Tan legend. It is the only extended anecdote, taking up about a third of what he has to say about Lao Tan, and he tells another version of the tale in his life of Confucius (*Shih-chi* 63.2142). He has also the story of the journey to the west, and the supposed identification with the Grand Historiographer Tan, which he doubts. There is also a tentative identification with Lao-lai-tzu, which we shall ignore since it seems peripheral to the problem. But Ssu-ma Ch'ien is able to add the information which is required for an official biography—names, place, office, and also the line of descent to his own time:

> Lao-tzu was a man of Ch'ü-jen village of Lai District of Hu Province in Ch'u. Surname: Li. Personal name: Erh. Style: Tan. He was a historiographer in charge of the archives of Chou. . . . (63.2139)
>
> Lao-tzu's son had the personal name Tsung. Tsung was a general of Wei, enfiefed in Tuan-kan. Tsung's son was Chu, Chu's son Kung. Kung's great-great-grandson was Chia. Chia held office under Emperor Wen of Han [179–157 B.C.E.] and Chia's son Chieh became tutor of Ang, Prince of Chiao-hsi, and so settled in Ch'i. (63.2142–43)]

All this must come from the tradition of a family which in Ssu-ma Ch'ien's own time claimed descent from Lao-tzu. If so, one would expect the ancestor to be, not a teacher without a surname on the margin of the Confucius legend, but someone with an official existence, such as the Grand Historiographer Tan. That the Lao-tzu of Ssu-ma Ch'ien's biography is a blend of the Lao Tan who taught Confucius and the Grand Historiographer Tan who visited Ch'in is an idea that goes back to the Ch'ing scholar Wang Chung (1744–94).[21]

More recent scholarship, without reaching agreement on this question, has continued to accumulate evidence, of varying weight but all pointing in the same direction, that the particulars in Ssu-ma Ch'ien's biography imply a date in the fourth century B.C.E. The ancestor's son Tsung is described as a general of Wei, which did not become a state until 403 B.C.E. The seven generations down to the time of Emperor Wen of Han reach back easily enough to 374 B.C.E., but not to an elder contemporary of Confucius. Ssu-ma Ch'ien could not have recognized the ancestor of the line as Lao Tan without also accepting the family tradition about his name and birthplace, which must therefore have been those of the introduction of the biography ("a man of Ch'ü-jen village of Lai District of Hu Province in Ch'u"). But Hu Province belonged to Ch'u only after 479 B.C.E., when it was won by the conquest of Ch'en.[22]

At first sight there seems to be an obvious weakness in the hypothesis that Ssu-ma Ch'ien took his information from the family of the Grand

Historiographer. It surely assumes that he confidently accepted the identification with Lao Tan, which he did not. However, let us try to put
ourselves in the position of the Grand Historiographer's descendants
under the Han. In the time of the Ch'in they had been proud of the
ancestor who prophesied its victory. This ancestor is also identified by
many with the author of a book which is increasingly influential. But
since the fall of the Ch'in the Grand Historiographer Tan has become a
liability while Lao Tan is a growing asset. In these circumstances it might
be politic to discover that ancestor Tan lived in P'ei, where the Han ruling
family came from, and to change the convention for writing his name,
replacing the graph Tan ("Bearer") with Tan ("Rimless"). It would then
be possible for Ssu-ma Ch'ien to be deceived by the family's claim to
descent from Lao Tan, in ignorance that it depends on the questionable
identification known to him from other sources.

Conclusion

We may now propose a scheme of five stages in the evolution of the
story:

1. A Confucian tale of the Master inquiring about the rites from a
    certain Lao Tan, very probably already known as an archivist of
    Chou. This tale, already current in the fourth century B.C.E., may
    be a historical reminiscence, or simply an exemplary story about
    the Master's humility in seeking learning wherever it is to be found.
2. The adoption of Lao Tan in the "Inner Chapters" of *Chuang-tzu*,
    towards 300 B.C.E., as one of the characters in the life of Confucius
    exploitabie as spokesmen of "Chuangism."
3. The appearance of *Lao-tzu* under the name of Lao Tan, taking ad-
    vantage of his authority as a teacher of Confucius. From this point
    he represents a philosophical trend ("Laoism").
4. The identification of Lao Tan with the Grand Historiographer Tan
    of Chou, who in 374 B.C.E. predicted the rise of Ch'in, and the inven-
    tion of the story of the journey to the west and of the writing of
    the book for Kuan-yin. The purpose was to win favor for *Lao-tzu*
    from the Ch'in. It may be guessed that the medium for this propa-
    ganda was the lost *Kuan-yin-tzu*. Stages 3 and 4 were completed by
    240 B.C.E.
5. The graphic adaptation of the name of Grand Historiographer to
    that of Lao Tan after 206 B.C.E. by the descendants of the former.
    The purpose was to make their ancestor welcome to the Han instead
    of the Ch'in. The personal details about the Grand Historiographer

thus became available as stiffening for the biography of Lao Tan by Ssu-ma Ch'ien. At the same period the classification of the Six Schools put "Laoism" and "Chuangism" under the common heading of "Taoism." Since Lao Tan was earlier than Chuang-tzu, he was established retrospectively as founder of the Taoist school.

Notes

1. Editors' note: This essay first appeared in *Studies in Chinese Philosophy and Philosophical Literature*, published by the Institute of East Asian Philosophies, Singapore, 1986, and reprinted in a volume with the same title by State University of New York Press in 1990. Reprinted here courtesy of Judy and Dawn Graham.

To maintain the formal coherence of this volume, some editorial changes have been made. Besides introductory remarks in the beginning, we supplied subheadings, standardized references to the *Chuang-tzu*, divided notes into footnotes and reference notes, appended references in a list at the end, placed characters in the index-glossary, and made minor semantic alterations to ensure greater clarity of text.

2. Editors' note: We added this translation from chapter 63 of the *Shih-chi*, based on Graham's own translation in the article, to give proper focus to his work. Other translations of the same text are found in Lau 1982, X–XI; Fung and Bodde 1952, 1:170–71.

3. Editors' note: The text *Chuang-tzu* divides into seven "Inner Chapters" (chs. 1–7), fifteen "Outer Chapters" (chs. 8–22), and eleven "Mixed Chapters" (chs. 23–33). Graham has shown that only the former had anything to do with the philosopher Chuang-tzu proper, while the latter two were edited in the third or even second century B.C.E. See Graham 1980.

4. See *Chuang-tzu*, ed. *Chuang-tzu yin-te*, Harvard-Yenching Sinological Index Series, Supplement No. 20 (Peking, 1947), 18/19/8–15 and 92/33/54–62; *Lü-shih ch'un-ch'iu chi-shih*, ed. Hsü Wei-yü, Peking 1955, 9.4 (9.13A) and 17.8 (17.30B).

5. *Chuang-tzu* 30/12/41–45, 35/13/45–53, 38/14/44–56, 39/14/56–60, 39/14/74–82, 55/21/24–38, 58/22/28–43.

6. Cf. Ch'ien 1951, 108. He notes that for the Six Classics the point has been made as long ago as the Sung by Huang Chen (1213–1280), for the Twelve Classics by Wang Yü commenting on the *Chuang-tzu chieh*

(*Chuang-tzu chi-ch'eng ch'u-pien* 19.299) of his father Wang Fu-chih (1619–1692).

7. Ed. *Ssu-pu ts'ung-k'an*, 20.10a. This seems to be a Confucian version of the episode found in *Chuang-tzu* 38/14/74–82.

8. Ed. *Ssu-pu pei-yao*, 3.1a. Lao Tan is also mentioned in 3.5b, 6.1a, 6.4b, 10.5b, and 10.6b.

9. Most commentators since Kuo Hsiang have agreed on this interpretation of the sentence. Lin Yun-ming in 1663 proposed to take *hsueh-tzu* in the sense of "disciples" ("Why does he go about collecting all those disciples?"). But there is no difficulty about understanding *hsueh-tzu* as "take you as model," "learn from you." Cf. *Huai-nan-tzu* 10 (*Huai-nan-tzu chu-shih*, Taipei 1973, 164), where the expression is used in the sentence "Lao Tan studied under Shang Jung." See also Lin Yun-ming, *Chuang-tzu yin*, in *Chuang-tzu chi-ch'eng ch'u-pien* 18.120.

10. *Chuang-tzu* 6/2/76, 6/2/83, 74/26/19, 81/29/16–51 passim.

11. Lao-lai-tzu, tentatively identified with Lao Tan in that biography, is equally blunt to Confucius in *Chuang-tzu* 74/26/18–24.

12. Ed. *Han-shih wai-chuan chin-chu chin-yi*, Taipei 1972, 5.225. The story also appears in the *Hsin-hsu*, ed. *Hsin-hsu chin-chu chin-yi*, Taipei 1975, 153.

13. The parallel is especially apposite if we take the mysterious Lao P'eng to have been an elder contemporary of Confucius, as does Chang Chi-t'ung (Ku 1963, 4:337f.).

14. Cf. the surely desperate attempts of T'ang Lan and Kao Heng to take Lao itself as the surname (Ku 1963, 1:332–35, 351–53).

15. See *Chuang-tzu* 38/14/44–56, 39/14/74–82, 61/23/1–42, 76/27/25–30.

16. Ma Hsü-lun had another interpretation: "Previously I thought of him as a man (in contrast with Heaven) but now he is not." Cf. 8/3/13: "Is it Heaven? Or is it rather man?" This is extremely attractive, but the modal *ch'i* normally precedes the main verb and I have not noticed examples in an auxiliary clause after *yi wei*. See Ma 1930, 3.5b.

17. Ed. *Hsün-tzu yin-te*, Harvard-Yenching Sinological Index Series, Supplement No. 22 (Peking, 1950). See also 79/21/22: "Chuang-tzu had a vision limited to Heaven and was ignorant of man."

18. I argue that chapter 33 ("T'ien-hsia") belongs with chapters 11 (66–74), 12 (1–6), 13 (1–45), 14 (1–5), and 15 in the latest stratum of the

book, expounding a political philosophy which is Taoist-centered but syncretistic. See Graham 1980; reprinted in Graham 1990, 313–21.

Editor's note: For a recent development of *Chuang-tzu* dating, see Roth 1991.

19. The dialogues are found in *Chuang-tzu* 62/23/23–42 and 76/27/25–30. The passages in 62/23/34–36 and 76/27/29 echo *Lao-tzu* 10, 25, and 41.

20. Or "the director in charge was pleased and said . . . ," following the proposal of Kuo 1962, 151 and translating the characters of the name. If the keeper of the pass is nameless, it can hardly be doubted that when he asked Lao Tan to write "for us," he is making the request on behalf of his state.

21. He expressed it in the *Lao-tzu k'ao-yi*, contained at the end of his *Shu-hsueh pu-yi*, ed. *Ssu-pu ts'ung-k'an*.

22. For the evidence of putting the Lao Tan of the biographical framework in the fourth century B.C.E., see Lo Ken-tse (who defended the identification with the Grand Historiographer Tan) in Ku 1963, 4:446–62. See also Dubs 1941, 1944, and Bodde 1942.

References

Bodde, Derk. 1942. "The New Identification of Lao Tzu." *Journal of the American Oriental Society* 62: 8–13.

———. 1944. "Further Remarks on the Identification of Lao Tzu: A Last Reply to Professor Dubs." *Journal of the American Oriental Society* 64: 24–27.

Ch'ien Mu. 1951. *Chuang-tzu tsuan-chien*. Hong Kong: Tongnam Printers.

Dubs, Homer H. 1941. "The Date and Circumstances of the Philosopher Lao-dz." *Journal of the American Oriental Society* 61: 215–21.

———. 1942. "The Identification of Lao-dz: A Reply to Professor Bodde." *Journal of the American Oriental Society* 62: 300–304.

Graham, A. C. 1980. "How much of *Chuang-tzu* Did Chuang-tzu Write?" *Studies in Classical Chinese Thought*. Journal of the American Academy of Religions Supplement 35: 459–501. Reprinted in Graham 1990: 283–321.

———. 1990. *Studies in Chinese Philosophy and Philosophical Literature*. Albany: State University of New York Press.

Ku Chieh-kang, ed. 1963. *Ku-shih pian*. 7 vols., Hong Kong: T'ai-p'ing.

Kuo Mo-jo. 1962. *Shih p'i-p'an shu*. Peking: K'o-hsueh ch'u-pan-she.

Ma Hsü-lun. 1930. *Chuang-tzu yi-cheng*. Shanghai: Shang-wu.

———. 1956. *Lao-tzu chiao-ku*. Peking: Ku-chi ch'u-pan-she.

Roth, Harold. 1991. "Who Compiled the *Chuang-tzu*?" In *Chinese Texts and Philosophical Contexts. Essays Dedicated to Angus C. Graham*, 79–128. Edited by
Henry Rosemont. La Salle, Ill: Open Court Press.

Waley, Arthur. 1934. *The Way and Its Power*. London: Allen and Unwin.

Wang Meng-ou. 1960. *Li-chi chin-chu chin-yi*. Taipei: T'ai-wan shang-chin yin-
shu-kuan.

2

The Lao-tzu Myth

Livia Kohn

Lao-tzu, the alleged Warring States philosopher and author of the *Tao-te-ching*, was elevated in Han bibliography to the status of "founder" of the "Taoist school." In the centuries that followed he became much more than that—an immortal, a cosmic deity, and the savior of humankind. Three main Han-dynasty groups contributed to this process in its earliest stages. First, there were individual seekers of immortality, the so-called magical practitioners (*fang-shih*). They adopted Lao-tzu as their patriarch and idealized him as an immortal, a particularly gifted human being who, by his own initiative and efforts, had attained the purity and power of the celestials. Second, the political elite, the imperial family and court officials, saw in Lao-tzu the personification of the Tao and worshiped him as a representative of their ideal of cosmic and political unity alongside the Yellow Emperor (Huang-ti) and the Buddha. Lao-tzu here was known as the Venerable Lord (Lao-chün) and became the object of formal imperial sacrifices. Third, popular religious cults, millenarian in nature and expecting the end of the world, identified Lao-tzu as the god who had continuously manifested himself through the ages and saved the world time and again. He would, they believed, come again as the messiah of the new age of Great Peace (T'ai-p'ing). Also called Venerable Lord or, in some groups, Yellow Venerable Lord (Huang-lao chün), this deified Lao-tzu was like the personification of cosmic harmony worshiped by the court but equipped with tremendous revolutionary power. As a messiah, he could overturn the present and reorganize the world, leading the faithful to a new state of heavenly bliss in this very life on earth.

All these forms of Lao-tzu were present in the second century C.E. After that, they merged into a single powerful deity, a personification of the Tao who guided immortality seekers in meditation, represented the center of the universe and its cosmic harmony, and revealed the secrets

41

of heaven to the leaders of organized Taoism. Lao-tzu, no longer the philosopher who withdrew from government service and emigrated to the west, accordingly from the fifth century onward received elaborate religious biographies that detailed his creation of the world, birth as a human being, and wanderings on earth. The following pages[1] discuss the deification of Lao-tzu and content of the Lao-tzu myth, detailing first the roles the god fulfilled in the later Han dynasty—as immortal, cosmic harmony, and popular savior. This section owes much to the outstanding scholarship of Anna Seidel. The second major section, then, describes the content and structure of his hagiography, focusing on the embellishments created around his cosmic stature and birth, his transmission of the teaching, and his journey to the west.

Lao-tzu In The Han Dynasty (206 B.C.E.–220 C.E.)

Lao-tzu as Immortal

The first to adopt Lao-tzu as their representative were the magical practitioners, wandering ascetics who strove to attain immortality through drugs, diets, and physical regimens, and who made a living with the help of pseudo-sciences, such as fortune-telling, astrology, medicine, and dream interpretation. They venerated the Yellow Emperor as the patriarch of various concrete techniques while seeing in Lao-tzu the foremost inspirational model for their quest. Lao-tzu thus became a teacher of the right way to live in the world while at the same time cultivating oneself and extending life. He was not yet a god and yet no longer a mere thinker, reclusive sage, or astrologer, but himself a practitioner of longevity who lived for several hundred years, maintained his vigor, and attained immortality by magic. He had developed full control over life and death, could foretell the future, and knew all about the patterns of the heavenly bodies. He could order demons about at will and wielded talismans and spells with ease.

While this understanding of Lao-tzu goes back to the Han dynasty, its first documentation is of a later date. It is indicated in the Lao-tzu biography in the *Lieh-hsien chuan* (Immortals' Biographies), attributed to Liu Hsiang of the Former Han. According to this, the Old Master was born during the Shang dynasty, served as an archivist under the Chou, was the teacher of Confucius, and later emigrated to the west. The main power that exalted him beyond ordinary mortals, however, was his nourishing on essence and energy, his ability to keep them in his body and not let them disperse—a quality the magical practitioners ardently pursued (Kaltenmark 1953, 62).

In addition, the immortal Lao-tzu is described in the *Shen-hsien-chuan* (Biographies of Spirit Immortals) of Ko Hung (261–341), an aristocrat and scholar of the early fourth century, who had a lively interest in all things Taoist and researched them with great acumen. For him the Tao could be reached through various physical and spiritual techniques, such as gymnastics, breathing exercises, diets, meditations, and alchemy. His major work, the *Pao-p'u-tzu* (Book of the Master Who Embraces Simplicity) is a vast compendium of these practices: protective measures against demons, ways of alignment with universal energies, energy absorption, pharmacology and herbal lore, the attainment of magical powers, and the preparation of "cinnabars" or elixirs of immortality (see Ware 1966; Sailey 1978). Ko Hung's biography of Lao-tzu reflects his attitudes toward the Old Master. As a scholar, he reports faithfully on the various accounts of Lao-tzu's life, citing a variety of sources. As an evangelist of the Tao, he praises Lao-tzu as an inspired teacher, a man versed in the intricacies of spontaneity, and a worthy sage to follow. As an immortality seeker, finally, Ko Hung represents Lao-tzu as a model for the efficacy and power of immortality techniques, placing him side by side with the herb-lord Ch'ih-sung-tzu (Master Redpine) and the sexual master Yung-ch'eng-tzu (Master Perfect Face).[2] Lao-tzu, in this vision, is a human being gifted by nature, the living proof of the possibility of reaching immortality, an inspiring example for the seekers (Maspero 1981, 395). As Ko Hung says,

By destiny Lao-tzu was endowed with a penetrating spirit and far-reaching foresight. The energy he had received at birth was unlike that of ordinary people. This caused him to become a master of the Tao; it gave him the support of the celestial gods and the following of the host of immortals.

Thus he came to reveal various ways of going beyond the world: the [alchemy of the] nine cinnabars and eight minerals; the [dietetics of] metallic wine and the golden fluid; the visualization of the mysterious and the simple and of guarding the One; the recollection of spirit and penetration of the hidden. . . .

Lao-tzu was basically a man of calm and serenity. Free from desires, he pursued only the prolongation of life. Thus it was that he lived under the Chou for a long time but never developed his rank or fame. He only wished to keep his inner light in harmony with the world of dust and grime, to realize nature within, and to leave once his Tao was perfected. He was indeed a true immortal. (Kohn 1996, 59)

Another expression of this understanding of Lao-tzu, in a more mythological form, is the story about his retainer Hsü Chia that Ko Hung tells. The retainer has served Lao-tzu for several hundred years and is following him when Lao-tzu approaches the pass during his emigration. Seeing that Lao-tzu is about to wander into distant lands and enticed by a beautiful woman he meets on the pass, he demands to be paid in full. Lao-tzu cannot afford the money, and Hsü Chia takes his claim to Yin Hsi, the Guardian of the Pass. Lao-tzu, when confronted with the situation, orders the man to open his mouth. His life-giving talisman drops out, Hsü Chia falls to the ground in a heap of bones. Lao-tzu's power established, Yin Hsi adjudicates the situation and Hsü Chia leaves, restored again to life (Kohn 1989, 55; 1991, 62; Schipper 1985, 43). The story shows Lao-tzu as the master over life and death. He has kept the servant alive by giving him a powerful talisman and through it has the power to remove and bestow life as he pleases. Lao-tzu here is a man with the magic of the immortals, perfected in the way the magical practitioners of the time thought ideal. As an immortal he is thus the living model of the magical practitioners, the active proof that their pursuit is valid and can be successfully completed. Lao-tzu, adopted by this group, thus rises to the status of master teacher and perfected immortal, still a man but of celestial standing, one who has power over life and death and can enter and leave the world at will.

Lao-tzu as Cosmic Harmony

The leading doctrine of the Han-dynasty elite was a teaching called "Huang-Lao" after the two senior representatives of its ideas, Huang-ti (the Yellow Emperor) and Lao-tzu. It centers on the Tao as the highest and most fundamental force of creation, which underlies all existence and orders humanity and the universe. The Tao pervades all, so that there is no qualitative distinction between the different levels of cosmos, nature, state, and the human body. Cultivation of one plane consequently must not only take into account the reverberations on all the others but also influences the entire system. The cosmos is seen as an integrated unity, in which the government of the state, the personal cultivation of the self, and the observation of natural and celestial cycles are different aspects of one and the same system (Major 1993, 12). Its ideal state is the perfection of "Great Peace," at which time all levels function in utmost harmony (Seidel 1984, 165).

Lao-tzu in this system, whose followers recited the *Tao-te-ching* as a manual of political and societal conduct (Seidel 1969, 31), appeared as the teacher of the Yellow Emperor. Credited in traditional mythology with the invention of the state and war, the Yellow Emperor was the first major creator of culture in the Confucian vision and the last of the pure rulers of the golden age according to Taoist myth. He was a sage and a ruler and a god, a culture hero, and also an immortal. Han stories about him abound, describing his war with Ch'ih-yu, the "Wormy Rebel" (see Lewis 1990), his cultural creativity, and his ascension to heaven in broad daylight on the back of a long-whiskered dragon (see Yü 1964). A mighty hero on his own, Huang-ti was yet represented as an ignorant fool when contrasted with Lao-tzu (Seidel 1969a, 51; 1969b, 228). Above and beyond him, Lao-tzu was a senior deity who knew all, a divine sage who had full intuition of the Tao and was truly at the source of creation. Only because of Lao-tzu's inspiration and wisdom could the Yellow Emperor undertake his enterprises and successfully ascend into the heavens. The culture of the world as well as the divinity of its creator all went back ultimately to Lao-tzu and the cosmic harmony of the Tao he represented. He was the only force that could ever bring back the benign and prosperous rule of the Yellow Emperor, the true representative of Great Peace (Seidel 1969b, 229).

Because of his veneration as a powerful force of creation, Lao-tzu's historical biography underwent significant changes. For example, he acquired an official lineage by being adopted as ancestor by the Li family. This accorded with a common custom under the Han, when many mythological figures were used by leading clans to raise their standing at the imperial court. The Li clan, previously unknown, rose to fame and fortune at this time, and the senior tutor Li Chieh, a native of southwest Shan-tung, consolidated his family's ascent by taking Lao-tzu as his clan's ancestor (Seidel 1969a, 18; 1969b, 222). In addition, Lao-tzu was associated with several historiographers, that is, astrologically trained officials who evaluated the celestial signs and recorded their impact on human affairs. The *Shih-chi* had already mentioned Lao-tzu's ability to examine the dynasty's virtue, and tentatively identified him with Tan, the Grand Historiographer of Chou, who lived around 350 B.C.E. In addition, Lao-tzu was now identified with Po-yang, astrologer under King Yu (r. 781–771 B.C.E.), thus making him a representative of celestial harmony who would come down to earth to identify heavenly signs whenever the need arose (Seidel 1969a, 30; Kusuyama 1979, 354).

In the second century, Lao-tzu became firmly established as the personification of the Tao. In 165 C.E., Emperor Huan offered an imperial sacrifice to him, traveling for this purpose to the birthplace of the historical Lao-tzu, where a temple had been erected. An inscription written for the occasion not only describes the sacrificial procedures but also documents the understanding people had of Lao-tzu at the time. It is called *Lao-tzu-ming* (Inscription for Lao-tzu) and dated to September 24,

165 C.E. (Seidel 1969a, 37; Maspero 1981, 394). The "Inscription" begins with a summary of the facts known about the philosopher Lao-tzu. It repeats the account of the *Shih-chi*, gives a concrete description of Lao-tzu's birthplace, and cites the *Tao-te-ching* as the major expression of his ideas. In addition, it praises Lao-tzu as the central deity of the cosmos, who was born from primordial energy, came down to earth, and eventually ascended back to the heavenly realm as an immortal. The text says,

> Lao-tzu was created from primordial chaos and lived as long as the Three Luminaries [sun, moon, stars]. He observed the skies and made prophecies, freely came and went to the stars. Following the course of the sun, he transformed nine times; he waxed and waned with the seasons. He regulated the Three Luminaries and had the four numinous animals by his sides. He concentrated his thinking on the Cinnabar Field, saw the Great One in his Purple Chamber,[3] became one with the Tao, and transformed into an immortal. (Seidel 1969a, 123)

Lao-tzu here is a celestial deity who moves freely among the stars and planets. Even when incarnate in a human body, his physical form is celestial, that contains wonderful palaces (Cinnabar Field, Purple Chamber) and deities (the Great Unity).

Next, the "Inscription" recounts the concrete circumstances that led to Emperor Huan's sacrifice and lists the credentials of the author, an offical named Pien Shao, for its compilation. All this is still by way of introduction to the actual praise offered to the deity, which joins the Lao-tzu vision of the immortality seekers with the understanding of Lao-tzu as a personification of the Tao and cosmic harmony. It says,

> Lao-tzu joins the movements of the sun and the moon, is at one with the five planets. He freely comes and goes from the Cinnabar Field; easily travels up and down the Yellow Court. He rejects ordinary customs, shadows his light, and hides himself. Embracing primordiality, he transforms like a spirit and breathes the essence of perfection.
>
> None in the world can approach his depth; we can only look up to his eternal life. Thus our divine emperor offers a sacrifice to Lao-tzu to document his holy spirituality. A humble servant, I strive in my turn to ensure his continued fame and thus engrave this stone to his greater glory. (Seidel 1969a, 128)

Lao-tzu as cosmic harmony was thus a deity venerated by the elite of the Han dynasty. This veneration was informed by various tendencies of the time, including the belief of the Huang-Lao school in the Tao as the central source of harmony informing government policy; the custom of adopting well-known mythological figures as ancestors of rising clans; the notion of Lao-tzu as a recurring sage who, as historiographer or astrologer, predicted the rise and decline of dynastic virtue; the immortality seekers' vision of Lao-tzu as a practitioner and master of long life; and the understanding of the Tao as the creative power of the universe underlying all creation and governing the planets as well as the world of humanity. All these different factors not only caused Lao-tzu to be identified with the Tao and seen as the representative of cosmic harmony on earth. They also developed the abstract notion of the Tao into a divinity of quasi-human form who was accessible to humanity as ancestor, adviser, and a model of sageliness.

Lao-tzu as Popular Savior

Lao-tzu as the savior of humanity was the logical correlate of this powerful cosmic divinity. As such he was taken up by various popular Taoist cults that emerged in the second century C.E. and, in the belief that the new age of Great Peace was at hand, contributed to the downfall of the Latter Han. One such cult, located in Shu (modern Ssu-ch'uan), has left behind a document that describes Lao-tzu as the incarnate power of the Tao that appears in every generation to support and direct the government of humanity. The *Lao-tzu pien-hua-ching* (Scripture of the Transformations of Lao-tzu) describes him:

> Lao-tzu rests in the great beginning,
> Wanders in the great origin,
> Floats through dark, numinous emptiness. . . .
> He joins serene darkness before its opening,
> Is present in original chaos before the beginnings of time. . . .
>
> Alone and without relation,
> He has existed since before heaven and earth.
> Living deeply hidden, he always returns to be:
> Gone, the primordial;
> Present, a man![4]

Lao-tzu here is the body of the Tao and the savior of humanity.[5] He represents the creative, ordering power of the universe that "transforms" the world. He has an unusual divine appearance, a sublimely divine nature, and nine distinct names to characterize his divinity. He is there and yet he is not. Like the Tao, he can be anything and everything, is flexible and yet stable. As the text says,

> Lao-tzu can be bright or dark, gone or present,
> Big or small, rolled up or stretched out,
> Above or below, vertical or horizontal, last or first.

> There is nothing he cannot do, nothing he will not accomplish.
> In fire he does not burn, in water he does not freeze.
> He meets with evil without suffering, confronts
>   disasters without affliction.
> Opposed, he is not pained, harmed, he is not scarred.

> Lao-tzu lives forever and does not die, but merely
>   dissolves his bodily form.
> Single and without counterpart, alone and without dependence,
> He is yet joined with all and never separate.
>
> (see Seidel 1969, 63)

Lao-tzu therefore is the Tao, and the Tao has always helped rulers to achieve and maintain perfect harmony in the world and it will again and again come down to do so. Therefore, Lao-tzu descends repeatedly to change human and natural life for the better, he undergoes endless transformations, not unlike Vishnu in Hindu mythology who appears in different avatars as the cycles of the world advance (see O'Flaherty 1975). Under different mythical rulers, Lao-tzu thus appeared using various different names, integrating classical myths about the advisers and teachers of sage rulers into the Lao-tzu story. For example,

> In the time of the sovereign Fu Hsi, he was called Master of Warm Vigor (Wen-shuang-tzu).

> In the time of the sovereign Shen-nung, he was called Master of Spring Perfected (Ch'un-ch'eng-tzu).

> In the time of the sovereign Chu-jung, he was called Master of Vast Perfection (Kuang-ch'eng-tzu). (see Seidel 1969a, 66)

In every generation, under every dynasty, Lao-tzu descends under a particular name to assist the ruler and guide the world to harmony. Now, according to the cult's belief, the world is coming to an end, and again Lao-tzu will descend and save humanity. Only this time, the government is so corrupt that the god does not appear to the ruler but rather to the simple and pure people in a distant corner of the empire. He instructs them in his proper worship and the right preparation for the new age to come:

> Give up all drunkenness and blood sacrifices,
> And you will be model followers of the Tao.
> Establish yourself firmly in tranquility and quietude,
> Fill your every pore with nonaction and nondesire,
> To be never shaken by afflictions—
> Then the Tao will come to support you well,
> And you will be saved!
>
> (see Seidel 1969a, 71)

Through a close relationship and direct communication with Lao-tzu, the local recipients of his revelation become the chosen people of the Tao. They follow its rules to the best of their abilities and thus can survive the impending cataclysmic changes to rebuild the world in the coming era of Great Peace.

Another revelation of the deified Lao-tzu, also in the second century and located in Ssu-ch'uan, was the transmission of the Covenant of Orthodox Unity (Cheng-yi) to the first Celestial Master, Chang Tao-ling, in 142 C.E. Ko Hung's *Shen-hsien-chuan* recounts the events:

> Chang Tao-ling entered Shu with his disciples and settled on Crane Cry Mountain (Ho-ming-shan), where he wrote a work on the Tao in twenty-four parts. Once, when he was in deep meditation, he had a vision of a celestial being descending in the company of a thousand wagons and a ten thousand horsemen, in a golden carriage with a canopy of feathers, drawn by a team of four dragons and a group of tigers. The host was numerous beyond count.
>
> The celestial introduced himself as an archivist [Lao-tzu], then again said he was the Lord of the Eastern Sea [divine ruler of the earth]. He bestowed on Chang the Tao of the most awesome Covenant of Orthodox Unity. Once Chang had received it, he found himself able to cure the sick. Thereupon the common people began to flock to him and venerate him as their master.[6]

Upon this revelation, Chang Tao-ling became the first Celestial Master (T'ien-shih). Organizing increasingly large numbers of followers, he strove to put an end to demon worship and blood sacrifices, replacing them with fasting, purification, and meditation (Kobayashi 1992, 23).

The cult concentrated on healing diseases and dispelling dangers, both with the help of incantations and talismans. The *Tao-te-ching* in this context was a direct manifestation of the Tao that could bestow magical powers and make people strong and even immortal, thus leading to the perfect harmony of Great Peace (Seidel 1969b, 222; Kobayashi 1992, 31).

The Celestial Masters have much in common with a third cult of a similar nature that sprang up also in the second century but in eastern China, on the Shan-tung Peninsula. It was known as the Great Peace (T'ai-p'ing) movement or as the Yellow Turbans, because its members wore yellow kerchiefs on their heads. Lao-tzu here appeared under the name Yellow Venerable Lord and was worshiped as the personification of the Tao, thus continuing the official Huang-Lao doctrine within a religious Taoist environment (Seidel 1969b, 228; Maspero 1981, 428). Followers of the Great Peace movement believed that the revelation of the Tao to their religious leader entitled him to rulership over the empire. Unlike the Celestial Masters, who understood themselves as spiritual advisers to mundane rule, they decided to replace the failing Han emperor (Seidel 1969b, 226; 1984, 168). Thus they rose in an armed rebellion in 184 C.E., all but toppling the Han empire and joining a long series of second-century peasant rebellions, both Taoist-inspired and secular (Seidel 1969b, 231–33).

During the Han dynasty, Lao-tzu therefore played a threefold role: as a master immortal and ideal model for magical practitioners; as a representative of the Tao and cosmic harmony, venerated by the elite and the court; and as a popular savior who reappeared in every generation to inspire the government and now manifested to leaders of popular cults. The deity Lao-tzu that grew out of the combination of these various figures was then seen as primarily identical with the Tao and one with the inner harmony of the cosmos. He lived forever and had power over life and death, just like a true immortal, but also took on human form and descended to earth, both to communicate with the people and to lead them to a new era of Great Peace. Lao-tzu from being a philosopher with a single lifetime on earth, however long, developed into a cosmic god who spent the lifetime of the universe appearing and vanishing to help people in their quest for perfection.

The Medieval Lao-tzu (5th–6th Centuries)

In the organized religious Taoism of the fifth and sixth centuries, Lao-tzu emerged fully as the highest god of the Celestial Masters. Being both identical with the Tao, and thus at the center of universal creation, and a god-turned-human in his exploits on earth, his hagiography took on new proportions and higher mythological dimensions. A full narrative was created that can be divided into three parts: Lao-tzu's birth as the Tao and on earth; Lao-tzu's transmission of the Tao to suffering humanity, both to the sage rulers of the past and in the *Tao-te-ching* to Yin Hsi; and Lao-tzu's journey to the west, his conversion of the peoples of Central Asia and India and appearance as the Buddha. The myth combines the Han-dynasty vision of Lao-tzu as cosmic god and savior with the mythized biography of the Buddha as it appeared in Chinese translation in the second century C.E. In addition, the myth also takes into account the ordination structure of the more fully organized religion, presenting a living example for the ideal Taoist life in the exploits of the highest god.

Lao-tzu's Birth

The first mythological account of Lao-tzu's birth is found in the *San-t'ien nei-chieh-ching* (Scripture of the Inner Explanation of the Three Heavens, TT 1205),[7] a Celestial Masters text dated to about 420 C.E. In its first scroll, it tells of the continued, active life of Lao-tzu as the Tao, ascribing to him three births: as the god of the Tao, from pure energy and as a celestial deity in heaven; in human form, as the ancient philosopher; and as the Buddha after his journey to the west. His mother is different in each case. First she is the Jade Maiden of Mystery and Wonder (Hsuan-miao yü-nü), a deity coagulated from pure primordial energies. As the text says,

> In the midst of emptiness and pervasion, great nonbeing was born. Great nonbeing transformed and changed into the three energies, the mysterious, primordial, and beginning. Intermingling in chaos, they followed each other and transformed to bring forth the Jade Maiden of Mystery and Wonder.
>
> After the Jade Maiden had been so created, the chaos energies congealed again to transform and bring forth Lao-tzu. He emerged from the left armpit of the Jade Maiden. At birth he had white hair, thus he was called Lao-tzu, "Old Child."[8] Lao-tzu is the Venerable Lord. (1.2b)

This Lao-tzu is the embodiment of the Tao. He arises at the dawn of creation and is born from a mother who is none other than the energies that make up himself, born supernaturally through her armpit and with the appearance of a wise old man. The god here may look human but he is still fundamentally a pure celestial.

His second birth brings Lao-tzu to life as an embodied human being. His mother is a human lady, known as Mother Li, and the birth story integrates the life of the philosopher. It is, however, set several centuries before his historically recorded lifetime—with the purpose of allowing Lao-tzu to travel to the west and attain birth as the Buddha, an event traditionally dated to 689 B.C.E. The *San-t'ien nei-chieh-ching* says,

> In the time of King Wu-ting of the Shang, Lao-tzu returned to the womb by entering Mother Li. During the pregnancy of eighty-one years, he continuously recited a sacred scripture. Then he parted her left armpit and was born. At birth he had white hair. Therefore she called him Lao-tzu, "Old Child." The "Scripture of the Three Terraces" (*San-t'ai-ching*) we still have today is the text Lao-tzu chanted in the womb. (1.3b)

Again Lao-tzu, although taking refuge in the womb of a human lady, is still a primarily supernatural figure. He is not conceived normally but enters the womb on his own initiative and in his own way. He is conscious even as an embryo and spends his time reciting sacred scriptures. More than that, he remains in the womb for a full human lifetime, emerging as an old man, ready to grow younger to teach the world the secrets of the Tao. In addition, the religious account explains that Mother Li was only apparently a human lady. It says:

> As regards his return to the womb in Mother Li, it must be understood that he himself transformed his body of pure emptiness into the shape of Mother Li. Then he took refuge in his own womb. There was never a real Mother Li. Unaware of this fact, people nowadays say that Lao-tzu took refuge in the womb of Mother Li. Such indeed is not the case. (1.3b)

Mother Li, the parent of the philosopher, has therefore become a new version of the Jade Maiden of Mystery and Wonder, a combination of energies put together by Lao-tzu for the express purpose of giving birth to himself. She bears the god for eighty-one years, the number of the highest totality of yang energy and the full lifetime of an ordinary person. Again Lao-tzu emerges from her left armpit, being both conceived and born asexually in the style of the virgin birth.[9] His age at birth accounts for the fact that he has white hair, possesses unusual wisdom, and is named "Old Child." It also adds to the claim of immortality and the notion that he reverses human fate and grows younger instead of older in the course of his life.

Lao-tzu's third birth takes place in India as the Buddha. It is recorded in the *Hsuan-miao nei-p'ien* (Esoteric Record of Mystery and Wonder), another fifth-century document of the Celestial Masters that survives in citations. Here we have,

> The wife of the king of India was called Ching-miao [Māyā]. Once, when she was taking an afternoon nap, Lao-tzu strode on the essence of the sun and entered her mouth. On the eighth day of the fourth month of the following year, he emerged through her left armpit. It was midnight. Having barely touched the ground, he took seven steps. From then on the Buddhist teaching came to flourish.[10]

This Taoist story integrates many details from the traditional birth story of the Buddha as it is found in Chinese in Chih Ch'ien's *T'ai-tzu jui-ying pen-ch'i ching* (Sūtra of the Origins and Deeds of the Prince in Accordance with All Good Omens).[11] The Buddha's mother, Queen Māyā, is given the Chinese name Ching-miao; the Buddha strides on a white elephant, capped by the sun, and appears to her in a dream during an afternoon nap; she is radiant and strong throughout her pregnancy then gives birth to the Buddha on the eighth of the fourth month; the divine child emerges from his mother's right hip and is immediately able to walk; taking seven steps, he announces his nobility to heaven and earth; later he attains enlightenment and begins the Buddhist teaching.

Closely imitating the Buddhist account, the Taoist myth of Lao-tzu's birth as the Buddha thus continues the two earlier births of the deity, in heaven and in China. Moving from the center of the uncreated universe to its most important created part (China), and on to the periphery in the west (India), the myth of the three births of Lao-tzu shows the universality of the Taoist teaching and ubiquitous validity of its power. Lao-tzu, equally present in heaven, in China, and in the west, represents the divine unity of the Tao that underlies all creation and unifies the world, however diverse its apparent multiplicity. He is the root of all existence and the prime source of true religion, born in human form to give succor to the world.

The Transmission of the Teaching

The second major activity of the god Lao-tzu is his teaching of the Tao on earth. This appears in the myth in two forms: in his repeated appearances to ancient mythical sovereigns, venerated in the Confucian tradition, as a teacher of culture; and in his transmission of the *Tao-te-ching* to Yin Hsi while crossing the pass for the west. In the first role, he is somewhat of a Confucian hero, being responsible for the overall progress of Chinese civilization; in his second role, he is the model for practicing Taoists, showing in an examplary way how sacred scriptures should be transmitted and how one becomes a Taoist initiate. Both modes of the teaching Lao-tzu are documented in sixth-century texts of the Celestial Masters school.

First, Lao-tzu as the teacher of mythical sovereigns appears in the *K'ai-t'ien-ching* (Scripture on Opening the Cosmos, TT 1437), a text that describes the creation and early development of the universe. It says,

> In the time of the sovereign Shen-nung [who first developed gricul-ture], Lao-tzu descended to be his teacher. Called Master of Vast Completion, he issued the *T'ai-wei-ching* (Scripture of Great Tenuity) to teach Shen-nung about the hundred plants and five grains. Shen-nung accordingly ordered the people to plant and reap those grains so that they could eat them instead of taking the lives of birds and beasts.
>
> After him, there was the sovereign Sui-jen [who first discov-ered fire]. Lao-tzu descended to be his teacher. He taught Sui-jen to drill wood and make fire, allowing the continuation of light even at night and enabling people to cook raw meat. It put an end to their rancid and bloody smells. (Kohn 1993, 14)

Thus no development of civilization went without the divine interven-tion of the Tao, here described as the deity Lao-tzu descending to give instructions in sacred scriptures. It did so under all the culture heroes of Confucian myth, who thereby are no longer independent agents but mere recipients of the Tao's orders. Lao-tzu is thus ultimately respon-sible for all forms of Chinese culture, providing the right impetus of cosmic energy at always the right time.

The second part of the myth that speaks about Lao-tzu as a teacher concerns the transmission of the *Tao-te-ching* to Yin Hsi. This story, to begin with, is not told in isolation but emerges as just one more instance of the deity delivering cultural and salvific impulses to suffering human-ity. Still, it is the high point of Lao-tzu's career during his second birth, the ultimate purpose for his incarnation in human form. As such, the story is developed to show the close interaction of Taoist master and disciple. It is told in the sixth-century biography of Yin Hsi, found today in a seventh-century encyclopedia known as *San-tung chu-nang* (Pearly Bag of the Three Caverns, TT 1139, 9.8b–14b).

It begins with Lao-tzu's arrival on the pass and the initial testing of Yin Hsi as his future disciple. The text tells the following story:

[Upon hearing that Lao-tzu had arrived], Yin Hsi tied on his seal of office and took his official tablet to receive the visitor with the proper formality.

"I am only a poor and humble old man," Lao-tzu said. "I live to the east of the pass, but my fields are on its western side. Tomorrow will be the day of the winter sacrifice. I wish to go and get some fuel, and that is all. Why does the honorable Guardian hold me?" (9.15b)

Despite this plea, Yin Hsi insists that Lao-tzu is much more than a farmer, which the latter duly admits. Then Yin Hsi asks to be taught. Lao-tzu, however, is not yet satisfied and tests his future disciple further by asking Yin Hsi to spell out his desire to pursue the Tao and to explain how he knew about Lao-tzu's true nature. Yin Hsi complies and launches into a lengthy description of his deep wish to realize the Tao, then recounts how his studies in astrology led him to recognize Lao-tzu's approach. Lao-tzu finally accepts him as a worthy disciple who has shown a long-standing inclination toward the Tao together with a strong determination not to be led astray (9.16a).

The myth here presents an exemplary interaction of master and disciple, reflecting the actual testing that aspirants of the Tao had to undergo before being admitted to the order. A new follower, when he first encountered the Tao and its organization, had to prove his inherent ability, determination, and loyalty; he had to state his wishes clearly before his elders and show that he had taken measures of his own toward realizing his goal. Similarly, followers had to pledge allegiance to the Tao and formally eschew all profit-making from their religious powers. The myth reflects this in a new retelling of the incident surrounding Lao-tzu's retainer, Hsü Chia, first described in Ko Hung's *Shen-hsien-chuan* cited above. The same story is told about the greedy retainer who collapses into a heap of bones and is helped back to life by Yin Hsi. But more than showing Lao-tzu's powers over life and death, it here serves to confront the uneducated servant Hsü Chia with the literate official Yin Hsi, the worldly with the spiritual, the greedy shaman with the pure Taoists, and by extension the vernacular versus the classical forms of Taoist ritual (Schipper 1985, 44). Any true ordinand, like Yin Hsi, has to commit himself fully to the Tao, giving up commercial interests and personal wishes.

The actual ordination takes place next when Lao-tzu transmits the *Tao-te-ching* together with several other texts, explanations, and precepts. Just as candidates of the Tao received practical methods and formal precepts together with the scriptures at ordination, so Yin Hsi in the myth learns to follow the Tao through oral explanations and behavioral precepts.[12] This, however, places him only at the bottom rung of the celestial ladder, and he still needs a period of intensive practice to reach the higher stages. Thus Lao-tzu gives Yin Hsi three years to perfect his Tao, after which he promises to meet him again in a "black sheep shop" in Ch'eng-tu (Ssu-ch'uan).[13]

Yin Hsi obeys and gives himself over to practicing full-time, then goes to find Lao-tzu. Again he needs the qualities of strong determination and utter trust in order to gain access to his master, who resides with a family in Ch'eng-tu and sends out a black sheep to the market as the agreed sign. Eventually the two meet again, and Lao-tzu examines his student to find him successful. He announces that Yin Hsi's immortal name is now listed in the perfected registers in the heavens and calls down a celestial procession that bestows upon Yin Hsi the proper garb of the immortals: a purple cap, a flying feathery skirt, cinnabar sleeves, and so on. He further bestows upon him the formal title "Master of the Beginning of the Scripture" and elevates him to the rank of "Highest Perfected."[14] In a culmination of the successful ordination, Lao-tzu next takes Yin Xi on an ecstatic journey through the universe, around the far corners of the world, to the paradises of P'eng-lai and K'un-lun, and into the nine heavens. Only after completing this mythological equivalent of the highest form of medieval Taoist practice, do the two sages set out on their concrete travel into the lands of the barbarians.

Yin Xi's three-year training period, his second meeting with Lao-tzu, and their joint travels represent the attainment of the highest ordination rank in medieval Taoism, that of Preceptor of the Three Caverns (Benn 1991, 96–97). Lao-tzu in this section of the myth is the ideal Taoist master, while Yin Hsi is the model Taoist follower. Lao-tzu as the Tao personified, gives his teaching to humanity; a divine savior, he descends into a human body to help all those willing to be saved, transmitting his teaching and the necessary instructions in a formal sequence of preparation, testing, training, and attainment.

Lao-tzu's Western Journey

The myth culminates in the two sages' travels to the west (Central Asia and India), where they convert the local population to Taoism. Summarily called "the conversion of the barbarians" (*hua-hu*), this part of the myth both in Yin Xi's hagiography and in the sixth-century version of the *Hua-hu-ching*, which survives partly in the *San-tung chu-nang* (9.14b–20b).[15] According to this, Lao-tzu and Yin Hsi go west and practice the Tao on a mountain in northern India. Their presence becomes known and the local "barbarian" king's curiosity is aroused. They exchange formal greetings and invite each other to banquets. While Lao-tzu is super-naturally able to feast the country's population for a long time, the king has trouble entertaining the enormous Taoist host of celestials and im-mortals. When his treasury is getting exhausted, he wonders whether Lao-tzu and Yin Hsi are really sages or rather demons in disguise. Fearing the latter, he has them burnt at the stake, thrown into boiling cauldrons, drowned in deep waters, and pierced by swords and lances. But the Taoists cannot be harmed

> "Are they finally dead?" the king asked.
>
> "No, Your Majesty," the runner reported. "When we threw them into the deep pool, dragon kings came to support them. The old man brings forth a radiance that fills the whole kingdom. They have not sunk and they are not dead. Oh, how can that be?!"
>
> The king was exasperated. "Is it possible that this Lao-tzu has control over celestial forces and sagely beings?" he asked his ministers. "If so, wouldn't it be better if we served him?" (*San-tung chu-nang* 9.13b)

The ministers agree and the king submits to Lao-tzu, who not only spreads his teaching but also acts to civilize the barbarians. In its eighth-century version, the *Hua-hu-ching* has him address them:

> "You barbarians are greedy and cruel! You make no difference be-tween kin and stranger and are intent only to satisfy your greed and debauchery! Not a trace of mercy or sense of social duty within you! Look at you! Your hair and beards are unkempt and too long! How can you comb and wash it? Even from a distance you are full of rank smell! How dirty your bodies must be!
>
> "Now that you are made to cultivate the Tao all these things will be great annoyances to your practice. I therefore order all of you to shave off your beards and hair. According to your native customs, all your garments are made of felt and fur. By teaching you the Lesser Way [Buddhism], I will by and by lead you to more cultivated manners." (ch. 1; Kohn 1993, 75–76)

This passage explains the strange customs of Buddhist practitioners as the civilizing efforts of the emigré Lao-tzu, the only way in which the primitive Indian "barbarians" can ever approach the purity of the Chi-nese Tao. Lao-tzu here is not only the god of the Tao incarnate, the savior of humanity in its purity, and the ideal model for Taoist practitioners. He is also the conquering hero, who pursues his quest, wins his kingdom, and sets up a codex of rules for his people. Like the hero, he does not attain his goal with ease but has to undergo a series of dangerous ordeals, tortures of fire, water, and weapons, which not by accident are the same as those suffered by sinners in hell. The hero Lao-tzu thus shows how the Tao serves to overcome even the deepest human suffering and bestows life in the midst of death. In addition, Lao-tzu as the Tao is also the paragon representative of superior Chinese culture who spreads humaneness and proper ritual formality among the non-Chinese and thus helps to create a more unified and civilized world.

Lao-tzu's exploits in the west reach a high point in the submission of the barbarian king, but they do not end there. Installing Yin Hsi as his representative, to be venerated as the "Buddha," he continues his proselytizing journey to many countries and eventually is born as the historical Buddha (Reiter 1990, 33). In the end, his mission accomplished, he returns to heaven, from where, in continuation of his role as the personified Tao, he again returns in China to reveal the Tao to the founder of the Celestial Masters and other Taoist leaders.

Conclusion

The Lao-tzu myth takes off from the narrative on the ancient philosopher in the *Shih-chi* and is first, during the Han dynasty, developed by three different social groups to varying effect. Magical practitioners emphasize Lao-tzu's longevity and ascetic discipline, describing him in terms of a successful practitioner and immortal. The political elite and the imperial court see in him the personification of the Tao, the representative of cosmic harmony on earth and in human society, while organized Taoist cults find in Lao-tzu their savior from an unbearable life, the harbinger of Great Peace, the god who has set the world right before and will continue to do so. By the fifth century, these three mythical strands have merged into one and characterize him as the highest god of the Celestial Masters. As this school of Taoism underwent further developments, so the myth of the god expanded and was reshaped. In its full extent, it can then be divided into three sections, concerning Lao-tzu's birth, his teaching among humanity, and his conversion of the western peoples. Throughout, Buddhist influence is felt, especially in the imagery of his emergence that imitates the birth of the Buddha and in the claim that his proselytization of the west caused the beginnings of Buddhism. The myth of the god supports the Taoist bid for universality, mirrors the process of Taoist ordination, and presents the Chinese insistence on cultural superiority vis-à-vis their western neighbors, expanding the cosmic power of the Tao outward in concentric circles. Lao-tzu, the ancient philosopher, even in his first biography depicted with characteristics that served the needs of the budding Taoist school, over the centuries continued to fill various roles required by the demands of different religious communities. While maintaining certain elementary characteristics and narrative events, his myth significantly changed in scope and meaning, transforming the god's shape in accordance with the flow of time.

Notes

1. This essay is based on a longer study of Lao-tzu in Taoist history and myth, which will appear under the title "Laozi in Taoist History."

2. For more on these immortals and their roles in religious Taoism, see Yamada 1989; Sakade 1985.

3. These are celestial palaces and energy centers in the body. Practitioners of early Taoist meditation united with the heavenly forces by empowering these centers with the presence of celestial deities. See Robinet 1993.

4. The text has survived only in manuscript and is not always legible. Found at Tun-huang (S. 2295), it is reprinted in Seidel 1969, 131–36, and Ōfuchi 1979, 686. It was written by a certain Wang Chou and revised in 612 by a monk of the Monastery of Mystery Metropolis in Ch'ang-an (Seidel 1969a, 60). It gives expression to the beliefs of a popular messianic cult in southwest China. A complete French translation of the text, on which I base my English version, is found in Seidel 1969a, 60–73.

5. For a more detailed discussion of Lao-tzu as the body of the Tao and god of popular Taoist cults, see Ishii 1983, 127; Maspero 1981, 396; Schipper 1978; 1994.

6. This follows the citation of the *Shen-hsien-chuan* in *T'ai-p'ing kuang-chi* 8. For a complete translation of Chang's biography, see Giles 1948, 60. Studies are found in Imbault-Huart 1884; Kobayashi 1992.

7. Texts in the Taoist Canon (*Tao-tsang*, abbreviated TT) are given according to Schipper 1975.

8. The word *tzu*, often used as a suffix for philosophers' names, is also a pronoun meaning "you" and the common word for "son" or "child."

9. The virgin birth is a common motif in myths and hero stories all over the world. Studies by Otto Rank, Lord Raglan, Joseph Campbell, and Alan Dundes are conveniently edited in Segal 1990. A collection of hero stories from various times and cultures is found in Leeming 1973.

10. This follows a citation from the *Hsuan-miao nei-p'ien* in Ku Huan's *Yi-hsia-lun* (Treatise on Barbarians and Chinese; dated to 467), which is contained in his biography in *Nan-shih* (History of the South) 75.

11. The text is contained in T. (Taishō Canon) 185, vol. 3.471–83. Texts in the Buddhist canon are cited after the Japanese Taishō Tripitaka edition (abbreviated T.), giving the serial number, the volume, and the page.

12. A detailed description of all the texts given to Yin Hsi according to the myth is found in the seventh-century *Hun-yuan chen-lu* (Perfect Record of Chaos Prime, TT 954). A study of this text is found in Kusuyama 1979, 393–422.

13. This is an important place in Taoism that even today is marked by a flourishing Taoist temple named after the black sheep (Ch'ing-yang-kung). See Yusa 1986.

14. The details of this part of the myth are desribed particularly in the twelfth-century *Yu-lung chuan* (Like unto a Dragon, TT 774) 4.2a.

15. The first version of the text goes back to about 300 C.E. and is mostly lost. Its third version, of the eighth century, has survived in a group of manuscripts found at Tun-huang. A fourth, illustrated version from the thirteenth-century has been edited in Reiter 1990. See Kohn 1995, 195.

References

Benn, Charles D. 1991. *The Cavern Mystery Transmission: A Taoist Ordination Rite of A.D. 711*. Honolulu: University of Hawaii Press.

Boltz, Judith M. 1987. *A Survey of Taoist Literature: Tenth to Seventeenth Centuries*. China Research Monograph 32. Berkeley: University of California.

Giles, Lionel. 1948. *A Gallery of Chinese Immortals*. London: John Murray.

Imbault-Huart, M. C. 1884. "La légende du premier pape des taoistes." *Journal Asiatique* 8.4: 389–461.

Ishii Masako. 1983. "Dōkyō no kamigami." In *Dōkyō*, ed. Fukui Kōjun et al., 1: 121–88. Tokyo: Hirakawa.

Kaltenmark, Maxime. 1953. *Le Lie-sien tchouan*. Peking: Université de Paris Publications. Reprinted 1988.

Kobayashi Masayoshi. 1992. "The Celestial Masters Under the Eastern Jin and Liu-Song Dynasties." *Taoist Resources* 3.2: 17–45.

Kohn, Livia. 1989. "Die Emigration des Laozi: Mythologische Entwicklungen vom 2. bis 6. Jahrhundert." *Monumenta Serica* 38: 49–68.

———. 1991. *Taoist Mystical Philosophy: The Scripture of Western Ascension*. Albany: State University of New York Press.

———, ed. 1993. *The Taoist Experience: An Anthology*. Albany: State University of New York Press, 1993.

———. 1995. *Laughing at the Tao: Debates among Buddhists and Taoists in Medieval China*. Princeton, N.J.: Princeton University Press.

———. 1996. "Laozi: Ancient Philosopher, Master of Longevity, and Taoist God." In *Religions of China in Practice*, ed. Donald S. Lopez Jr., 52–63. Princeton, N.J.: Princeton University Press.

Kusuyama Haruki. 1979. *Rōshi densetsu no kenkyū*. Tokyo: Sōbunsha.

Leeming, David A. 1973. *Mythology: The Voyage of the Hero*. Philadelphia: J. B. Lippincott Company.

Lewis, Mark E. 1990. *Sanctioned Violence in Early China*. Albany: State University of New York Press.

Major, John S. 1993. *Heaven and Earth in Early Han Thought: Chapters Three, Four, and Five of the Huainanzi*. Albany: State University of New York Press.

Maspero, Henri. 1981. *Taoism and Chinese Religion*. Translated by Frank Kierman. Amherst: University of Massachusetts Press.

O'Flaherty, Wendy D. 1975. *Hindu Myths: A Sourcebook Translated from the Sanskrit*. Baltimore, Md: Penguin.

Ōfuchi Ninji. 1979. *Tonkō dōkei: Zuroku hen*. Tokyo: Kokubu shoten.

Reiter, Florian C., ed. 1990. *Leben und Wirken Lao-Tzu's in Schrift und Bild: Lao-chün pa-shih-i-hua t'u-shuo*. Würzburg, Germany: Königshausen & Neumann.

Robinet, Isabelle. 1993. *Taoist Meditation*. Translated by Norman Girardot and Julian Pas. Albany: State University of New York Press.

Sailey, Jay. 1978. *The Master Who Embraces Simplicity: A Study of the Philosophy of Ko Hung (A.D. 283–343)*. San Francisco: Chinese Materials Center.

Sakade Yoshinobu. 1985. "Hōso densetsu to Hōsokyō." In *Chūgoku shinhakken kagakushi shiryō no kenkyū*, ed. Yamada Keiji, 2: 405–62. Kyoto: Jimbun kagaku kenkyūjo.

Schipper, Kristofer. 1975. *Concordance du Tao Tsang: Titres des ouvrages*. Paris: Publications de l'École Française d'Extrême-Orient.

———. 1978. "The Taoist Body." *History of Religions* 17: 355–87.

———. 1985. "Vernacular and Classical Ritual in Taoism." *Journal of Asian Studies* 65: 21–51.

———. 1994. *The Taoist Body*. Translated by Karen C. Duval. Berkeley: University of California Press.

Segal, Robert A., ed. 1990. *In Quest of the Hero*. Princeton, N.J.: Princeton University Press.

Seidel, Anna. 1969a. *La divinisation de Lao-tseu dans le Taoisme des Han*. Paris: École Française d'Extrême Orient. Reprinted 1992.

———. 1969b. "The Image of the Perfect Ruler in Early Taoist Messianism." *History of Religions* 9: 216–47.

———. 1978a. "Der Kaiser und sein Ratgeber." *Saeculum* 29: 18–50.

———. 1978b. "Das neue Testament des Tao." *Saeculum* 29: 147–72.

———. 1984. "Taoist Messianism." *Numen* 31: 161–74.

Ware, James R. 1966. *Alchemy, Medicine and Religion in the China of AD 320*. Cambridge, Mass.: MIT Press.

Yamada, Toshiaki. 1989. "Longevity Techniques and the Compilation of the *Lingbao wufuxu*." In *Taoist Meditation and Longevity Techniques*, ed. Livia Kohn, 97–122. Ann Arbor: University of Michigan Press.

Yü Ying-shih. 1964. "Life and Immortality in the Mind of Han-China." *Harvard Journal of Asiatic Studies* 25: 80–122.

Yūsa Noboru. 1986. "Seito seiyōkyū seijōsan oyobi shisen ni okeru dōkyō kenkyū no genshō." *Tōhōshūkyō* 68: 86–98.

Zürcher, Erik. 1959. *The Buddhist Conquest of China: The Spread and Adaptation of Buddhism in Early Medieval China*. 2 vols. Leiden, The Netherlands: E. Brill.

3

Lao-tzu in Six Dynasties Taoist Sculpture

Yoshiko Kamitsuka

Understood in its widest sense,[1] Taoist sculpture includes all images of holy figures worshiped in Chinese religion, the gods of the stars, of water and thunder, of mountains and the earth, as well as army heroes and many more. It also includes Taoist art work found in temples throughout Chinese history, the statues of Taoist deities known from texts and artistic objects.[2] To limit the inquiry, this essay concentrates on early medieval images of Lao-tzu as the highest Taoist god, known then as the Highest Venerable Lord (T'ai-shang lao-chün) and the Heavenly Worthy of Primordial Beginning (Yuan-shih t'ien-tsun). The period under discussion is known as the Six Dynasties, or as the division of North and South. Lasting from the third to sixth centuries C.E., it was the time when Buddhism gained a firm hold in Chinese culture and when organized Taoist doctrine and practice first developed. The northern part of the country was ruled by a non-Chinese Hunnish people, the T'o-pa, who called their dynasty the Wei (Northern Wei) and had their capital at Lo-yang. The indigenous Chinese government had fled south and established itself in Chien-k'ang (modern Nanking). A number of different dynasties succeeded each other here, most important among which were the Liu-Sung (420–479) and the Liang (502–557).

The role of religion in the two parts of China differed significantly. In the south, it was transmitted mainly by the aristocrats or gentry, who followed the philosophical teachings of Confucius or Lao-tzu and saw Buddhism as an attractive new alternative. Religious practice tended to come out of philosophical convictions; it was not centralized but depended on local leaders. Both organized Taoist and Buddhist groups were growing slowly, seeking upper-class followers and leading the common people with a belief in a better world. Among Taoist leaders, Lu Hsiu-ching (406–477), member of the gentry, literatus, and adherent of

63

the Celestial Masters, made especially significant contributions to the organization of the Taoist teaching.

In the north, all religion was state-sponsored and depended on the government's approval. Philosophies ranked far below practicable doctrines and organizational models that could support T'o-pa rule. Adapting Chinese statecraft, the foreign rulers sought out religious leaders who could offer them an integrated way of governing. Both Buddhists and Taoists were successful at different times in gaining the confidence of the rulers and had their creeds established as state religions. Notable among the Taoists was K'ou Ch'ien-chih (365–448) of the Celestial Masters school, who with a set of new revelations founded a theocracy that lasted for several decades.[3] The common people, if they were not led to rebellion by millenarian preachers, were subject to a local administration that was carried to a large extent by officially authorized clergy, either Buddhist or Taoist.

Against this background, Taoist sculpture developed predominantly in north China. It both provides concrete evidence and furthers our understanding of early religious Taoism among the common people. Its foremost object or highest god was the deified Lao-tzu, who had developed from an ancient philosopher and the alleged author of the *Tao-te-ching*. He was the giver of revelations, the recipient of sacrifices and worship, and was known as the Highest Venerable Lord. As such, he was the Tao, the underlying force of the universe, "dispersed—pure energy, embodied—a man," as a second-century work put it. With the introduction of Buddhist statues, this personified Tao was increasingly depicted in human form and venerated like a Buddha or popular deity. How exactly he was seen and approached, how the format of his depiction developed over time, shall be the subject of the following pages. I will begin with a preliminary survey of the development and nature of Taoist sculpture, then focus on the inscriptions found on various objects to examine the beliefs expressed in them and the function they had in medieval Chinese society.

The Emergence of Taoist Sculpture

The oldest extant literary evidence for the existence of Taoist sculpture is from the fifth century, the time of Lu Hsiu-ching and K'ou Ch'ien-chih. No immediate records about sculptural activities associated with these men survive from their time, but the seventh-century Buddhist polemicist Shih Fa-lin associates them with artistic efforts in his *Pien-cheng lun* (In Defense of What Is Right). He says,

Thinking about it, before the dynasties of the Liang, Ch'en, Ch'i, and Wei [of the sixth century], there was only the worship of sacred scriptures, which were kept in hollow gourds or small baskets. Originally there were no images of the Heavenly Worthy.

As both Master Jen in his *Tao-lun* [On the Tao] and Mr. Tu in his *Yu-ch'iu* [In Pursuit of the Obscure] say, "The Tao has neither matter nor form; it is the pure essence of yin and yang." Similarly the *T'ao yin-chü nei-chuan* [Inner Biography of Recluse T'ao] states: "He [the patriarch T'ao Hung-ching] set up both Buddhist and Taoist institutions on Mao-shan [Mount Mao near Nanking] and paid homage in both every day. In the Buddhist halls there were sacred statues, which the Taoist temples did not have."

Moreover, Wang Ch'un states in his *San-chiao-lun* [On the Three Teachings]: "Taoists recently have come to do well nigh anything for their livelihood. In order to gain more followers, they have even imitated Buddhists in their creation of sacred images. These so-called statues of the Heavenly Worthy show the god with two perfected to his right and left and are placed in the center of Taoist halls of worship. Attracting a greater number of followers with these, the Taoists are able to make a living. Lu Hsiu-ching of the Sung dynasty was among those image-makers." (T. 2110, 52.535a;[4] see Ch'en 1963, 268–69)

According to this passage, originally Taoists did not have religious images because "the Tao has neither matter nor form." This is also evident from the Taoist argument presented in the polemical text *Shih san-p'o lun* (Examining the Essay on the Threefold Destruction) by the Buddhist monk Seng-shun (fl. 500). According to him, a defender of Taoism says, "The barbarians do not believe in emptiness and nonbeing, therefore when Lao-tzu emigrated he had them make statues of his form and with their help converted them" (T. 2102; 52.52b). While, therefore, according to high doctrine, Taoists were not supposed to make images, the general populace had few scruples of this kind. Increasingly exposed to Buddhist statues, people fashioned Taoist images too, beginning, as the texts have it, in the fifth century in the environment of Lu Hsiu-ching. Other Buddhist texts critical of the Taoist religion strongly allege that Taoists plagiarized Buddhist images. As Chen Luan says in his *Hsiao-tao lun* (Laughing at the Tao) of the year 570: "Taoists sometimes make statues of the Venerable Lord with two bodhisattvas in attendance. One is Vajragarbha; the other, Avalokiteśvara" (T. 2103; 52.146b). He here identifies the two attendants of the Tao with Buddhist deities and polemically attacks Taoism. Chen Luan, as other Buddhists engaged in the medieval religious debates, thereby places all Taoist sculpture firmly in the shadow of the foreign religion.

While Lu Hsiu-ching was actively organizing the religion in the south, K'ou Ch'ien-chih strove to purge and rejuvenate the movement of the Celestial Masters in the foreign-dominated north and, in the 430s, succeeded in establishing a Taoist theocracy by becoming the leading official under Emperor T'ai-wu of the Northern (T'o-pa) Wei. After the latter had been formally ordained as a Taoist by receiving sacred talismans and registers, all emperors of the northern dynasties followed suit and, as the records emphasize, had images fashioned of the Heavenly Worthy and the host of immortals for their personal worship. In this part of China, Taoist sculpture therefore first appeared through K'ou Ch'ien-chih's influence and the ensuing political popularity of the religion. Literary sources thus place the emergence of Taoist sculpture in the fifth century, while Buddhist polemics criticize it as a cheap imitation of their artwork. On this background, what actual works of Taoist sculpture survive and what are their particular characteristics?

Early Taoist Images

In comparison to extant Buddhist works of art, Taoist images of the Six Dynasties are few in number. As far as I can ascertain, at present about fifty Taoist works, as opposed to over 2,500 Buddhist images, are known to survive in actuality or in rubbings, or are mentioned in inscriptions on stone or metal, listed in chronological order in table 3.1.[5] Among them, only four go back to the fifth century, while twenty-five come from the first half of the sixth century, and twenty from its second half. This roughly matches the literary evidence that places the first works of Taoist sculpture in the time of Lu Hsiu-ching and K'ou Ch'ien-chih. Also, all extant or known objects are clearly from the north. This has to do with the fact that the T'o-pa, in an effort to win the divine support of their ancestors, were eager religious builders, sponsoring creations also for the great Buddhist cave temples. Taoist steles and images, it seems, were thus primarily an offshoot of Buddhist sculptural activity in the north.

The oldest extant example of a Taoist sculpture is the Buddho-Taoist tablet sponsored by Wei Wen-lang of the year 424.[6] It is a four-sided object, one facet of which shows a Taoist image and inscription while the other three are covered with Buddhist materials, showing the complex integration of Buddhism and Taoism at the time. It is today preserved in the

Yao District Museum of Shensi Province, which also holds several similar works (nos. 26, 28, 32, 33, 37 in table 3.1) that usually have two Taoist and two Buddhist sides. The four-sided stele of the year 570 (no. 43), which is mentioned in a Ch'ing-dynasty source, is clearly described as being "respectfully created with two faces depicting ten Buddhist images and the other two depicting eight Taoist images" (*T'ao-chai tsang shi-chi* 14.3a).

From the perspective of art history, images and inscriptions that integrate the two religions go back to the creation of four-sided objects in the developing Chinese Buddhist community. A different Buddha or bodhisattva was depicted on each of the four faces, as for example in the work dated to 566, found at the Sheng-mu Monastery, where the Buddha Śākyamuni appears in association with Maitreya, Avalokiteśvara, and Amitābha (Matsubara 1961, 222). Certain donors, sponsoring the creation of a four-sided work, must have felt it appropriate to include Taoist images on the sides. For them, the Taoism current at the time, it seems, was merely a variant of the more dominant Buddhist religion. Their worlds overlapping, Buddhas, bodhisattvas, and venerables were apparently seen as different aspects of the many deities available to succor poor mortals. Wei Wen-lang's Buddho-Taoist stele and the image of the Buddha, Lao-tzu, and several bodhisattvas, sponsored by Li T'an-hsin and his brothers (no. 37), both have inscriptions that refer to their donors as "followers of the Buddha."

That such "followers of the Buddha" in their devout creation of Buddhist art should also include the images of Taoist deities may seem strange at first glance. Closer examination, however, reveals that this mixture and even integration of Buddhism and Taoism documents the popular understanding of the two religions. Ordinary people who were not doctrinal specialists of either creed were blissfully unaware of the subtle variants and sophisticated ranking of their doctrines and philosophies. Instead of being hampered by minor differences, they overcame the distinctions and focused on the common points between the religions, creating a uniquely Chinese form of Buddhism and developing Taoism in their own way.

The Taoist God

All extant sculptures show the highest Taoist god, sometimes alone, sometimes with two attendants. Many of them also have inscriptions, indicating which deity is depicted and giving his or her formal title. The work sponsored by Wei Wen-lang merely says that it is "a work showing both Buddhist and Taoist images." The expression "Taoist image" (*tao-hsiang*), which occurs here for the first time, is the natural counterpart to

TABLE 3.1

Taoist Bas-Relief Steles and Images

No.	Date	Object/Name of sponsor	Present location
1.	424	Buddho-Taoist stele of Wei Wen-lang	Yao District Museum
2.	496	Sovereign Venerable Lord of Yao Po-to	Yao District Museum
3.	500	Stele of Yang Hsiang-chao	Yao District Museum
4.	500	Stele of Yang Lang-hei	Yao District Museum
5.	505	Stele of Feng Shen-yü et al.	Lin-t'ung District Museum
6.	508+	Three Worthies at Shih-hung Monastery in Fu-chou	Yung-ch'ing wen-k'u
7.	513	Heavenly Worthy of Chang Hsiang-tui	Peking Library (rubbing)
8.	512+	Stele of Wang Shih-pao	Yao District Museum
9.	512+	Stele of Wu Hung-piao and brothers	Yao District Museum
10.	514	Stele of Chang Luan-kuo	Yao District Museum
11.	515	Two Worthies of Chiao Ts'ai	Boston Museum of Fine Arts
12.	515	Three Worthies of Mr. Kai	Osaka Municipal Museum of Art
13.	517	Stele of Sixteen Citizens	Shensi Provincial Museum
14.	519	Stele of Wei Tao-kuan et al.	Lin-t'ung District Museum
15.	520	Stele of Ch'i Shih-chen	Yao District Museum
16.	521	Stele of Ch'i Ma-jen	Yao District Museum
17.	521	Three Worthies with Inscription	Literary sources
18.	522	Lao-tzu and the Buddha of Yang Ch'ü-jen	Literary sources
19.	524	Stele of Mr. Wei	Literary sources
20.	526	Stele of Kuo Fa-lo et al.	Peking Library (rubbing)
21.	527	Stele of the Nun Wang A-shan	Museum of Chinese History, Peking
22.	532	Stele of Fan Nu-tzu	Peking Library (rubbing)
23.	534	Two-sided stele	Osaka Municipal Museum of Art
24.	NWei	Four-sided stele from Louguan Monastery near Hsi-an	Literary sources
25.	NWei	Bronze stele of standing Venerable	Tokyo National Museum
26.	NWei	Stele of Hsia Hou-tseng	Yao District Museum
27.	NWei	Venerable of Ch'i Ma-jen	Hsi-an Forest of Steles
28.	NWei	Stele of Seventy Citizens	Yao District Museum
29.	548	Highest Venerable of Mr. Ts'ai	Kyoto University Institute for Humanistic Research (rubbing)
30.	554	Four-sided stele	Osaka Municipal Museum of Art

No.	Date	Object/Name of sponsor	Present location
31.	557	Buddho-Taoist stele of Chiang Tu-lo	Ssu-ch'uan, Chien-yang
32.	559	Stele of Chiang A-lu	Yao District Museum
33.	Chou	Stele of Lei Hsiao-pao	Yao District Museum
34.	561	Venerable Lord of Ma Lo-tzu	Museum of Chinese History
35.	561	Stele of Fu Lan-hsi	Yao District Museum
36.	562	Stele with inscription	Shodo Museum, Tokyo
37.	562	Buddha, Highest Venerable, and bodhisattvas; Stele of Li T'an-hsin and brothers	Yao District Museum
38.	564	Venerable Lord of Yao Tao-ni	Literary sources
39.	565	Venerable Lord of Chiang Ts'uan	Peking Library (rubbing)
40.	567	Heavenly Worthy of Ch'üan Ho-tsao	Literary source
41.	568	Venerable Lord of Tu Ch'ung-?	Tokyo Fine Arts University
42.	569	Venerable Lord of Ts'ai Ch'en-hu	Literary sources
43.	570	Four-sided stele	Literary sources
44.	572	Heavenly Worthy of Li Yuan-hai	Peking Library (rubbing)
45.	576	Venerable Lord of Meng A-fei	Peking Library (rubbing)
46.	578	Stele of Ma T'ien-hsiang	Peking Library (rubbing)
47.	NQi	Stele of Ma Ch'i, Abbot of Great Capital Monastery	Lo-yang Museum of Ancient Arts
48.	Chou	Three Worthies	Osaka Municipal Museum of Art
49.	Chou	Four-sided stele	Fujii Yurin, Kyoto

"Buddhist image" (*fo-hsiang*), a term that had been in use earlier. More specific references to Taoist images, in addition, name the deity depicted: Sovereign Venerable Lord, (Highest) Venerable Lord, or Heavenly Worthy (of Primordial Beginning). An example for the first is the second-oldest object, Yao Po-to's stele of the year 496 (no. 2). It says specifically that it was "respectfully created as a stele to honor the Sovereign Venerable Lord."

Among the many works, furthermore, whose inscriptions refer to the Taoist god as the "Venerable Lord" (nos. 27, 34, 38, 39, 41, 42, 45), the Venerable Lord of Tu Ch'ung-? of the year 568 (no. 41) is unusually crafted. Thirty-five centimeters in height, this work focuses on a large central image of Lao-tzu (see figure 3.1).[7] The deity is clad in a thick robe and wears a formal square headdress. He has a straight triangular beard. His right hand holds a fly-whisk made from a deer-tail, while his left rests on his thigh, holding a tablet. To his sides stand two attendants,

Figure 3.1

The Venerable Lord of Tu Ch'ung-?
(Tokyo University of Fine Arts and Music, no. 41), dated 568.

Statue of the god Lao-tzu owned by Tokyo University of Fine Arts and Music.
Photographed and reprinted with permission.

each grasping a jade audience tablet. The group is placed on a lotus-type platform, guarded to the right and left by lions, with an incense burner in front of the platform. The donor's parents are depicted and named in an inscription in the lower section. On the back of the stele, an inscription is written in characters that each fill one exact square, begin-ning with the words "the Taoist follower Tu-Ch'ung-? . . . . " Among all Taoist sculptures and inscriptions of the medieval period, this work is exceptional in its exactitude and formality, expressing the deep mystical sensibility of its creator and sponsor in the serenity and beauty of its image. This is a rare and outstanding work of art indeed. Aside from this, two steles do mention Lao-tzu by the name Highest Venerable Lord, of which Venerable Lord is an abbreviation (nos. 29, 37). Two further objects refer to the highest deity of the Tao as the Heavenly Worthy (nos. 7, 40) and one uses the full form of this title, Heavenly Worthy of Pri-mordial Beginning (no. 44).[8]

Two important observations may be gleaned from this information on the titles of the Highest God. One, there is no obvious relation be-tween the name in the inscription and the iconography of the image. Whether the god is named Venerable Lord (Lao-chün) or Heavenly Worthy (T'ien-tsun) makes no difference in the way he is shown. More-over, in the beginnings of Taoist art, as both early finds and literary evi-dence suggest, all images were fundamentally imitations of Buddhist pictures and differences even between Taoist and Buddhist figures are not clear. Once a more Taoist style developed, the predominant character-istics of the figures were their Chinese-style robes and headdresses, and the presence of beards and side burns. As the *Fo-tao lun-heng* (Balanced Discussion of the Buddhist Way) says, "the Heavenly Worthy wears a golden headdress on his head, is clad in a yellow robe, has white hair hanging from his temples, and holds a jade tablet in his hand" (T. 2104, 52.381c). This matches the appearance of the figures discovered so far. The specific Taoist looks of the figures, it appears, evolved gradually during the late Six Dynasties and became iconographically consistent in the sixth century. But while Taoist images became distinct from their Buddhist counterparts, still no difference was made between the Vener-able and the Heavenly Worthy.

The second observation is that many donors in the inscriptions name themselves "Taoist," "Taoist follower," or "Taoist priest," showing an active self-awareness of themselves as practicing Taoists. The titles "Taoist fol-lower" (*tao-min*, found in nos. 2, 27, 34, 40, 41, 42, 44) and "Taoist" (*tao-shih*, found in no. 7) both indicate a faithful believer in the Tao and prac-titioner of the organized Taoist religion. "Taoist priest" (*nan-kuan*, in nos. 38, 39), on the contrary, parallels "Taoist priestess" (*nü-kuan*) and refers to a specialized religious official in the hierarchy of the communal organization. People sponsoring religious images were therefore active adepts of the Taoist path.

To summarize: The most important characteristic of early Taoist sculpture is its close similarity to Buddhist works of the same period. Even where the self-awareness of the Taoist donor is evident and where the figures are depicted with Chinese-style garb, beard, and accessories, the fundamental similarity to the Buddhist model remains unchanged. Inspired in the beginning by the unprecedented rise of Buddhist statues in the fifth century, early Taoist sculpture clearly developed under the overwhelming impact of the foreign religion.

The Yao-Family Stele

What, then, was the purpose of fashioning such religious images? How, specifically, did people understand the role of the images in their lives?

An answer to these questions is found in the inscriptions on the objects. They tend to give information on five points: (1) the date of the carving, (2) the name of the donor, (3) the dedication of the object, (4) the identity of the sculptor, and (5) the religious beliefs of the donors. In addition, they often mention the purpose of the particular stele, the occasion and circumstances of its creation, and the process of its production. Before we look at the overall picture, however, let us examine in more detail an object with an extensive inscription, the Sovereign Venerable Lord of Yao Po-to (no. 2), dated to 496 and today in the Yao District Museum.[9]

This work, commissioned by the Yao family, has text inscribed on all four faces. While the front inscription is well known among scholars of Chinese calligraphy for its unusual style, neither the text on the other three faces nor the object as a whole—which until recently was considered an example of Buddhist art since scholars were unaware of Taoist art as a class of its own—have received proper scrutiny from a Taoist viewpoint. The front panel presents three rather sketchy figures carved in a niche in the stone (figure 3.2). Below them is a lengthy and still legible inscription containing a eulogy on the "Great Tao, which creates and nurtures the myriad beings" and which is most clearly manifest in Lao-tzu, here named Li Erh. Yao Po-to and his brothers state that they had this work fashioned to express their joy in the wonderful creation of the world through the Tao and Lao-tzu's salvific activities in it. Much of the text thus refers to the deity's exploits, mentioning his nobility, his encounter with the Guardian of the Pass, his transmission

FIGURE 3.2

Sovereign Venerable Lord of Yao Po-to
(Yao District Museum, no. 2), dated 496.

Statue of Yao Po-to, plate number 62, *Chugoku shodo zenshu*, volume 2, Wei, Jin, Nanbeichao. Property of Yao District Museum. Photograph in Heibonsha 1986, 2:62. Used with permission.

of the *Tao-te-ching*, and his conversion of the barbarians. In addition, the text furnishes some concrete details on the production of the object. The Yao family, it says, came from Pei-ti District in southeastern Shensi and, in true accordance with their heritage as "descendants of [the sage emperor] Shun," had given outstanding official service for many generations. A similar text on the reverse side adds the title "First Ancestor" (*shih-tsu*) to the list of renowned forebears of the clan. This "First Ancestor," as evident in the *Chin-shu* (History of the Chin Dynasty), was Yao Yi-chung, father of Yao Ch'ang, the founder of a local kingdom called the Later Ch'in. The Taoist devotees who had the stele made were therefore of eminent heritage—an exception among the donors, who were usually commoners.

The more immediate purpose of the work was "above to honor the emperor, below to support the ancestors and relatives for seven generations." This is a typical statement found in many Taoist objects of the time. In fact, among the texts deciphered so far, thirteen mention the emperor as a recipient of their good wishes, another thirteen focus on the ancestors for seven generations, and fourteen speak about their relatives. The emperor is, of course, the current ruler of the T'o-pa Wei, and the emphasis placed on him shows the continuing role of Taoism as a form of state religion at the time. The ancestors are the direct forebears of the clan and most often named summarily, but on occasion the specific names of deceased parents or grandparents are also mentioned. The relatives, finally, represent the more immediate household and family, indicating a practical concern for the present. This format is typical for Taoist art and seems to have been standardized over time.

On the left face of the Yao-family stele, two prayer incantations are engraved. The first runs:

> May we soar freely through the great void,
> Where sounds of Brahma resonate,
> Be friends with the immortals,
> And pause to look at the great Jade Capital!

This clearly expresses, in rather poetic language, the hope that the sponsors of the stele, including their ancestors, should find a way out of this world and ascend to the world of the immortals.

The second prayer says,

> May the governors and rulers
> And all the officers who keep the earth in order
> Guide the people with bright virtue. . . .

> May the good teaching be spread widely,
> And the people follow it in happiness
> Looking up with hope. . . .
> May they have their wishes realized
> And their lives extended!

This presents the vision of a religiously inspired government that would bring peace to the earth and each individual. It is of a this-worldly and practical nature, showing the hopes and wishes of the living members of the Yao family—unlike the first incantation, which is both about living people and deceased ancestors, praying for immortality for all.

In addition, the text expresses the family's hope that this image of the Sovereign Venerable Lord might beautifully radiate on the mountain side.

> For unending kalpas in the future,
> May it never be moved from this location,
> And always allow easy contact
> With the divine immortals.

This shows that the stele was made to be set up in a mountain spot where it served as a manifestation of the celestials on earth. It would allow easy contact and communication between earthlings and heavenly beings, including the family ancestors-cum-immortals. Through their intercession, in turn, all the family's present hopes would eventually be realized. The more ancient and primitive belief in sacred mountains as communication centers between ancestors and descendants is here linked with Taoist doctrine and the vision of the immortals. Lao-tzu as the Sovereign Venerable Lord in this context has the important role of mediator between the natural world on earth, in which he appears carved in stone, and the spiritual world of the heavens, where he appears in his true celestial form.

On the right face of the stele is another incantation, which immediately reflects Six Dynasties Taoist thought.

> We pray that
> All the members of Taoist Yao Po-to's family—
> His three forebears and five ancestors,
> His fathers and mothers of seven generations,
> All his relatives, long deceased or dead lately—
> If currently in the three bad rebirths,
> May speedily be rescued and liberated!

> May they forever be separated from
> The suffering of the dark hell prisons,
> And ascend to the Southern Palace,
> The true home of the immortals!
> Should they, again, be reborn as humans,
> May they have lords and kings for their
> fathers!

This prays for the liberation of the family's ancestors from all suffering in the "three bad rebirths" in the underworld prisons or hells, as a hungry ghost, or as an animal. Instead, they should ascend to the Southern Palace where the souls of the dead are purified and given new, immortal bodies. After serving their term in heaven or in hell, if ever they should be reborn on earth, it is hoped that they will be in noble or royal families, living a blessed life of ease.

This kind of this-worldly, practical orientation in the ancestral cult is typical for the religious texts and activities of the time. A very similar incantation is, in fact, found in the *Lao-chün yin-sung chieh-ching* (Scripture of Recited Precepts of the Venerable Lord, TT 785),[10] a text of thirty-six Taoist rules, revealed to K'ou Ch'ien-chih in the year 415. The context here is a detailed set of instructions how "Taoist youngsters, priests, male and female followers should burn incense and offer prayers" (Rule 21, 11a). Most commonly invocations like these were used in formal religious ritual, such as the Golden or Yellow Register Rite or the Rite of Mud and Ashes.[11] Participants typically began with the burning of incense and the noisy clapping of teeth in order to establish communication with the divine. Then a formal invocation of repentance would be recited while the sinner touched his head to the ground in supplication. Undergoing long monotonous penances, believers hoped to gain salvation for themselves and their ancestors. The central portion of such rites was the prayer invocation. It commonly contained a petition for the pardon of one's sins and a request for permission to ascend to the immortals after death; a prayer on behalf of one's ancestors to have them freed from hell; and a prayer for the salvation of all people, living and dead, for peace on earth, and for the well-being of the emperor. Such ritual invocations, known from the literature, closely match the inscriptions found on the Yao-family stele—which thus provides concrete evidence that such rituals were in fact practiced at the time.

The four faces of the Yao-family stele together contain the longest inscription of any Taoist object known to date. In content, it ranges from praise for the Sovereign Venerable Lord and the vision of the immortals' realm to the practicalities of the ancestral cult and hopes for a better life on earth. It actively integrates all these different concepts, showing the richness and complexity of medieval Taoism.

Inscriptions in General

Typically Taoist inscriptions are remakably similar to their Buddhist counterparts. As mentioned previously, the wish "above to honor the emperor, below to support the ancestors and relatives for seven genera- tions" is a typical statement found in both, often supplemented by the desire to help "all living beings," a trend inspired by Mahāyāna Bud- dhism. In addition, the expression "third teaching of the dharma under the dragon flower tree" occurs occasionally, indicating the hope that the future buddha Maitreya would descend and create a better world. There are also mentions of "spontaneously appearing food and clothing," "Three Treasures," "purple lotus," "Three Worlds," and other terms that go back to Buddhist concepts and were only gradually integrated into Taoism.[12] They appear most frequently in the inscription of the Vener- able Lord of Chiang Ts'uan (no. 39).

In answering the earlier question what purpose the fashioning of these religious images served, subtle differences emerge from object to object. A common goal apparently was to record the achievements of one's ancestors, but some steles place a higher emphasis on the cohesion of living clan members, while others express mourning for the dead and focus on their memory. In general, benefit was expected for both the emperor and the ancestors, but often it was the death of a close relative that occasioned the stele. Prayers typically indicate four major concerns:

1. Rescuing the souls of the dead from the three bad rebirths and transferring them to heaven
2. Ensuring the happiness of currently living family members
3. Supporting the imperial family and the political stability of the country
4. Liberating all living beings in the universe from suffering

Less frequent, but still worth noting, are two additional points:

5. Securing a beneficial condition for ancestors in case of human re- birth
6. Getting ready for the coming of the messiah

The production of Taoist images in medieval China therefore began as part of the ancestral cult and was often occasioned by the death of an immediate family member. In addition to expressing personal grief, the image sometimes assumed a deeper religious significance as a token of the donor's personal hope for immortality and eternal life. It could, moreover, be used to record the achievements of a family's ancestors and was a way to express wishes for peace on earth and the liberation of all beings. From grief to personal hope, from family concerns to state affairs and universal salvation, Taoist sculpture reveals the gradual expansion of personal concerns and thereby the deepening of religious feelings in medieval China.

Last, analyzing the production of images and their inscriptions from a spatial and temporal axis, one finds that the concerns expand from the self to the family, to the state, and finally to all beings suffering in the Three Worlds of birth and death. The scope of concern widens with every step. In terms of time, too, the main focus begins with the self, then extends into the past to the ancestors of seven generations, and finally moves forward into the future to the family's descendants. It thereby joins the three periods of past, present, and future in one continuous line. The production of Taoist images, together with the performance of Taoist rituals, was thus firmly rooted in the lives and beliefs of the medieval Chinese.

Chinese Gods, Buddhas, and Immortals

From the evidence introduced so far it may seem that medieval Taoist sculpture was largely an imitation of Buddhist models. Looking at the phenomenon more closely, however, it becomes clear that Buddhism itself underwent several changes in its adaptation to Chinese indigenous religion after it was introduced in the first century C.E. Growing distinctly Chinese roots in Chinese society and culture, Buddhism relied heavily on indigenous models and was welcomed first as a different form of the belief in immortality. Thus Buddhism began its Chinese career under strong Taoist impact, both ritually and iconographically.

Ritually, the first Buddhist worship recorded in the dynastic histories took place in a first-century ceremony jointly dedicated to the Buddha Śākyamuni, the Yellow Emperor, and Lao-tzu. Duke Ying of Ch'u, the younger brother of Emperor Ming (r. 58-75 C.E.), is said to have chanted incantations for the Yellow Emperor and performed services to the Buddha (*Hou Han-shu* 42). Similarly, Emperor Huan in 65 C.E. had an altar erected in the palace, where he offered sacrifices to the Buddha and Lao-tzu (*Hou Han-shu* 7). It is not clear whether any images were used in these ceremonies and, if so, of what type they were. Nevertheless the fact that the Buddha, the Yellow Emperor, and Lao-tzu were worshiped jointly reflects the same kind of Buddho-Taoist integration that is evident from later steles. The earliest indigenous Chinese form of Buddhism is, therefore, a cultural mix from its very beginning.

Iconographically, too, Buddhist images in the earliest stages were matched with representations of traditional Chinese deities, such as the Queen Mother of the West, the Lord King of the East, the Yellow Emperor, and the God of Agriculture. As Yü Wei-chao and Kominami Ichirō have shown, paintings on stone pillars in a tomb at Yi-nan show the Lord King and Queen Mother in the east and west, and have Buddhist figures, often young men in monk's garb with halos around their heads, in the north and south. The murals of a tomb at Ho-lin, moreover, show the same figures in the east and west but have an "immortal riding on a white elephant" in the south and a picture entitled "Relics" in the north. In both cases, images of the Lord King and the Queen Mother are indigenous and Taoist, while the pictures of the other figures are clearly Buddhist (Yü 1980, 68–74; Kominami 1983, 517–29). Similarly, numerous mirrors were found in tombs that originally showed only Chinese immortals,[13] but as time went along they became more Buddhist, showing buddhas, apsaras (goddesses), and bodhisattvas. One mirror, for example, has a buddha figure together with mythical animals; another shows a buddha in the company of a flying celestial and a rising phoenix (Mizuno 1968, 20–27). A similar phenomenon is also apparent on other mirror decorations that depict the Money Tree, associated with the earth god cult, and the Spirit Bottle, a characteristic of the immortals (Yü 1980, 75; Kominami 1993, 290–94).

Buddhism was thus, at its first introduction, integrated into the Chinese world as a new form of immortality belief and, as the visual evidence shows, merged actively with native ideas. By the Six Dynasties, however, it had taken root and was developing an independent worldview and iconography, experiencing a great boom in the fifth century, from which the growing Taoist religion received its inspiration. The close similarities among works of art accordingly stand as a direct continuation of the early form Buddhist art took on Chinese soil. The mutual integration and joining of the traditions gave rise to the particularities of Taoist sculpture, showing Lao-tzu on par with the Buddha as the highest venerable of the Taoist religion. Worshiped with the Yellow Emperor and the Buddha since the Later Han dynasty, Lao-tzu and the ideas he stood for represented an important gateway for Buddhism into Chinese culture. Even central notions, such as *buddha, bodhi, nirvāṇa*, were translated first with the help of terms from the *Tao-te-ching*. Both the identification of the ideas of this text with Buddhist doctrines and that of Lao-tzu with the Buddha contributed greatly to the specific Chinese understanding of Buddhism. They also led to Taoist sculptures of the Venerable Lord and the Heavenly Worthy created during the Six Dynasties. The Buddha Śākyamuni, accepted into Chinese culture, thus was divinized and popularized along the same lines as the deified Lao-tzu, just as the mutual interchange between the beliefs produced the unique flavor of medieval Chinese religion.

Hopes for Ancestral Happiness

Taoist sculpture in medieval China follows Buddhist models not only in its format but also in its particular understanding of ancestor worship. The common expression "ancestors for seven generations" is originally of Indian Buddhist origin and in China is first linked with the hope that one's forebears might be speedily rescued from the sufferings of the three bad rebirths in the medieval *Yü-lan-p'en ching* (Ullambana Sūtra).[14] However the expression may have been meant in this text, ordinary Chinese practitioners interpreted it in their own particular way. As the T'ang-dynasty commentator Tsung-mi (780–841), patriarch of several Buddhist schools, explains correctly, the original Buddhist idea of "seven generations" does not refer to one's direct patrilineal ancestors for seven generations but to the parents who have raised one for the past seven lives (*Yü-lan-p'en ching-shu*; T. 1792, 39.508a). Rather than referring to the traditional Chinese ancestral cult, the phrase was originally linked with the belief in transmigration. The common people of medieval China, not being versed in theory but rooted in ancestor worship, gave the expression a more indigenous twist, leading to prayers for blessings for their patrilineal ancestors of seven generations.

The Taoist phrase in this usage appears not only on art work but, in different variants ("seven ancestors," "seven generations," "seven mysteries"), also in scriptures. Here it is closely linked with the traditional Chinese belief that deeds of ancestors and descendents are mutually related, one being responsible for the suffering or good fortune of the other. While the notion that the happiness of one generation depended on the good and bad deeds of another is entirely Chinese, the number seven most commonly found in its context is definitely of Indian origin. The *Dīghanikāya* (Long Sayings), a collection of the Buddha's sermons, for example, frequently says,

> He was well born on both sides, of pure descent through the mother and through the father back through seven generations, with no slur upon him, and no reproach, in respect of birth. (Rhys-Davids 1969, 146)

This is contrary to traditional Chinese ancestor worship, which was based on a lineage of five generations (including the self) and required mourning and memorial services for relatives still personally known. Unlike in India, no particular importance is attached to ancestors up to seven generations, a number introduced to China only through Buddhism.

Integrating therefore the Indian numbering and the Buddhist belief in karmic retribution with Chinese ancestor worship and the notion of mutual responsibility over generations, a new form of both Buddhist and Taoist worldview took shape. The idea that the ancestors up to seven generations had to be rescued from the sufferings of the underworld— again a notion that was introduced from India—moreover went far beyond the framework of the formally organized religions and entered deeply into Chinese popular belief. Buddhist and Taoist steles, in this context, represent one among several practical measures taken to ensure the best possible fortune all around. There is no question that the salvation of self and ancestors was the most serious concern of donors in early medieval China. Not only are good wishes for the ancestors expressed most frequently in the inscriptions, but the back of one stele (no. 22) even depicts how a deceased family member is judged by Yama, the king of hell, and given a suitable punishment for his bad deeds during life. In accordance with the doctrine of karmic retribution, one's ancestors must undergo punishment in the hells, but this punishment, according to the belief, was eased or even expiated through the merit accumulated by having a stele made.

Taoist devotional steles, far from being pure works of art, played a key role in Chinese religious life whose vibrancy and scope went far beyond the boundaries of either Buddhist or Taoist formal doctrine and organization. While Buddhism underwent a transformation under Chinese cultural impact, Taoism developed its particular ideas and practices under Buddhist influence. Both together, merging with popular ancestor worship, created the unique religiosity of medieval China. Taoist sculpture, grown under Mahāyāna auspices as much as on the basis of Taoist scriptures, represents a lively and immediate expression of this religious consciousness.

Notes

1. Editors' note: This article is an abbreviated version of the author's detailed study on Taoist sculpture (Kamitsuka 1993). It was translated by Livia Kohn and edited with the generous help of Elizabeth ten Grotenhuis.

2. Editors' note: A study of the literary evidence on the fashioning of Taoist images is found in Reiter 1988. An extant statue, probably dating from the eleventh century, is described in Erdberg 1941. A study of Taoist sculpture in relation to visualization and healing practices is found in Sakade 1994. Laozi statues extant in American collections are the subject of Pontynen 1980a, 1980b, 1983.

3. A detailed record of K'ou's activities and the history of Taoism under these rulers is found in the "Record on Buddhism and Taoism" in the *Wei-shu* (History of the Wei Dynasty). An abbreviated version is contained in the *Sui-shu* (History of the Sui Dynasty), in the section on "Taoist Texts and Scriptures."

Editors' note: For an English discussion of the theocracy, see Mather 1979; a translation of the historical chronicles is found in Ware 1933. For a more detailed analysis of the relationship between the two religions at this time, see Kohn 1995.

4. Editors' note: Texts in the Buddhist canon are cited after the Japanese Taishō Tripitaka edition (abbreviated T.), giving the serial number, the volume, and the page.

5. Editors' note: Works from later periods are more numerous than this, and many are also collected in U.S. museums, notably the Field Museum of Natural History in Chicago (collected by Berthold Laufer in 1908–10), the Freer Gallery of Art in Washington, D.C., and the Museum of Fine Arts in Boston. See Pontynen 1983.

6. For a description and discussion of this object, see Yao 1965, 134–38; Han and Yin 1984, 46; Chang 1992, 83–87.

7. For more details on this object, see Ōmura 1915, 379; Matsubara 1966, 211.

8. On this latter work (no. 44), see particularly Matsubara 1966, 219; Ch'en et al. 1988, 39.

9. For different analyses of this work, see Yao 1965; Matsubara 1966, 42; Heibonsha 1986, 2:210; Han and Yin 1987; and Chang 1992.

10. Editors' note: Texts in the Taoist canon (*Tao-tsang*, abbreviated TT) are given according to the numbering in Schipper 1975.

11. Details on the performance of such rites are fuond the *Wu-shang pi-yao* (Esoteric Essentials of the Most High, TT 1138), the first Taoist encyclopedia, dated to 574.

12. Editors' note: For a study of Buddhist terms in early medieval Taoism, see Zürcher 1980.

13. Editors' note: For early images of immortals on mirrors, see Loewe 1979. A study of the development of immortals in art is found in Spiro 1991. On Chinese/Taoist images as vehicles for the early reception of Buddhism, see Wu 1986; James 1986.

14. T. 686, 16.779–80. This text concerns the festival for the dead and the spirits. It is of medieval origins and, although its date and provenance are problematic, probably existed when Taoist sculpture developed.

Editors' note: For a thorough study of this text and the rituals associated with it, see Teiser 1988.

References

Chang Yen. 1992–93. "Chūgoku Senseishō Yōken no hirin." Translated by Wang Chien-hsin. *Bukkyō geijutsu* 205: 77–89 and 211: 101–23.

Ch'en Kuo-fu. 1963. *Tao-tsang yüan-liu k'ao.* Peking: Chung-hua.

Ch'en Yüan, Ch'en Chih-chao, Tseng Ch'ing-ying, eds. 1988. *Tao-chia chin-shih lüeh.* Peking: Wen-wu Publishers.

Erdberg Consten, Eleanor von. 1942. "A Statue of Lao-tzu in the Po-yün-kuan." *Monumenta Serica* 7: 235–41.

Han Wei and Yin Chih-i. 1984. "Yao-hsien Yao-wang-shan te fo-tao hun-ho tsao hsiang-pei." *K'ao-ku yü wen-wu* 1984–85: 46–51.

Han Wei and Yin Chih-ku. 1987. "Yao-hsien Yao-wang-shan ti tao-chiao tsao hsiang-pei." *K'ao-ku yü wen-wu* 1987.3: 18–26.

Heibonsha, ed. 1986. *Chūgoku shodō zenshū.* Tokyo: Heibonsha.

James, Jean M. 1989. "Some Iconographic Problems in Early Daoist-Buddhist Sculpture in Chian." *Archives of Asian Art* 42: 71–76.

Kamitsuka Yoshiko. 1993. "Nanbokuchō jidai no dōkyō zōzō." In *Chūgoku chūsei no bunbutsu*, ed. Tonami Mamoru, 225–89. Kyoto: Kyoto University, Jimbun kagaku kenkyūjo.

Kohn, Livia. 1995. *Laughing at the Tao: Debates among Buddhists and Taoists in Medieval China.* Princeton, N.J.: Princeton University Press.

Kominami Ichirō. 1983. "Bukkyō chūgoku denpa no ichiyōsō: Zuzō haichi kara no kōsatsu." In *Tembō asia no kōkogaku: Higuchi Takayasu kyōju taikan kinen ronshū*, ed. Higuchi Takayasu, 515–25. Tokyo: Shinchōsha.

Kominami Ichirō. 1993. "Shinteiko to Tōgo no bunka." *Tōhō gakuhō* 65: 223–312.

Loewe, Michael. 1979. *Ways to Paradise: The Chinese Quest for Immortality.* London: George Allen and Unwin.

Mather, Richard B. 1979. "K'ou Ch'ien-chih and the Taoist Theocracy at the Northern Wei Court 425–451." In *Facets of Taoism*, ed. Holmes Welch and Anna Seidel, 103–22. New Haven, Conn.: Yale University Press.

Matsubara Saburō. 1966. *Chugoku bukkyō chōkokushi kenkyū*. Tokyo: Yoshikawa Kōbunkan.

Mizuno Seiichi. 1968. *Chūgoku no bukkyō geijutsu*. Tokyo: Heibonsha.

Ōmura Seigai. 1915. *Shina bijutsushi chōsohen*. Tokyo: Bussho kankōkai.

Peking Library Corsortium, ed. 1989. *Pei-ching t'u-shu kuan-tsang Chung-kuo li-tai shih-k'o t'a-pen hui-p'ien*. Cheng-chou, PRC: Chung-chou Publishers.

Pontynen, Arthur. 1980a. "The Deification of Laozi in Chinese History and Art." *Oriental Art* 26: 192–200.

———. 1980b. "The Dual Nature of Laozi in Chinese History and Art." *Oriental Art* 26: 308–13.

———. 1983. "The Early Development of Taoist Art." Ph.D. dissertation, University of Iowa, Iowa City.

Reiter, Florian C. 1988. "The Visible Divinity: The Sacred Image in Religious Taoism." *Nachrichten der deutschen Gesellschaft für Natur- und Völkerkunde Ostasiens* 144: 51–70.

Rhys-Davids, T. W. 1969. *Dialogues of the Buddha*. Sacred Books of the Buddhists, vol. 2. London: Luzac & Co.

Sakade Yoshinobu. 1994. "Ki to dōkyō shinzō no keisei." *Bungei ronsō* 42: 256–93.

Satō Chisui. 1977. "Hokuchō zōzō meikō." *Shigaku zasshi* 86.10: 1–47.

Schipper, Kristofer. 1975. *Concordance du Tao Tsang: Titres des ouvrages*. Paris: Publications de l'École Française d'Extrême-Orient.

Shih Fu. 1961. "Chieh-shao liang-chian pei-ch'ao tao-chiao shi-tsao xiang." *Wen-wu* 1961/12: 54–55.

Spiro, Audrey. 1991. "Shaping the Wind: Taste and Tradition in Fifth-century China." *Ars Orientalis* 21: 95–116.

Teiser, Stephen. 1988. *The Yü-lan-p'en Festival in Medieval Chinese Religion*. Princeton, N.J.: Princeton University Press.

Ting Ming-yi. 1986. "Tsung Chiang Tu-lo chian Zhou Wen-wang Fo-tao tsao hsiang-pei kuan pei-ch'ao tao-chiao tsao-hsiang." *Wen-wu* 1986/3: 52–62.

Tsukamoto Zenryū. 1975. "Gishin bukkyō no tenkai." In *Tsukamoto Zenryū zenshū* 3: 1–50. Tokyo: Daitō Publishers.

Ware, James R. 1933. "The *Wei-shu* and the *Sui-shu* on Taoism." *Journal of the American Oriental Society* 53: 215–50.

Wu Hung. 1986. "Buddhist Elements in Early Chinese Art." *Artibus Asiae* 47: 263–352.

Yao Sheng. 1965. "Yao-hsien shih-k'e lüeh-chih." *K'ao-ku* 1965/3: 134–51.

Yü Wei-chao. 1980. "Tung-han fo-chiao t'u-hsiang k'ao." *Wen-wu* 1980/5: 68–77.

Zürcher, Erik. 1980. "Buddhist Influence on Early Taoism." *T'oung-pao* 66: 84–147.

Part II

Chinese Interpretations

A Tale of Two Commentaries:
Ho-shang-kung and Wang Pi on the *Lao-tzu*

Alan K. L. Chan

Of all the commentaries on the *Tao-te-ching*, those by Ho-shang-kung (probably second century C.E.) and Wang Pi (226–249) are by far the most important. Whereas the former acted as the undisputed guide to the Taoist classic up to the T'ang period, Wang Pi subsequently became the premier spokesman for philosophical Taoism. Later commentators might disagree with them, but they could hardly have accessed the text without them. Rooted in a Han context, the Ho-shang-kung commentary fuses together cosmological, religious, and political insights to form a comprehensive vision of Tao. Self-cultivation, in particular, is linked directly to government. Like Ho-shang-kung, Wang Pi also found in the *Lao-tzu* an antidote to the ills of society and a blueprint for political reform. But with the fall of the Han, new questions demanded a rethinking of the Tao. Focusing on the concepts of "nonbeing" (*wu*) and "naturalness" (*tzu-jan*), Wang responded with a bold and innovative reformulation of Taoist philosophy. Attention to the context, under which the two commentators stood, helps clarify not only their understanding of the *Lao-tzu*, but also their self-understanding as interpreters of the classical tradition.

Ho-shang-kung's *Lao-tzu Chang-chü*

Ho-shang-kung: Legend and Commentary

Traditionally, the Ho-shang-kung commentary is reckoned a work of the Former Han dynasty. Little is known of its reputed author, whose name means literally an old man or master who dwells by the riverside. Legends relate that he "appeared" during the reign of Han Wen-ti (r. 179–157 B.C.E.) and made his home along the banks of the "river," presumably the Yellow River, where he gained a reputation as an expert in the *Tao-te-ching*. Emperor Wen, himself a keen student of the Taoist classic, sent an envoy to seek advice from the "Old Master by the River."

What is interesting is that Ho-shang-kung refused to answer the emperor's questions, claiming that the teachings of the *Lao-tzu* are too profound and exalted to be explained from a distance. Understandably annoyed, Emperor Wen went personally and sternly reminded him that no one was above the royal domain. Without a word, Ho-shang-kung "rose high into the air," and revealed his true identity as a divine emissary. After a prompt apology and convinced of his sincerity to be instructed in the teachings of the Tao, Ho-shang-kung finally presented his commentary on the *Tao-te-ching* to the repentant emperor (see Chan 1991b). The story of Ho-shang-kung is significant because it harbors a strong political message. Even the emperor must submit to the rule of Tao, and by implication defer to Taoist experts. The commentary ascribed to Ho-shang-kung is equally explicit in its political design, although there is also a religious dimension to it. This latter has led some scholars to suppose that it should be dated after the Han, when the Taoist religion was more fully established (Kusuyama 1979; Kobayashi 1990, 241). Without rehearsing the arguments here, suffice it to say that the Ho-shang-kung commentary probably dates to the latter part of the Han dynasty, when indeed both religious and political concerns pervaded the Taoist imagination. Although it may not have been a product of Emperor Wen's time, there is little concrete evidence to trace it beyond the Han era (Chan 1991a, 107–18).

In terms of style and interpretive orientation, the commentary subscribes to the dominant scholastic trends of the Han. Called simply the *Lao-tzu chang-chü*, it belongs to the genre of *chang-chü* literature, which one may paraphrase as commentary by "chapter and verse." Such commentaries display strong philological acumen and often attempt to provide an exhaustive reading of the classics, breaking down the original into parts and mapping out the meaning of words and semantic units by identifying their perceived referents. A word or concept may be seen to refer to particular objects in nature, or to have a basis in specific historical experiences, including events and persons of the mythological past. Meaning, in this framework, is thus essentially "referential" and translates into a network of "correspondences" which delimits the boundaries of interpretation. The same hermeneutical orientation characterizes Ho-shang-kung's work. The *Lao-tzu* opens with the famous words: "The way that can be spoken of is not the constant Way." Whereas the Tao that can be disputed refers to "the way of classical expertise and of the teachings of government," the author explains, the "constant Tao" means "the way of naturalness and long life."[1] By identifying the precise reference, the meaning of the original is rendered concrete and specific. This brings into view also the practical significance of Taoist teachings. But is Ho-shang-kung saying that the *Lao-tzu* is concerned solely with a program of self-cultivation aimed at "long life," which opposes any form of political engagement?

Self-cultivation is important, but "the way of naturalness and long life" does not exclude politics; on the contrary, it offers a superior guide to government. Put differently, there is a polemical side to the commentary as well. The Taoist way can bring about renewal where Confucian and other methods, relying on "classical expertise" and "teachings of government," have failed. If the *Lao-tzu* denounces "benevolence" and other virtues (e.g., ch. 18), it is not because virtue as such is to be abandoned; rather, the point is to rectify harmful errors and to establish the "true"—that is, Taoist—meaning of virtue so as to effect spiritual and political change. Similarly, the Confucian conception of the sage may be deficient—for which reason the *Lao-tzu* did not hesitate to say, "exterminate the sage" (ch. 19)—but this only drives home the point that false prophets must give way to true sages, whose being mirrors the workings of Tao. From this perspective, even classical learning need not be dismissed as opposed to Taoist teachings; the real problem is the kind of distortions put on the classics by misguided scholars. Viewed in the light of Tao, illuminated by it, the classics should also conform to "the way of naturalness and long life."

Having criticized the prevalent view of learning (e.g., ch. 48), a higher mode of understanding is put forward; and having found the Confucian model wanting, the commentary proposes that the secret to good government lies in Taoist self-cultivation. As the T'ang scholar Lu Te-ming (556–627) observed, Ho-shang-kung "composed the *Lao-tzu chang-chü* . . . to instruct Emperor Wen, in which he set out the key to self-government and the government of the country" (Lu 1985, ed., 63). In the words of the commentary itself, when the *Lao-tzu* refers to "the government of the sage," it means precisely that "the sage governs the country [*chih-kuo*] in the same way he governs himself [*chih-shen*]."[2]

Cosmological Underpinnings

Central to Ho-shang-kung's understanding is a cosmological interpretation of Tao. In itself, the "constant" Tao is transcendent and thus ineffable. If so, on what basis can it be said to mean "the way of naturalness and long life"? Logically, "nameless" is perhaps all that one can say about it. But the *Lao-tzu* also says that the "nameless" is "the beginning of heaven and earth" (ch. 1). For Ho-shang-kung, far from being obfuscating or inconsistent, this provides the necessary key to unlocking the mystery of creation. The reason why the Way cannot be named is that it has no shape or form. By "beginning," furthermore, the *Lao-tzu* means that the Tao "emits the vital energy [*ch'i*] and gives rise to change." As a result, heaven and earth came into being, and by virtue of the power of life they have received, they in turn produced the "ten thousand things," that is, all beings. Like a "mother," as the *Lao-tzu* suggests (e.g., chs. 1, 25, 52), the Tao not only created the world but nourishes it with its powerful energy.

By means of what may be called a cosmological turn, the concept of Tao is connected with the genesis of the cosmos. The claim of transcendence is not undermined; it is, however, interpreted from the perspective of the Tao's creative power. When the *Lao-tzu* makes use of such concepts as "nothingness" or "nonbeing" (*wu*) and "emptiness" (*hsü*) to underscore the transcendence of Tao, Ho-shang-kung argues, they must not be interpreted "nihilistically" to mean an absolute absence. The Tao may be described as "empty" or "nothing" in just the same way it is called "nameless"; that is to say, without shape or form. "All beings are born of nonbeing," the *Lao-tzu* declares (ch. 40); but this can only mean that "the Way is without form, and beings are therefore said to be born of nonbeing." Clearly, to Ho-shang-kung, the more important point is that the "formless" creates form, as the cosmic energy emanating from Tao brings forth all forms of life. The emptiness of Tao, in other words, properly understood, is but another way of affirming the fullness of the vital energy.

In this respect, the commentary brings to bear the Han cosmological view that the cosmos is constituted and sustained by vital *ch'i* energy, the life force of human beings and the universe (Schwartz 1985, 179). Differentiated into the two primary forms of yin and yang, the vital energy is seen to pervade all levels of existence. Undoubtedly, Ho-shang-kung shared the view, common in Han literature, that the "lighter," more rarefied yang energy "rose" to form heaven, while the "heavier" yin congealed and solidified to become earth. In the *Lao-tzu*, we are told that "the Way gave birth to the One; the One gave birth to the Two; the Two gave birth to the Three; and the Three gave birth to the ten thousand things" (ch. 42). The apparent simplicity of this famous cosmogonic account belies its difficulty. Grammatically, both number and tense are not specified in the original (e.g., D. C. Lau translates, "two begets three"). Any potential ambiguity, however, is fully resolved in the Ho-shang-kung commentary. What the Tao produced at the beginning was the "One." The "One" generated yin and yang, which "gave birth to the harmonious, the clear, and the turbid." These three forms of energy then differentiated to form heaven, earth, and man, which "together produced the ten thousand things" (ch. 42).[3]

The "One"

The concept of the "One" is especially important to Ho-shang-kung. At first glance, it appears just another term for Tao. But the "One" is always distinguished from Tao in the commentary. If the Way is like a "mother," then the metaphor of the "son" applies easily to the "One." "The world has a beginning, which acts as the mother of the world," the *Lao-tzu* says; and, "having known the mother, one then knows the son" (ch. 52). "Beginning" and "mother" of course refer to Tao; equally without hesitation, Ho-shang-kung states, "the son is the One."

The "One" must not be turned into an abstract concept, into a kind of metaphysical "oneness," however. Fundamentally, it is defined in the commentary as the "core" or "essence" of Tao (ch. 1). It is also equated with "virtue." Far from the moralistic interpretation favored by Confucians, "virtue" is seen to stem directly from a dispensation of Tao. "The Way gives birth to them; virtue rears them," according to the *Lao-tzu* (ch. 51). Ho-shang-kung comments: "The Way gives birth to the ten thousand things. Virtue is the One. The One directs the flow of energy and nurtures them." What does this mean? Ho-shang-kung is careful to explain, "The One was produced by Tao at the beginning. It is the essential energy or vital essence [*ching-ch'i*] of the great harmony" (ch. 10; ch. 21). Thus, the "One" is the original substance of life itself, energy in its most pure and potent form. From the microcosmic to the macrocosmic levels, existence ultimately hinges on the "vital essence" of Tao. "Heaven obtained the One and became clear; earth obtained the One and became tranquil" (ch. 39). To Ho-shang-kung, this passage (also in ch. 10, comm.) must have been particularly revealing. Heaven and earth attain their natural, pristine state only in "virtue" of the "vital essence" with which they have been endowed. Viewed from another angle, reconstructing Ho-shang-kung's reasoning, this is why the "One" must be understood concretely as energy: To be able to bring about the flourishing of heaven and earth, it must itself be a powerful agent of change.

Moreover, the *Lao-tzu* goes on to say, "spirits" or "gods" (*shen*) are likewise dependent on the "One" to become efficacious, which makes them the numinous beings that they are. The fact that spiritual beings have a place in the Taoist universe should not be surprising. In traditional China, religious disbelief concerned only a small minority. What is of greater interest is that the "gods" themselves are shown to be *ch'i* essences, a manifestation of the power of Tao. Further, the various constituents of the cosmos are now integrated into a structured whole. Heaven and earth, spirits and humans, are all connected by the "One"; channels of communication become open as the "vital essence" flows through the universe. Differences arising from energy differentiation are not denied, but the spiritual and the physical can no longer be regarded as separate categories. This applies not only to heaven and earth, but to human beings as well. In religious terms, this means that just as heaven has its divine luminaries and earth has its nature spirits, so human beings have their spiritual essences.

Long Life and Naturalness

According to the *Lao-tzu*, "The spirit of the valley never dies; it is called the mysterious female" (ch. 6). These cryptic remarks present little difficulty to Ho-shang-kung:

> "Valley" means to nourish. If one could nourish one's spirits, one would not die. "Spirit" means the spirits of the five inner organs. . . . If the five inner organs are all damaged, then the five spirits will be gone. This means that the way of immortality lies in the mysterious female. "Mysterious" refers to heaven; in man it is the nose. "Female" refers to earth; in man it is the mouth. (ch. 6)

The commentary is characteristically specific, and again reflects its rootedness in a Han setting. It goes on in some detail to identify the "five spirits" and the organs to which they are attached in the human body. The reference to the "nose" and "mouth" brings into sharp relief that the energy-essence is visualized concretely as breath. Details aside, the human body is thus understood as a "sacred vessel" (ch. 29), animated by indwelling spirits. If life is constituted by energy, death occurs when it dissipates or, which amounts to the same thing, when the spirits depart from the body and "return" to their cosmic source. The same basic understanding, indeed, applies to the full spectrum of human experience. Sickness and health, for example, depend on the influence of the "five spirits"; anger and other emotions are but stirring of the energy within; and even such phenomena as success and failure, fortune and misfortune, can be approached from the perspective of the operation of the vital energy.

In principle, because the human body proves to be a veritable spiritual force-field, and since the vital energy as such cannot be extinguished, the possibility of immortality must therefore be affirmed. This, to Ho-shang-kung, reflects a central concern in the *Lao-tzu* (e.g., chs. 7, 16, 33, 44, 50, 55, 59). Further, if the Tao is eternal, and if the "One" makes possible embodying the Tao, it would follow that human beings can truly aspire to "return to the infinite" (ch. 28). What may not be immediately clear and which the commentary serves to explain, is that embodying the Tao means literally possessing spiritual essences in one's body. So long as they remain in the body, death simply cannot happen. Nevertheless, this does not render the *Lao-tzu* a manual for immortality. On the contrary, Ho-shang-kung seems to believe that any striving for life, and still less life everlasting, would contradict the very point the text is trying to make. All things "obtained the One" and came into existence; conversely, without that which gives them life, they naturally die (ch. 39). Ho-shang-kung's commentary here is decisive: "This states that the ten thousand things ought to follow their (allotted) time of life and death, and must not only want to live perpetually for time without end" (cf. Boltz 1985).

A new and significant turn in Ho-shang-kung's thinking can thus be detected, which repositions the commentary from cosmology and religion to focus on Taoist practical philosophy. While immortality proves to have a basis in the Tao, it does not follow that human beings should be consumed by longings for it. Life and death form a part of the transformation processes which constitute the Taoist world. Death, as much as life, belongs to the realm of "naturalness," that which is "so of itself" (*tzu-jan*), a concept which Ho-shang-kung positively identifies as the key to Taoist wisdom. The "constant Way," one must not forget, is not just about "long life," but "the way of naturalness and long life."

Guarding the One

In what sense can "naturalness" be said to complement "long life"? Two separate claims need to be distinguished here. On the one hand, if the concept of naturalness is taken seriously, any attempt to prolong life by artificial means is doomed to failure and must be rejected. On the other hand, if careful steps are not taken to preserve life, the natural flow of things is also interrupted. Together, these interrelated concerns help define Ho-shang-kung's principal interest in "self-government and the government of the country." The natural life span of an individual, given the cosmological underpinning of the commentary, is evidently determined by one's energy endowment. Individual differences notwithstanding, human beings have been given a proper "mandate" (*ming*) to prosper and live long. While the energy endowment may be "thick" or "thin" (ch. 1), this does not detract from the "virtue" of Tao, which ensures natural fullness and abundance. From this perspective, naturalness turns out to be the basis of long life, while "longevity" (*shou*) refers to one's allotted life span (e.g., chs. 35, 42, comm.).

There are, however, obstacles which may jeopardize one's natural longevity. If the body is destroyed, the "five spirits" disperse; if the body is harmed, the spirits hasten their departure. For this reason, the body must be well taken care of, and the conditions, under which the vital essence may be adversely influenced, must be clearly identified. Actual longevity, in other words, reflects not only a richly endowed body but also a well-maintained abode of the spirits. This entails certain practical considerations about the enemies of long life. Ho-shang-kung warns that the body, in particular the sensory and reproductive organs, can easily succumb to temptations, become "perverse," and cause death (ch. 50). But despite the countless guises in which they appear, in the final analysis the ills of humanity can be traced to the problem of desires. This is why the *Lao-tzu* repeatedly emphasizes having few desires (e.g., chs. 3, 12, 19, 80). Of all the desires that threaten to cut short one's "mandate," Ho-shang-kung singles out avarice and lechery to be most injurious to one's vital essence (e.g., chs. 9, 10, 22, 26, 29, 36, 41, 44, 46, 59). Whereas the former is sure to give rise to deviousness and endless worries, sexual indulgence—in Ho-shang-kung's gender specific terms— depletes a man's store of vital essence, by which semen is also constituted. Having diagnosed the disease, Ho-shang-kung then proceeds to prescribe a cure. To be free from the tyranny of desires, there is no better way than to abide by what the *Lao-tzu* has termed "nonaction" (*wu-wei*).

The commentary defines nonaction specifically as the diminishing of desires (ch. 48). It is characterized by both "emptiness" and "fullness," conceived concretely in terms of the operation of vital energy. The concept of "emptiness" best describes nonaction, in that energy in its rarefied state naturally fills up empty space. The "One," Ho-shang-kung writes, "shuns where it is filled and dwells in the empty" (ch. 35). Yet, when infused with energy, what was "empty" becomes "full." Attention, in other words, must be shifted from obtaining the "One" to safeguarding its presence. As the commentary continues, "If one finds joy and delights in Tao, the One will stay put"; otherwise, it will move on like a "passing guest." This, in general terms, is what Ho-shang-kung means by "embracing the One" (chs. 3, 10), "concentrating on the One" (ch. 55), and more typically "guarding the One" (*shou-yi*; e.g., chaps. 20, 22, 27, 81).

Translated into a Taoist theory of self-cultivation, nonaction, defined as "guarding the One," means that the body must be kept "empty"— that is, pure of defilements—so that the spirits are not harmed. More than once, Ho-shang-kung emphasizes that "governing the body" consists of abandoning desires, making the "five inner organs" pure and ensuring that the spirits remain in the body (e.g., chs. 5, 11, 16, 72). To "guard the One," a careful diet and other forms of abstinence are recommended (ch. 10). Overexertion or agitation weaken the energy endowment and put one's longevity at risk. The precious vital essence should only be used sparingly; if it is not belabored, "the five spirits will not suffer and consequently one can last long" (ch. 59; also ch. 33). Besides abstinence and moderation, breathing exercises also contribute to Taoist self-cultivation. From the basic observation that shortness of breath signals unease, if not "disease," breathing control can help ensure an easy and even circulation of *ch'i* energy. Ho-shang-kung is quite specific on this score:

> Exhaling and inhaling, the successive breaths of the nose and mouth should be continuous and subtle, as if one could preserve them and yet as if they were not there. One's breathing should always be leisurely and at ease, and not rushed or exhausting. (ch. 6; also ch. 12)

At one point, the commentary notes that in circulating the vital essence, breathing should be done such that "the ears do not hear it" (ch. 10). If the mind is calm and "empty" to such an extent that the ears no longer hear the sounds of arousal and the eyes do not see the colors of desire, then it becomes "full," truly mindful, and is able to "hear" and "see" the inaudible and invisible, the wonder of Tao.[4] In contrast to sensory experience ruled by desires, this may be called "reverse hearing" and "inward vision" (chs. 15, 33, 52).

The Ruler and the Sage

In later Taoism, "inward vision" or more generally the practice of "guarding the One" developed into a sophisticated religious discipline (Kohn 1989a). But this does not bear directly on Ho-shang-kung's understanding of the *Lao-tzu*. Although nonaction in the sense defined above can secure the "One" and thus vitality and long life, it remains rooted in "naturalness" and largely impervious to any artificial regime designed to gain immortality. Moreover, the author makes every effort to bring out the underlying ethical insights of the original. For example, according to Ho-shang-kung, heaven and earth are enduring because they remain "calm and tranquil" and do not expect any "reward" for their "service" to humanity—a lesson *Lao-tzu* "intended to teach man" (ch. 7). Similarly, the fact that the "sage" can "last long and face no danger" is not due to esoteric practice but simply to his humility (ch. 22). And this is the real lesson of Taoism. If one is full of himself, he can never be empty; and no diet or technique of meditation can help him safeguard the One.

Despite its potential universal significance, this lesson is meant specifically for the ruler. This may be considered a third turn in Ho-shang-kung's commentary, from cosmology and self-cultivation to the art of rulership. In fact, the ruler is identified consistently as the subject of *Lao-tzu*'s discourse (e.g., chs. 38, 45, 46). The message to the ruler begins with self-cultivation and its ethical implications. Emptiness of desires is always reflected in concrete behavior: no glutton or lecher can claim to have secured the "One"; boastfulness and dishonesty are by definition opposed to Tao and must be counted as enemies of "naturalness and long life." Desires and excesses, however, do not only violate the natural order at the personal level, but extend their destruction to society at large. Social disharmony and political disorder are therefore but symptoms of the same disease which disrupts the "virtue" of Tao. This forms the basis of the claim that to govern a country is fundamentally no different from nourishing and preserving one's vital energy. The enlightened ruler, Ho-shang-kung argues, understands the value of nonaction in both "self-government and the government of the country" (ch. 43; also chs. 29, 37).

At the political level, what the *Lao-tzu* teaches is that government must be based on the ruler's own "emptiness." In theory, the efficacy of nonaction raises little question. Just as sounds "of the same tone resonate with each other" (ch. 23), the people would "naturally" respond to the ruler. Reflecting the principle of "correspondence" common in Han thinking, it is assumed that nonaction from "above" initiates a process of transformation that diminishes desires "below" (e.g., chs. 3, 37, 57). Yet how persuasive is this kind of theory in a world beset with violence at every turn? What if, as Ho-shang-kung himself asks, "in applying the Way to teach and transform the people, they do not conform but turn to hypocrisy and deceit?" (ch. 74). The ideal of reciprocity is not denied, but Ho-shang-kung is also attentive to the practical demands of government. Interventionist policies of both the Legalist and Confucian variety only trouble the people and exhaust precious resources (ch. 60). He rejects heavy taxation (ch. 75), reliance on harsh laws and stiff punishments (ch. 74), and above all war (e.g., chs. 30, 31, 68). Confucian policies with their emphasis on benevolence and proper conduct to him are imposing arbitrary distinctions and artificial standards. In particular, the kind of ritual action and rules of propriety so central to the Confucian enterprise is taken to task for "lacking in substance," which amounts to a recipe for hypocrisy (ch. 38).

Does nonaction, then, entail anarchy, a total absence of political authority? To Ho-shang-kung, this was never a serious option. Rather, potential disturbances should be stopped before they develop into serious problems (ch. 64). Politically, if a recalcitrant few were to unsettle the harmony of the realm, the ruler should "respond with his imperial laws to seize and kill them. No one would then dare to commit any violation" (ch. 74). Does this contradict the critique of Legalist methods? The commentary is careful to add: "Lao-tzu deplored the fact that the king at that time did not first try to transform the people with the Way and virtue, but resorted immediately to penalties and punishment." In this way, a concrete program of government begins to take shape. The general operating principle calls to mind the kind of Taoist political philosophy, called "Huang-Lao" thought, which flourished in the early Han and whose teachings are often summed up by the phrase, "to rest with the people" (Twitchett and Loewe 1986, 693; Peerenboom 1993). While basic sustenance should be ample and available to all, nonessential items are best contained. As the *Lao-tzu* instructs, "Do not value goods that are hard to come by" (ch. 3). The commentary specifies: "This means that the ruler does not value priceless jewels. Precious metal is left in the mountains; pearls and jade are cast into the deep" (cf. ch. 64). Controls on the supply side will have an impact on demand. If the conditions are favorable, according to this argument, the people will become calm, "restful," and not troubled by desires.

Just as naturalness in self-cultivation does not mean leaving the body unguarded, nonaction in government cannot be without decisive leadership and timely mediation. The use of strong medicine does not alter the basic premise. Since human beings are the "sacred things" of the world, the sanctity of life must remain inviolate. Still, Ho-shang-kung cannot ignore the competing claims of ethical and political life. Confronted with the power of desires, concrete steps must be taken to prevent the individual or society as a whole from losing the "One." Precisely because the sanctity of life must be protected, timely and forceful measures are required of the ruler. Nevertheless, having sided with order and the public good, must not the possibility of abuse also be considered? To prevent public officials from abusing their power, Ho-shang-kung advises that the ruler maintain complete control (chs. 36, 65). But then, who prevents the ruler from violating the people's trust himself? Ideally the ruler should submit to the Taoist sage, who is no ordinary mortal but carries an exceptionally rich energy-endowment which renders him superior (ch. 1). No amount of effort or learning can make one a Taoist sage; one is either born a sage or not at all. Indeed, the "virtue" of the sage is so great that "not even the son of heaven could make him a servant" (ch. 56). Embodying true "emptiness," utterly independent and devoid of self-interest, in theory the sage alone could be entrusted with the government of the empire.

Sages, however, are rare. Fortunately, their teachings are recorded in the classics and explained by expert commentators. The Ho-shang-kung commentary was never an "academic" exercise undertaken to satisfy speculative interests. The way of "naturalness and long life" seeks not merely to explain the constant Tao, but more importantly to ensure that the ruler remains responsive to and responsible for the people. If the ruler realizes that his best interest is to abide by "emptiness," he naturally governs by nonaction. For this reason, while immortality does not overshadow the needs of government, the dire consequences of losing the "One" are heavily underlined (e.g., comm. chs. 30, 42, 55, 71, 76). For the same reason, Ho-shang-kung insists that "troublesome" policies must be eliminated. What is "troublesome" basically expresses a state of confused "turbidity" (from which, interestingly, the English word "trouble" is also derived) in the vital essence. If purity or emptiness is not restored, a powerful "turbulence" will arise and with it a reign of violence and disorder. If the "One" is secured, however, nonaction finds expression in "pure," spontaneous action, which not only ensures the well-being of the individual but proves an unfailing guide in the management of complexities.

Wang Pi's *Lao-tzu-chu*

Wang Pi and Profound Learning

Best known in the West as a leading proponent of "Neo-Taoism," Wang Pi is remembered in Chinese sources as a brilliant interpreter of the *Lao-tzu* and the *Yi-ching*, and a founding member of "Profound Learning," *hsuan-hsueh*. The word *hsuan*—literally, a deep, dark red color—is taken from the *Lao-tzu* to signify the profundity or "mystery" of the Tao. Drawing from the Taoist classics and building particularly on the concept of "nonbeing" (*wu*), Profound Learning is credited—or discredited, in which case it may be better rendered "Dark Learning"—for having advanced a revival of Taoist philosophy which challenged the Confucian orthodoxy. Wang Pi and others "expounded on the *Lao-tzu* and *Chuang-tzu*, and established the view that heaven, earth, and the ten thousand things all have their root in nonbeing" (*Chin-shu* 43.1236; see Lin 1977, Lynn 1994). It gained wide currency and consequently, "Lao-tzu and Chuang-tzu came to occupy the main road, and competed with Confucius for the right of way" (*Wen-hsin tiao-lung* 4.18).

To orthodox Confucians, no doubt, Profound Learning seemed a dangerous heresy. But Wang Pi never saw himself as a "Taoist" in the sectarian sense of the word, especially if this implies "anti-Confucian" sentiments. To borrow from the *Lun-yü* (15.29), for which Wang also provided a commentary, he aimed only at "broadening the Way," by bringing to light its full meaning. There is ultimately only one Tao, although articulated differently by Confucius, Lao-tzu, and other ancient sages. The task of the interpreter is to bring out the common ground between them, to disclose the profound unity of the classics. Profound Learning, as a type of learning aimed at explicating the meaning of Tao, has nothing "dark" or "mysterious" about it. Firmly rooted in the teaching of the sages, it appears dark only because scholars had not come to view the classics in the right way. To place them in a proper light, Wang Pi not only put forward a new interpretation, but spearheaded a fundamental critique of Han learning.

The latter, as we have seen, is characterized by its "chapter-and-verse" method of interpretation. As one critic complained, scholars of the *chang-chü* school had become obsessed with "precious details, play on fine words and clever arguments, which destroy the form and substance of the classics" (*Han-shu* 30.1723). When coupled with the fact that scholarship had become a prerequisite for official appointment and thus an avenue for material gains, it is not difficult to see why intellectuals committed to the idea of "learning for the sake of oneself" (*Lun-yü* 14.24)—that is, self-improvement and moral development—would be alarmed by what seemed rampant abuses of classical learning. In this context, the question of interpretation attracted considerable attention in Profound Learning, and occasioned a major debate on the relationship between "words and meaning." Wang Pi was not the only one involved, but his contribution is substantial and bears directly on his understanding of the *Lao-tzu*.

On Words and Meaning

The basic question is raised in the *Yi-ching*: "Writing does not completely express what is said, and what is said does not completely express the (intended) meaning [will].[5] If so, does this mean that the ideas of the sages cannot be discerned?" (*Hsi-tz'u* 1; Lou 1980, 2:554). Common experience might suggest that spoken words, and worse still writing, often fail to express intense feelings or difficult ideas. Wang Pi, however, defended the possibility of understanding:

> Images are that which yields meaning. And words are that through which the images can be understood. To fully express what is meant, there is nothing better than images; to fully bring out the images, there is nothing better than words. Words are born of images; thus one can search through the words to view the images.

Images are born of meaning or ideas; thus one can search through
the images to view the meaning. (*Chou-yi lüeh-li*; Lou 1980, 2:609;
Lynn 1994, 31)

The seemingly hierarchical distinction between "words" and "images" is necessitated by the structure of the *Yi-ching*, but not essential to
the argument. A variety of means may be employed to express meaning.
Whether by means of graphic images or words of explanation, the important point remains that meaning is always mediated. But having
affirmed the importance of words and images, Wang Pi introduces a
new argument:

Thus, words are the vehicle through which images are understood;
once the images are grasped, the words themselves are forgotten.
Images are that which holds meaning; once the meaning is grasped,
the images themselves are forgotten.

Written signs are thus necessary but not sufficient; they are important
instruments but not the end itself. While mediation is required, understanding transcends the media through which meaning is brought to
mind. "For this reason," Wang Pi concludes, "those who keep only to
the words have not attained the image; those who keep only to the
images have not attained the meaning" (Lou 1980, 2:609).

The Han approach is fundamentally wrong because it fails to recognize the reality of ideas. By reducing meaning to reference, it is in effect
denying that written works have a "world" of their own. This can only
lead to a fragmented reading, albeit loaded with "precious details," which
not only sacrifices depth for an artificial breadth, but violates the coherence and unity of the classics. Thus, Wang Pi is adamant that words and
images can hinder understanding if they are turned into icons with
preestablished meanings extraneous to and independent of the texts
themselves. They must be "forgotten" in the sense that understanding
is possible only if one can, as it were, read between the lines to penetrate
into the world of ideas that breathes life into the words and images. For
"chapter-and-verse" scholars, including Ho-shang-kung, of course, this
does not make any sense at all, for to them sense is derived from reference. There is "nothing" between the lines, and what is not objectively
identifiable cannot have any meaning.

Wang Pi thus turns out to be quite an iconoclast. From a hermeneutical perspective, his view of the *Lao-tzu* differs from Ho-shang-kung's in
many respects. Most noticeably, the latter's concern with long life is

entirely absent in the former. Where it occupies the foreground in the text, Wang Pi consistently directs attention to the Tao itself. For example, the image that "one who dies but does not perish" (ch. 33) is seen to express the central idea of the limitlessness and inexhaustibility of Tao: "Although one dies, the Way by which life is made possible does not perish." Similarly, he has little interest in cosmological and religious details. For example, whereas for Ho-shang-kung the "sacred vessel" of the world refers to human beings with indwelling spirits, Wang Pi argues differently: "'Sacred' means without form and without limit; 'vessel' is made by unifying different things. Without form yet unified, it is therefore called a 'sacred vessel'" (ch. 29). Reference is not the issue; more critical to understanding is the sense in which the image expresses a deeper idea, an idea which in this instance Wang Pi goes on to relate to "naturalness." Other examples can be cited, but what accounts for the differences between the two commentaries is clearly the prior assumption about meaning and the consequent perspective from which the text has been viewed. The "spirit of the valley" (ch. 6), as we have seen, discloses to Ho-shang-kung a map of the spiritual body and a guide to naturalness and long life. For Wang Pi, the words bring to mind rather the image of "the middle of the valley," which suggests the idea of "nonbeing" or "nothingness." Once the chains of reference are broken, the commentator is free to pursue the perceived deeper meaning of the text. Together, nonbeing and naturalness form the twin foci of Wang Pi's *Lao-tzu* commentary.

The "Nonbeing" of Tao

What does *wu* mean? Grammatically, the word functions both as a transitive verb and as a noun. *Wu* and its opposite *yu* mean basically "not having" and "having" something, and "nothing" and "something." Disagreement, however, arises when they are extended to represent metaphysical concepts. If *wu* means "nothingness" or, as many scholars prefer to translate, "nonbeing," does it have a positive meaning, or even reference? In Ho-shang-kung's commentary, it is viewed positively in terms of *ch'i* energy. Even if "nothing" can be seen or described, "something" is certainly there to bring about created order. Can the same be said for Wang Pi's understanding? Inasmuch as *yu* is most simply rendered "being" at the ontological level, *wu* may be translated "nonbeing." This does not, however, prejudge its meaning or rule out other translations.

In agreement with Ho-shang-kung, Wang Pi recognizes the transcendence of Tao. On the opening words of the *Lao-tzu*, he writes:

> The Way that can be spoken of and the name that can be named
> point to things and represent forms, which are not constant. Hence
> (the constant Tao) cannot be spoken of and cannot be named. (ch. 1)

Unlike Ho-shang-kung, Wang Pi is not concerned with what the constant Tao stands for, but with the logic of *Lao-tzu's* argument. The same
approach marks his understanding of Tao as the "beginning" and
"mother" of all things:

> All beings originate from nonbeing. Thus, before there are forms
> and names, the Way then is the "beginning" of the ten thousand
> things. When there are forms and names, the Way then "brings
> them up, nourishes them, makes them secure and stable" [*Lao-tzu*,
> ch. 51]; it is their "mother." This means that the Way in its formless-
> ness and namelessness originates and completes the ten thousand
> things. They are thus originated and completed, but do not know
> why this is so. (ch. 1)

Characteristically, ideas from different parts of the *Lao-tzu* are drawn
together in the commentary to bring out the perceived unity of the text.
The transcendence of Tao is to be affirmed on account of its formless-
ness and ineffability. But in relation to beings, the Tao is conceived as
both absolute beginning and teleological end. The latter, an extension of
the idea of an overarching presence and purpose of Tao, makes possible
the transition from metaphysics to ethics. But Wang Pi adds a third point,
that the presence of Tao is hardly noticeable—a point of particular importance to his interpretation of Taoist practical philosophy.

    The theme of transcendence is linked directly to the inadequacy of
language and its implication for understanding. "Names," Wang Pi states,
"serve to determine form. Completely undifferentiated and without
form, the Way cannot be pinned down and determined" (ch. 25). Although such words as "deep," "wondrous," and "great" may be useful
in providing glimpses of the Tao, "they do not exhaust the meaning of
the ultimate" (*Lao-tzu chih-lüeh*; Lou 1980, 1:196; see Wagner 1986; Rump
1979, xxviii). Even the word "Tao" is to be used with caution and not
turned into a divisive and limiting "name" (ch. 25). Indeed, "If one speaks
of Tao, one loses its constancy; if one were to name it, one misses its
truth" (Lou 1980, 1:196).

    Having pointed out the inadequacy of language, however, as in the
debate on "words and meaning," Wang Pi cannot allow the further claim
that understanding of Tao is impossible. Although the idea of transcen-

dence remains central, it does not represent the whole picture. "One may want to speak of nonbeing, but things become complete through it" (ch. 14; also ch. 6). Philosophically, Wang Pi argues, "As nonbeing cannot be made manifest by nonbeing itself, it must be mediated by beings" (*Yi-ching hsi-tz'u* comm.; Lou 1980, 2:548). While the "nonbeing" of Tao cannot be compromised, this should not obscure the fact that its power or "constancy" is manifested in nature. In this way, a dialectical reading of the *Lao-tzu* begins to take shape, by which Wang Pi is able to affirm both understanding and the possibility of following Tao in individual action and government.

The Logic of Creation

According to the *Lao-tzu*, "The Way gives birth to One," which in turn produces "Two," "Three," and the myriad creatures (ch. 42). Like Ho-shang-kung, Wang Pi is convinced that the concept of "One" promises to shed light on the wonder of Tao. Unlike Ho-shang-kung, however, he is not convinced that "One" can be equated with the vital essence which generated yin and yang and initiated the process of creation at the "beginning":

> The ten thousand things and the ten thousand forms ultimately go back to "One." On what basis do they come to be "One"? Because of nonbeing. From nonbeing comes "One." . . . Since it is called "One," how can it be without words? With words and with "One," how can there not be "Two"? With "One" and "Two," "Three" is thus born. From nonbeing to being, all numbers end here. (ch. 42)

The analysis of the way in which "Two" and "Three" come into being is indebted to the *Chuang-tzu* (ch. 2); but the main argument here is that the multiplicity and diversity of things can ultimately be traced to a single source. Yet, what is the relationship between "nonbeing" and "One," and how can the asserted unity of creation itself be justified? If creation cannot be understood simply in terms of particular agents of change, what does Wang Pi have to offer in its place?

To reconstruct Wang Pi's argument, we may again contrast it with Ho-shang-kung's interpretation. First and foremost, the concept of "One" does not refer to any entity or substance. The parallel between numbers and things should already give an indication of Wang's approach. "Two" is inconceivable without "One," but "Two" does not follow from "One" in the same sense that an original vital energy produced yin and yang. Significantly, "beginning" is not taken as a temporal reference, but as indicating conceptual priority. "Things are born and then nurtured, nurtured . . . and then made complete," Wang Pi writes; but "what causes them to be born?"

> It is Tao. What nurtures them? It is virtue. . . . For things which are born, and for efforts which are made complete, there are always causes. As there are causes, then none is not caused by Tao. Thus when (the argument is) pushed to the limit, we again come to the ultimate Tao. On account of their (immediate) causes, they are therefore each accorded different titles. (ch. 51)

The myriad things and affairs have their proper place and reasons in the larger architecture of Tao, but before they can be understood the prior condition for their being must be recognized. The Way constitutes the absolute "beginning" in that all beings have causes and conditions which can be shown logically to derive from "One." By tracing the chain of beings from particular, contingent causes to a necessary foundation, Wang Pi is able to account for the unity of creation without resorting to the language of time and being. Indeed, the argument cannot be complete if "beginning" is conceived as an expression of time, or the "One" in terms of a first being or original substance. If the possibility of infinite regress cannot be admitted, the idea of a first being or substance seems self-defeating. The proper conclusion, in other words, can only be *wu*, what being is not. This is not the place to decide the merit of the argument; suffice it to note that for Wang Pi the question of beginning cannot be resolved unless the absolute otherness of Tao is taken seriously. Dialectically understood, the concept of "One" ultimately rejoins that of nonbeing.[6] Cosmological interpretations in general and Ho-shang-kung's in particular are thus philosophically untenable, for they project a false image of "nonbeing." It is entirely appropriate to portray Tao conceptually and metaphorically as "beginning," "One," or the "root" of all beings; but serious misunderstanding arises when what is conceptual or metaphoric is misread literally to represent a kind of original substance or energy. Clearly not to be identified as a formless and nameless "something," Wang Pi's argument points persuasively to "nonbeing" as a negative concept, which sets the Tao apart from the domain of beings.

Principle of Nature

If Wang Pi were only interested in metaphysics, his analysis of the *Lao-tzu* would probably have ended here. But the emphasis on "nonbeing" does not downplay ethics. As Wang Pi explicitly relates, "Things of this world all have life by virtue of being; the origin of being is rooted in nonbeing. If one were to attain the fullness of being, one must return to nonbeing" (ch. 40). The more theoretical discussion is integral to his Taoist practical philosophy. In the language of ethical theory, what is deemed truly the case is also the basis for what ought to be the case. As the "constancy" of Tao constitutes a pristine order, it defines the terms and direction of Taoist ethics and politics. If present realities deviate from this order, as Wang Pi believes they do, it becomes imperative to recover what is "true," to reorient human thinking and action by modelling after Tao, and in this sense to "return" to it.

The "sage," the *Lao-tzu* maintains, "knows without having to set foot outside his door, and sees the way of heaven without having to look through his window" (ch. 47). Wang Pi explains:

> The Way has its great constancy, and principle has its ultimate end. By holding fast to the way of old, one can master the present; though living in the present, one can know the beginning of antiquity. This is why the sage knows without having to set foot outside his door or look through his window. (ch. 47)

The idea of "principle" (*li*), the way in which the "great constancy" of Tao is manifested, translates into patterns, structures, and laws. The regularity of the seasons, the movement and positioning of the stars, and other natural phenomena which constitute the "way of heaven," thus all testify to the presence of Tao (e.g., chs. 9, 73). The question is, How does this pertain to the world of human affairs?

The determination of "principle" suggests that the basis for "acting" is "knowing." Yet the reasons for acting and being cannot be located outside the self. The sage "knows" without having contact with the phenomenal world because "true" knowledge, not to be confused with the mastery of information or skills, stems directly from the realization of one's "nature." This, indeed, is but a logical extension of the analysis of Tao as "nonbeing." If the Tao were a supreme "something," then knowledge of it would be indispensable; but in the light of "nonbeing" where there is literally "nothing" to know, a different view emerges. Building on *Lao-tzu*'s insight that "man models after earth; earth models after heaven; heaven models after Tao; Tao models after the naturally-so" (ch. 25), Wang Pi carefully develops the idea of "naturalness" (*tzu-jan*):

> "Model after" means to follow specific rules. Man does not act contrary to (the rules of the) earth, and thus he is [obtains] completely safe; this is what is meant by "modelling after earth." Earth does

not act contrary to heaven, and thus it can [obtains the ability to] support all things; this is what is meant by "modelling after heaven." Heaven does not act contrary to Tao, and thus it can [obtains the ability to] shelter all things; this is what is meant by "modelling after Tao."

Tao does not act contrary to what is naturally so, and thus it obtains (the realization of) its nature [*hsing*]. To model after what is naturally so means to follow the rules of the square while inside the square, and to follow the rules of the circle while inside the circle; that is, to adhere without exception to what is naturally so. *Tzu-jan* is a term for what cannot be designated, an expression for the ultimate. . . . Thus, they model after one another. (ch. 25)

The "is" evidently implies "can," and both are understood in terms of human nature (*hsing*); literally, what one has "obtained" from Tao. Moreover, this is also the meaning of virtue. As Wang Pi states, "The Way is the cause or reason of things; virtue is what they have obtained from Tao" (ch. 51).[7]

Conceptually, "nature" or "virtue" can be traced to "One" as well, which at the ontological level suggests "what is true [*chen*] in man" (ch. 10). This is based on *Lao-tzu's* claim that all beings come into existence in virtue of having "obtained One" from the "beginning" (ch. 39). In this regard it is not enough to define human nature as the desire for food and sex, or in terms of particular moral qualities as philosophers have done before. Basic "principles" which constitute and regulate life processes are important, but they, too, logically stem from "One." The "essence," the *Lao-tzu* declares, is perfectly true or real (ch. 21). According to Wang, this means that if things "return" to the "deep"—that is, if one models after the emptiness of Tao—"then the ultimate of what is essential and true would have been obtained, and the nature of the ten thousand things would have been settled." The fact that "man models after earth" and ultimately *tzu-jan*, far from endorsing an external standard, thus completes the analysis of Tao by driving home the "oneness" of nature. The concept of naturalness is important because it alone can adequately account for the order of nature without violating the principle of nonbeing. "Essence" or true nature cannot be externalized. If creation cannot be traced to a godlike something, whose image or substance would presumably inform the nature of beings, the argument can only be that things are "naturally so," an integral whole at the foundational level. This is why Wang Pi insists that although beings are originated and completed by Tao, they do not know why it is so.

Naturalness and Nonaction

In view of its transcendental ground, the "naturally-so" must be said to be "an expression for the ultimate"; in relation to beings, however, it is pregnant with practical possibilities. According to the *Lao-tzu*, "Heaven and earth are not benevolent" (ch. 5). Wang Pi comments,

> Heaven and earth abide by *tzu-jan*. Without their doing or making anything, the ten thousand things themselves govern one another and put their affairs into order. Thus, (heaven and earth) "are not benevolent." Benevolence necessarily involves setting up and changing things, dispensing favors and doing things for them. If things were thus set up and changed, they would lose their true nature. With favors and (discriminating) action, then things would not be equally preserved. . . . Do nothing [*wu-wei*] to the ten thousand things, and they will be at ease in their own functions; then indeed nothing will not be self-sufficient. (ch. 5)

This distinguishes naturalness from the Confucian predilection for benevolent intervention. More precisely, bearing in mind Wang Pi's nonsectarian stance, while benevolence may be the most admirable of conducts (ch. 19), it pales by comparison with nonaction (*wu-wei*), a concept which Confucius himself recognizes and applies to the highest sage (*Lun-yü* 2.1, 15.4). One strong message that emerges from all the classics, as Wang Pi firmly believes, is that ethically and politically naturalness expresses itself in nonaction.

As an explanatory tool, the concept of *wu-wei* helps pinpoint the sense in which one can be said to model after Tao, and thus to realize nature. Following *Lao-tzu*'s statement that "those who follow the Way" are "the same as the Way" (ch. 23), Wang Pi establishes a ground for nonaction:

> The Way, in its formlessness and nonaction, sustains and completes the ten thousand things. Therefore, those who follow the Way take nonaction as their master [or, dwell in nonaction]. . . . Then, things will obtain their true nature and become one with Tao. (ch. 23)

Obviously, nonaction has little to do with total inaction, but intimates the workings of Tao. Human beings, "on account of their immediate causes" (ch. 51), can initially be seen to follow the way of heaven and earth, in the sense that the seemingly haphazard ways of human life conform to specific patterns. The deeper idea, however, is not to model artificially after something else, but "to take nonbeing as the basis of all functions," so that virtue may be completely utilized (ch. 38) and all beings "be at ease in their own functions" (ch. 5).[8]

As an expression of nonbeing, nonaction is categorically free from the store of competing interests and ideological investments that bind action in the sociopolitical world. Thus the *Lao-tzu* stresses that the pursuit of Tao "decreases" everyday until it reaches nonaction, where paradoxically "nothing is left undone." This means "to return to emptiness and non-being," according to Wang Pi. "With action [in the sense defined above], there is bound to be loss"; by nonaction, in contrast, affairs in the order of nature are accomplished effortlessly and spontaneously (ch. 48).

What does one stand to "lose"? The recurrent theme of loss joins together the Taoist critique of desires and the promise of nonaction. Driven by desires, one risks losing one's true nature. The direction of Taoist ethics thus lies in "decreasing" one's desires and any false sense of self that engenders them until one reaches the tranquil depth of empti-ness and nonbeing. The *Lao-tzu*, presenting us with yet another paradox, announces that "the sage desires to have no desires, and does not value goods that are hard to obtain" (ch. 64). Wang Pi identifies the real ethical problem: "Desires, however slight, give rein to striving and conflict; goods that are hard to obtain, however small, give rise to greed and thievery" (cf. ch. 44). Naturally humble and generous, the *Lao-tzu* also says of the sage, without partiality or any concern for selfish gain, he finds self-fulfilment (ch. 7). This, as Wang Pi succinctly relates, is but to say that he embodies nonaction in his person.

The important distinction, of course, is that the sage never strives to achieve these "virtues"; rather, like an "infant," whose wholesome nature has not yet been deformed by the cancerous growth of desires (ch. 55), he naturally models after Tao and realizes the "highest virtue" (ch. 38). This is possible because the Tao itself is "constant in having no desires" (ch. 34). From these words, according to Wang Pi, we arrive at a clear idea of the Taoist model of naturalness:

> The ten thousand things all come into being because of Tao. Having been born this way, they nonetheless do not know the reason. Thus, when the world is constant in having no desires, the ten thousand things each and all obtain their proper place or station, as if the Way had done nothing for them. (ch. 38)

By demonstrating the interrelatedness of *Lao-tzu*'s central insights, Wang Pi weaves together a coherent account of Taoist philosophy. The concept of "One" remains at the center, bridging the transcendence of

Tao and the order of the Taoist world. Its natural sense of being the beginning and smallest of all suggests readily—especially in the light of the meaning of *wu*, which encompasses both "not having" and "not being"— the priority of having "less" on the ethical level. Indeed, much of Taoist ethics hinges on the claim that having more or what is bigger is not necessarily better. Once the sense of having "more" is linked to the endless ties and longings which render human beings prisoners in their own world, the Taoist calculus of "profit and loss" becomes transparent (chs. 22, 23). Meaningful gain, in this context, can only be measured on a scale of freedom, by the extent to which one is not being fettered by desires, or not having the kind of interest-seeking thought/action which invariably precipitates conflict and disorder. In having less, and this is perhaps the distinctively Taoist contribution, the world is seen to be naturally simple and whole, noncontentious and self-sufficient. This is the virtue which the world has obtained from Tao. As part of the natural order, human beings should logically reflect the same base of quiescence and completeness. To Wang Pi, this speaks more eloquently than any cosmological proof that human nature is modelled after Tao, which is to say "true" and "naturally so," a state of simplicity and wholeness that is realized through nonaction.

The Politics of Nonaction

The same principles apply to both ethics and politics. Thus, when the *Lao-tzu* describes how the people in an ideal Taoist community are content in their simple ways and, among other things, have no cause to resort to instruments of war (ch. 80), Wang Pi cuts directly to the underlying idea: "They do not have desires and wants." In government, the *Lao-tzu* says, it is important that "the people be kept constantly without knowledge and without desires" (ch. 3). Not to be misconstrued as a kind of political technique designed to manipulate or coerce, this means that they be allowed "to safeguard their true nature." To sharpen the point that what passes for knowledge in the world misses the mark of *tzu-jan*, the *Lao-tzu* more strongly asserts, "Those who were good at working the Way in ancient times did not try to make the people smart, but to keep them dumb" (ch. 65). "Smart," in this context, must be understood in the sense of having "many cunning schemes and clever skills," which corrupt natural simplicity; the word "dumb," on the other hand, "means not having knowledge and guarding their true nature, which is to say to follow what is naturally so." This was how the sage kings governed, and this is how the rulers of the present can establish once more the rule of Tao. Government, too, must in the final analysis abide by naturalness and nonaction.

The sage ruler naturally never puts himself first or claims credit for his accomplishments. Consequently, the people are not aware that he has brought order and well-being to the world, assuming that the good fortune they enjoy has come about spontaneously. In this sense, according to Wang Pi, the *Lao-tzu* speaks of the "highest" ruler as being merely "known" by the people. Only those who are unable to govern by nonaction turn to benevolent action, which endears them to the people; they are not only known but praised. With praise, however, blame also arrives. At a still lower level, there are those who fail to govern by benevolence but rely on force and cunning instead. They may command fear and outward compliance, but they are certainly resented and cannot effect genuine, lasting peace (ch. 17; also chs. 5, 27, 38). It is only when the people are naturally in order, as opposed to obeying orders imposed from without, that the Taoist political ideal may be realized.

For Wang Pi, Taoist government must aim constantly at "honoring the root and putting to rest the branches":

> Govern the country with Tao, then the country will be at peace. Govern the country with rectitude, then military expediency will arise. . . . In governing the country with Tao, one honors the root so as to put the branches to rest. In governing the country with rectitude, one establishes punishment and laws to tackle the branches. If the root is not established, the branches will be sparse. If the people are not taken care of, the result will inevitably be armies being used with strategic expediency. (ch. 57)

The people must be supported; this is one meaning of "honoring the root and putting to rest the branches." This would mean that the people be allowed to work their fields and enjoy the fruits of their labor. The plenitude of nature is not in doubt—having "obtained" the virtue of Tao, heaven and earth naturally provide for all beings—but greedy and ruthless governments disrupt the order of nature. To maintain a peaceful environment, in which the people prosper and are content, Wang Pi's *Lao-tzu* advises against excessive taxation, heavy punishment, war, and other taxing measures (e.g., chs. 72–76). Whereas reliance on laws and punishment "to profit the state" is entirely misguided and "will only lead to loss" (ch. 36), military intervention must remain a last resort to weed out violence and disorder (ch. 30). To further the work of supporting the people and to uproot abuses from the political system, as Wang Pi also insists, officials must be appointed on the basis of ability (ch. 3), and not by reputation or family background as was commonly the case in third-century China.

All these are important tools, but like words and images they remain means and may prove counterproductive if confused with the end. From the larger Taoist perspective, government is not unlike the work of a farmer, who needs only ensure that the course of nature is not prevented from coming to fruition (ch. 59). More precisely, Wang Pi explains,

> The nature of the ten thousand things is constituted by *tzu-jan*. Therefore, it can be followed but not acted upon, be allowed to complete its course but not held by force . . . any attempt to forge it into something else is bound to end in failure. . . . The sage realizes the nature of *tzu-jan*, and guides the ten thousand things to come to flourish in their natural state. Thus, he follows and respects their nature, and does not artificially act upon or interfere with it. He eliminates what causes them to be deluded, and removes what acts to seduce them. Thus, their mind is not confused and they naturally attain their true nature. (ch. 29)

Surely, to borrow from the Mencius, no ruler would want to model after the fool who pulled up his young plants by force to help them grow. To follow *tzu-jan* means that one does not arbitrarily try to alter or "improve" nature. To preserve the integrity of nature, the sage and by extension the ruler would, however, make sure that obstructions to human flourishing are removed. The argument returns thus to the basic Taoist claim of nonaction and the diminishing of desires. Desires must be firmly "put to rest," so that the "root" may grow; put another way, taking full advantage of the suggestiveness of the metaphor, the people would never find genuine peace and contentment if the "root" of all social and political problems is not eradicated.

Ultimately the ruler himself must embrace nonaction so as to establish a model to transform the people—that is, to enable those under the spell of desires to reclaim their true nature. Specific policies or techniques of government are secondary and must be "forgotten" if nonaction were to be realized. Government by nonaction is not "mysterious," however. It does not involve mystical or esoteric practices, but rests on the claim that the transforming power of Tao, defined in terms of naturalness and exemplified by the ideal sage-ruler, would spontaneously permeate the mind and heart of the people. There is perhaps a degree of optimism to this view, but one which to Wang Pi is well justified. This is because the all-encompassing order of *tzu-jan* extends to the sociopolitical level. The institution of family and state is not extrinsic to nature. More specifically, the hierarchical structure of sociopolitical institutions reflects the principles governing the Taoist world. This explains *Lao-tzu's* claim that

Taoist self-cultivation, which Wang Pi again relates to realizing one's true nature, has a direct impact on the well-being of the family and the country (ch. 54). This also explains why the text ranks the king as one of the "four great ones" after Tao, heaven, and earth (ch. 25; see also chs. 39, 42).

In this respect, Wang Pi the iconoclast thus turns out to be quite a conservative. The sociopolitical framework as a whole must be carefully conserved because it forms an integral part of the natural order. While the king occupies a privileged position, it is also the case that the art of rulership can now be defined in terms of Taoist principles. Embodying these principles, the ideal sage naturally serves as a model for all rulers to emulate. But equally if not more important, the way of the sage can also be invoked in judgment of governments; that is to say, once the principles are understood, they offer an objective standard by which actual performance can be measured. On this account, for Wang Pi, the *Lao-tzu* and the other classics are in complete agreement.

Notes

1. Quotations from the Ho-shang-kung commentary are based on two modern critical editions, Cheng 1971 and Wang 1993. English translations are my own; compare Erkes 1958. Translations of the *Lao-tzu* are adapted from Lau 1980. A good introduction to both commentators is Robinet 1977.

2. Ch. 3. Some versions have a slightly different reading. Due to space constraints, textual variation and emendation will not be indicated in this discussion. Though important, they do not affect the general argument presented here.

3. Although the author was clearly influenced by the "correlative" cosmology prevalent in the Han period, this does not mean that he had simply imposed an existing theory on the text. The *Lao-tzu* states, "The ten thousand things carry yin on their backs and yang in their arms" (ch. 42). As a commentator, Ho-shang-kung is concerned to fill in the details, to make sure there is no misunderstanding, and in so doing to lay bare the Taoist understanding of creation. As opposed to some other yin-yang theories which may posit a "great ultimate" or "heaven" at the "beginning," the argument here is that creation cannot be understood apart from Tao, and in particular, the "One." For a general account of Han cosmology, see Needham (1956) and Henderson (1984).

4. According to a T'ang Buddhist source, Ho-shang-kung equates the words "invisible, inaudible, subtle" in ch. 14 with "essence, spirit, energy." This is not found in the extant versions of the commentary, however. See Wang 1993, 55.

5. Technically, meaning need not be restricted to intention, but the word *yi* signifies primarily "meaning" as embodied in "ideas" and thus involves the notion of "will." Note also that the discussion here is limited to written communications. All quotations from Wang's writings are from Lou's critical edition (1980).

6. This would suggest, as Wang Pi points out also, that "One" is not a number; precisely "because it is not a number, numbers are made complete." Without dimensions and therefore cannot be "counted," the concept of "One" signifies "the great ultimate of change" (Lou 1980, 2:547).

7. "Virtue," Wang Pi elaborates, "means 'to obtain'. Constantly without losing what has been obtained, there will be benefit without harm. Thus, the name 'virtue' is used. How does one come to obtain virtue? Because of Tao. How does one completely utilize virtue? By taking nonbeing as [the basis of all] functions" (ch. 38).

8. The ethical relevance of "nonbeing" also entails a mode of being characterized by "emptiness" (*hsü*). "Although heaven and earth are vast," Wang Pi writes, "they take nonbeing as their heart. Although sages and kings are great, they take emptiness as their master" (ch. 38). While the word *hsü* performs the same semantic function as *wu* in relating the transcendence of Tao, it also suggests a sense of "quiescence" (*ching*), which helps bring out the meaning of nonaction. As Wang makes the philosophical connection, "As a rule, being arises from emptiness; movement arises from quiescence" (ch. 16).

References

Boltz, William G. 1985. "The *Lao-tzu* Text that Wang Pi and Ho-shang-kung Never Saw." *Bulletin of the School of Oriental and African Studies* 48: 493–501.

Chan, Alan K. L. 1991a. *Two Visions of the Way: A Study of the Wang Pi and the Ho-shang-kung Commentaries on the Lao-tzu*. Albany: State University of New York Press.

Chan, Alan K. L. 1991b. "The Formation of the Ho-shang-kung Legend." In *Sages and Filial Sons: Mythology and Archaeology in Ancient China*, ed. Julia Ching and R. W. L. Guisso, 101–34. Hong Kong: Chinese University Press.

Cheng Ch'eng-hai. 1971. *Lao-tzu Ho-shang-kung-chu chiao-li*. Taipei: Chung-hua shu-chü.

Erkes, Eduard. 1958. *Ho-shang-kung's Commentary on Lao-tse*. Ascona, Switzerland: Artibus Asiae.

Henderson, John. 1984. *The Development and Decline of Chinese Cosmology*. New York: Columbia University Press.

Kobayashi Masayoshi. 1990. *Rikuchō dōkyōshi kenkyū*. Tokyo: Sōbunsha.

Kohn, Livia, ed. 1989a. *Taoist Meditation and Longevity Techniques*. In cooperation with Yoshinobu Sakade. Ann Arbor: University of Michigan, Center for Chinese Studies Publications.

———. 1989b. "Guarding the One: Concentrative Meditation in Taoism." In *Taoist Meditation and Longevity Techniques*, ed. Livia Kohn, 123–56. Ann Arbor: University of Michigan, Center for Chinese Studies Publications.

Kusuyama Haruki. 1979. *Rōshi densetsu no kenkyū*. Tokyo: Sōbunsha.

Lau, D. C. 1980. *Lao Tzu Tao Te Ching*. Harmondsworth, England: Penguin Books.

Lin, Paul J. 1977. *A Translation of Lao Tzu's Tao Te Ching and Wang Pi's Commentary*. Ann Arbor: University of Michigan, Center for Chinese Studies Publications.

Lou Yü-lieh, ed. 1980. *Wang Pi chi chiao-shih*. 2 vols. Peking: Chung-hua shu-chü.

Lu Te-ming. 1985 ed. *Ching-tien shih-wen*. Shanghai: Ku-chi ch'u-pan-she.

Lynn, Richard John. 1994. *The Classic of Changes: A New Translation of the I Ching as Interpreted by Wang Bi*. New York: Columbia University Press.

Needham, Joseph. 1956. *Science and Civilisation in China*. Vol. 2: *History of Scientific Thought*. Cambridge: Cambridge University Press.

Peerenboom, R. P. 1993. *Law and Morality in Ancient China: The Silk Manuscripts of Huang-Lao*. Albany: State University of New York Press.

Robinet, Isabelle. 1977. *Les commentaires du Tao to king jusqu'au VIIe siècle*. Paris: Presses Universitaires de France.

Rump, Ariane. 1979. *Commentary on the Lao-tzu by Wang Pi*. In collaboration with Wing-tsit China. Honolulu: University of Hawaii Press.

Schwartz, Benjamin I. 1985. *The World of Thought in Ancient China*. Cambridge, Mass.: Harvard University Press.

Twitchett, Denis, and Michael Loewe, eds. 1986. *The Cambridge History of China*.

Vol. 1: *The Ch'in and Han Empires, 221 B.C. – A.D. 220*. Cambridge: Cambridge University Press.

Wagner, Rudolf G. 1986. "Wang Pi: 'The Structure of the Laozi's Pointers' (*Laozi weizhi lilüe*)." *T'oung Pao* 72: 92–129.

Wang K'a. 1993. *Lao-tzu Tao-te-ching Ho-shang-kung chang-chü*. Peking: Chung-hua shu-chü.

5

Later Commentaries:
Textual Polysemy and Syncretistic Interpretations

Isabelle Robinet

In the Chinese tradition, the *Tao-te-ching* has been considered a political, literary, philosophical, and religious document.[1] Its brevity, conciseness, and rhymed phrases have facilitated its use as a sacred and liturgical text by certain Taoist groups. Its rich topics for meditation have inspired philosophical and metaphysical reflections. Its obscure expressions, moreover, have given Taoists plenty of occasion to illustrate their practices of longevity and immortality. The text is cited by all groups in the Chinese tradition—by Confucians, Buddhists, and Taoists alike—and is undoubtedly one of the great classics of ancient China. It was also the subject of about seven hundred commentaries, beginning with Han Fei-tzu in the third century B.C.E. and continuing to the present day—incorporating throughout a whole variety of different tendencies and interpretations.

Historically, three major types of commentaries can be distinguished: technical or specialist readings, mainly of the early centuries C.E.; philosophical exegeses, such as the Ch'ung-hsuan (Twofold Mystery) vision of the T'ang dynasty (618–906); and inner alchemy interpretations, primarily of the Sung dynasty (960–1260). Among the first (see table 5.1), we have the famous work of Ho-shang-kung, a legendary figure of the second century C.E., whose work was probably put together several centuries later, and the *Hsiang-erh*, the main work on the *Tao-te-ching* by the Celestial Masters. Among the second, there are the standard edition of the text by Wang Pi (226–249 C.E.), the master commentator of the text, and the interpretations by major Twofold Mystery thinkers, such as Ch'eng Hsuan-ying and Li Jung of the early T'ang, who read the *Tao-te-ching* in the light of Buddhist logic. It is among the third group, since the Sung dynasty, that the greatest number and variety of interpretations is found and from which the following analysis will draw most frequently.

TABLE 5.1

Tao-te-ching Commentaries in Chronological Order

Name	Date	Edition
B.C.E.		
Han-fei-tzu	d. 230	Han-fei-tzu
Yen Tsun	2nd c.	TT 693
2nd century C.E.		
Ho-shang-kung	2nd c.	TT 682
3rd century C.E.		
Wang Pi	226–249	TT 690
Hsiang-erh	ca. 250	Tun-huang ms., Jao 1956
Chieh-chieh		in citations
7–9th centuries		
Ch'eng Hsuan-ying	fl. 650	TT 711ms., , Yen 1983
Li Jung	fl. 660	TT 722
Emp. Hsuan-tsung	r. 713–756	TT 677, 678, 679
Li Yueh	8th c.	TT 692
Tu Kuang-t'ing	850–933	TT 725
Lu Hsi-sheng	fl. 888–904	TT 685
11th century		
Ssu-ma Kuang	1019–1086	TT 689
Wang An-shih	1021–1086	
Ch'en Ching-yüan	1025–1094	TT 714
Lü Hui-ch'ing	1031–1100	TT 686
Su Ch'e	1039–1112	TT 691
Wang P'ang	1042–1076	TT 706
12th century		
Emp. Hui-tsung	r. 1101–1126	TT 680
Ch'en Hsiang-ku	fl. 1101	TT 683
Lu Chiu-yuan	1139–1192	
Chao Shih-an	fl. 1152	TT 724
Shao Jo-yü	fl. 1159	TT 688
13th century		
Pai Yü-ch'an	fl. 1209–1224	Tsung-shu chi-ch'eng
P'eng Ssu	fl. 1229–1251	TT 708
Lin Hsi-yi	ca. 1210–1273	TT 701
Tu Tao-chien	1237–1318	TT 702
Tung Ssu-ching	fl. 1246–1260	TT 705 (collection)
Wu Ch'eng	1247–1331	TT 704
Yang Chih-jen	fl. 1287	TT 685

Name	Date	Edition
Teng Yi	fl. 1298	TT 687
Liu Wei-yung	fl. 1299	TT 723
Chao Ping-wen		TT 695
Chao Chih-chien		TT 719
14th century		
Emp. Tai-tsu	1328–1398	TT 676

Here we can distinguish philological from ideological interpretations, but before we do so, let me make some remarks on commentaries and interpretation in general.

Commentaries as Exemplary Readings

As Borges has said, a book—and the *Tao-te-ching* is that no less than any other—"is not a closed entity; it is a relationship." It is in fact a dialogue, a relational play between the book and the reader, the object of the reading and its subject as well as the subject of the book. This relational play imposes a task on the reader. The reading modifies the book and invites its recreation; it is an unending work of remaking, trying to assure that nothing of the original richness is lost. But the book in its own turn also modifies the reader; its different interpretations create groups of readers and schools of readings. In the case of the *Tao-te-ching*, more than in many others, Western readers must overcome distances of cultural background while Chinese readers must struggle with the thought habits of a distant historical period. The commentaries on the text accordingly attempt to reapproach the reading of a work that has become distanced by the passing of time and by the misty origins of its author. They develop a sense of contemporality that can be received by people of their own time and is relevant to their world, a world more likely than not dominated by a vastly different kind of thinking, such as Confucianism or Buddhism. To dissolve the distance between the period and culture, in which the text evolved, the reader of another time must either make the text contemporaneous to the reader or make the reader contemporaneous to the text. This is the task commentaries typically set for themselves, aiming at translating the text into a more current language while circling around its obscurities, lessening its paradoxes, and reducing its originality. They reshape the old document for a newer taste, frequently using syncretistic forms of interpretation. Difficulties and incoherencies of the text are frequently simply left aside, replaced by paraphrases and semi-translations.[2]

The *Tao-te-ching* is a particularly attractive object for commentaries, because it is contradictory and abrupt and contains unintelligible phrases such as "spirit of the valley" (*ku-shen*) and "mysterious female" (*hsuan-p'in*). Its various incoherencies may be due partly to later alterations, but Chinese culture has typically rejected the dissection of its classical texts and treated them as an integrated whole. It has thus been largely unacceptable to the Chinese to explain inconsistencies simply through textual alterations, the loss of phrases or sections, and the overlapping of different compilers of the same document. They do not see gaps in transmission and senseless, unintelligible phrases in a historical, analytical way but treat the *Tao-te-ching* as a consciously created document and develop its shortcomings to advantage—creating a higher depth of sense, a mystery to unravel. Obscure expressions then become metaphors for things unknown that can be solved in innumerable creative ways, quite in the same manner as T. Todorov describes the interpretative process when speaking about Rimbaud (1978, 82). It is for this very reason that the *Tao-te-ching* has earned its elevated rank among Chinese classics. Its text, one might say, will never be definite, its obvious surface meaning will forever be found insufficient, and its words can only be approached as starting points of an inquiry that creates sense, however secondary, from its words.

The *Tao-te-ching* supports continuous interpretation. Does that mean we are dealing with a text that will say whatever one wants it to? No, certainly not. However multiple the approaches and interpretations, not all variant readings are possible. One may even go so far as to give a general reading of the text, to which all commentators agree. Such a reading is found in Tung Ssu-ching's "Collected Interpretations" (TT 705) of the thirteenth century. According to him, the *Tao-te-ching* centers around nonaction, serenity, and spontaneity, and advises people to live in weakness and softness and respond in emptiness or receptivity; they should be free from strife and competition, forget their self, the world, and all opposites. Most commentators would readily support these as the central concepts of the text. Beyond this basic consensus, however, the text is multifaceted, polysemic, and has multiple layers of meaning. Often phrases can be read in more than one way, containing a surplus of intention that seems to cry out for interpretation. Terms like "spirit of the valley," for example, consist of words that belong to the common domain; what they lack, as Todorov has said about Nerval, are "explicit discursive associations" (1978, 81). We do not know what connection unifies the words or phrases into wholes, nor what justifies the particular order in which they appear. Numerous are the evocative images in the text that float about, as Michel de Montaigne (1533–92) has it, "fluttering, flying, moving—truly alive." There is an abundance of symbolic figures, which remain unconnected, inexplicable, and obscure.

This pervading polysemy of the text is due only in part to its being written in classical Chinese. As Ricoeur has shown, words in Western languages too have multiple meanings that become apparent as they are applied in language (1969, 94–95). The difference from classical Chinese lies in the frequency and intensity of the multiple references. In other words, while our language tries, with some exceptions, to forestall the polysemy of any given word through the context in which it is used, the Chinese tend to indulge in the active encouragement of polysemic readings by placing words into a context that does not define them unequivocally. What is more, they prefer contexts that render this polysemy fully evident and use it as an established procedure in writing, in the same way as they enjoy the use of metaphors, allusions, and discontinuities, both in literary and artistic works. Often even the quality of literature lies in the active encouragement of the polysemy of a given word by placing it into a context that does not define it unequivocally but encourages the reader to pursue the meaning until its intention becomes fully evident.

The central subject of the *Tao-te-ching*, the Tao or absolute, is by nature inaccessible through language, as Lao-tzu says. The language used to speak about it, full of enigmas, breakups, incoherencies, may have this precise function, which is that it tries to speak of that which no human speech can ever expose, to transmit a certain truth—or The Truth—with the help of riddles, symbols, allusions, and metaphors. The nature of this truth is such that it cannot be stated directly, a point emphasized repeatedly by the important early commentator Wang Pi. The obscure points of the text are therefore geared specifically to sharpen the reader's mind, a tendency that makes the *Tao-te-ching* similar to mystical and alchemical materials, both Eastern and Western.

Again Todorov's statement about Rimbaud applies: what is remarkable in the *Tao-te-ching*, both in function and discourse, is "the very possibility of hesitation between a typographical error and an intentional formulation" (1978, 82). This openness, this multiplicity of possible meanings, is moreover often maintained by the commentators and turned into a procedure and a general rule of reading. There are some clear examples where commentaries intentionally read the work on several levels at the same time. The Taoist Chao Shih-an, for example, in his "Collected Interpretations" (TT 724) of the year 1152, distinguishes three possible applications of the text: the mystical way of nonaction in complete oblivion; the methods of long life, of which Lao-tzu was the earliest practitioner; and the political order of governing the empire (14.13b, 7.36b). Similarly Teng Yi, in his "Three Interpretations" (TT 687) of the late thirteenth century, unravels the text on three levels: the textual, philological interpretation; the cosmological understanding of the Tao, including spiritual practice; and the technical, alchemical reading that focuses on virtue (*te*) and its specific practical application.

Directions of Inquiry

In reading the *Tao-te-ching*, it is useful to rely on Todorov's analysis of interpretation and commentary (1978). He begins by making a distinction between inquiry into truth and inquiry into meaning, that is, reading the text teleologically to support a particular understanding of the world regarded as the truth, or reading it to find an underlying intention inherent in the work, with no predetermined outcome. When interpretation is regarded as part of an inquiry into truth, it sets itself, from the very beginning, a clear point where it wants to arrive, such as, for example, Christian exegesis. The text is used to support a predetermined teaching, and the ultimate sense is imposed on the original meaning from the outside. Among the commentaries on the *Tao-te-ching*, this is the case particularly in the *Hsiang-erh*, a communal Taoist reading of the third century that has survived in a manuscript recovered from Tun-huang (Robinet 1977, 40–48), and among interpretations in terms of longevity techniques, mainly of the twelfth and thirteenth centuries (Robinet 1977, 49–55). But such works are few and usually also contain other forms of interpretation, due to the fact that there were in general a great variety of orientations in ancient China—unlike in the West, where different forms of patristic exegesis, however heavily contested, had a common basis in Christian doctrine. The absence of one central dogma, the multiplicity of teachings, and the variety of languages created by the many different schools (especially among alchemists), make unified, single-minded commentaries on the *Tao-te-ching* the exception.

Inquiry into meaning, on the contrary, can take place on various levels. It includes philological interpretation of the meaning of specific terms that inquires into the meaning of the text as a whole free from predetermined truth, the search for its original meaning or the intention of the author. This mode of interpretation implies the idea of a unified intention, an objective meaning, a "true sense." This concept is not very active in *Tao-te-ching* commentaries either, because they tend to be more concerned with multiple levels of reading than with unifying intention. Also, the search for one sense forever runs into difficulties due to the inherent incoherencies and discontinuity of the text. Ideological interpretation seeks to put an end to what Todorov calls "pragmatic ambiguity" or a plurality of values. This form of interpretation varies among *Tao-te-ching* commentaries according to the different intellectual traditions of ancient China, such as Legalism, Confucianism, Profound Learning, Buddhism, Taoism, Neo-Confucianism, and so on. It is also often apparent in specific interpretations that use the *Tao-te-ching* mainly to support personal ideas, exploiting the authority of the great old text to add strength to a particular kind of thinking that in itself is quite new. The best-known cases of this kind are the commentaries by Wang Pi and Yen Tsun. Here the new work contains two texts of equal value: that of the original author and that of the commentator. Still, the two are linked, and one cannot translate either without reference to the other.

Yet another kind of reading prefers textual coherence and uses structural or intratextual interpretation. Recreating a consistent body of thought, this mode of commentary uses specific expressions to clarify the various elements of the text in relation to an assumed "overall thinking" of the original author. Here the *Tao-te-ching* is interpreted text-internally, with phrases in one section being read in the light of phrases from another, one chapter understood in the light of the next. Such commentaries are rhythmically interspersed with the original, transposing its words and phrases from one part to another. A further method of reading involves supplying individual chapters with an interpretative paragraph, then connecting the whole by looking at the sequence of chapters and their meaning in context. This is done particularly by Ch'eng Hsuan-ying (TT 711; Robinet 1977, 96–204) and Chao Chih-chien (TT 719), while Lü Hui-ch'ing uses both the latter methods in conjunction (TT 686).

Generally speaking, Chinese commentaries are therefore more philosophical or ideological than scientific or analytical. They proceed less by strict analysis and hardly ever disect the text into smaller and subtler units by means of, for example, grammatical interpretation. Rather, they typically develop an overall synthesis that revives the original function of language: to speak and to show, to create a new vision on the basis of the old. This new vision can be either one of depth or one of breadth. In the case of an in-depth vision, a completely new philosophy is superimposed on the original text, as in the case of Wang Pi, who was a strong independent thinker but left behind no independent works, only commentaries. In the case of a broad-spectrum vision, certain great compilers pull together whole anthologies of commentaries and subcommentaries, giving a wide range of possible meanings and fanning the original out broadly. A good example for this is Tu Kuang-t'ing's "Great Sage Meaning" (TT 725) in forty-eight chapters.

While texts in the West, therefore, are frequently read either to support a particular worldview or with the goal of finding an underlying intention or true sense, the Chinese tradition overall has favored a multiplicity of meanings. Some commentaries recreate the original in the light of contemporaneous concerns, linking grammatical analysis, philosophy, soteriology, and religious (and even political) practice in one sweeping whole. Their reading is as multivalent as their original; and their synthesis often gives a veritable plethora of interpretation rather than specific meanings. To understand the commentaries to the *Tao-te-ching* in more detail, I will discuss different primary modes of Chinese readings of the text, dividing them mainly according to philological (grammatical) and ideological (philosophical) readings. Philological readings address the format of the text overall, its phrases and variants in punctuation, and the specific meaning of individual words. Ideological readings are divided according to Taoist, Buddhist, and Confucian, representing the major intellectual traditions of imperial China.

Philological Readings

Variants in Format

The first concrete problem any discussion of the *Tao-te-ching* and its commentaries faces is the fact that the original was transmitted in different versions, which means that not all commentators worked with the same basic text. Fortunately, the versions they worked with commonly do not show substantial differences—with the exception of a version contained in the "Systematic Explanations" (TT 697).[3] Certain commentators took special notice of this problem of philological analysis, notably the great erudite Ch'en Ching-yuan of the eleventh century, who dedicated an entire study to it (TT 714). Another commentator of the same mettle is P'eng Ssu, an alchemist of the thirteenth century and student of Pai Yü-ch'an, who wrote a comprehensive comparison of the variants contained in twenty-five different *Tao-te-ching* editions (TT 708). Beyond these two great masters, some commentators, such as Emperor Hsuantsung of the T'ang (TT 677, 2.3b), discussed textual details at selected spots, but most interpreters of the *Tao-te-ching* took only very occasional note of basic editoral variants.

Another difficulty one faces is in the inner organization of the text. Does it have one part or two? Is it divided into chapters or not? And how many chapters? The answers to these questions vary greatly. Most commentators opt for a division into two parts and eighty-one chapters, following the commentary of Ho-shang-kung, one of the earliest standard works. But there are others. The historian and politician Ssu-ma Kuang (1019–1086), for example, rejects the division in two parts, the *Tao-ching* and the *Te-ching*, arguing that the Tao and the virtue interpenetrate each other (TT 689). Ch'en Hsiang-ku, following him, treats the text as one fluid whole (TT 683). In terms of chapter numbers, there are editions in 78 (Li Yueh of the T'ang; TT 692), 72 (Yen Tsun of the Han; TT 693), 67 (Emperor T'ai-tsu [1328–1398]; TT 676), and 68 chapters (Wu Ch'eng [1247–1331]; TT 704). Because the celebrated commentator Wang Pi did not interpret chapters 31 and 66, their authenticity was frequently doubted. Others have added titles to the chapters, either adopting those first proposed by Ho-shang-kung or creating their own, as in the case of Chao Shih-an and Pai Yü-ch'an (TT 724).

The variants in editions and textual organization have contributed greatly to differences in the commentaries' formats. They are explored in most detail in works that concern themselves exclusively or primarily with philological analysis. Among those, specialization is common. Commentators favoring grammatical analysis tend to focus on the separate discussion of specific words, expressions, and phrases, while those giving ideological readings focus on divisions between chapters. They have the tendency to prefer a synthesis, to give language back its original function, to speak and to show. Lu Hsi-sheng, Shih Yung, Tu Tao-chien, and Lin Hsi-yi all belong among this group—it is their kind of work that makes commentaries in China a literary category in their own right.

Philological Readings: Punctuation and Phrases

Classical Chinese texts have no punctuation. The division of sentences and phrases depends on the reader, and the meaning of the text follows from its punctuation. A famous example is the first chapter of the *Tao-te-ching*. Depending on whether one punctuates after *wu* (nonbeing) and *yu* (being)[4] or after *ming* (name), the text reads differently. In the first case, we have:

> Nonbeing names the origin of heaven and earth;
> Being names the mother of all things.

In the second case, the two lines read,

> The nameless [nonbeing-name] is the origin of
>   heaven and earth;
> The named [being-name] is the mother of all things.

The same pattern continues in the next two lines. Here we have either

> Therefore, in continuous nonbeing one wishes to see
>   the subtlety;
> In continuous being one wishes to see the outcome.

or, on the contrary,

> Therefore in continuous nondesire [nonbeing-wish],
>   one can see the subtlety;
> In continuous desire [being-wish], one can see the
>   outcome.

This last version is strengthened by the occurrence of the expression "continuous nonbeing" in the *Chuang-tzu*, a fact that emphasizes the high philosophical content of the term. The first reading, on the other hand, is supported by the fact that the Ma-wang-tui manuscript has a particle after "nondesire" and "desire." Commentators through the centuries have interpreted the lines in both ways and heatedly argued about them. It was especially readers of the Sung dynasty, such Ssu-ma Kuang, Wang An-shih (TT 724, 1.19ab), and his son Wang P'ang (TT 706, 1.3a–4b), who preferred the first reading, while Wang Pi favored the latter, followed later by the alchemist Pai Yü-ch'an (TT 724, 3.3a), the Taoist Niu Miao-ch'uan (TT 724, 1.24b, 1. 31ab, 3.11b, 4.7b), and many others.

Li Yueh's commentary of the T'ang dynasty gives an example of ideosyncretic personal punctuation. The last lines of chapter 25 usually read

> Man models himself after earth,
> Earth models itself after heaven,
> Heaven models itself after the Tao,
> The Tao models itself after so-being.

He, however, changes the punctuation to after "human being" and proposes the following new version:

> What models itself after earth is earth,
> What models itself after heaven is heaven,
> What models itself after the Tao is the Tao—
> This is so-being. (TT 692, 2.6b)

Unlike the first example, which supports both readings equally and is debated in various editions of the text, this second case shows the flexibility of the text even to traditional Chinese readers. Although standards existed throughout history, individuals have always cherished their particular vision and easily found room for expressing it with the help of the text. As in the second case, punctuating even one word later can give an entire section a completely different meaning, change the cosmology and metaphysics of the text into something utterly new.

The Meaning of Words

Many commentaries begin their exposition by discussing the exact meaning of a phrase or term, using various ways. A common method is the introduction of homophones, words with the same sound but different meanings. For example, Wang Pi says, "The Tao, that is *tao*, to guide" (ch. 38); Tu Tao-chien has, "the Tao, that is *tao*, to walk" (TT 702, 3.1b). A more metaphorical and complex interpretation is given to obscure words, of which there are many in the *Tao-te-ching*. The second word in chapter 10, for example, is *ying*, a form of vital or spiritual energy. It occurs in the line

Can you support (*tsai*) the spiritual energy and material soul (*ying-p'o*) and embrace the One without letting go?

According to Ho-shang-kung, *ying* should be understood as *hun* (spirit soul) because it occurs together with *p'o*, the material soul. Ch'en Ching-yuan further supports this by saying that *ying* means "coming and going" and therefore indicates the spirit soul, which moves about freely (TT 714, 2.6a). This reading has been adopted by most commentators, but there are exceptions. Li Jung, for example, cited by Wu Ch'eng finds that *ying* means "to preserve" and the phrase *ying-p'o* refers to a special practice of "preserving the material soul" (TT 704, 1.14b). Teng Yi has yet another reading, thinking that the two words indicate the sun and the moon (TT 687, 2.4a).

Similarly, the phrase *Shih-san*, "ten three," in chapter 50 is read sometimes "thirteen," sometimes "three out of ten." "Thirteen" is then taken to refer to the constituents of the body, which are again identified differently by different authors. They are the nine orifices and four members according to Han Fei-tzu, the three passages, nine orifices, and the mind following Ho-shang-kung, and the five inner organs, five members, plus the three energy centers in the head, torso, and abdomen known as the "cinnabar fields" in the reading of Li Yueh (TT 292, 3.9a). The "three out of ten," on the other hand, are understood to indicate three people out of every ten or 30 percent of the population.[5]

Also, entire lines or sections are interpreted differently because different meanings are given to one or the other word. For example, the very first line of the book, "The Tao that can be told is not the eternal (*ch'ang*) Tao," is sometimes read "The Tao that can be told is not the ordinary Tao" because *ch'ang* has both meanings (TT 724, 4.20ab). Ch'eng Hsuan-ying of the seventh century almost always begins his comments with a textual note of this kind. Wu Ch'eng, a thirteenth-century academy scholar, critical editor of several classics, and writer of the preface of the *Yung-lo ta-tz'u-tien* (Great Yung-lo Encyclopedia), also places foremost importance on terminological and philological explanations. Lin Hsi-yi (ca. 1210–1273), author of the "Oral Interpretations," similarly pays special attention to language. In chapter 7, for instance, he gives particular value to the expression *wu-ssu*, "nonpersonal" or "without personal interests," in the description of the sage. To him this "nonpersonal" quality is not merely, as commonly understood, the public-spirited, generous nature of the sage but indicates "a spirit that does not contain anything," a psychological realization of the "true emptiness" of the Buddhists, pure no-self (TT 701, 1.21a). He moreover emphasizes that in reading Taoist texts it is necessary to apply different standards of and values from those used in the Confucian classics (2.1b, 3.2a). In dealing with the *Tao-te-ching*, he accords particular metaphorical value to its most obscure and paradoxical expressions, seeing them as intentional obfuscations. "Lao-tzu and Chuang-tzu," he says, "actively used words that caused indignation and astonishment among the people" (1.7a). Accordingly he finds many basic intentions of the author behind the various smoke screens of the text.

Individual words of the *Tao-te-ching* have therefore been given close attention among commentators of the text, leading to varieties in interpretation and opening horizons for new visions of the work. Words having multiple meanings are especially often chosen for explanation, giving the commentator a chance to expand the text in directions that he chooses himself. Philological interpretations, whether discussing format, punctuation, or individual words and phrases, therefore, are never just that. Instead of remaining mere textual notes, they always lead on to theoretical speculation, allowing the commentator to see his concerns and those of his time in the ancient document.

Ideological Interpretations

Taoist Visions of Longevity Practices and Inner Alchemy

Salvation in Taoism has always been closely linked with physical practices leading to longevity, such as gymnastics, breathing exercises, dietetics, sexual techniques, and circulating *ch'i* energy around the body. Used as a preparatory stage for meditations and mystical states in the early religion, they were integrated into a coherent system called inner alchemy (*nei-tan*) since the T'ang dynasty.

Both a physical and a mental disciple, inner alchemy centers on the sublimation, fine-tuning, and animation of both the body and the mind. It begins with a rather gross bodily state represented by an inner form of energy known as essence (*ching*), which appears as sexual energy, as semen in men and menstrual blood in women. The first stage of inner alchemical refinement is then the transformation of essence into *ch'i* energy, the stuff of pure vitality. This, in turn, is further transmuted into spirit, and from there into emptiness. This transformation is at the same time accompanied by the increase within the adept of eternal light that existed prior to the universe. Originally residing only as a spark within, this light gradually comes to suffuse and illuminate the entire body-and-spirit of the adept. The mental processes taking place here not only consist of transforming the inner image of the body but also involve the development of a multidimensional consciousness. To this end the texts require the adept to undergo a form of mental gymnastics, during which he must both overcome the literal meanings of the teaching and perfect the swift and fluid passage from one level of thinking to the next, from one concept to the next, thus dynamizing and unifying the mental and physical process in its entirety (see Robinet 1989, 1995).

The *Tao-te-ching* has frequently been interpreted in terms of either longevity practices or inner alchemy. One of its earliest and most influential commentaries, of approximately the second century C.E., interprets the text in the light of the former: the one attributed to Ho-shang-kung, the Master on the River (TT 682). In many instances, this commentator understands the text in terms of Taoist longevity practices known as "nurturing the vital energy." One uses various breathing and dietetic techniques to increase the staying power of one's vital energy, so that eventually it becomes impervious to the decay that normally comes with old age and allows one to last even beyond the death of the body. Against this background, Ho-shang-kung understands the the obscure phrase *hsuan-p'in*, usually rendered "mysterious female," as "the mysterious and the female." "The mysterious" refers to heaven, while the "female" refers to earth, and the phrase indicates the way one inhales the yang energy of heaven (breath) through the nose and ingests the yin energy of earth (food) through the mouth. The expression as a whole then stands for the way human beings communicate with heaven and earth by means of their physical organs, respiration and nourishment.

An anonymous commentary called *Chieh-chieh* (Systematic Explanation), which probably stems from the third century C.E., is the most organized exposition of the *Tao-te-ching* in terms of longevity techniques

(Robinet 1977, 49–56). But the tradition went beyond it, reappearing for example with further developments in Li Yueh's work under the T'ang. He interprets "mysterious female" along the lines of Ho-shang-kung but also sees the "thirteen" mentioned in chapter 50 as the "thirteen points of life and death" in the body, that is, the five inner organs, three cinnabar fields, the head, and the four extremities (TT 692, 1.4a, 3.9a). Chang Chung-ying of the thirteenth century similarly follows Ho-shang-kung in his reading of chapter 6 and goes on to understand chapter 10 in practical terms. "Support the spiritual energy and material soul" for him means to "purify the essence and the breath" (TT 724, 11.26b–27a, 15.1b, 16.12b–13a).

Inner alchemy commentaries follow similar lines. The thirteenth-century writer Teng Yi, for example, sees inner alchemical practice as the equivalent of virtue (*te*), the practical application of the Tao, and places it as the final of the three levels, on which he interprets the text—the philological, the cosmological, and the inner alchemical (TT 687, 1.10ab, 1.15b–16a). Chao Shih-an uses almost two complete pages to interpret the first chapter of the text in inner alchemical terms (TT 724, 2.18a–19a). Niu Miao-ch'uan, also of the thirteenth century, gives various explanations for "mysterious female." Not only an allusion to the practice of embryo respiration, it might also refer to the "original One" in the system of inner alchemy, the point in the kidneys from which the inner alchemical work begins (TT 724, 11.36a–37b). Yang Chih-jen, writing in 1287, on the other hand, reads the phrase as "the mysterious and the female" and interprets it alchemically to refer to the lead and mercury and, in terms of the *Yi-ching*, as the trigrams Li and Kan (fire and water). The expression stands further for dragon and tiger, east and west, yang and yin—designating different levels of the alchemical work. He says,

> When one practices the exercise, Kan and Li increase and diminish throughout the body, the wind and the clouds rise and disperse through the seven orifices. The true energy spreads, no longer warm or cold; pure yang circulates, no longer of life or death. This is the effect of the mysterious and the female. (TT 724, 11.38a)

Along the same lines, Liu Wei-yung's commentary of the year 1299 begins with diagrams that illustrate the text in cosmological and practical terms. Here the "spirit of the valley" designates the place where the spirits of the inner organs are located; the "thirty spokes of the wheel" corresponds to the secret numbers of the organs; and "the mysterious and the female" refers to the left and right kidneys, following an age-old Taoist tradition (TT 723, 1.1b).

Inner-alchemical interpretation of the text follows the work of the Taoist master Pai Yü-ch'an (fl. 1209–1224), whose commentary survives in citations and has been collected in the *Ts'ung-shu chi-ch'eng*. His entire work is interspersed with invocations of instances when, according to the schedule prescribed for inner-alchemical refinement, one should purify and sublimate one or the other form of energy in order to attain the Tao: moving from the personal body, to the heart-and-mind, the inner nature, the spirit, and so on. This form of asceticism is what he finds referred to in the text, when Lao-tzu traces a progression of cultivation from the self through the family and the village to the state and the empire (ch. 54). He finds a reference here to internal-psychological rather than external-social realities. Thus, in the same vein, for him the notions of action in nonaction, affairs of no-affairs, and taste without tasting (ch. 63) describe the mind-and-heart, inner nature, and spirit, in this order. Expressions such as "act without imposition," "be withdrawing," "not desire to display excellence" (ch. 77) he links with the rigors of inner-alchemical practice. One must, in turn, forget the self, the heart-and-mind, inner nature, and spirit to reach to the Tao (*Ts'ung-shu chi-ch'eng*, p. 21).

Pai Yü-ch'an identifies the Tao as the heart-and-mind of the cosmos (p. 21), the soul of the world, which is the "gate of heaven and earth" (p. 2). All opposites, male and female, white and black, are seen in relation to inner-alchemical categories, the spirit, inner nature (*hsing*), and destiny or the mandate of life one is ordered to have by heaven (*ming*; ch. 28, p.8); metaphors of simplicity and no-mind—such as the infant (ch. 55, p. 15), unknowing (ch. 65, p. 18), and freedom from disease (ch. 71, p. 20)—are related to the concepts of no-thinking or no-mind, originally adopted from Buddhism. Even the "people who grow old and die" are interpreted as a mental state, as the total absence of conscious thought (ch. 80, p. 22).

In summary, commentaries oriented toward Taoist longevity practices prefer to read the obscure phrases of the *Tao-te-ching* in terms of physical organs and activities, while inner alchemists tend to see references to processes and dynamic movements within individual chapters and through larger portions of the text. The reading of Pai Yü-ch'an, in particular, shows the primary concerns of Sung Taoists: the transformation from a physical into a spiritual being through rhythmical phases of transformations with the help of physical and meditational practices.

Buddhist Thought: Being and Nonbeing

In contrast to inner alchemy, Buddhist thought is more concerned with metaphysics and the workings of the human mind. Buddhist or

Buddhist-inspired thinkers typically place great emphasis on the notion of nonbeing and its identity or close conjunction with the notion of being. That is to say, they focus on the fundamental absence of any underlying substantial basis of the universe and on the absolute value of emptiness and nonbeing, while at the same time acknowledging the concrete reality of the phenomenal world as a necessary guide to enlightenment and truth. By clarifying conceptions, and by gradually reorganizing perception, Buddhists hope to get people to see the world as it really is and realize their true Buddha-nature.

In terms of *Tao-te-ching* commentaries, Buddhists therefore concentrate on the notion of nonbeing and its relation to the Tao and the world. The first to focus on this notion, however, was not himself a Buddhist but Wang Pi (226–249), who read the text in the light of Profound Learning, the predominant Chinese philosophy of his time (TT 690; Rump and Chan 1979). He has been accused of overemphasizing nonbeing, the latent, underlying cause of all, to the detriment of being, reality, and existence. In fact, for him the Tao "is nonbeing" (ch. 8), "all beings owe their existence to it" (ch. 11), and "to realize themselves all beings have to return to nonbeing" (ch. 41). Nonbeing is the underlying ground, the foundation, of beings, their source and their end. Wang Pi thus imbues nonbeing, the underlying substratum of life, with a strength it had never had before, challenging later Buddhists to redefine the term in their own way.

Although many commentaries to the *Tao-te-ching* were written by Buddhists—Kumārajīva (d. 416) and Seng-chao (384–414), and even Emperor Wu of the Liang (r. 502–550)—they are mostly lost and remain only in fragments. In their wake, though, there was an entire school of *Tao-te-ching* interpretation, known as Twofold Mystery, that took up the dialectic of the Buddhist school known as Madhyamaka (Middle Way). Flourishing in the seventh century under the T'ang, it was represented mainly by Ch'eng Hsuan-ying and Li Jung and represents a thinking that strives for a balance between being and nonbeing, the *via positiva* and the *via negativa* in approaching the Tao, rejecting each in turn because any form of comprehension in relation to the ultimate truth of the Tao can only be a means, never an end. The *Tao-te-ching* in this vision goes beyond both, its mystical immersion passing through the dialectic interplay of being and nonbeing and finding its realization in a mutual negation that is at the same time their coincidence—and that of all opposites, spiritual and phenomenal.

In the light of the highest Truth, all negation vanishes because it does not exist except in relation to affirmation. Similarly all affirmation is eliminated because it can only be valid as long as there is some form of negation. Going beyond both, followers of Twofold Mystery reject all that can be thought and named as ultimately inadequate. Doing so, they reach the stage of the first "mystery," expressed in the first chapter of the *Tao-te-ching* as

> The nameless is the origin of heaven and earth;
> The named is the mother of all things.

Abolishing both, the nameless and the named, nonbeing and being, the absolute and phenomena, thinkers of Twofold Mystery find the first establishment of the Middle Way. This stage, however, is in turn overcome when they attain the level of "complete oblivion," a state that goes beyond both, the negation of affirmation (not named, not being) and the negation of negation (not nameless, not nonbeing). This is the second "mystery," the step that leads to complete oneness with the Tao.

The school traces itself back to the Taoist Sun Teng of the fourth century and lasts until the Sung dynasty, when it is represented by Chao Shih-an (fl. 1152; TT 693) and Shao Jo-yü (fl. 1135; TT 688; Robinet 1977, 131). It represents the strongest Buddhist influence on any reading of the *Tao-te-ching*. But others also place a high emphasis on nonbeing. Emperor Hui-tsung (r. 1101–1126), for example, takes up the Buddhist distinction between phenomena (the world of concrete phenomena) and principle (the world of the numinous) and associates it with being and nonbeing in the *Tao-te-ching* (TT 680, 1.1a–2a). For him, being then becomes "eternal being" and gains a transcendent quality as existence-as-such, while nonbeing becomes "eternal nonbeing," the totality of creative power of the Tao. This division, a metaphysical reinterpretation of being and nonbeing based on Buddhist terms and idea, he then uses to understand the first line of the *Tao-te-ching*, where the Tao that cannot be told is defined as the "eternal Tao."

Chao Ping-wen of the early thirteen century similarly equates eternal nonbeing with the true emptiness of the Buddhists, while seeing eternal being as the wondrous existence of all phenomena, an existence that transcends all limits and all negation (TT 695, 1.3ab). Yet another proposition along the same lines is found in the work of Chao Chih-chien, who sees the Tao as highest nonbeing and its first evolution, the One, as being or transcendent existence (TT 719, 4.13b). Tu Tao-chien of the early fourteenth century adds the thinking of the *Yi-ching* (Book of Changes) to this concept. Eternal nonbeing here is without opposite, without limit, the Nonultimate, which yet at the same time is the Great Ultimate, the central creative pole of the universe. Nonbeing is the numinous world before beings, the state "before heaven;" eternal being, on the contrary, designates the "two principles [yin and yang] and the myriad beings," the state "after heaven" as it manifests in the phenomenal world. The *Tao-te-ching*, Tu says, expresses the same basic idea in terms of being and nonbeing where the *Yi-ching* uses the notions of movement and tranquility (TT 702, 1b, 2b).

Chinese philosophical discourse as it is strongly influenced by Buddhism thus tends to emphasize the ideas of being and nonbeing in the *Tao-te-ching* and develops them in linkage not only with phenomena and principle but also more transcendent concepts, such as not-being and not-nonbeing (TT 689, 1.2a; TT 691, 2.21b). Usually this form of discourse remains quite separate from the more technical Taoist vision of inner alchemy. Only Tung Ssu-ching (fl. 1246–1260) establishes a connection between the two. "Nonbeing," he says, "is the spirit, while being is the vital energy." In their interaction they correspond to what inner-alchemical texts describe as "the hidden and the manifest" (TT 705, pref. 6ab).

Confucian and Neo-Confucian Readings

Confucian thought is commonly seen as the opposite or complement of Taoist philosophy because it is concerned largely with the world and society, emphasizing the betterment of man within the family and state. It places a high value on virtues and their realization, favors learning rather than forgetfulness, and sees human life and work as defined by social relations, not through some spiritual entity, such as the Tao. Nevertheless, Confucian thinkers have always highly esteemed the *Tao-te-ching* for its deep philosophical insight, and commentators variously have interpreted the text in a Confucian light.

The work of Lu Hsi-sheng (fl. 888–904) is one of its most Confucian readings. His basic thesis is that the ancient Confucian sages, such as Fu Hsi, King Wen, and Confucius, as well as all Confucian classics basically accord with the ideas of Lao-tzu. To show this, he cites the *Yi-ching*, the *Li-chi* (Book of Rites), and the *Lun-yü* (Analects), showing their basic agreement with different passages of the *Tao-te-ching*. The statement, for instance, that "one may know the world without going out of doors" (ch. 47) he understands in terms of the Confucian process of the extension of wisdom as described in the "Great Learning" (*Ta-hsueh*) chapter of the *Li-chi* (TT 685, 3.12b–13b). According to this, one must first rectify one's mind and verify one's thoughts, then one can bring order to the family, the state, and eventually the empire (Vandermeersch 1980, 2:707–8). Similarly he conflates the statement "if kings and barons held on to the nameless Tao, all things would be in order" (ch. 32) with the line "govern the state with correctness" (ch. 57) and arrives at the Confucian doctrine of the "rectification of names," which claims that when all names, titles, and functions correspond perfectly to their actual reality, the state is in good order (TT 685, 2.15b, 3.23b). He thereby gives a Confucian reading to passages seen by the ancients as quite contrary to this philosophy.

Another line of Confucian-inspired interpretation links self-cultivation and government. Among *Tao-te-ching* commentators, this is first proposed by Ho-shang-kung, who develops his thinking on the double level of Taoist practice and political thinking. Many later thinkers have under-lined this pattern as the most fundamental explanation of the text, com-ing back time and again to a vision of political harmony quite in line with Confucian thought. Among them, Emperor Hsuan-tsung of the T'ang (r. 713–756) is probably the most well known (TT 677), but it is also found in the work Ch'en Ching-yuan (1025–1094) who uses it as its essen-tial approach (TT 714). Yet another way of seeing Confucian thought in the *Tao-te-ching* is to begin with the basic complementarity of the two schools. Wang P'ang (1042–1076), the son of Wang An-shih, for example, compares Confucianism to the spring and summer, the time of activity and growth, while Taoism is the fall and winter, the time of fruition and harvest, a period that sees the hiding and rest of vegetation (TT 706, pref.6b, 5.24a, 6.18a). Unlike Wang Pi, who thought that Confucius never spoke about nonbeing because he incarnated it while Lao-tzu discussed it because he incarnated being, Wang P'ang understands being and nonbeing as interdependent, with Confucius and Lao-tzu each empha-sizing one part.

Joining the different philosophies, syncretistic commentators tend to come back to certain powerful phrases of the classics. Among the sayings of Confucius, they often use "heaven does not speak yet the seasons pass"; from the works of Mencius, they take "spirit of exulta-tion" (2A/2; Vandermeersch 1980, 2:521) and "all things are within me." Most frequently, however, they rely on the *Yi-ching*, from which they commonly cite "going to the depth of principle and inner nature one arrives at the mandate of heaven," a passage taken from one of its pre-Han commentaries, the *Shuo-kua* (On the Hexagrams; see TT 683, 1.5a; TT 685, 2.3a). Also referred to as the "recovery of inner nature," the Han-dynasty passage is later used to link T'ien-t'ai Buddhism (which identifies the Chinese idea of inner nature with Buddha-nature) with Confucian thought. This link is made, among others, in the work of Li Ao (772–841), a precursor of Neo-Confucianism. The expression also appears in more technical Taoist works, such as the *T'ien-yin-tzu* (Master of Heavenly Seclusion, TT 1026, 2a) by the T'ang Taoist Ssu-ma Ch'eng-chen (647–736). It appears in the *Tao-te-ching* commentaries by Ch'eng Hsuan-ying (TT 711, 4.20a, 16.11a), Lu Hsi-sheng and Wang P'ang. Su Ch'e (1139–1112), brother of the famous poet Su Tung-po, makes it the central theme in his commentary, written, of all things, to show a Buddhist monk how Buddhism and Confucianism work together!

For Wang P'ang, inner nature is the central pivot. The seat of human transcendence, it is identified with the "uncarved block" of the *Tao-te-ching* and with the "spirit of exultation" of Mencius. "Going to the depth of inner nature" along the lines of the *Yi-ching* is then also equated with the "recovery of destiny" (*fu-ming*) in the *Tao-te-ching* (ch. 16). The Confucian *Yi-ching*, Buddhism, and Taoism are thus merged into one integrated philosophical whole. Just as Wang P'ang plays with mixed expressions from all three schools of thought throughout his work, so Su Ch'e interprets the philosophies as though they teach the same thing and uses the *Shuo-kua* passage cited above to illustrate and summarize Taoist personal asceticism. For him, inner nature is ultimate reality in a Buddhist sense. It is the residence of the Tao in human beings, so immense that it can fill heaven and earth (like Mencius's "spirit of exultation"). Neither life nor death have any impact on it; it suffers neither increase nor diminution. The destiny of the individual, the life he or she is ordered to have by heavenly mandate (*ming*), in this context, is the transcendent aspect of inner nature (*hsing*), its wondrous, supernatural dimension. Inner nature thus remains within a domain of language, which destiny surpasses (TT 691, 1.10a, 14b, 19a).

Some commentators also find in inner nature the central creative pole of the universe and ultimate point of primordial origin, the Great Ultimate of the *Yi-ching* (Chu Po-hsiu in TT 724, 11.13b). For others, inner nature goes beyond even that (Hsiu Hsiu-an in TT 724, 20.30a). Then again, there are thinkers who find the human equivalent of the Tao in the original heart-and-mind, in spirit, revealing a double line of influence, both Buddhist and Neo-Confucian. Chao Shih-an, writing in 1152, is a pioneer of this tendency. For him, the mind is the Tao, the fundamental nonbeing (TT 724, 12.24a). Similarly, Tu Tao-chien (1305) sees the mind as the creative pivot that exists before heaven and earth, the ultimate root of all (TT 702, 1.5b, 2.5a, 4.2a). The alchemist Pai Yü-ch'an, too, explains the mind as the "root of the universe" (TT 724, 12.24a), while Yü Ch'ing-chung places it before the cosmos (12.34a), and Shao Jo-yü understands it as the energy of primordial chaos within human beings (TT 688, 1.12a).

Shao follows specifically the Mādhyamika thinking adopted in the school of Twofold Mystery, but also links the *Tao-te-ching* with the "Doctrine of the Mean" (*Chung-yung*) chapter of the *Li-chi*, citing Mencius, Confucius, Chuang-tzu, and various inner alchemists in the process. Chao Shih-an similarly uses the "Doctrine of the Mean" and Mencius's "spirit of exultation" to explain the basic principles of Taoist practice, linking Confucian thought with the Taoist understanding of primordial energy. His vocabulary is Neo-Confucian and heavily Buddhist ("true nonbeing," "true emptiness"), while his understanding of being and nonbeing continues Twofold Mystery thinking. Questions of sudden versus gradual enlightenment, debated hotly among Buddhists, are approached in this mode, and he applies negations of negations in best Mādhyamika fashion. References to inner alchemy are also found frequently in his work, especially in the interpretation of expressions like "spirit of the valley" and "mysterious female" in terms of Taoist practices (TT 724, 23.15ab, 2.14ab, 2.9ab, 2.16a–18b, 7.36b, 11. 12a–17b).

Another form of syncretism among *Tao-te-ching* commentaries is found in the work of Ch'en Ching-yuan, dated to 1072. He aims to develop a synthesis between the "three teachings" and the various earlier commentaries to the text. His work accordingly is a mixture of Neo-Confucian philosophical distinctions, such as between "below forms" (physical) and "above forms" (metaphysical; TT 714, 1.3b);[6] originally Buddhist notions, such as the distinction between the constituting foundation and the outer functioning activity; and mystical ideas of Profound Learning and religious Taoism, such as "complete forgetfulness." He discusses the dialectic between being and nonbeing, recalls the understanding of Ho-shang-kung, and alludes to practices of energy circulation. He distinguishes between ancient interpretations of the *Tao-te-ching*, which focused on the double level of self and state, and contemporary exegeses, which concentrate on the behavior of the individual in both moral and mystical practice (TT 714, 1.18b, 4.2b, 2.12ab, 1.18a–19b, 2.7a–9a).

Ch'en's commentary is of particular interest because it tries to connect the *Tao-te-ching* with commentaries of different schools, with other Taoist texts, and with the Confucian classics. Among Taoist texts, he uses ancient works, such as the *Chuang-tzu* and the *Huai-nan-tzu* (Writings of the Prince of Huai-nan; TT 1184), and also religious scriptures, such as the *Yin-fu-ching* (Scripture of Hidden Correspondences, TT 108) and the *Hsi-sheng-ching* (Scripture of Western Ascension, TT 725). Among Confucian classics, he cites the works of Confucius and Mencius together with the *Yi-ching* and the *Shih-ching* (Book of Songs). With this powerful combination, he produces a general recapitulation of the many different ways in which the *Tao-te-ching* was seen and read and understood.

Conclusion

Inner alchemy visions of dynamic processes of refinement and perfection, Buddhist categories of the constituting foundation and its outer functioning, inner nature and the mind, Confucian ideas of human virtues and their spread from individual to empire, and Neo-Confucian concepts, such as the material force—they all have been applied to the *Tao-te-ching* to explain the text, make it relevant for contemporaneous concerns, and maintain an active connection with the past. Its ancient and often obscure expressions, such as "mysterious female" and "recovery of destiny," are taken up again and again to illustrate new ideas and practices. What all the different commentaries have in common is their effort to diachronically link the present with the past and/or synchronically join the thought of the *Tao-te-ching* with that of other teachings. The procedure in either case is to make certain key terms evident, terms that might be specific technical expressions (as taken from Buddhism, for example) or metaphorical images, such as the "mysterious female" or the "spirit of the valley." In all cases, the point of departure is the text itself, the *Tao-te-ching*, which remains an open work, continuously reinterpreted in commentaries and citations, and forever generating new meanings. It is as if the text contained, latent and hidden, all forms of thinking and philosophy that ever developed in traditional China. It is used both to bestow prestigious antiquity to current ideas and to validate old concepts by imbuing them with contemporary meaning.

The commentaries clearly reflect the manifold tendencies in the history of Chinese thought. They contain metaphysical discussions among Taoists and Buddhists on the nature of nonbeing, the transcendent absolute, and being, the existence of all. They show the different mystical interpretations of inner nature, the residence of ultimate reality within human beings, and of mind, the spirit-like quality of the psyche. They link the text with physical and alchemical practices, rewrite it in political, mystical, cosmological, and philosophical terms. And they mix all these together, never allowing one form of explication to exclude another, often joining different visions in one and the same exegesis. Only rarely do they focus on a single key notion or essential term. Usually they circle around a number of basic ideas, using them all at different times when they consider it fit. The *Tao-te-ching*, reinterpreted in its commentaries over the ages, is thus a prime text for the continuous unfolding of syncretism in traditional China, supported by thinkers of all different schools and forever reconfirmed in its original polysemy.

Notes

1. Editors' note: This article is a slightly revised version of Robinet 1984. It was translated by Livia Kohn.

2. Examples are Lu Hsi-sheng's work (TT 685) of the ninth and Lin Hsi-yi's commentary (TT 701) of the thirteenth century. Texts in the Taoist Canon (*Tao-tsang*, abbreviated TT) are given according to the number in Schipper 1975.

3. The newly found Ma-wang-tui version also differs in many respects from the traditional texts commentators used, but it was unknown to them.

4. The translation of *wu* and *yu* as nonbeing and being is very unsatisfactory. Basically, *wu* is a negative indicating the absence of something, while *yu* is its opposite, showing that something is there. By philosophical extension, "*wu*" indicated the absence of visible and material being and "*yu*" its presence (in Neo-Confucianism), or again the absence or presence of any substantial being of the universe (in Taoism and Buddhism). In any case, the negation contained in the term as well as its affirmative counterpart, implies a determination. *Wu* is the foremost concept in the *via negativa* of Chinese mystics.

5. See Lu Hsi-sheng in TT 685, 3.16a; Ssu-ma Kuang in TT 689, 3.5a; Shao Jo-yü in TT 688, 3.13b.

6. The same distinction is already made in the T'ang commentary by Lu Hsi-sheng (TT 685, 1.9b, 3.6a) and in that by Emperor Hsuan-tsung (TT 679, 1.12b).

References

Jao Tsung-i. 1956. *Lao-tzu hsiang-erh-chu chiao-ch'ien*. Hong Kong: Tong Nam Printers. Reprinted Shanghai: Wen-yin, 1992.

Ricoeur, Paul. 1969. *Le conflit des interprétations*. Paris: Seuil.

Robinet, Isabelle. 1977. *Les commentaires du Tao to king jusqu'au VIIe siècle*. Paris: Mémoirs de l'Institute des Hautes Études Chinoises 5.

———. 1984. "Polysémisme du texte canonique et syncrétisme des interprétations: Étude taxinomique des commentaires du *Daode jing* au sein de la tradition chinoise." *Extrême Orient — Extrême Occident* 5: 27–47.

———. 1989. "Original Contributions of *Neidan* to Taoism and Chinese Thought." In *Taoist Meditation and Longevity Techniques*, ed. Livia Kohn, 295–38. Ann Arbor: University of Michigan, Center for Chinese Studies Publications.

———. 1995. *Introduction à l'alchimie intérieure taoiste: De l'unité et de la multiplicité*. Paris: Editions Cerf.

Rump, Ariane, and Wing-tsit Chan. 1979. *Commentary on the Lao-tzu by Wang Pi.* Honolulu: University of Hawaii Press.

Schipper, Kristofer. 1975. *Concordance du Tao Tsang: Titres des ouvrages.* Paris: Publications de l'École Française d'Extrême-Orient.

Todorov, T. 1978. *Symbolisme et interprétation.* Paris: Seuil.

Vandermeersch, Leon. 1980. *Wangdao ou la voie royale.* 2 vols. Paris: École Pratique d'Extrême-Orient.

Yen Ling-feng. 1983. *Ching-tzu ts'ung-chu.* Taipei: Hsueh-sheng.

6

The Tao-te-ching in Ritual

Livia Kohn

As early as the first century B.C.E., the *Tao-te-ching* was considered a sacred text that should be recited to the greater benefit of self and state. By the second century C.E., it was the central text of the Celestial Masters, who not only recited it for its magical effect but also based their behavioral precepts upon it. In the later Celestial Masters group at Lou-kuan, moreover, it became the central focus of Taoist practice, both meditational and liturgical, and played an important role in the formal ordination of priests. Three stages and forms of the *Tao-te-ching* in ritual can be distinguished: its recitation, begun under the Han and continued actively in religious Taoism; its veneration in devotional practices and meditation, first documented in a fifth-century text; and its role in Taoist ordination as it developed fully in the sixth century. The following pages will look at these three forms in turn.

Reciting the *Tao-te-ching*

The Han dynasty was founded under the auspices of the legend of the Master of the Yellow Stone, according to which an old man appeared to the noble Chang Liang and handed him a book on strategic warfare that decided the campaign in favor of Liu Pang, the dynasty's founder (see Bauer 1956). The old man, a supernatural immortal, was part of the growing mythology that also divinized Lao-tzu at the time. Early Han rule greatly favored the theories of the *Tao-te-ching*, politically interpreted as a policy of nonaction or *laissez-faire*. In addition, Empress Tou, the mother of Emperor Ching (r. 151–141 B.C.E.), not only had Taoist advisers but also placed great store in the text and for the first time had it known by the formal title "classic" or "scripture" (*ching*). Emperor Ching, under her influence, issued an edict that recommended its regular recitation all over the empire (Seidel 1969, 24). Recitation of an important text or classic was not only the favored method of learning in a culture that had limited access to written materials but also an expression of devotion and an exercise in self-cultivation. Another text commonly recited at the time, for example, was the "Classic of Filial Piety" (*Hsiao-ching*), which was not only short and easy to memorize but also inspired people to behave in an obedient and deferential manner toward their elders. In the same way, the recitation of the *Tao-te-ching* in the Han dynasty helped people to be more contented with their role, gave them tranquility in their dealings with the world, and increased their understanding of the subtleties of the universe.[1]

In addition to its favorable position at court, the *Tao-te-ching* in the Han dynasty was also popular among two kinds of people: literati without official status and lesser officials working on the local level (Kimura 1959, 627). Both groups greatly venerated the text and taught it to the people in their communities, causing a gradual maturation of its ideas in the popular mind. Thus Yen Tsun of the first century, a learned fortune-teller, gave popular lectures on the *Tao-te-ching* at night (Seidel 1969, 27). He also wrote a commentary to the text, which has survived in the Taoist canon (TT 693;[2] Robinet 1977, 11). An-ch'i Sheng, a practitioner of immortality, taught the text to several local officials, who in turn spread it among their colleagues and families (Seidel 1969, 27). Philosophers of the later Han, such as Hsiang Hsiu, recited it continuously to gain inspiration to behave tranquilly and to be socially conscious. Several well-situated men even took it as a guide to distributing their fortunes among the poor (Seidel 1969, 31). Spread among the wider populace through the instruction by freelance literati and local officials, the text was soon picked up as a major sacred scripture by the growing popular Taoist cults. It was then no longer seen as the work of a philosopher, however saintly, but as the revealed emanation of the pure Tao. As such, it was no longer called the *Lao-tzu* or the *Wu-ch'ien-wen* (Text in Five Thousand Words) but known as the *T'ai-shang hsuan-yuan tao-te-ching*, the "Highest Scripture of the Tao and Its Virtue Originating in Mysterious Primordiality" (Seidel 1969, 91). Nor was it merely applied as a guide to personal and political conduct; instead its primary use was found in the magical efficacy of its pure words, which could bring good fortune, exorcise demons, and cure diseases.

The Celestial Masters

This application of the *Tao-te-ching* is best known from the organized Taoist school of the Celestial Masters, founded in 142 C.E. by Chang Tao-ling in southwest China. Their main religious practice was the healing of diseases as the first step to the mastery of longevity techniques and the attainment of immortality. To this end they established so-called chambers of silence, where the sick would retreat to reflect on their wrong-doings, and organized the faithful under group leaders or libationers, who presided over the regular recitation of the *Tao-te-ching*. The Celestial Masters used the text as a religious scripture, in a practice not unlike the Buddhist chanting of sūtras, with the aim of gaining magical powers from the holiness of its pure words (Kobayashi 1992, 31). The *Tao-te-ching* thus played a more ritual than doctrinal role; it was a magical document that could bestow the powers of the Tao and make people not only healthy but, if recited frequently enough, turn them into immortals.

To ensure the proper efficacy of *Tao-te-ching* recitation, practitioners had to be morally pure. Accordingly, the Celestial Masters also used it as the inspiration for certain behavioral rules. These rules are connected with the *Hsiang-erh* commentary to the *Tao-te-ching*, a text describing the contemporaneous interpretation of the text (see Bokenkamp 1993). It is attributed to Chang Lu, third Celestial Master and grandson of Chang Tao-ling, who lived in the early third century.[3] The precepts listed are of two kinds: a group of nine precepts providing general rules of behavior based on the philosophy of the *Tao-te-ching*; and a group of twenty-seven precepts, which present a mixture of general rules, behavioral regulations, and temporal taboos.

The first nine are as follows:[4]

1. Practice nonaction.
2. Practice being soft and weak.
3. Practice guarding the female and never move first.
    These are the highest three practices.
4. Practice being nameless.
5. Practice being pure and tranquil.
6. Practice doing only good.
    These are the medium three practices.
7. Practice having no desires.
8. Practice knowing when to stop.
9. Practice yielding and withdrawing.
    These are the lowest three practices.
    (1a; see also Bokenkamp 1993, 50)

Taking classical phrases and technical terms from the *Tao-te-ching*, these precepts provide general guidelines to Taoist behavior without applying them to any concrete context. They are ranked in three different levels, each having one major *Tao-te-ching* doctrine as its central guideline and two lesser teachings as support. They begin with the highest level, where adepts have already attained an advanced stage and can perfect themselves through the practice of nonaction. This is supported by the injunction to be soft and weak at all times and guard the female, that is, to show reticence and never push themselves forward. Ideal Taoists of this level are withdrawing and serene, acting only if forced to by circumstances and never imposing their subjective will on the world.

The three medium-level precepts are addressed to practitioners who have not yet attained complete nonaction but are firmly on the way there. They are admonished to remain nameless, that is, without fame in the world, to develop purity and tranquility, and to do good in everything they undertake. Such people are ideally dedicated fully to the service of the Tao, working for the community without expecting any personal rewards, and living in purity and tranquility.[5] On the lowest or introductory level, finally, practitioners begin by trying to remain free from personal desires and learning when to stop. This means that they try to refrain from violently bending nature and society to their will. Instead they yield to others and adapt to the environment, withdrawing their personal wishes in favor of a greater harmony with the world and the Tao. Taken together, these nine precepts give a succinct, if abstract, vision of the goal of Taoist practice and its steps: freedom from desire through control of personal inclinations leads to an unassuming and humble personality, which in turn paves the way for the attainment of complete nonaction and oneness with the Tao. A human being is created that is full of regard for his fellow men and selflessly serves the greater good of all.

In addition, the early Celestial Masters had twenty-seven more specific precepts to prohibit certain kinds of behavior, again ranked in three groups (Bokenkamp 1993, 51). Here, the highest set represents a guide to active service of the Tao. Adherents are never to forget the divine law and must keep strictly within its boundaries. They must not pursue worldly goods or reveal the group's esoteric teachings. As advanced practitioners, if not actually leading members of the community, they must also abstain from killing and eating animals as well as from harming and diminishing their own energy. In addition, they are guided to be aware of the cosmic constellations, paying attention to the astrological energy currently dominant and never harming it, thus obeying temporal taboos that raise the practitioners' awareness of their role in the larger cosmos. The rewards are apportioned accordingly: those who obey the highest rules become immortals, all others will extend their years and live happily ever after.

The medium-level precepts, before the highest attainment, encourage members to develop a helpful and positive attitude within the community, show humility and yield to the needs of others. People are urged to keep their sensual pleasures and ambitions in check, never pursuing fame and praise. They should also remain faithful to the group and neither consult nor study writings from outside, the so-called false texts. The group of lower precepts, finally, is more introductory, guiding people to behave in accordance with the community rules and with deference to their fellow members. They are warned not to strive for positions beyond their status, leave the military well alone, and abstain from sacrifices for the popular gods—the demons and the spirits of the dead, whom the Taoists considered impure and defiled (Strickmann 1985, 188). Members should also learn to be modest, never boasting of being Taoist sages, and maintain humility and calmness even in quarrels or when criticized.

These various rules of the Celestial Masters served to direct member's personalities and lifestyles toward higher Taoist purity and raised group awareness and cohesion among the faithful. The *Tao-te-ching* played a central role in keeping the followers together, both through its daily recitation and through the active behavioral guidelines it afforded. The Celestial Masters used the text actively to create a feeling of difference vis-à-vis any outsiders, with whom contact was limited and should never involve revelation of in-group secrets.

Recitation and Immortality

Other early Taoist groups similarly venerated and recited the *Tao-te-ching*, just as later organized Taoists studiously followed the practice of the text. Among the early groups, a local cult in Ssu-ch'uan has left behind a manuscript that describes the transformations of the deified Lao-tzu and includes a set of his instructions. The *Lao-tzu pian-hua-ching* (Scripture on the Transformations of Lao-tzu) says,

> Day and night you must remember me,
> And I will not suddenly let you go.
> Waking and dreaming you must think of me,
> And I will appear to prove your faith. . . .

> Be upright and guard your self,
> And I will know you as one of the good.

> I have given you a text.
> If you wish to know me,
> Recite the "Five Thousand Words" ten thousand times,
> Then you can see my head and know my body [the Tao],
> Come softly to be one with me![6]

Lao-tzu here instructs his followers to remember him constantly, insisting that they develop a continuous awareness of the Tao and the spiritual nature of the universe. If they attain this concentrated meditative state, he promises, he will never leave them without his support and they will find his guidance everywhere. Just as in the practice of the Celestial Masters, so here too joining the Tao mentally and being morally upright are integral parts of Taoist practice, without which the Tao will not stand by or come to help. Lao-tzu then mentions his scripture, calling it the "Five Thousand Words" and instructing the faithful to recite it ten thousand times. This recitation will help toward attaining the desired state of constant remembrance and lead to the visualization of, and even union with, the deity.

The practice of reciting the *Tao-te-ching* continued to spread not only among the learned, who used it as a guide to proper moral and spiritual behavior, and among the religious cults, who saw it as a magical means toward immortality and mystical union. It also entered the circle of individual immortality practitioners and alchemists, where it was generally considered quite efficacious (Yoshioka 1959, 123). Ko Hung, however, the learned alchemist of the early forth century, finds it insufficient. He says:

> The *Tao-te-ching* may actually come from Lao Tan but it is only a general discussion and a rough outline of our topic [of immortality]. Its contents in no way allow a complete exposition of the matter that could be employed as support for our pursuit. Merely to recite this scripture without securing the essential process would be to undergo useless toil. How much worse in the case of texts inferior to the *Tao-te-ching*![7]

This rejection of *Tao-te-ching* recitation in itself is telling evidence for the commonality of the practice among Taoist adepts at the time. It shows how different schools and lineages made use of the text for their own ends, to increase virtue and gain magical powers, and how a certain rivalry existed among both practices and practitioners.

Nonetheless, in the fifth century, the recitation of the *Tao-te-ching* was a prominent practice of immortality seekers. It is mentioned in the story of Lao-tzu transmitting the *Tao-te-ching* to Yin Hsi, the Guardian of the Pass, a classical example for the ideal relationship between Taoist master and disciple. Here Lao-tzu rejects Yin Hsi's demand to join him on his further travels and says,

> In order to follow me, you first have to attain the Tao. But your many impurities are not eradicated yet, so how can you follow me on my distant wanderings? For the present, recite the "Text in

Two Sections" [the *Tao-te-ching*] ten thousand times. Then your Tao will be perfected and you can follow me on my distant wanderings.[8]

Yin Hsi did as he was ordered and recited the *Tao-te-ching* ten thousand times over a period of three years. As a result, he "gained eternal life and the state of no death." According to another source, he "attained inner sincerity in his essence and pervasion in his meditation so that he could pervade the mystery."[9] Later Taoists imitated this but in a more mythological manner—they flew off to heaven as immortals upon reciting the *Tao-te-ching* ten thousand times.[10] According to the *Chen-kao* (Declarations of the Perfected, TT 1016) of approximately the year 500, for example, a certain Old Lord instructed three members of the Chou family, the father and two sons, to recite the *Tao-te-ching*. The father and elder brother succeeded in reciting the text ten thousand times and flew off as celestials. The younger brother, however, only reached 9,733 times and did not attain immortality (5.6a; Yoshioka 1959, 123). Yet, even without flying off to heaven, the recital of the *Tao-te-ching* endowed the practitioner with magical powers and an invulnerability to harm, for which a classical example is described in the *Lao-tzu hua-hu-ching* (Scripture of Lao-tzu's Conversion of the Barbarians). The story tells of a western king's attempt to burn the Taoists alive. Then it says,

> They burned them for over forty days. Then the wood was exhausted and the fire went out. But Lao-tzu and Yin Hsi were unharmed. They sat calmly on the glowing embers and recited the Scripture as before. (*San-tung chu-nang* 9.18b–19a)

To sum up, the recitation of the *Tao-te-ching* as a religious practice began during the Han as an educational and spiritual undertaking, followed by certain circles at court as well as by lesser officials and freelance literati. Spread into the wider populace, it was then taken up by organized Taoist cults, who made it into a more magical than educational technique. In this context, recitation of the text was actively linked with certain behavioral precepts and thus with the formal status as a faithful believer in the Tao. In addition, the practice was taken up by immortality practitioners and believed to afford transformation into a celestial and the acquisition of magical powers—but only if performed ten thousand times without slackening. Fewer recitations, though not harmful, did not afford ultimate success. The *Tao-te-ching*, no longer a mere guide to good moral and spiritual behavior, thus advanced to the status of ritual chant and magical incantation. As such it was used, in a highly ritualized fashion, in the formalized context of organized Taoist groups.

The *Tao-te-ching* in Meditation

In due course the practice of reciting the *Tao-te-ching* was further integrated into organized Taoist meditation practice. Here the text was used in visualization rituals that included purification procedures, the burning of incense, and the calling down of celestial guardians. It was closely linked with the devotional visualization of Lao-tzu, first described of Lao-tzu in Ko Hung's alchemical work, the *Pao-p'u-tzu*:

> His family name is Li, his personal name Tan, his courtesy name Po-yang. His body is nine feet tall, of a yellow coloring. He is bird-mouthed and has an arched nose. His bushy eyebrows are five inches long, his ears measure seven inches. There are three vertical lines on his forehead, his feet are marked with the eight trigrams, and he stands on a golden turtle.

> His residence is a high tower of gold, where the rooms are lined with jade and the steps are of silver. His clothing is of multi-colored cloudy vapors, and his hat is tiered, and he holds a pointed sword. He is furthermore attended by 120 yellow divine lads. To his left are 12 blue dragons, to his right are 36 white tigers. Before him go 24 vermilion birds, and to his rear follow 72 dark warriors. His vanguard consists of 12 heavenly beasts; his rearguard, of 36 evil-dispellers. Above him hover thunder and lightning with flashes and brilliances. (ch. 15; see Ware 1966, 256–57)

This is a typical example for Taoist visualization practice. The deity is named with precision; he or she has an unusual physical appearance and is dressed in wondrous colorful garb. Unusually tall, his physical features show his celestial stature, especially in the symbolic lines he has on his forehead and his feet. Garbed in cloudy vapors, he is brilliant and wears a hat of nine levels that symbolizes heaven.

The deity is further surrounded by palaces of gold and gems and accompanied by an entourage of divine attendants and numinous beasts, all numbered in groups of twelve. The animals mentioned are originally starry constellations, showing that Lao-tzu's residence is in the heavens. The vermilion bird and the dark warrior, depicted as a combination of a turtle and a snake, are the symbolic animals of the south and north respectively (Major 1986, 65). The heavenly beast (*ch'iung-ch'i*), an ox-like creature covered with bristles, and the evil-dispeller (*pi-hsieh*), a one-horned furry deer with a long tail, moreover, are baleful constellations associated with demonic powers. Their service to Lao-tzu in such great numbers documents his power even over the inauspicious forces of the universe and enhances the description of the splendor in which he resides at the very center of the universe. Lao-tzu as the visible god of the Tao here not only represents its extraordinary nature and supramundane value, but also the central position it occupies in the creation and continued existence of the universe. Attaining a true vision of this central force leads to long life, power, and omniscience.[11]

Following the southern alchemical traditon, the school of Highest Clarity (Shang-ch'ing), which places high emphasis on visualization and ecstatic travels to the heavens (see Robinet 1984; 1993), identifies Lao-tzu as the central deity of the head, where he resides in central cavity called Ni-wan Palace or Grotto Chamber. This in turn is identical with the upper Cinnabar Field in the body and Mount K'un-lun in the cosmos, the central axis of the world and paradise of the immortals (Maspero 1981, 350). The palace belongs among the so-called Nine Palaces in the head and is located three inches inside from the mid-point between the eyebrows. To enter it, one passes first through the Hall of Light (Kohn 1991b, 236). Lao-tzu resides here as the Yellow Venerable Lord joined by the lords Wu-ying and Pai-yuan to his left and right (Robinet 1984, 1: 129). He is the powerful deity of the center that rules the Nine Heavens of the universe, wanders easily about Mount Kunlun, and has full control over the human body (Maspero 1981, 371; Yamada 1989, 20). To visualize him, adepts begin by reciting the *Tao-te-ching*, then proceed as follows:

> Recite the scripture three times, then close your eyes and hold your breath. Visualize the Palace of the Hall of Light with pink terraces and green chambers on the left, yellow towers and purple gateways on the right.
>
> Next, visualize the Palace of the Cavern Chamber, a golden room with purple coverings. On the left see Lord Wu-ying, on the right Lord Pai-yuan, both dressed in flowery purple caps, dragon skirts, and phoenix robes.
>
> In the center, see the Yellow Venerable Lord. He looks like a newborn infant and is dressed in a flowery robe with yellow embroidery. The three gods sit next to each other, facing outward. Once you see them in your head, call out their names to establish communication.[12]

Only after the scripture has been recited can the deity be fully visualized. Closing his eyes, the adept moves gradually inward, seeing the Hall of

Light, a beautiful palace with magnificent buildings, then goes on to inspect the Cavern Chamber, where besides marvelous furnishings he also sees the gods. Moving from the periphery to the center, he first spies the two attendants Wu-ying and Pai-yuan. Then he sees Lao-tzu in the middle, looking fresh like a newborn baby yet dressed in a flowery celestial robe. The god here represents the Tao in its two aspects as the creative power of the universe that is always new and as the ruling force of the universe that presides over life and death with imperial splendor.

Meditative Recitation

In addition, the *Tao-te-ching* itself also stood at the center of a ritualized meditation. According to a fifth-century text that appeared as a preface to the text, the *Tao-te chen-ching hsü-chueh* (Introductory Explanations to the *Tao-te-ching*),[13] Lao-tzu gave detailed instructions on how to properly venerate the scripture. Adepts should purify themselves thoroughly and enter a special meditation chamber, where they burn incense, straighten their robes, bow to the ten directions, and actively visualize Lao-tzu and his major assistants, Yin Hsi (the Guardian of the Pass) and Ho-shang-kung (the Master on the River and commentator on the *Tao-te-ching*). Only in the venerable presence of these divine personages, is the *Tao-te-ching* to be opened. Its recitation must further be preceded by a formal prayer, by which the adept calls upon the Lord of the Niwan Palace, the central representative of the gods, to descend. As the divinity approaches, the room undergoes mysterious changes: a radiance as of seven jewels spreads, doors and windows open spontaneously. A link of light to the higher spheres is thus established, through which the practitioner floats up and away into the purple empyrean. Finding himself among the stars, he has the sun and moon at his sides and approaches the divine immortals to gain immortality for himself—and not only for himself but also for his ancestors of seven generations.

After this invocation, when the adept has placed himself firmly among the celestials, he proceeds with the ritual. The text says,

> Finish the recitation, then clap your teeth and swallow your saliva thirty-six times. Visualize the green dragon to your left, the white tiger to your right, the red bird in front of you, and the dark warrior at your back.
>
> Your feet stand between the eight trigrams, the divine turtle and the thirty-six masters bow to you. In front, you see the seventeen stars, while your five inner organs give forth the five energies and a network pattern streams across your body.

On three sides you are joined by an attendant, each having a
retinue of a thousand carriages and ten thousand horsemen. Eight
thousand jade maidens and jade lads of heaven and earth stand
guard for you. (sect. 5; Kohn 1993, 174).

Clapping one's teeth and swallowing saliva are part of the standard
Taoist meditation ritual, symbolic forms of announcing one's communication with the deities. Next, as in the visualization instructions cited
earlier, the adept is to place himself in the cosmic center by seeing himself surrounded by the four mythical animals of the four directions and
placing his feet firmly on the eight trigrams of the *Yi-ching* (Book of
Changes). Everyone bows to him, and he is fully established among the
stars, and his body has become a pure constellation of light and energy
pattterns. Then he sees himself supported by attendants, one on each
side and behind him, who in turn, as in an imperial procession, are joined
by thousands of followers and servants. Now that the celestial position
of the meditator at the center of the cosmos is firmly established, he can
recite the *Tao-te-ching* in its truest environment and to its greatest effect.

The *Tao-te-ching* in meditation thus continues the recitation practice
in conjunction with the visualization of the deified Lao-tzu as a god in
the center of the body and the universe. As a body divinity, Lao-tzu
resides in the head and looks like a newborn baby, symbolizing the vital-
izing power of the Tao and its state of eternal youth. As a universal god,
Lao-tzu is in the center of the heavens, surrounded by starry constellations and supported by gods and other celestials. Here he symbolizes
the Tao as creative force that continues to regulate the universe from its
central axis. In the meditation ritual, the practitioner places himself in
the same position, identifying with both the Tao in his body (to give him
longevity) and the Tao at the center of the universe (to make him a member of the celestial host). In both cases he is either supported by chanting
the *Tao-te-ching* or performs the rite in preparation of its recitation. The
adept becomes both the embodied and celestial Tao by concentrating on
Lao-tzu in his head and placing himself at the center of the cosmos.
Thus he attains immortality and finds himself in the highest celestial
position, surrounded by divine attendants and mythical beasts. The *Tao-
te-ching*, in the context of Taoist visualization ritual, is thus both means
and object of the adept's union with the Tao.

Ordination through the *Tao-te-ching*

In the fifth century, there were five distinct schools of organized
Taoism, one in north, the others in south China. First, there were the

northern Celestial Masters under the foreign T'opa Wei rulers, who established Taoism as a state religion based on the revelation of a set of precepts known as the "New Code" to K'ou Ch'ien-chih in 415 (see Mather 1979) and, toward the end of the century, created a major Taoist center at Lou-kuan, focusing largely on the veneration of Lao-tzu and the recitation of the *Tao-te-ching*. Second, their southern counterparts, also called Celestial Masters, continued to follow the rules of Chang Tao-ling while reorganizing their community through a tighter hierarchy and more elaborate rituals. Their creed centered on the transmission of formal registers, that is, lists of the names of gods that would protect initiates, and the healing of diseases through exorcisms and talismans (see Kobayashi 1992).

In the south, there was further, third, the school of the Three Sovereigns (San-huang), whose teaching focused on the creation of social harmony through the writing of talismans and their worship in formal rituals. Its members also engaged in visionary forms of divination, trying to determine the best way to a harmonious society along the lines of the Great Peace ideal (see Andersen 1994). Fourth, the Numinous Treasure (Ling-pao) school focused on the veneration of specially revealed scriptures and the performance of public rituals for the salvation of all beings. This school shows the heaviest Buddhist influence (see Zürcher 1980). The school of Highest Clarity, finally, with its extensive descriptions of the higher heavens and the gods and its detailed instructions on how to travel to them ecstatically, concentrated on individual practice and the full attainment of immortality in the heavenly realms. Its practice was most sophisticated and its texts were the most literary; it was considered the highest among the schools.

In the early sixth century, these five Taoist schools, as part of an overall move toward reunification of the empire and the creation of a unifying orthodoxy, integrated their different teachings into one systematic and hierarchical whole, which we call integrated Taoism. At this time, the standard structure of Taoist ordination first developed, beginning with the transmission of registers and formal initiation of lay practitioners under the auspices of the southern Celestial Masters, then moving on to a more complex ordination hierarchy in this order: *Tao-te-ching* followers (northern Celestial Masters), Three Sovereigns, Numinous Treasure, and Highest Clarity. Each school was given a position in the system, with its scriptures and practices designating a particular rank. As a Taoist attained each rank, he would receive the respective school's scriptures, vow to observe new precepts, learn different rituals and meditations, and obtain a suitable formal title that indicated his rank in the celestial hierarchy above.[14]

Tao-te-ching *Followers*

Tao-te-ching followers represent the second level of this system, succeeding the basic initiation of the southern Celestial Masters and completing their training. A practitioner at this level was on the borderline between remaining a householder and becoming a recluse of the Taoist religion. The level goes back to the teaching of the northern Celestial Masters as it developed especially in their center at Lou-kuan, located in the foothills of the Chung-nan mountains southwest of modern Hsi-an. Lou-kuan was allegedly Yin Hsi's old home, given to him as a reward for official service by an early Chou ruler. Keen on astronomy and the observation of earth energies, Yin Hsi set up an observatory, from which the name Lou-kuan, "Lookout Tower," derives. From there he espied the purple energy of Lao-tzu on his way to the west and duly had himself stationed at the pass to become his disciple. He then invited the sage to his home, where the *Tao-te-ching* was finally transmitted.

Lou-kuan first became a Taoist center under the guidance of a member of the Yin family named Yin T'ung (398–499) in the early fifth century; it was firmly placed on the Taoist map by Wang Tao-yi (447–510) in the 490s. Under his direction, not only were the buildings and halls of Lou-kuan repaired and greatly expanded, but a major collection of Taoist scriptures and ritual manuals was undertaken, including both northern and southern materials, notably those of the Highest Clarity and Numinous Treasure schools. As a result, Lou-kuan played a central role in the sixth-century integration of Taoism, and many of its masters were prominent at the imperial court both under the northern and the T'ang dynasties.[15]

The teaching of the Lou-kuan group centered specifically on Lao-tzu and saw the *Tao-te-ching* as the main vehicle to salvation. Many legendary masters are accordingly described as having attained immortality through recitation of the text (Chang 1991, 87–88), and the veneration of both Lao-tzu and Yin Hsi remained a central feature of the school. But Lou-kuan Taoists were also influenced by Buddhist teachings, which grew popular at this time. They believed that people were rewarded or punished in their lives because of good or bad karma stored up from the past or accumulated by their ancestors. They could improve their karmic situation not only by venerating Lao-tzu through prayers and the production of statues, but also through the moral practice of following the (originally Buddhist) "five precepts" against killing, stealing, lying, sexual misconduct, and intoxication. These precepts guaranteed a proper life now and good rewards in the future. As one of their major texts, the

Lao-chün chieh-ching (Precepts of the Venerable Lord, TT 784) puts it: "Male and female followers of pure faith who uphold and obey the precepts will find the world a happy place and never know sorrow or distress" (19a; Kohn 1994, 206).

In addition, Lou-kuan Taoists practiced recitation of the *Tao-te-ching*, ideally ten thousand times, and the worship of Lao-tzu as the highest god to overcome the limitations of earthly existence and ascend to the ranks of the immortals. They learned the basic doctrine that the Tao, in its concrete manifestation in energy and the five phases, was originally part of both physical nature and the human body but spoilt by people's passions and desires. "Scattered yang becomes light; spread-out energy forms the six roots of the senses. From this, life and death arise: because the Tao is scattered and divided. Thus people leave the root and rush after the branches," the *Hsi-sheng-ching* (Scripture of Western Ascension, TT 726) explains, a mystical description of highest Taoist aspirations also of Lou-kuan provenance (Kohn 1991a, 93). Advanced practitioners of Lou-kuan thus pursued immortality through the purification of their bodies and minds, using various longevity techniques and meditational methods in the process: dietetics and energy control, talismans and visualizations, ecstatic excursions to the heavens and alchemy (Chang 1991, 99). The *Tao-te-ching* in Lou-kuan practice was thus pivotal both for lay followers, who received the text and followed the five precepts, and for advanced practitioners, who chanted it ten thousand times and founded their pursuit of immortality upon it. The *Tao-te-ching*, as uttered by the god Lao-tzu, here was a sacred scripture in the fullest sense, activated in various ways in the community of believers.

Tao-te-ching *Precepts and Related Scriptures*

When Lou-kuan Taoism was merged into integrated Taoism, its practitioners became "*Tao-te-ching* followers" and were ranked on the second level of ordination. The teaching of Lou-kuan then represented the highest form of Celestial Masters Taoism and served as the transition stage to other forms of practice, such as talismanic rituals and ecstatic exursions. Typically, *Tao-te-ching* followers were advanced lay followers who were preparing to leave the householder's life but had not yet done so (Jen 1990, 316). Their progress was divided into two stages. First they learned basic meditation and recitation techniques, worshiped Lao-tzu and Yin Hsi as their major patriarchs, and observed a group of ten precepts that included the five basic rules and a set of guidelines to help practitioners to live in harmony with their families and their communities, striving for the liberation and salvation of all beings.[16] Second, they took additional precepts and received more detailed instructions on the *Tao-te-*

ching, undergoing an ordination ceremony that named them Preceptors of Lofty Mystery and bestowed upon them a variety of exegetical, devotional, and technical materials linked with the text:

1. Major early commentaries on the *Tao-te-ching*, such as the physiological interpretation of Ho-shang-kung and the *Hsiang-erh* of the Celestial Masters
2. Technical interpretations of the text, such as the *Lao-tzu nei-chieh* (Inner Explication of the *Tao-te-ching*) and the *Lao-tzu chieh-chieh* (Detailed Explanations of the *Tao-te-ching*), which both survive only in citations (Kusuyama 1979, 199)
3. Philosophical and mystical exegeses of specifically Lou-kuan provenance, such as the *Hsi-sheng-ching*, which contains Lao-tzu's oral instructions to Yin Hsi (see Kohn 1991a), and the *Miao-chen-ching* (Scripture of Wondrous Perfection), a philosophical work on proper Taoist behavior in self-cultivation and public service (see Maeda 1987)
4. Practical manuals on *Tao-te-ching* meditation and ritual, such as the *Lao-tzu chung-ching* (Central Scripture of Lao-tzu, TT 1168) on the looks and functions of the body gods;[17] and the *Wu-ch'ien-wen ch'ao-yi* (Protocols for the Audience of the *Tao-te-ching*), a technical manual on ritual practice that is lost today (Benn 1991, 85)
5. Formal hagiographies of Lao-tzu and Yin Hsi, such as the *Kao-shang Lao-tzu nei-chuan* (Highest Essential Biography of Lao-tzu; lost) and the *Wen-shih nei-chuan*, which describe the progress of the Tao on earth and the first formalized transmission of the *Tao-te-ching*

Conclusion

The *Tao-te-ching* has played an important role in Taoist ritual from the very beginning. Its early history can be described according to five phases. First, in the Han dynasty, it was considered a valuable inspirational document, the recitation of which would give moral guidance and spiritual succor. As such it was used not only at court but also by the educated among the people, from whom it eventually spread to organized Taoist cults. In a second stage, these organized groups, especially the Celestial Masters, recited the *Tao-te-ching* as the revealed emanation of the pure Tao and treated it like a magical spell that could grant good health, freedom from demons, and immortality. As such, the text was chanted on a daily basis and linked not only with formal ritual practices but also with different sets of precepts, which aimed to ensure the ritual purity of the practitioner.

Third, among organized Taoist schools of the early middle ages, the *Tao-te-ching* was recited in a meditative context, linked with visualization of the deified Lao-tzu. Ten thousand recitations were believed to guarantee access to heaven and immortality. In the Lou-kuan center of the northern Celestial Masters, fourth, Lao-tzu and the *Tao-te-ching* stood at the center of Taoist belief and practice, and from there were integrated into the complex ordination hierarchy of integrated Taoism during the sixth century. Here, fifth, it was the key scripture of the so-called *Tao-te-ching* followers, who stood at the second level of the hierarchy, and was associated with a set of ten precepts, certain visualization and ritual practices, and accompanied by a group of supportive and interpretative documents that were transmitted along with it.

The *Tao-te-ching*, from the recorded sayings of the "Old Master," thus advanced to be the central scripture of a major Taoist school, a basic text that every aspiring Taoist had to worship, study, and recite. Playing a key role in Taoist medieval ordination, it has continued to be of central importance throughout Taoist history, even to the twentieth century (Hackmann 1920, 169). The *Tao-te-ching* as a ritual text has pervaded religious Taoism from its very beginnings to the present day, inspiring believers and guiding adepts to the higher purity of the Tao.

Notes

1. The *Tao-te-ching* is still applied today; for example, in a daily reading at a construction company in Taipei, where it serves to give employees a sense of value and a feeling of tranquility.

2. Texts in the Taoist canon (*Tao-tsang*, abbreviated TT) are given according to the number in Schipper 1975.

3. The text survives in a Tun-huang manuscript (S. 6825; Ōfuchi 1979, 421; Jao 1956; Mugitani 1985, index. See also Boltz 1982).

4. The precepts are in *Lao-chün ching-lü* 1a–2a (Scriptural Precepts of the Venerable Lord, TT 786; see Jen and Chung 1991, 566).

5. Purity and tranquility are important concepts in the later tradition, where they form the center of the *Ch'ing-ching-ching* (Scripture of Purity and Tranquility, TT 620; trans. in Kohn 1993, 25–29).

6. Tun-huang ms. S. 2295, repr. Seidel 1969, 131–36. French translation in Seidel 1969, 70; see also Yoshioka 1959, 122.

7. *Pao-p'u-tzu* 8.4b–5a (Book of the Master Who Embraces Simplicity). See Ware 1966, 142.

8. This passage is taken from Yin Hsi's essential biography, the *Wen-shih nei-chuan*, cited in *San-tung chu-nang* 9.10b (A Bag of Pearls from the Three Caverns, TT 1139).

9. Following *Hsi-sheng-ching* 1.11ab (Scripture of Western Ascension, TT 726); trans. in Kohn 1991a.

10. See *Lao-chün ts'un-ssu-t'u* (Visualization Charts of the Venerable Lord), ed. *Yün-chi ch'i-ch'ien* 47.17ab (Seven Tablets in a Cloudy Satchel, TT 1032). Ten thousand recitations will cause the practitioner to reach the cloudy realm by being received in an immortal's chariot. See Yoshioka 1959, 124.

11. The ritual was also used as a form of divination in the school of the Three Sovereigns. See Andersen 1994, 12.

12. This follows the Highest Clarity text *Tz'u-yi wu-lao pao-ching* 26a (Precious Scripture of the Five Old Ones of the Female One, TT 1313). See also Yamada 1989, 30.

13. Tun-huang manuscript, S. 75 and P. 2370.

14. The system is not well studied to date. See Yoshioka 1959, 126; Benn 1991, 82.

15. For a survey discussion of Lou-kuan and its Taoists, see Ch'ing 1988, 430; Jen 1990, 219; Chang 1991.

16. Recorded in the *Shih-chieh-ching* (Scripture of the Ten Precepts, TT 459), the first five of the ten precepts are against killing, debauchery, stealing, cheating, and intoxication. The second five are positive vows, such as "I will maintain harmony with my ancestors and kin and never do anything that harms my family!" and "When I see someone unfortunate, I will help him with my strength to recover good fortune!"

17. The text is also contained *Yün-chi ch'i-ch'ien* 18–19. For a study, see Schipper 1979.

References

Andersen, Poul. 1994. "Talking to the Gods: Visionary Divination in Early Taoism." *Taoist Resources* 5.1: 1–24.

Bauer, Wolfgang. 1956. "Der Herr vom gelben Stein." *Oriens Extremus* 3: 137–52.

Benn, Charles D. 1991. *The Cavern Mystery Transmission: A Taoist Ordination Rite of A.D. 711.* Honolulu: University of Hawaii Press.

Bokenkamp, Stephen. 1993. "Traces of Early Celestial Master Physiological Practice in the *Xiang'er* Commentary." *Taoist Resources* 4.2: 37–52.

Boltz, William G. 1982. "The Religious and Philosophical Significance of the 'Hsiang-erh Lao-tzu' in the Light of the Ma-wang-tui Silk Manuscripts." *Bulletin of the School for Oriental and African Studies* 45: 95–117.

Chang Wei-ling. 1991. "Pei-ch'ao chih ch'ien lou-kuan tao-chiao hsiu-hsing-fa ti li-shih k'ao-ch'a." *Tao-chiao-hsüeh t'an-so* 4: 67–117.

Ch'ing Hsi-t'ai. 1988. *Chung-kuo tao-chiao-shih.* Ch'eng-tu: Ssu-ch'uan jen-min.

Hackmann, Heinrich. 1920. "Die Mönchsregeln des Klostertaoismus." *Ostasiatische Zeitschrift* 8: 141–70.

Jao Tsung-i. 1956. *Lao-tzu hsiang-erh-chu chiao-ch'ien.* Hong Kong: Tong Nam Printers. Reprinted Shanghai: Wenyin, 1992.

Jen Chi-yü. 1990. *Chung-kuo tao-chiao-shih.* Shanghai: Jen-min.

Jen Chi-yü and Chung Chao-p'eng, eds. 1991. *Tao-tsang t'i-yao.* Peking: Chung-kuo she-hui k'e-hsüeh ch'u-pan-she.

Kimura Eiichi. 1959. *Rōshi no shin kenkyū.* Tokyo: Sōbunsha.

Kobayashi Masayoshi. 1992. "The Celestial Masters Under the Eastern Jin and Liu-Song Dynasties." *Taoist Resources* 3.2: 17–45.

Kohn, Livia. 1991a. *Taoist Mystical Philosophy: The Scripture of Western Ascension.* Albany: State University of New York Press.

———. 1991b. "Taoist Visions of the Body." *Journal of Chinese Philosophy* 18: 227–52.

———, ed. 1993. *The Taoist Experience: An Anthology.* Albany: State University of New York Press.

———. 1994. "The Five Precepts of the Venerable Lord." *Monumenta Serica* 42: 171–215.

Kusuyama Haruki. 1979. *Rōshi densetsu no kenkyū.* Tokyo: Sōbunsha.

Maeda Shigeki. 1987. "Rōshi myōshinkyō shōkō." *Waseda daigaku daigakuin bungaku kenkyūka kiyō* 14: 21–32.

Major, John S. 1986. "New Light on the Dark Warrior." *Journal of Chinese Religions* 13/14: 65–87.

Maspero, Henri. 1981. *Taoism and Chinese Religion.* Translated by Frank Kierman. Amherst: University of Massachusetts Press.

Mather, Richard B. 1979. "K'ou Ch'ien-chih and the Taoist Theocracy at the Northern Wei Court 425–451." In *Facets of Taoism*, ed. Holmes Welch and Anna Seidel, 103–22. New Haven, Conn.: Yale University Press.

Mugitani Kunio. 1985. *Rōshi sōjichu sakuin*. Kyoto: Hōyu shoten.

Ōfuchi Ninji. 1979. *Tonkō dōkei: Zuroku hen*. Tokyo: Kokubu shoten.

Robinet, Isabelle. 1977. *Les commentaires du Tao to king jusqu'au VIIe siècle*. Paris: Mémoirs de l'Institute des Hautes Études Chinoises 5.

———. 1984. *La révélation du Shangqing dans l'histoire du taoisme*. 2 vols. Paris: Publications de l'École Française d'Extrême-Orient.

———. 1993. *Taoist Meditation*. Translated by Norman Girardot and Julian Pas. Albany: State University of New York Press.

Schipper, Kristofer. 1975. *Concordance du Tao Tsang: Titres des ouvrages*. Paris: Publications de l'École Française d'Extrême-Orient.

———. 1979. "Le Calendrier de Jade: Note sur le *Laozi zhongjing*." *Nachrichten der deutschen Gesellschaft für Natur- und Völkerkunde Ostasiens* 125: 75–80.

Seidel, Anna. 1969. *La divinisation de Lao-tseu dans le Taoisme des Han*. Paris: École Française d'Extrême-Orient. Reprinted 1992.

Strickmann, Michel. 1985. "Therapeutische Rituale und das Problem des Bösen im frühen Taoismus." In *Religion und Philosophie in Ostasien: Festschrift für Hans Steininger*, ed. G. Naundorf, K. H. Pohl, and H. H. Schmidt, 185–200. Würzburg, Germany: Königshausen and Neumann.

Ware, James R. 1966. *Alchemy, Medicine and Religion in the China of AD 320*. Cambridge, Mass.: MIT Press.

Yamada Toshiaki. 1989. "Dōbō shinson shikō." *Tōhōshūkyō* 74: 20–38.

Yoshioka Yoshitoyo. 1959. *Dōkyō to bukkyō*. Vol. 1. Tokyo: Kokusho kankōkai.

Zürcher, Erik. 1980. "Buddhist Influence on Early Taoism." *T'oung-pao* 66: 84–147.

Part III

Modern Readings

7

Influential Western Interpretations
of the *Tao-te-ching*

Julia M. Hardy

The *Tao-te-ching* has acquired a widespread and diverse Western audience, and it appeals to readers on a variety of levels. Many have found it to provide solutions to Western religious, philosophical, and social problems. Today's scholars of Taoism tend to view these popular Western interpretations of the *Tao-te-ching* critically; however, earlier scholarship has been a major source for current popular understandings of the text. This survey of influential Western interpretations of the *Tao-te-ching* identifies three historical phases characterized by different interpretive agendas. The first, which I mention only briefly, covers the eighteenth and nineteenth centuries, and is concerned mainly with comparison of the *Tao-te-ching* with Christian doctrine. Comparisons with Christianity continue in the next phase, which begins around 1915, but a clear shift in the understanding of the text occurs, and the *Tao-te-ching* is often employed as an instrument to criticize Western thought and values. It is during this second period that scholarly participation in the appropriation of the *Tao-te-ching* for Western needs is most common. The third and final phase is that of recent scholarship on the *Tao-te-ching* (late 1970s and early 1980s); it is marked by a serious attempt to avoid appropriation and create an interpretation based on Chinese sources.

Earliest Interpretations: The *Tao-te-ching* and Christianity

The earliest known Western translation of the *Tao-te-ching* was a Latin version produced by Jesuit missionaries in China, and presented to the British Royal Society in 1788. The translators' stated intent was to show that "the Mysteries of the Most Holy Trinity and of the Incarnate God were anciently known to the Chinese nation" (Legge 1962, xiii).

Speculations about Christian doctrine hidden within the *Tao-te-ching* were a popular topic among missionaries, and the first scholarly studies of the text, commencing fifty years later, continued these speculations.

In 1820, J. P. Abel-Rémusat, in his "Mémoire sur la vie et les ouvrages de Lao-tseu," published the bizarre claim that the Hebrew consonants signifying Yahweh are represented by three Chinese characters in the opening lines of chapter 14.[1] Abel-Rémusat also interpreted Tao in a way that was compatible with his understanding of the God of Christianity. He stated that Tao, like logos, conveys "the triple sense of Supreme Being, reason, and word [la parole]" and described it as first cause and creator, "primordial reason, the intelligence which formed the world, and rules it like the spirit rules the body" (Julien 1842, xii). In 1842, Abel-Rémusat's student, Stanislas Julien, called his teacher to task on a number of issues when he published a complete French translation. In the introduction he demonstrated the fallacy of Abel-Rémusat's strange hypothesis about chapter 14, and questioned his understanding of Tao. According to the Chinese, said Julien, "the Tao is devoid of action, thought, judgment, and intelligence" (1842, xiii). Julien's work was based on substantial scholarly underpinnings; his interpretation relied on the Chinese commentaries, and he was the first Western scholar whose concern was to present an authentically Chinese understanding of the text.

Like Julien, James Legge, who published the first reliable English translation in 1891, avoided attempts to impose Christian theology onto the text. However, in his introductory remarks, Legge made his sympathies clear and proclaimed Lao-tzu wrong about many things about which Christian doctrine was right (1962, 21, 29), not actually interpreting the text but simply measuring it against preconceived standards. According to Legge, because Lao-tzu was fundamentally wrong on these crucial issues, the degeneration of any school of thought based on Lao-tzu is inevitable—as is evident, he said, in subsequent forms of popular Taoism (Legge 1962, 29–30). Legge, Julien, and Abel-Rémusat were by no means the only nineteenth-century interpreters; through 1905, there were thirteen different translations into English alone (e.g., Legge 1891, Carus 1898, Giles 1905; see Welch 1965, 4). Julien's approach was ignored in most of these translations, and explicit comparisons with Christianity were the norm.

Western Adaptation: Confronting the Mystery of Tao

During the second major phase of Western interpretation, the *Tao-te-ching* was received no longer as Christian revelation in an alien form or a misguided oriental attempt at wisdom, but in its own right. Nevertheless, religious and philosophical questions remained important, and comparisons with Christianity, even when not explicit, were still influential in interpreting the text. One religious question many interpreters asked was whether or not Tao had qualities that could be associated with Western concepts of supreme deity. Despite the admonition of the first lines of the text—that Tao cannot be defined or understood—scholars speculated frequently about the nature of Tao: Is Tao a mystical Absolute, a form of Supreme Being, the creator of the world, or something else?

Some insisted that Tao was something entirely different from the Christian God. Marcel Granet, in his influential *La pensée chinoise*, said, "Chinese wisdom has no need of the idea of God" (1968, 478). In Chinese thought, he insisted, "there is no creator. Nothing was created in the world, and the world was not created" (1968, 275). "Tao was never conceived as a transcendent reality. . . . Tao is merely the impersonal principle of all sanctity" (1968, 477). Needham cited Granet emphatically, stating: "Chinese ideals involved neither God nor Law" (1956, 290), and described the Chinese universe as ruled, not by "fiats issued by a supreme creator-lawgiver," but by "an ordered harmony of wills without an ordainer" (1956, 286–87). Others interpreted Tao differently. There were those who viewed Tao as a kind of supreme being that, even if not directly equated with God, had many qualities associated with him. The French scholar Max Kaltenmark, in his *Lao-tzu and Taoism*, described Tao as "a superior reality that transcends the perceptible and imperceptible modalities of being." He regarded Tao as creator and "first cause" of the universe: Tao "causes all creatures to be born," although "its role is not always presented as directly procreative" (1969, 38). For Kaltenmark, Tao was a "mysterious being" that could be apprehended not only through mystical encounter but also nourished as a presence within the individual "Holy Man" as "life principle" (1969, 60).

Henri Maspero, who died in Buchenwald in 1945, was doubtless a great influence on Kaltenmark; Kaltenmark wrote the preface to Maspero's posthumously published works. Maspero's description of Tao is subtly different from that of Kaltenmark—his Tao is more impersonal—but he, like Kaltenmark, viewed the goal of mystical experience as an encounter with the Absolute (1981, 422). Maspero understood the *Tao-te-ching* to contain veiled references to techniques for producing ecstasic "mystical union with the impersonal Tao" (1981, 30). He analyzed mysticism as a religious phenomenon in some detail, and concluded that all its forms—including Taoist—shared a common structure. The interpretations differ, but the experiences are "identical" (1981, 426). Not unlike modern perennialists, Maspero apparently assumed that the experiences were identical because the Absolute is always the same, and is simply interpreted differently according to the cultural background of the experient.

Other interpreters strongly disagreed with the notion of Tao as an absolute being. In an essay entitled "What is Taoism?" Herrlee Creel criticizes Maspero's statements about the identity of all mystical experience, asserting the importance of distinguishing between Western and Taoist mysticism (1956, 140). In the West, Creel states, the prevailing view recognizes a special relationship between humanity and the universe, but in Taoism, there is no such special relationship. Continuing this point in a later essay, he argues that Tao is more ordinary—existing even in "ordure and urine" (*Chuang-tzu*, chap. 7; 1970, 31)—than extraordinary, and that it is certainly not a manifestation of a divine spark within each human being. With this stance Creel criticizes a number of previous interpretations of Tao by Westerners, his final passage poetically expressing his disdain for the need that compels some scholars to impose some notion of the Absolute onto Tao:

> Let others be awed by the lofty remoteness of absolute knowledge, and spend their lives in pursuit of it like quixotic knights seeking the Grail; the Taoist does not believe it. Let others honor the universe by endowing it with human qualities, calling it "infinite mind" or "absolute reason." The Taoist, with an apparent simplicity that is wholly deceptive, with the approach to the ridiculous that always characterizes the sublime, calls it The Great Clod. (1970, 36)

Where Creel is primarily concerned with criticizing those who distort Tao by likening it to familiar understandings of deity, Wing-tsit Chan[2] objects to critics who claimed that Tao was irrational, mystical nonsense. In the introduction to his translation, Chan writes that Tao "is mysterious only in the sense of subtlety and depth, not in the sense of irrationality" (1963, 9). He pronounces Joseph Needham "fundamentally correct" in his equation of Tao with the "Order of Nature," which as nonbeing brings being into existence.

> The traditional idea that a supreme supernatural being, Heaven, is the ruler of the universe is replaced by the doctrine that *the universe exists and operates by itself.* (1963, 10; italics mine)

Chan adds that while many Westerners assume that "nonbeing" implies absence, Lao-tzu proved that nonexistence can exist—a radically new concept which transformed Chinese philosophy. In attempting to explain the complex relationship between Tao, being, and nonbeing, he defers to the words of Fung Yu-lan:[3]

> Since the Tao is unnamable, it therefore cannot be comprised in words. But since we wish to speak about it, we are forced to give it some kind of designation. We therefore call it Tao, which is really not a name at all. That is to say, to call the Tao Tao, is not the same as to call a table table. . . . Tao is not itself a thing. (1966, 95)
>
> Anything that comes to be is a being, and there are many beings. The coming to be of beings implies that first of all there is Being. These words, "first of all," here do not mean first in point of time, but first in a logical sense. . . . Tao is the unnamable, is Nonbeing, and is that by which all things come to be. Therefore, before the being of Being, there must be Nonbeing, from which Being comes into being. What is here said belongs to ontology, not to cosmology. It has nothing to do with time and actuality. For in time and actuality, there is no Being; there are only beings. (1966, 96)

Fung here argues that Tao cannot be compared to any cosmological supreme being. Tao is not a being but "lies beyond shapes and features" (1966, 94). Unlike Chan, who objects to any association of the *Tao-te-ching* with mysticism, Fung insists that the absence of an Absolute does not render a mystical interpretation of the text irrelevant. He presents an understanding of mysticism based on the notion of self-cultivation so fundamental to Chinese thought and most commonly associated with Confucianism rather than Taoism. Fung defines transcendence as the process of reaching one's full potential as a human being. The best method for approaching the final stage of this process is silence—"not to talk about it" (1966, 340)—the silence implied by the opening lines of the *Tao-te-ching*. Hence, for Fung, the *Tao-te-ching* is a mystical text, but mysticism is not the pursuit of some irrational end: "Mysticism is not the opposite of clear thinking, nor is it below it. Rather it is beyond it. It is not anti-rational, it is super-rational" (1966, 342).

Tao as a Way of Life

The *Tao-te-ching* appealed to many Western interpreters simply as a philosophy of life, as advice on values and behavior in the ordinary, everyday world. Some associated mysticism, and religion in general, with superstition and ignorance. They read the *Tao-te-ching* as a philosophy that could take the place of religion. Others, like Waley and Fung, interpreted the text in both mystical and practical terms.

Arthur Waley was not the first to translate Tao as "Way," but his *The Way and Its Power*, first published in 1934, marked the beginning of a widespread Western understanding of the text as a manual explicating the value of a particular way of life. In the detailed introduction to his translation that is slightly longer than the translation itself, Waley places the *Tao-te-ching* in the context of the transition from a religion based on divination and sacrifice, centered on the ruling nobility, to a recognition of the moral autonomy of the individual. From this perspective, the *Tao-te-ching* shares with many other texts of its period an emerging concern with individual morality and the notion of self-cultivation. According to Waley, each text represents a particular school of thought as to how this self-cultivation might best be undertaken. The *Tao-te-ching* represents the voice of those who recognize the power of desirelessness, humility, passivity, lowliness, imperfection, stillness, and intuition. While Waley discusses mysticism in the *Tao-te-ching*, even comparing Taoist mystical practices to Indian yoga (1934, 116–20), he emphasizes the role of this mysticism in the service of self-cultivation.

In contrast, Wing-tsit Chan questions whether even union with Tao need be regarded as a mystical experience. For him, "the chief subject of the book is how to live, including ethics, government, and diplomacy" (1963, 10) and its "main objective... is the cultivation of virtue or *te*" (1963, 11). While he acknowledges that Taoism "no longer exists as an independent philosophical system" in China, he attributes to Taoist philosophy— "tightly woven into the fabric of Chinese life"—a number of positive characteristics of the Chinese people, including: "rugged individualism," "love of spiritual tranquility and mental peace," "simplicity of life," "withdrawal in order to advance," "wisdom in silence," "wealth in seeming poverty," and "love of nature" (1963, 29–30).

Fung likewise emphasizes the understanding of the *Tao-te-ching* as a way of life. As already mentioned, he links mysticism with the cultivation of the human potential for good, not with union with an Absolute as described by, for example, Maspero. Fung articulates a preconception about Chinese thought that was embraced by other Western interpreters of the *Tao-te-ching* during this period when he says, "The Chinese people take even their religion philosophically" (1966, 3). Unlike Western philosophy, Feng insists, Chinese philosophy is a lived philosophy; its purpose is not simply to "acquire... knowledge," but to "develop . . . character" (1966, 10). Fung even goes so far as to say, "In the world of the future, man will have philosophy in the place of religion. This is consistent with Chinese tradition" (1966, 6).

Another Chinese interpreter, Lin Yutang,[4] agrees, stating that from the Chinese point of view, the West has no philosophy:

> We need a philosophy of living and we clearly haven't got it. The Western man has tons of philosophy written by French, German, English, and American professors, but still he hasn't got a philosophy when he wants it. (1942, 569)

The problem with Western philosophers, according to Lin, is that they search for facts, rather than values (1942, 570). Facts only confuse people; values help them lead rewarding lives. Lin then recommends the *Tao-te-ching* to Westerners in search of a philosophy of life, saying, "If one reads enough of this Book, one automatically acquires the habits and ways of the Chinese":

> It teaches the wisdom of appearing foolish, the success of appearing to fail, the strength of weakness and the advantage of lying low, the benefit of yielding to your adversary and the futility of contention for power. (1942, 579)]

What Chan, Fung, and Lin have in common is their belief that the *Tao-te-ching* was a strong, positive force in Chinese civilization, containing a wise and effective philosophy of life that could easily be recommended to the West. From this position it was only a short step to the notion that the text could represent the solution to a number of Western problems.

A Chinese Antidote to Western Problems

Lin, among several interpreters of the *Tao-te-ching* who suggested specific reforms of Western thought and values based on the text, believed that it could be used as a therapeutic alternative to Western thought. An incident characteristic of this position is reported in Richard Wilhelm's introduction to his German translation of the *Tao-te-ching*, first published in 1915. Here he tells the story of a séance at a Lao-shan monastery, which was abruptly interrupted when Lao-tzu announced that "he had just been called to London (*Lun*) in England (*Ying*), where they needed him" (1985, 10). By the early twentieth century, Wilhelm poetically proclaimed, "the threads that were first spun by Lao Zi are beginning to be woven into the cultural fabric of Europe" (1985, 10).

Wilhelm was the first to use the disease analogy, but only to hint that Lao-tzu could be an antidote for a sick Western society, as when he contrasted the "satanic powers" of Faust—like "those of the Titan of the

West"—to the more favorable powers of the eastern Lao-tzu (1985, 88). It was not until the onset of World War II some decades later that this kind of interpretation came to the fore. In 1942, Lin wrote:

> If I were asked what antidote could be found in Oriental literature and philosophy to cure this contentious modern world of its inveterate belief in force and struggle for power, I would name this book. . . . [Lao-tzu] has the knack of making Hitler and the other dreamers of world mastery appear foolish and ridiculous. . . . And furthermore, if there is one book advising against the multifarious activities and futile busy-ness of the modern man, I would again say it is Laotse's *Book of Tao*. (1942, 579)

Lin was a resident of the United States for thirty years, and a refugee from China's own contentious situation; he did not condemn the West so much as modernity and accordingly expressed deep admiration for Emerson, Whitman, and Thoreau. Blaming scientific materialism, as exemplified by the notion of "objective" experimentation, for the problems of modernity, and also the absence of a "philosophy of the rhythm of life" (1942, 579), Lin honored Lao-tzu as a source for an alternative philosophy.

The most vocal and prolific advocate of Taoism as an antidote to the disease of the West was British biochemist Joseph Needham. In the second volume of his *Science and Civilisation in China*, he presents a thorough critique of modern Western thought and offers in its place an "organic naturalist" philosophy based on the *Tao-te-ching* and other early Chinese texts. Needham argues that the *Tao-te-ching* represents the thoughts of a "primitive agrarian collective" opposed to the feudal nobility ruling at that time (1956, 100). Discontented scholars, along with artisans who had come to understand nature through the power of "manual operations," formed a union that gave birth to incipient Chinese forms of democratic socialism and science.[5] Needham compared the powers-that-be of the modern West with the ancient feudal lords, whose "Confucian and Legalist social-ethical thought-complex was masculine, managing, hard, dominating, aggressive, rational and donative," and encouraged his readers to follow the ancient Taoists who "broke with it radically and completely by emphasizing all that was feminine, tolerant, yielding, permissive, withdrawing, mystical and receptive" (1956, 59).

Needham thus proposed that Westerners change their way of thinking from the customary dualistic, mechanistic mode, in which "a *deus* always had to be found for a *machina*," to the Chinese organic mode in which "the parts, in their organizational relations, whether of a living body or of the universe, were sufficient to account, by a kind of harmony of wills, for the observed phenomena" (1956, 302). According to his Chinese "organic naturalism," everything in the universe is interrelated, and participates in a "colossal pattern" that is self-motivating and self-sustaining (1956, 280–81). Following Granet's understanding, he suggests that this Chinese idea of Order promotes a healthy sense of respect for others and for the natural world. Needham's interpretation of the *Tao-te-ching*, and of Chinese philosophy in general, was shaped by his critical attitude toward modernity, his utopian image of the ancient Taoists, and his vision of the potential for an ethical and communal practice of science to serve as a tool for human redemption. More than any other scholarly interpreter, Needham appropriated the *Tao-te-ching* in service of his own agenda—his interpretation was shaped by his perceptions of the situation and needs of the modern West (Hardy 1990, 30–33). His understanding of ancient Taoism and Chinese history was skewed by this agenda, but he struck a chord in Western consciousness and his work elicited considerable popular response.

Holmes Welch took a different but equally powerful approach to interpreting the *Tao-te-ching* as an antidote to the disease of the West. He concludes his study, *Taoism: The Parting of the Way*, with an imaginary discourse given by Lao-tzu to twentieth- century Americans. In response to an inquiry about the source of America's problems, Welch's modern-day Lao-tzu begins with advertising and public relations, which damage character by creating desires and distorting facts. The solution he proposes is an "anonymity program": each company should have a representative "who would do what he could to keep people from learning about its good products and good works" (1957, 166). Following this, Lao-tzu raises the problem of the educational system, which perverts character by emphasizing defeat and victory in both its modes of teaching and its sports programs. Next he criticizes foreign policy, arguing that the United States should "relinquish the role of world leadership" to the United Nations. Above all, political representatives should not act superior, for "superiority is the form of aggression which is hardest to forgive because it is hardest to requite" (1957, 169). Instead,

> train your ambassadors to droop a little, drift a little, appear a little stupid, miss opportunities to promote your interest, and give other peoples a chance to laugh at your expense. (1957, 170)

As did many other Western interpreters during and after World War II, Welch thus suggests that the teachings of Lao-tzu could discourage people from making war upon one another—even as the *Tao-te-ching* was originally intended to do when written during the Warring States period in China (1957, 176–78). Some might be surprised that this modern Lao-tzu, while advocating pacifism, does not propose nonviolence, or inaction, in all situations. "Force is sometimes necessary," he says instead—but a force undertaken only with great regret and sadness (1957, 171). In addition, Welch points out Lao-tzu's "important message" for the "unsuccessful people" of America:

> That they are wise to be obscure; that there is a standard by which here and now they are better than most of the successful people who seem so far above them. . . . [Lao-tzu] makes it possible for them once more to think well of themselves. (1957, 175–76)

He concludes his work on "Tao Today" with a long quotation from chapter 80 of the *Tao-te-ching*, the section that describes the primitive utopia long favored in romantic Western interpretations of Taoism, again emphasizing his vision of the Tao as the solution for Western problems.

Scholars like Welch, Needham, and Lin Yü-tang with their understanding of the text as an antidote to the diseases of Western civilization have had a substantial influence on the popular reception of the *Tao-te-ching*. Particularly in recent years, popular interpreters have continued to use the text to criticize certain aspects of Western culture and to offer alternatives based on it. Scholars, on the other hand, have become more concerned with producing an authentically Chinese understanding of the ancient text.

Recent Scholarship: Addressing the Biases of the Past

Although much effort during the second period was directed toward appropriative interpretations of the *Tao-te-ching* to cure Western ills, there was also much solid and unbiased scholarship before 1980 that laid the groundwork for current *Tao-te-ching* studies. Here the emphasis is on understanding the text as it has been interpreted by the Chinese and within the context of Chinese history and culture, while attempting to eliminate the biases of the first and second periods of Western reception.

Continuity between the Tao-te-ching *and Later Taoist Religion*

For two thousand years Taoism has existed in China as a religious institution, with priestly functionaries, ritual practices, gods and goddesses, heavens and hells, and all the accoutrements of religious organization. In the Taoist religion, Lao-tzu is revered as a god, and the *Tao-te-ching* is one of thousands of texts in the Taoist canon. In the late 1970s and early 1980s, some scholars began to point out that all this rich material was being virtually ignored in favor of the philosophy expressed in ancient texts like the *Tao-te-ching* (see Strickmann 1979, 164–67). The reason for this, they argued, was a bias in favor of a philosophical interpretation of Taoism that had proven immensely attractive to Western thinkers and created an idealized vision of ancient China.

This attraction and idealization were, moreover, part of an overall Western attitude of "orientalism," which was unveiled as the dominant bias toward Eastern cultures by Edward Said (1979). According to him, Westerners are fascinated with the ancient traditions of Oriental cultures, judging them to be the only true expressions of Eastern peoples, which are deploringly corrupt today. Western scholars, explorers, and diplomats accordingly set out to recover and restore these ancient traditions; thus archeological explorations and the study of classical texts go hand in hand with colonial ambitions. As Said says,

> [The Orient] is known, then invaded and possessed, then recreated by scholars, soldiers, and judges who disinterred forgotten languages, histories, races, and cultures in order to posit them . . . as the true classical Orient that could be used to judge and rule the modern Orient. (1979, 92)

Stimulated by the general shift in Western scholarship away from the idealized ancient "Orient" and toward an appreciation of current and local cultures, the attention of researchers in Taoist studies focused away from the classical texts and onto later Taoist religious scriptures and ritual. However, this was not entirely new. Research on the later religious aspects of Taoism had begun decades before, with Maspero a great pioneer in this area, followed by Kaltenmark, Schipper, and others. The relationship between the "philosophical Taoism" of the *Tao-te-ching* and later "religious Taoism" similarly had been a lively topic of scholarly debate as well, and virtually every major scholar weighed in on this issue. Some, like Creel, argued that there was no relationship, that "religious Taoism" bore no resemblance to the refined thought expressed by the early classics. Others, like Maspero, believed that there existed a direct continuity between all forms of Taoism. The debate has continued (see Thompson 1993), but in the meantime the focus of scholarly research has shifted clearly toward later religious manifestations of Taoism (see Seidel 1990; Overmyer et al. 1995).

Two scholars who have recently attempted to demonstrate a continuity between the *Tao-te-ching* (and the Taoism of the period in which it was written) and later religious Taoism are Norman J. Girardot and Livia

Kohn. In his *Myth and Meaning in Early Taoism*, Girardot presents considerable evidence for a "structural continuity"—not an "identity" (1983, 276)—between archaic Chinese mythology, the philosophy of the *Tao-te-ching*, and later Taoist religious ritual. He criticizes what he believes to be a false distinction between Taoist philosophy and Taoist religion, since "when post-Han Taoism became conscious of itself as an organized religious movement it creatively drew upon a preexisting history of religious ideas most closely associated with the early classical texts" (1983, 276).

Girardot's argument echoes the earlier issue concerning the relationship between Tao and concepts of God; he suggests that the distinction between the *Tao-te-ching* and later Taoism rests on false assumptions about the nature of religion. Girardot argues that the *Tao-te-ching* is a religious text even though it may not be focused on supernaturalism, transcendence, or immortality. Based on Clifford Geertz's notion of "religion as a cultural system," Girardot defines religion as "a system of symbolic thought and action that is 'focused on salvation' and is interpretively grounded in mythical or cosmological 'formulations of a general order of existence'" (1983, 6; using Lessa and Vogt 1965, 204).

According to him, "early Taoist thought is most adequately understood in terms of its relation to a mythological theme of creation, fall, and 'salvational' return" (1983, 6). He says,

> Tao as the Beginning is an enduring and sustaining presence in the world; and, even though it is hidden or lost to man, it is possible to return to an indentification with the source of all meaning and life. Tao, as the source and ground of nature, constantly "returns" (see chap. 40) [of the *Tao-te-ching*] to the conditions of the beginning in the sense of a periodic reiteration of the cosmogony. (1983, 49)

To him, salvation in the *Tao-te-ching* is not associated with "a specific, once-and-for-all Christian flavor of savior, permanent eschatological redemption, or transcendental immortality" (1983, 6). Rather, it is part of a cyclical process in which one periodically returns "to an identification with the source of all meaning and life" (1983, 49).

Neither is the creation described in the *Tao-te-ching* comparable to creation in the biblical sense; yet it is an integral aspect of the Taoist religious experience, a continuous, cyclical process or *creatio continua*:

> The return to the chaos condition . . . is not presented as an absolute end but as a method of constantly starting over again in the world. Returning to the beginning is not just to maintain, once and for all, the fetal or precosmic condition but to be reborn into

the human world. Because of his periodic journeys back in time as an emulation of the cyclic regeneration of the Tao, the Taoist remains fresh and whole. The sage lives creatively in the world by knowing the secret of creation. (1983, 76)

There is no creator god in early Taoism: its "essential mystical intentionality seems to favor the idea of creation *always lacking any creator separate from the creation*" (1983, 64; italics mine). Girardot uses terms familiar to Western readers in discussing early Taoist religion as expressed in the *Tao-te-ching*, but turns the familiar structures upside down. Mystical union is possible without an absolute reality to unite with, and creation is possible without a creator. The "fall" is a fall into order, and salvation is a return back into chaos, not an escape into some heavenly otherworld. Girardot concludes that there is a definite continuity between early and later Taoism, based on the structure of movement from creation to fall and on to salvational return, which persists in the later religion even though it embraces a system in some ways more familiar to the West.

Livia Kohn has demonstrated a different sort of continuity between early and later Taoism in China. In *Early Chinese Mysticism: Philosophy and Soteriology in the Taoist Tradition*, she argues that mystical, philosophical understandings of the *Tao-te-ching* did not end when the Taoist religion began. She posits that the "quietistic, naturalistic" tradition, as based on the ancient Taoist philosophical texts, eventually joined with "the meditational concepts and techniques of Buddhism" to form a third kind of Taoism, in addition to "philosophical" and "religious" Taoism, a mystical tradition she calls "Lao-Chuang":

Lao-Zhuang [Lao-Chuang] begins where philosophical Taoism ends—it comments on the ancient philosophies and makes use of them in other contexts, relating their ideas to concerns current at various times and using their images, metaphors, and philosophical terminology for purposes of its own. (1992, 5–6)

This tradition did not become institutionalized, according to Kohn, but rather "remained independent and oriented toward the individual. It was primarily intellectual, not devotional, and was carried by the literati and aristocratic elite" who were unhappy with contemporary politics (1992, 7).

Kohn's theory best accounts for the link between later Taoism and the arts, and for individuals in Chinese history who have been associated with Taoism even though they have not been participants in the Taoist church. For example, many Chinese poets make reference to the

Tao-te-ching and the *Chuang-tzu*, as well as to Buddhist concepts, in expressing poetically what Kohn describes as "Taoist mystical philosophy."
These poets were often disgruntled Confucian officials, and they easily
fit Kohn's description of those unhappy members of "the literati and
aristocratic elite" who "remained independent and oriented toward the
individual," and whose Taoism was "primarily intellectual, not devotional" (1992, 7). The interpretation of the *Tao-te-ching* preserved by what
Kohn calls the Lao-Chuang tradition is more similar to that of popular
Western interpretations than that of most recent scholars, but her interpretation is based on thorough research on Chinese sources.

Historical versus Scriptural Interpretation

As early as 1934, Waley had pointed out that many Western translations of the *Tao-te-ching* were biased towards a scriptural interpretation—
that is, they were primarily concerned with conveying an ahistorical,
spiritual meaning of the text. In contrast, Waley's translation and interpretation were historical in that he took into account the cultural context and original meaning of the text at the time it was written. Waley's
approach has been the model for a number of recent translations. Of
these, the only one to be supported by extensive theoretical and methodological, rather than philological, underpinnings is that of Michael
LaFargue. In *Tao and Method*, he employs the form-critical method first
developed in biblical studies to reconstruct the *Sitz-im-Leben* of the
"Laoist" school and thus recover the "original meaning" of the text (1994,
76). Because his views are expressed in a chapter in this volume, I will
not discuss them further except to comment on one aspect of this work:
the relevance of his interpretation to modern Western life.

The only recent scholarly interpreter of the *Tao-te-ching* to discuss
this issue, LaFargue with his historical interpretation flies in the face of
the popular Western image of Taoists as misfits who reject society; his
Taoists are more like Confucians in that their primary concerns are issues
of rulership. He convincingly argues, however, that his interpretation
of the *Tao-te-ching* need not decrease its relevance to the modern Western
reader. This text of a scholarly class of "Laoist *shih*-idealists" still represents a "moral resistance" against a "dehumanizing social environment,"
a resistance founded on the notion of "organic harmony" (1994, 295).
LaFargue addresses those who fear the loss of Lao-tzu as the voice of
the rugged individualist, and who resent the implicit and explicit associations with hierarchy revealed by the text and maintained in this analysis.
He reminds us that there are many people "whose responsibilities give
them some degree of authority over others" (1994, 297). Modern Western readers can apply the Laoist concept of the "ruler," not simply to

high officials, but to any person in a position of authority—"from the highest CEO to the night supervisor at MacDonald's." He proposes that the *Tao-te-ching* could be a model for an "idealistic ethos" of leadership, an ethos he believes America desperately needs (1994, 299–300).

Logic and Mysticism

Whether demonstrating the continuity of the *Tao-te-ching* with so-called religious Taoism or seeking a historical understanding of the text, Girardot, Kohn, and LaFargue continue to posit the existence of mysticism within early Taoism. Chad Hansen, to the contrary, expresses strong objections to any mystical interpretation of the text and favors a vision of the Tao as a linguistic pointer of logic. This view, in its turn, is countered by A. C. Graham, in conjunction with Kohn and LaFargue, arguing that Taoist mysticism is not like Western mysticism, and that mysticism is possible without the belief in a metaphysical Absolute—the key objection Hansen has to this view. More specifically, Hansen, in his *A Daoist Theory of Chinese Thought*, accuses all Western scholars, past and present, of a bias based on the understanding of Tao as an Absolute, and expresses his intention to remove from the *Tao-te-ching* all taint of mysticism or Buddhism caused by this bias. He argues that almost all English translations add a definite article to the subject of the first line of the text and capitalize it ("the Tao") but that there is nothing in the Chinese text to indicate the grammatical accuracy of this rendition. It could just as well be that the text reads "a tao, "any tao," "some taos," or "taos" (1992, 215, 402n26).[6] The implication of "the Tao" is that something exists called "the constant Tao," though it is nameless: the ineffable Absolute of mystics.

Hansen's translation of the term eliminates any sense of Tao as an absolute being. He regards *tao* not as a metaphysical construct but as a "form of discourse." According to Hansen, the term refers to a form of discourse about guiding behavior that is common to all the early Chinese schools of thought: "The guiding ideal of this classical period of Chinese thought is to get a constant *dao* [*tao*]—a form of discourse that reliably guides behavior" (1992, 5). The response of the *Tao-te-ching* to this search for a constant *tao*, says Hansen, is to conclude that no constant guiding discourse is possible. The *Tao-te-ching* simply "analyzes the way in which discourse *daos* shape and polish us and our behavior" (1992, 209). His radically different interpretation results in a unique perspective on the text:

> Daoism is a *dao* about *dao*; it discourses about discourse, prescribes about prescription. It is a series of theories about *daos*. Laozi . . . wants to escape the socializing effects of language. (1992, 210)]

From this point of view, the meaning of the first line becomes, simply, "any prescriptive system put into words gives inconstant guidance" (1992, 216).

On the other hand, Kohn, La Fargue, and Graham have expressed the opinion that a mystical interpretation of the text is possible without positing Tao as a metaphysical reality. Kohn argues that "mystical traditions, however similar structurally, are fundamentally different. *Their absolutes are not one*" (1992, 38; italics mine). While she states that "the [Taoist] absolute is the Tao," she also emphasizes that Taoist mysticism is a worldly mysticism very different from what Hansen describes: "Oneness or union with the Tao is . . . natural to begin with, and becomes more natural as it is realized through practice . . . [it] is astounding only in the beginning" (1992, 12). Its focus and goal is not the mystical experience itself, but "transformation of body and mind" (1992, 11). Another non-stereotypical interpretation of Tao appears in A. C. Graham's *Disputers of the Tao*, which makes it very clear that "no Chinese thinker conceives the One and the constant as Being or Reality behind the veil of appearance" (1989, 222). Taoist mysticism is accordingly a practice with very practical goals: "The Taoist relaxes the body, calms the mind . . . frees the current of thought . . . lets his problems solve themselves" (1989, 234).

Graham blames Western misinterpretations of the *Tao-te-ching* on the fact that its readers are asking the wrong question. The question should not be the Western "What is the truth?" but the Chinese "Where is the Way?" (1989, 3). For him, too many interpreters probe the text trying to decode mysterious statements, which they believe reveal the nature of some ultimate reality, when in fact the *Tao-te-ching* is about values and a philosophy of life. It deconstructs traditional dichotomies like rich and poor, useful and useless, weak and strong, and teaches a practice that leads to a spontaneous awareness of a mature sense of values. In this spontaneous awareness lies the mystical experience.

LaFargue likewise insists that the *Tao-te-ching* does not refer to an "ineffable absolute" (1994, 268) and denies all religious claims of transcendence as the key to truth. Instead he describes the transcendent as an "aesthetic center" with a "surplus of meaning":

> This surplus of meaning is what makes Laoist Tao (and the focal centers of many other religions) "ineffable." Tao is not a symbol whose real referent is a metaphysical reality or principle. (1994, 288)

LaFargue prefers to substitute "the good" for the "transcultural objective Absolute, as the epistemological foundation for worldviews and religions" (1994, 269) because it is founded in experience rather than in principles, and theories about it are open to critical reflection. LaFargue's concept of "the good" is a challenging proposition for scholars of religion; its consideration goes far beyond the scope of this analysis (see LaFargue 1992). Be it only said that he, like other recent interpreters, is not hostile to the notion of Taoist mystical experience but also confines that experience to the realms of practice and practicality.

The deliberate appropriation of the *Tao-te-ching* as an antidote to Western problems has been virtually nonexistent among recent scholars, having given way to focus on the text within its Chinese cultural context. Still, many recent scholars of the *Tao-te-ching* have definite agendas based on personal opinions and personal needs and are unlikely to state those agendas. Graham's exceptional admission in this regard is refreshing:

> My personal philosophizing has always for better or worse influenced and been influenced by my reading of Chinese texts. We all seem to have some post-modernist vision of shaking up and realigning the conceptual scheme of the West. (1991, 297)

Hidden attitudes can make the process of evaluating biases in recent interpretations of the *Tao-te-ching* very difficult. Hostility toward opposing points of view is sometimes evident, as in the case of Hansen's attitude toward mysticism, but the agenda behind the hostility is usually difficult to discern. Because of the shortage of direct statements about these "post-modernist vision[s]," and also because most recent studies are lengthy and highly complex, recent scholarship on the *Tao-te-ching* is unlikely to have an immediate impact on popular understandings of the text—despite its dedication to correcting earlier misinterpretations.

Conclusion: Bad Scholarship—Good Religion?

Based on the interpretations of the second period of *Tao-te-ching* scholarship, popular books about Taoism, as well as input from other sources (notably Chinese and other Asian martial arts instructors), a popular understanding of Taoism has emerged in the West. Despite their titles, the most widely read popular books on Taoism—*The Tao of Pooh* (Hoff 1982), *The Tao Is Silent* (Smullyan 1977), *The Tao of Physics* (Capra 1975), and *The Dancing Wu-li Masters* (Zukav 1979)—have little to say about the *Tao-te-ching*. Quotations from the *Chuang-tzu* are far more frequent, and no attempt is made to distinguish between the philosophies of the two. Likewise these books tend to make no distinctions between

Buddhism (particularly Zen), Taoism, and even sometimes Hinduism. The following quotation from Fritjof Capra's *Tao of Physics* is indicative:

> Although these [Hinduism, Buddhism, and Taoism] comprise a vast number of subtly interwoven spiritual disciplines and philosophical systems, the basic features of their worldview are the same. (1975, 19)

> They all emphasize the basic unity of the universe which is the central feature of their teachings. The highest aim for their followers—whether they are Hindus, Buddhists or Taoists—is to become aware of the unity and mutual relation of all things, to transcend the notion of an isolated individual self and to identify themselves with the ultimate reality. (1975, 24)

Popular texts like Capra's assume that the *Tao-te-ching* mystically conveys a universal meaning that can serve as a solution to the problems of today's world. Despite the oversimplifications and outright errors made in these works, readers devour them for their philosophy, humor, and spiritual inspiration.

Taoism in the West today is not at all like Chinese Taoist religion. Very few Westerners have adopted its gods and goddesses, although there are a few organizations, such as the Tai Chi Society (Master Moy Lin-Shin) and Daoism of America (Master Charles Belyea), that have installed altars in their centers, worship Taoist gods, and celebrate Taoist (and Buddhist) festival days. Likewise, usually only those Westerners who practice Ch'i-kung, Tai-chi ch'üan, Inner Alchemy (as taught by Mantak Chia), or other forms of Taoist meditation and longevity, regard the *Tao-te-ching* as a manual explicating specific techniques. More typically, Western proponents of the text are not eager to form Taoist religious organizations because they interpret Taoism to be directly opposed to such institutions. Rather, they interpret the *Tao-te-ching* as an alternative to certain aspects of Western culture and/or religion. Some resist organized religious institutions in the belief that the text describes a way to be religious without having to go to church. Others object to the Western notion of God and understand the *Tao-te-ching* to be about an impersonal deity—absolute, immanent, or both. They may be equally likely to infer that it is about no deity at all and read the *Tao-te-ching* as an ethical expression that is independent of motivations like the divine retribution and eternal damnation they deem undesirable.

Many are also attracted to the notion of Tao as a way of life, a way of maintaining a kind of countercultural existence apart from, or in resistance to, mainstream values and institutions. Readers may be especially attracted to the reversal of values in the *Tao-te-ching*, to the notion that the useless can be useful, stupidity can be smart, ugly can be beautiful, and so forth. Many of the students with whom I have read the book over the years have been particularly persuaded by this aspect of the *Tao-te-ching*, as they feel personally trapped by an overemphasis on commercialism and a social orientation toward economic success; they often read the *Tao-te-ching* as a manifesto declaring freedom from these values. Seeing in it a philosophy opposed to mainstream institutions and religious organizations, they are undoubtedly influenced by earlier scholarly interpretations, such as those by Lin, Needham, and Welch, that emphasize the role of the text as an antidote to Western ills.

Yet other readers approach the *Tao-te-ching* as the spiritual expression of an ecological worldview. To them it supports notions of the interconnectedness of organic and inorganic matter and denies human dominion over nature, placing humanity solidly within the natural world instead.[7] Some of these readers admire antitechnology passages in the text and embrace it in service of a neo-Luddite agenda, while others employ it as a tool for expressing the importance of using technology and science in an ecologically sound manner.

Needham has been particularly influential among those who associate the *Tao-te-ching* with science. Needham's view that the observation of nature is an integral part of early Taoism is an important part of Capra's thesis in *The Tao of Physics* about parallels between "Eastern Mysticism" and modern physics. One can also hear echoes of Needham in Capra's description of the old paradigm that he claims modern physics is now replacing, a paradigm not only scientifically wrong but socially destructive. This was

> the view of the universe as a mechanical system composed of elementary building blocks, the view of the human body as a machine, the view of life as a competitive struggle for existence, the belief in unlimited material progress . . . [and] the belief that a society in which the female is everywhere subsumed under the male is one that is "natural." (1975, 325)

Like Needham, Capra believes that scientists are capable of creating a new ecological and humanistic view of the world, based on scientific proof of the unity of all matter. Capra suggests that, because of new discoveries in physics, a "new vision of reality [is] coalescing to form a powerful force of social transformation" (1975, 341). The persuasive style of his justification of a religious perspective in scientific terms is a major reason for the popularity of his work.[8] Still, for Capra and other popular interpreters, the implications of Tao in modern physics are brilliantly positive and even utopian, leaving out any mention of the fact that some of the same physicists they praise for their "Taoist" ideas contributed to the creation of nuclear bombs.

On the other hand, not everyone regards the impact of Tao on Western culture as an unmixed blessing. People like Michael Billington criticize the overly optimistic embrace of Tao, blaming the "cultural collapse" of the West on the "rock-sex-drug counterculture . . . heavily doused with Zen Buddhism, Taoism, and other forms of 'Chinese Mysticism'" (1994, 76). Due to the influence of this quasi-mysticism on scientists like Niels Bohr, Wolfgang Pauli, Carl Jung, Julian Huxley, and most especially Joseph Needham, he argues, the "irrational cult of environmentalism" has emerged as the "dominant paradigm of society and government." The result of this "perversion" has been that:

> The view of man as a rational being in the image of God, defined by his creative capacity to scientifically transform and advance his environment through higher-order technologies, has been largely replaced by the view of man as a mere beast, subject like any beast to the relative scarcity of resources available to a fixed level of technology. (1994, 76)]

Billington's words serve as a stern warning to idealists who assume that the *Tao-te-ching* will automatically have the same mystical, holistic, and positive impact on any reader.

Still, despite the opposition of people like him (a small minority when it comes to Western visions of the *Tao-te-ching*), and despite the frequent objections of scholars to the distortions in understanding of Chinese religion typical of most popular texts,[9] I personally do not think popular interpretations of the *Tao-te-ching* are entirely bad. I believe that we are witnessing changes in Western thought brought about by these interpretations which, while they may be the product of "bad scholarship," may be at the same time "good religion." I share with some earlier scholars like Needham and Welch, and with almost all popular interpreters, the opinion that certain values and modes of thought that predominate in the West are unhealthy. I regard the wave of new translations and *Tao-te-ching* related books[10] as a positive indication that there is widespread interest in nurturing other, healthier values and modes of thought such as those extolled by Welch, Needham, Fung, Lin, Capra, Hoff, and many others. Western interpretations of the *Tao-te-ching* may too often be grounded in bad scholarship, but, in my opinion, they frequently make good religion.

Notes

1. Schipper notes that he heard this same notion "as a boy in Holland, from the vicar at catechism" (1992, 3).

2. Wing-tsit Chan (1901–94), a notable scholar of Confucianism, was born in Canton, earned his Ph.D. from Harvard, and taught philosophy at Dartmouth College and Columbia University.

3. Fung Yu-lan (1895–1990) earned a doctorate in philosophy from Columbia University, but did not become a U.S. immigrant after his studies were completed. He only came back once, in 1946, as a visiting professor at the University of Pennsylvania.

4. Lin Yutang was born in Fukien Province in 1895. Although raised as the son of a Chinese Presbyterian minister, he repudiated Christianity in early adulthood. He studied at Harvard, and was a visiting professor at the Universities of Pennsylvania and Hawaii, but established his fame primarily as a writer of popular texts on Eastern religion. In 1966, he moved to Hong Kong, where he died a decade later.

5. Needham's ideas have been roundly criticized by many sinologists, most comprehensively and cogently by Nathan Sivin (1978; 1985).

6. Both Wing-tsit Chan and Richard Wilhelm's 1985 translator (from the German) defy the standard convention and use Tao without the definite article while yet continuing to capitalize the term. My practice in this article follows theirs. I first encountered the notion of eliminating the "the" in a popular work by Da Liu, unfortunately titled by inattentive editors, *The Tao and Chinese Culture*. Liu's reasoning is that the definite article transforms "a growing and vital reality" into an "intellectual abstraction" (1979, 2–3). Hansen's argument is much more radical.

7. For articles on Tao and the environment, see the journals *Environmental Ethics* and *Philosophy East and West*.

8. Capra's book was first published in 1975 and underwent revised editions in 1983 and 1991.

9. Debates between scholars and readers of popular interpretations

on various electronic discussion groups are frequently acrimonious and bitter. In 1994, a discussion group on Taoism broke out into a "flame war" of such proportions that the sponsors chose to close it down and institute in its place a group limited only to scholars and "serious" students of Taoism.

10. The 1995 edition of *Books in Print* lists about ninety books with titles of "Tao of" or "Tao and." Only a few of these are written by academics, and their subjects range from money, sex, relationships, mothering, cooking, and conversation to computer programming, sailing, architecture, teaching, and leadership. In addition, there are over thirty translations of the *Tao-te-ching* listed under that title, and about twenty-five books that have titles beginning with "Taoist" or "Taoism."

References

Abel-Rémusat, J.P. 1820. "Mémoire sur la vie et les ouvrages de Lao-tseu, philosophe chinois du VIe siècle avant nôtre-ère." *Mémoires de l'Academie des Inscriptions et Belles-Lettres* 7: 1–54.

Billington, Michael. 1994. "The Taoist Perversion of Twentieth-Century Science." *Fidelio: Journal of Pottery, Science and Statecraft*, Fall 1994: 76–96.

Capra, Fritjof. 1991 [1975]. *The Tao of Physics: An Exploration of the Parallels Between Modern Physics and Eastern Mysticism* Boston: Shambhala.

Carus, Paul. 1898. *Lao-tze's Tao-teh-king: Chinese English with Introduction*. Chicago: Open Court Publications.

Chan Wing-tsit. 1963. *The Way of Lao Tzu*. New York: Bobbs-Merrill.

Creel, Herrlee. 1956. "What Is Taoism?" *Journal of the American Oriental Society* 76: 139–52.

———. 1970. *What Is Taoism? and Other Studies of Chinese Cultural History*. Chicago: University of Chicago Press.

Fung Yu-lan. 1966 [1948]. *A Short History of Chinese Philosophy*, ed. Derk Bodde. New York: Free Press.

Giles, Lionel. 1905. *The Sayings of Lao Tzu*. London: John Murray.

Girardot, Norman J. 1983. *Myth and Meaning in Early Taoism: The Theme of Chaos (Hun-tun)*. Berkeley: University of California Press.

Graham, A. C. 1989. *Disputers of the Tao: Philosophical Argument in Ancient China*. LaSalle, Ill.: Open Court.

———. 1991. "Reflections and Replies." In *Chinese Texts and Philosophical Contexts:*

Essays Dedicated to Angus C. Graham, ed. Henry Rosemont Jr. 267–322. LaSalle, Ill.: Open Court.

Granet, Marcel. 1968 [1934]. *La pensée chinoise*. Paris: Éditions Albin Michel.

Hansen, Chad. 1992. *A Daoist Theory of Chinese Thought: A Philosophical Interpretation*. Oxford: Oxford University Press.

Hardy, Julia M. 1990. "Archaic Utopias in the Modern Imagination." Ph.D. dissertation, Duke University.

Hoff, Benjamin. 1982. *The Tao of Pooh*. New York: E. P. Dutton.

Julien, Stanislas. 1842. *Le livre de la voie et de la vertu*. Paris: Imprimérie Royale.

Kaltenmark, Max. 1969. *Lao Tzu and Taoism*. Translated by Roger Greaves. Stanford, Calif.: Stanford University Press.

Kirkland, Russell. 1992. "Person and Culture in the Taoist Tradition." *Journal of Chinese Religions* 20: 77–90.

Kohn, Livia. 1992. *Early Chinese Mysticism: Philosophy and Soteriology in the Taoist Tradition*. Princeton, N.J.: Princeton University Press.

LaFargue, Michael. 1992. "Radically Pluralist, Thoroughly Critical: A New Theory of Religions." *Journal of the American Academy of Religion* 60: 693–716.

———. 1994. *Tao and Method: A Reasoned Approach to the Tao-te-ching*. Albany: State University of New York Press.

Legge, James. 1962 [1891]. *The Texts of Taoism*, vol. 1. New York: Dover.

Lin Yutang. 1942. *The Wisdom of China and India*. New York: Modern Library.

Liu, Da. 1979. *The Tao and Chinese Culture*. New York: Schocken Books.

Maspero, Henri. 1981 [1971]. *Taoism and Chinese Religion*. Translated by Frank A. Kierman Jr. Amherst: University of Massachusetts Press.

Needham, Joseph. 1956. *Science and Civilisation in China*. Vol. II: *History of Scientific Thought*. Cambridge: Cambridge University Press.

Overmyer, Daniel L., David Keightley, Edward Shaughnessy, Constance Cook, and Donald Harper. 1995. "Chinese Religions: The State of the Field (II)." *Journal of Asian Studies* 54: 314–95.

Said, Edward. 1979. *Orientalism*. New York: Vintage Books.

Schwartz, Benjamin I. 1985. *The World of Thought in Ancient China*. Cambridge, Mass.: Harvard University Press.

Schipper, Kristofer. 1992. "The History of Taoist Studies in Europe." Paper presented at the International Symposium on the History of European Sinology, Taipei.

Seidel, Anna. 1990. "Chronicle of Taoist Studies in the West 1950–1990." *Cahiers d'Extrême-Asie* 5: 223–347.

Sivin, Nathan. 1978. "On the Word 'Taoist' as a Source of Perplexity, with Special Reference to the Relations of Science and Religion in Traditional China." *History of Religions* 17: 303–29.

————. 1985. "Max Weber, Joseph Needham, Benjamin Nelson: The Question of Chinese Science." In *Civilizations East and West: A Memorial Volume for Benjamin Nelson*, ed. E. V. Walter, V. Kavolis, E. Leites, and M. C. Nelson, 37–49. Atlantic Highlands, N.J.: Humanities Press.

Strickmann, Michel. 1979. "On The Alchemy of T'ao Hung-ching." In *Facets of Taoism: Essays in Chinese Religion*, ed. Holmes Welch and Anna Seidel, 123–92. New Haven, Conn.: Yale University Press, 1979.

Smullyan, Raymond M. 1977. *The Tao is Silent*. New York: Harper & Row.

Thompson, Lawrence G. 1993. "What is Taoism? (With Apologies to H.G. Creel)." *Taoist Resources* 4.2: 9–22.

Waley, Arthur. 1958 [1934]. *The Way and Its Power: A Study of the Tao-te-ching* and Its Place in Chinese Thought. New York: Grove Press.

Welch, Holmes. 1965. *Taoism: The Parting of the Way*. Boston: Beacon Press.

Welch, Holmes, and Anna Seidel, eds. 1979. *Facets of Taoism: Essays in Chinese Religion*. New Haven, Conn.: Yale University Press.

Wilhelm, Richard. 1985 [1915]. *Lao Tzu, Tao-te-ching*: The Book of Meaning and Life. London: Arkana/Penguin Books.

Zukav, Gary. 1979. *The Dancing Wu Li Masters: An Overview of the New Physics*. New York: William Morrow.

The Thought of the Tao-te-ching

Benjamin Schwartz

The text known in ancient China as the *Lao-tzu* after its alleged author, and later as the *Tao-te-ching*, is one of the most frequently translated and yet one of the most difficult and problematic texts in all of Chinese literature.[1] It has been described as many things: a handbook of prudent mundane life philosophy, a treatise on political strategy, an esoteric treatise on military strategy, a utopian tract, or a text that advocates "a scientific naturalistic" attitude toward the cosmos. Many elements suggestive of these various interpretations are indeed present in the work. However, to the extent that they are, they have their locus within a vision that I would maintain is as mystical as any orientation to which that term has been applied in any other culture. In the following, I shall therefore begin with precisely the mystical dimension of the *Tao-te-ching*, to then pursue its views on nature and possible tendencies of "scientific" naturalism, its understanding of humanity and human society, and, finally, its political perspective. The thought of the *Tao-te-ching* emerges as multifaceted and endlessly adaptable to many-layered interpretations. Yet its mystical dimension remains essential.

Mysticism and Organic Order

Among students of comparative religion, there seems to be some consensus concerning the earmarks of mystical orientations in religion. In all of them we find some notion of "ground of reality" or ultimate aspect of reality or a dimension of "nonbeing" (naturally all metaphors when applied to the ineffable are suspect), which cannot be discussed in the categories of human language. It is a reality or dimension of reality beyond all determinations, relations, and processes which can be described in human language. Yet the mere assertion of the existence of such a reality does not in itself constitute mysticism. It is rather the profound faith or "knowledge" in the sense of gnosis that this reality—incommunicable in words—is nevertheless the source of all meaning for human beings, which makes mysticism in some sense a religious outlook. The "mystery" is not an absence of "knowledge" but a kind of higher direct knowledge of the ineffable source of all that lends existence meaning. It thus refers to a plenitude rather than to an absence, but a plenitude beyond the grasp of language. In most orientations which have been called mystical there is, then, the assumption that finite humans or some finite humans can achieve oneness or some kind of mystic union with the ultimate ground of reality.

All the above factors are, I think, present in and even central to the visions of the *Tao-te-ching*. Yet again, there is no such thing as mysticism in general. Taoism is obviously as *sui generis* as is Mahāyāna Buddhism, Brahmanism, Sufism, and Christian and Jewish mysticism. The ineffable reality itself cannot, in principle, be differentiated, since it is by definition beyond all definition, but the paradoxical fact remains that most mysticisms have, of course, attempted to use language to convey their truth. To the extent that they do so, their dominant metaphors and the ways in which they relate their mysticism to all aspects of their cultural heritage and historical situation profoundly color their entire vision. Here the orientations of the culture become fully operative.

Beginning, therefore, with the mystical dimension of Taoism, one is immediately struck by the use of the word "Tao" as the dominant term. How does a term, which in Confucianism refers mainly to social and natural order, indicate a mystic reality? Let me make two observations at the outset. First, as a mystical text, like similar works, the *Tao-te-ching* is not deeply committed to the term itself: "I do not know its name, so I style it the *Tao*. If forced to name it, I would call it *great*" (ch. 25).[2] And second, when the *Tao-te-ching* uses the term "Tao" to refer to the world of "determinate being," to the world of the "ten thousand things," it still retains its meaning of encompassing order.

How, then, may a word which refers to *order* come to have a mystical meaning? In the modern West, words which refer to "impersonal order," or "structure," to use the most common contemporary metaphor, seem to suggest the very antithesis of the mystical. A structure is something totally transparent to our analysis. We know what it is made of and how it is put together. Ideally, it should contain no mysteries. But the concept of order found in China is not a structure in this sense. It is the total organic pattern, not at all something "built up" out of parts. I am, of course, well aware that even in the modern West, the literal sense of the word "structure" as "something that has been built" has been largely abandoned. We thus speak of "emerging structures," and this seems to imply a *gestalt* emerging as a totality. Still, so long as one thinks of an order, whether spatial or temporal, as an immanent whole, one notes that it is composed of a multitude of separate components and relations and yet what holds the whole together is not in the parts. It is the elusive whole that holds the parts together. To the extent that there is an order, there is also some kind of ungraspable principle or unity at its heart. Indeed, in a dynamic order, the elements and the relations may undergo great change, as in the processes of biological growth, and yet the principle of unity will remain.

Much of what I have said here reminds us of Needham's conception of the dominance of "organismic philosophy" in China (1956). However, one must ask—what does the word "organism" mean? What is the nature of the whole which envelops and determines the parts? At one point, Needham flatly states that one would not wish to deny that ancient Taoist thought had strong elements of mysticism (1956, 35). On the whole, however, he is painfully anxious to disassociate his conception of organism from mystical implications. He thus states that in the Chinese conception of organism, "the parts, in their organizational relations whether of a living body or the universe were sufficient to account by a kind of harmony of wills, for the observed phenomena" (1956, 302). He then, however, adds, "the cooperation of the component parts of the organism is not forced but absolutely spontaneous, even involuntary."

Now, "harmony of wills" and "cooperation" are terms that seem to suggest separate entities which "voluntarily" come together to cooperate by express design. The image suggests that the parts somehow exist as "individuals" before they come to "cooperate." Needham, however, hastens to erase this impression by implying that in fact the "organizational relations" are really logically prior to the parts, and he makes it quite clear that the cooperation of the parts is, in fact, "involuntary" and really determined by the whole. All these terms—organizational relations, organizing principle, organism, process, and so on—seem to point to some kind of determinable knowledge about something quite definite, while the *Tao-te-ching* apparently insists that what accounts for the order as a whole as well as the "spontaneous" behavior of the parts is itself beyond language. What, indeed, is an "organizing principle" *an sich*? If a term like "organizing principle" is meant to refer to anything describable and definite, it is not the Tao in its ineffable aspect of nonbeing. The *Tao-te-ching*, however, prefers not to name the unnameable or to imply any knowledge of "how it works."

The Tao

The mysticism of the *Tao-te-ching* does not rest on a theistic metaphor. The insistence on the word *tao* represents a striking departure from the centrality of the word "heaven" in other forms of Chinese thought of the period. The word *heaven* here often carries with it some sense of a conscious, guiding force; it remains the central term even in the *Lun-yü* (Analects) of Confucius. Heaven may already be immanent in the processes of nature, its presence in nature may manifest itself in the way of nonaction, yet in its relation to the human world, heaven still seems to have intentional and providential associations. Thus, in generally preferring the word "Tao" to the word "heaven" to express the ultimate, the *Tao-te-ching* may be fully aware of the associations with deliberate action (*yu-wei*) clustering about the term *heaven*. In the very first passage of the text as it is now arranged, we find the statement, "the nameless is the beginning of heaven and earth." Elsewhere we find it stated with regard to the Tao that, "I know not whose son it is; it seems that it precedes the High God" (ch. 4). Here heaven and earth are not the ultimate. One can make determinate statements about them and, like all determinate things, they are finite and perhaps not eternal. There is, in fact, a definite implication that the whole determinate universe may arise in time and disappear in time. The theme of the inaccessibility of the ultimate reality to language is a basic theme in the *Tao-te-ching* and in the *Chuang-tzu*, and here we are again forcefully reminded of the early emergence in China of the "language" question. Confucius deeply believed in language as providing an image of true order and Mohism groped toward the notion of a new, improved language which would provide a new and more precise picture of the world in all its particularities. The *Tao-te-ching*, while not casting doubt on the language describing the natural order (although it does indeed cast doubt on the received language descriptive of the human order), finds that that which makes the determinate Tao possible lies beyond all language.

What the *Tao-te-ching* dwells on is the impermanent, finite nature of all the determinate realities of which one can speak. Hence the ringing assertion in the first line of the text as now constituted:

> The Tao of which one can speak
> Is not the eternal [or permanent?] Tao;
> The names which one can name
> Are not the eternal name. (ch. 1)

This is not Vedanta. The world of our ordinary experience does not seem to be a cosmic illusion (*māyā*) projected by the absolute. In addition to the Tao in its unnameable dimension, there is Tao in its aspect as the "speakable" and there are the "ten thousand things," which can be named. Indeed, the image of the world which can be named is in the *Tao-te-*

ching quite "commonsensical." Yet a major characteristic of this world, however real, is its impermanence related to its determinate finitude.

The Tao in its aspect of the ineffable eternal is nondeterminate and nameless. It cannot be identified with anything nameable. It is *wu* or nonbeing. I translate this word here with a term often used in Western writings on mysticism, since it seems to correspond adequately to its use in the translation of mystical literature in other cultures. *Wu* is a reality which corresponds to no determinate finite entity, relation, or process which can be named. Yet it is eminently "real" and the source of all finite reality. The neutral belief in such a reality would not constitute mysticism, but the *Tao-te-ching* is indeed not neutral.

Some thirty of the eighty-one chapters of the book deal with the mystic dimension and they are among the most poetic and rhapsodic in the entire text. Here, as elsewhere in mystical literature, we find the constant paradoxical effort to speak about the unspeakable.

> Born before heaven and earth—silent and void,
> It stands alone and does not change.
> Pervading all things, it does not weary. (ch. 25)

> Gaze on it, there is nothing to see,
> It is called invisible.
> Listen to it, there is nothing to hear,
> It is called the inaudible.
> Grasp it, you cannot hold it,
> It is called the ungraspable.
> It is called the form of the formless,
> The image of the imageless. (ch. 14)

> The Tao is broad, reaching left and right;
> The ten thousand things depend on it for life.
> Yet it does not desert them.
> It accomplishes its task,
> Yet claims no merit. (ch. 34)

> You cannot keep it close, you cannot keep it far off.
> You cannot benefit it nor can you name it. . . .
> You cannot ennoble it or debase it. (ch. 56)

The point at which Taoism, like other mysticisms, takes on its own specific character as Taoism is that mysterious region where the world of nonbeing comes to relate to the world of the determinate, the individuated, and the related, or perhaps literally in Chinese, to the world of the "there is" (*yu*). We have already noted that in the first chapter of the *Tao-te-ching* one of the main factors which divides being from nonbeing is the eternity of nonbeing and the transience and finitude of being. There is, however, no implication that the transient and finite is either "unreal" or intrinsically "evil" as such.

The dominant metaphor which emerges here, as in the case of other mystical outlooks, is crucial to the entire vision. In the *Tao-te-ching*, we thus find the statement, "the nameless is the beginning of Heaven and Earth; the named [or nameable?] is the mother of the ten thousand things" (ch. 1). The use of the metaphor of the mother is most striking. It reminds us of the centrality of the biological-generative metaphor even in the earliest Chinese religious orientation and of the highly positive familial, nurturing associations which surround this term. It suggests a definitely benign and affirmative view not only of the principle of individuation but of the world of entities which have been brought into being. This mysticism does not negate nature. It affirms nature. Here we find a striking contrast with early Buddhism with its revulsion against the principle of individuation and its deep apprehension of the differentiated cosmos as a realm of suffering. The thought of the text, like that of the *Lun-yü* and the *Chuang-tzu*, has for some reason been able to attain a lofty indifference to the question of creaturely suffering so dominant in early Buddhism. Such an attitude allows one to relate to nature in wholly affirmative terms.

The use of the metaphor of the mother, however, also calls our attention to another major theme of the *Tao-te-ching*—its exaltation of the feminine as the symbol of the principles of nonaction (*wu-wei*) and "spontaneity" (*tzu-jan*), which link the world of nature to its source in nonbeing.

> The spirit of the valley never dies;
> This is called the mysterious female.
> The gateway of the mysterious female
> Is called the root of heaven and earth.
> It continues on as if ever present,
> And in its use, it is inexhaustible. (ch. 6)

Here the symbol of the valley whose nature is wholly determined by its empty space and its passive receptivity to all that flows into it seems to be related to the sexual and generative role of the female. The female role in sex is ostensibly passive. Yet the "female conquers the male by stillness; in stillness she occupies the lower position" (chap. 61). Essentially, it is the female who plays the leading role in the procreative process.

She acts "by not acting" in both the sex act and in generation. She thus represents the nonassertive, the uncalculating, the nondeliberative, nonpurposive processes of generation and growth—the processes by which the "empty" gives rise to the full, the quiet gives rise to the active, and the one gives rise to the many. The female is the epitome of nonaction. While nonbeing is itself unnameable, one nevertheless has the impression throughout that the passive, the empty, the "habitual," and the nonassertive aspects of nature are emblematic of and point toward the realm of "nonbeing." In the *Tao-te-ching*, the nonhuman cosmos and even the "natural" aspects of human life operate in this spontaneous and nonactive fashion. Therefore, one can say that nature abides in the Tao and that in nature there is no rupture between nonbeing and being. The nonactive aspect of nature is the manifestation of the Tao in its "nonbeing" aspect, and nature thus abides in the Tao.

Nature and "Scientific" Naturalism

Nature in the *Tao-te-ching* is processes not guided by a teleological consciousness. Despite the pathos suggested by the use of the image of the mother with its nurturant associations, the Tao is not consciously providential. "Heaven and earth are not benevolent; they treat the ten thousand things as straw dogs" (chap. 5). Heaven and earth do not concern themselves with the weal or woe of individual humans or of other creatures. One indeed may say that Lao-tzu's nature is an order that runs spontaneously and without deliberate planning or premeditation. This indeed is its glory and its mystery.

Then again, the nature which appears in the *Tao-te-ching* is the nature of our ordinary experience and nothing more. There are observations of natural processes in the book. There is a particular preoccupation with the dyadic opposites of nature—masculine and feminine, dark and light, weak and strong, hard and soft, dynamic and passive—which reminds us of similar concerns in Anaximander and Heraclitus. One already finds the notion of yin and yang in its abstract meaning of the general principle of dyadic complementary and/or opposition. These observations and ideas probably belong to the accepted current views of nature in the intellectual world of the time. An examination of the passages involved indicates, however, that the point is never that of simply making a "scientific observation." There is no evidence whatsoever (such as we find in abundance in the Mo-tzu) of any desire of the *Tao-te-ching*'s author to know the causes of separate things and events or to use scientific knowledge for technical purposes.

The treatment of dyadic opposites in the text, while having no necessary relationship to "scientific inquiry," does, to be sure, raise a problem from the point of view of the mystic core of the book. While the terms of the various dyads are often treated as equal, they are sometimes given unequal weights, indicating the presence of an unexpected moralistic torque, which would create a problem from both a "value-free scientific" as well as a "mystical" point of view. Lau has pointed out the obvious and striking "asymmetry" in the *Tao-te-ching* view of the female versus the male, the weak versus the strong, the soft versus the hard, and the passive versus the active (1958, 2). In all cases, the first term of the dyad is definitely "preferred." It enjoys a higher "ontological" status, just as water is preferred to stone; it seeks lowly places, and it is, in a more profound sense, stronger than stone.

When dealing with organic life, there is the powerful metaphor of the superiority of infancy.

> Man when born is soft and weak;
> When he dies, he is hard and solid.
> The ten thousand things—grass and trees—
> Are born soft and supple.
> When they die, they are withered and hard.
> Therefore, the hard and the strong are the
>   companions of death;
> The soft and weak are the companions of life. (ch. 76)

Elsewhere, the infant is portrayed as full of an unformed and undifferentiated potency. The *Tao-te-ching* is not asserting that the unfavored sides of these dyads are not parts of the order of nature. Rather, it seems to assert that things emerge from nonbeing in their soft, undefined, fluid, and therefore truly potent states. They are thus, at least in some sense, closer to the heart of the Tao. As they progress to hardness, crystallization, and clear differentiation, they are more isolated and cut off from the source of being. In the end, death which allows creatures to "return to the mother" releases them from their hardness and isolation. It is, however, clear that all of this reflects the continuing overwhelming concern of the *Tao-te-ching* with human life and hence the presence of a somewhat inconsistent "humanism," which it seems to share with its predecessors. The mysticism of the text is thus closely linked to the injunction in the imperative mode, "Abide by the soft!" This injunction clearly indicates that the discussion of the "dialectic" of nature reflects not any concern with scientific investigation, but an abiding interest in restoring a "natural" way of life for human beings during their sojourn within the kingdom of the ten thousand things. It is, indeed, an impulse which is in deep tension not only with any alleged "scientific" propensity but with mysticism to the extent that mysticism points to a realm "beyond good and evil." The *Tao-te-ching* is not entirely free from "value judgment."

A word must also be said about the general attitude toward "learning" and "knowledge" in the *Tao-te-ching*. In responding to passages such as,

> He who engages in learning daily increases.
> He who deals with the Tao daily decreases,
> Decreases further until he attains nonaction. (ch. 48)

Needham states that "what they [the Taoists] attacked was Confucian scholastic knowledge of the ranks and observances of feudal society— not the knowledge of the Tao of nature" (1956, 33). Now, one need not doubt that the *Tao-te-ching* devalues the Confucian knowledge of ranks and observances, but there is again no evidence whatsoever that it recommends the pursuit of knowledge of nature's workings. There is, in fact, some evidence to the contrary.

When the *Tao-te-ching* attacks the "knowing the beautiful as beautiful" and further asserts that "the five colors blind the eye, the five notes deafen the ears, and the five tastes injure the palate" (ch. 12), I suspect that it sees the careful observation, dissection, and analysis of the differentiated characteristics of the world of nature as closely connected with the human fixation on ever more differentiated and varied consumer pleasures and for "goods which are hard to come by." The observer of nature cannot be indifferent to an accurate observation of "sense data." The text thus seems mainly concerned that the sharp discrimination of these sense qualities is intimately linked to the obsessive desire for sensual pleasure.

The desire for such goods, whether by feudal rulers or the masses who emulate them, are as much a part of the "artificial" civilization which the *Tao-te-ching* rejects as are "ranks and observances." Thus, when it says that the sage is "for the belly and not for the eye" (ch. 12), we may interpret this fairly literally. The belly refers to the simplest satisfaction of basic biological needs, while the eye refers to the careful discrimination of the outer sensual qualities of things so necessary to "sophisticated" pleasure. The careful and close observation of the properties of things may well have been associated with the craftsmen who created the "unnatural" luxuries of high civilization.

On the other side, there is the telling passage in which the *Tao-te-ching* asserts that

> Without stepping out of one's door,
> One knows the world.
> Without looking out of the window,
> One sees the way of heaven.
> The further one goes, the less one knows. (ch. 47)

Here the knowledge referred to seems to be mystic gnosis; it would appear that purely empirical knowledge of any kind is depreciated. The kind of careful "observation of nature," of which Needham speaks, was certainly to flourish in China. Yet there seems to be little ground for assuming that it had anything to do with the vision we find in the *Tao-te-ching*. On the contrary, the systematic and careful "scientific" observation of nature would seem to be precisely one of those highly deliberate, calculating, and intentional projects which in no way corresponds to the spirit of nonaction. Again, this does not mean that the *Tao-te-ching* and particularly the *Chuang-tzu* were not *au courant* of the ideas of nature available in their time. It means, however, that the notion that they were fundamentally concerned with the devotion of energy to the "scientific" observation of nature either as an end in itself or as a means to technical ends remains totally unproven.

The Human Realm

Lau has asserted that the *Tao-te-ching*, like other ancient Chinese philosophical texts, was fundamentally interested in advocating a way of life and that here, as elsewhere, "no fast line was drawn between morals and politics" (1958, 356). Although I have here begun my consideration of the book with a focus on its mystical dimension, I would not deny its fundamental concern with the human realm. It is, in fact, the relationship between these two dimensions—both of them equally important—that constitutes the heart of the vision as well as of the problematic aspects of this vision. To the extent that human beings as creatures "abide" in the Tao, they are part of that world of nature which the *Tao-te-ching* affirms. All the instinctive, "autonomous" aspects of man's biological life operate within the realm of nonaction, and one might say that human life on its simplest, vegetative "programmed" level unites the human to the Tao and may be considered good. One might also say that the urge to preserve life on this level is also good. Here is where we find the Yang Chu strain imbedded in the *Tao-te-ching*.[3] The ordinary, unreflective, nondiscriminating man immersed in the routines and habits of a simple life who clings to the sweetness of "mere living" is, at least on one level, at one with the Tao.

I say "on one level," because there does seem also to be the infinitely higher level of the gnosis of the Taoist sage. The emphasis on the prudent, "mundane" clinging to mere living is illustrated throughout the book. While one possesses life, one savors it, yet one is ready to leave it without regret. To the extent that threats to life come from war, political ambition, strife, and the competition for power and wealth, or even from the self-conscious pursuit of moral programs of "uplift," as in the case of both Confucianists and Mohists, these threats arise out of the pathologies of civilization and should be avoided at all costs.

> Your name [in the sense of reputation] or your person—
>   which is dearer to you?
> Your person or your goods—which is worth more?
> Know where to stop, be content with your lot
> And you will not be disgraced.
> Know when to stop and you will meet no danger.
> Then you can then live long. (ch. 44)

> Cause the people not to treat death lightly
> And not to wander off to distant places. (ch. 80)

As for the inevitable pains inflicted by the Tao and the prospect of death by natural causes, the Taoist sage in *Tao-te-ching* seems prepared to accept them with the utmost equanimity. He accepts his destiny to live and his destiny to die. Despite the appreciation of life, the *Tao-te-ching* at one point even states that "the reason I have trouble is that I have a body. When I no longer have a body, what trouble have I?" (ch. 13). Lau finds that since "survival is assumed without question to be the supreme goal of life," this passage clearly "goes against the general tenor of the book" (1963, 42). This remark, however, strongly reflects Lau's own unwillingness to take seriously the centrality of the book's mystical dimension. Survival may be the supreme goal in life, but to the man of gnosis able to identify with nonbeing, life itself with its ever-present threat of trouble is not the supreme value. He will not sacrifice life for illusory goods, but he is quite prepared to abandon it when his time comes.

The word *hsing* for "human nature" does not occur in the *Tao-te-ching*. One suspects that, as a mystic who believed that at least some had the power to become "one with the Tao," its author shied away from any tendency to fix human capacities within any finite groove. The word *hsing* had become linked with the question of the innate capacity to conform to a normative social order, which the *Tao-te-ching* rejects. Nevertheless, its entire discussion of human affairs is based on the premise

that the "natural" desires of people who abide in the Tao are in themselves limited and simple. So long as they are not exposed to the lures of
false desires and aspirations, they can be kept in their pristine natural
state.

> Not to value goods which are hard to come by
> Will keep the people from theft.
> Not to display that which is desirable
> Will keep the people's minds from being confused. . . .
> The sage empties their minds and fills their bellies;
> Weakens their wills and strengthens their bones.
> He sees to it that they constantly
> Remain without knowledge and without desires. (ch. 3)

"Emptying the mind" (a term also applicable to the Taoist sage) means
removing all the false goals and projects of higher civilization and re-
turning the mind to the pervasive sway of the Tao. "If we are without
desires people will themselves become simple [like the uncarved block]"
(ch. 57). Again, "desires" in this context do not seem to mean the simple
satisfaction of biological instinctive needs for food, sex, and shelter, but
the kinds of desires and needs created by civilization. The "filling of the
belly" is the very antithesis of the gourmet's calculating project of invent-
ing ever new ways of interesting his jaded palate.

At this point, however, the inevitable question arises: How does the
breach with the Tao occur in the human sphere? The first answer seems
to be that it is due to the rise of civilization. It is thus quite correct to call
the *Tao-te-ching* a "primitivist" tract, an attack on the entire project of
civilization. But why does civilization arise? Here our focus shifts to the
mysterious emergence within the human mind of an unprecedented
new kind of consciousness that seems to exist nowhere else in nature.
Somehow within the Eden of the Tao, there arises the deliberative, analytic mind which has the fatal capacity to isolate the various forms,
constituents, and forces of nature from their places in the whole in which
they abide, to become fixated on them, to make them the objects of newly
invented desires and aspirations. The human mind itself becomes,
through this new consciousness, isolated from the flow of the Tao and
finds its meaning in asserting its separate existence against the whole.
An entire new world of conscious goals is posited—goals of new sensual
gratifications, pleasures, wealth, honor, power even the goal of individual
moral perfection. Thus, the "great artifice" is born (ch. 10).

As we have seen, the hard, the assertive, the strong, and the ugly
exist in nature itself, but in nature they are not isolated from their oppo-

sites or from the whole. This new deceptive consciousness has, however, the power of isolating them and fixing them. It itself becomes an
embodiment of the hard, the analytical, the aggressive, and the self-
encapsulated. It brings all things into hard, clear focus, removing them
from the harmonious hazy state in which they naturally abide. Among
the discriminations now made are the clear discriminations between the
beautiful and the ugly, the good and the bad.

> The world knows that the beautiful is beautiful,
> Thus the ugly is posited.
> Everyone knows the good as good,
> Thus the evil is posited. (ch. 2)

In nature, all opposites are mutually dependent, and yet in the sphere
of ethics and aesthetics, we would absolutize one of the poles and attempt
to eliminate the other. The other pole is, however, never destroyed. It
simply also stands out in its isolated clarity. The true evil here is the
conscious intent to pursue the "good" in isolation as an end in itself. In a
state of nature, the ugly and the "not good," whatever that may be, are
imbedded in the harmonious whole. While the hardness and strength
are part of the "ecology" of the Tao, they are in nature transfigured by
the higher good of spontaneity and nonaction in which they abide. There
is a long passage which describes a decline from the highest "embodiment of the Tao" (virtue, *te*) to a complete alienation from the Tao (the
point of reference seems to be to the sage-ruler).

> The man of highest virtue does not manifest his virtue,
> Therefore, he has virtue;
> The man of lowest virtue [is concerned] not to lose virtue,
> Therefore, he is without virtue. (ch. 38)

The possessor of the highest virtue is unconscious of it and, one might
say, without any self-consciousness. Thus, the virtue simply manifests
itself in all his behavior. There then somehow emerges the self-conscious
concern with the possibility of "losing virtue." The highest virtue is
nonaction without deliberate consideration—a term which seems to
mean something like a conscious concern with specific sequences of
action. The man of lower virtue is, therefore, conscious of such specific
consequences and must be concerned with not losing his virtue. He is
thus already in the realm of deliberate action.

The Confucian man of benevolence (*jen*) who may represent the
highest level of the lowest virtue, then, acts with conscious intent of

becoming good but he still does not dwell on the specific consequences of his acts. In Lau's translation of the *Tao-te-ching*, he is not, however, without "ulterior motive" in the broadest sense of the term. The man of righteousness (*yi*), one step further down, is wholly oriented to the external consequence of his acts. We then make the plunge to those whose action is based on the contrived rules of ritual propriety (*li*), conceiving of it as an instrument for controlling society "out there." Here we already have the kind of person who, when others do not respond to the sway of ritual, will "bare his arm and use force" (ch. 38). We note in all this not only a decline from nonaction to deliberate action, but also from the inner to the outer—from inner virtue to external machinery. From the assertion of the ego in "goodness" one descends to the assertion of the ego manifesting itself in aggression, greed, and violence. The connecting link between Confucian benevolence and wickedness is the goal-directed consciousness.

In such paradoxical statements, as when the *Tao-te-ching* proclaims "that when the six family relations are no longer in harmony, one has filial piety and parental kindness" (ch. 18), one notes that, so long as this deliberate, deceptive consciousness had not arisen, the harmonious pattern of family and social life as described by Confucius may have in fact existed "naturally" as it does among the programmed "social" animals. Did the harmony break down because of the emergence of moral depravity, which led men to be highly conscious of the need for virtue? Or were both self-conscious morality and moral depravity fruits of the same deliberative and purposeful consciousness? Do they both derive from the same "tree of knowledge of good and evil"? It would seem that the latter was, in fact, the case. Benevolence, righteousness, skill, and the search for utility all grow from the same root. As the text says,

> Cut off benevolence, abandon righteousness,
> And the people will return to filial piety and kindness;
> Cut off skill and abandon utility,
> And robbers and thieves will disappear. (ch. 19)

The *Tao-te-ching* does indeed attack the more obvious evils of civilization in a prophetic spirit:

> The people are hungry;
> It is because those above devour too much in
>   taxes. (ch. 75)

> The court is corrupt,
> The fields are overgrown with weeds.

> The granaries are empty,
> Yet there are those dressed in finery
> With swords at their sides and filled with food
>   and drink. (ch. 53)

> Where troops have encamped,
> There will brambles grow. . . .
> In the wake of mighty armies,
> Bad harvests follow without fail. (ch. 30)

Yet these obvious social evils seem to be quintessentially part of the project of civilization as such and the false human consciousness which lies behind it. If this false consciousness originated anywhere, it would seem to have originated first among the Confucian culture heroes who dreamed of "improving on nature" by concentrating attention on the "good" and the "beautiful." It was inevitable that others would arise to assert their egos against the Tao in even cruder and more direct ways. The particular animus of the *Tao-te-ching* against ritual propriety seems to reflect the belief that these rules and prescriptions are contrived out of the Confucian realization that benevolence and righteousness as moral influences will simply not work against the more obvious evils of society. Hence the need to contrive all the external rules of ritual.

The Political Perspective

Can we then say that the *Tao-te-ching* represents a primitive anarchism and a total rejection of political order and hierarchy? In the West, we would generally associate this with any primitivism. Yet the fact remains that the text abounds in advice and exhortations addressed to rulers. Some interpreters indeed firmly believe that it is primarily a treatise on statecraft and even on military strategy. The text itself provides us with no historic account of any devolution from a state of nature to the rise of civilization, although many passages in the *Chuang-tzu*, which seem closely allied to the *Tao-te-ching* outlook, provide such accounts. We thus read of an ancient state of affairs in which men

> lived the same as birds and beasts, grouped themselves side by side with the ten thousand things. Who then would know anything about "gentleman" or "petty man"? Dull and unwitting, they had no wisdom, so their virtue did not depart from them. . . .
>
> However, along came the sages, huffing and puffing after benevolence, reaching on tiptoe for righteousness, and the world for the first time had doubts. (*Chuang-tzu* 9; Watson 1968, 105)

Here indeed we seem to have something like a primitive harmonious anarchy followed by the unaccountable rise of a new notion of good and evil among those called the sages. It is not implied even here that the sages were the evil "kings and priests" of the Western eighteenth-century Enlightenment. They were bent on benevolence, righteousness, and world improvement, but in them the insidious consciousness of deliberate action first emerged.

It is also interesting to note that even the author of this passage takes for granted the existence of a political order in the state of nature. He assumes that even then there had been the exemplary Taoist sage-ruler Ho Hsü, who had maintained humankind in its pristine innocence through the power of his virtue. In the *Tao-te-ching*, we find the universal rule mentioned as one of the four fundamental components of the cosmos—the Tao, heaven, earth, and kingship (ch. 25). Here we have a clear illustration of how the pervasive cultural orientation toward the mediating role of sage-rulers is present even in the *Tao-te-ching* strain of Taoism with its strong "humanistic" concern. One might say that in a true Taoist society, the authority of the truly Taoist universal king may be as "natural" as the presence of the dominant male in the group life of many higher mammals. However one may account for the origins of human civilization, it is suggested throughout the text that only Taoist sage-rulers can reverse the pathology of civilization. The *Tao-te-ching*, indeed, offers advice not only to potential "universal kings" but even to the princes of states of ancient China. As in the case of Confucius and Mo-tzu, the compiler of the text does not seem to believe that the masses can save themselves, exposed as they are to both the seductions of civilization and the oppressions inflicted by civilization. Having been exposed to false consciousness, the masses participate in it fully and long to share in the goals of their masters. They can hardly transcend their environment. If civilization began with the false consciousness of the proto-Confucius sages of the past, it is now only sages who have achieved the higher mystic gnosis who can save the mass of people from the pathologies of civilization.

The Taoist sage alone can put an end to the artificial projects of civilization and allow the majority of people to return to a state of nonaction. It is possible that living as he did in the third century B.C.E., the compiler of the *Tao-te-ching* may have shared the faith of Mencius and others that the time was ripe for the rise of a new universal king who would transform the world through the radiating power of his gnosis, although there is no evidence in the text for the notion of any Tao of history. The belief in the radiating, almost magical power of the Taoist sage is even present in the *Chuang-tzu*, where figures such as the hideous Ai T'ai-to must fight off the people who flock about him drawn by the radiance of his spiritual power (Watson 1968, 72). Beyond this, however, we are not told how the sage will obtain political power in the first place. Obviously, the Taoist sage does not plan or contrive to obtain it. In the explicit words of the text, the empire will be won by "refraining from deliberate action" (ch. 57). What we have here is the mystical hope that the "world" will somehow naturally gravitate to the orbit of the sage-ruler who embodies the mystic power or virtue of the Tao.

The discussions of how the Taoist sage-ruler actually rules seem to alternate between depictions of his mystical powers or virtue (*te*) and what might be called his "policy" orientations which are, of course, described mainly in negative terms. "As for the best ruler," the text says, "the people simply know that he is there" (ch. 17). His being there is not a vacuous presence, however, since his self-effacing quality, his sub-missiveness, his utter impartiality, as well as his refusal to intervene in the lives of his subjects in order to display his providential concern (for example, "he treats them as straw dogs" [ch. 5]) are all qualities which come to permeate the lives of those he rules.

Yet in addition to these descriptions of the ruler's radiant charisma, there are many negative "policies." He does not advance men of worth. He empties the minds of the people of the useless knowledge that leads to the multiplication of false needs. He refrains from war to the extent possible. A large state ruled by a sage can, by its conciliatory, humble, and considerate policies (holding itself in the lower position like the female), induce small states to seek its protection. Small states ruled by sages renouncing power and pride can win the protection of such large states without in any way resenting it (ch. 61). Thus, the traditional prob-lem, as expressed strongly by Mo-tzu, of the relations of the large and small states is resolved or dissolved amicably without recourse to war. The passage which most vividly projects the *Tao-te-ching*'s vision of the good society is in chapter 80:

A small settlement [community] with few inhabitants.
Even though they have labor-saving implements,
See to it that they are not used.
See to it that they take death seriously
And do not wander far off.
　　Although they may have boats and carts,
See to it that no one rides them.
　　Though they have arms and weapons,
No one will drill with them.
See to it that they return to the knotted cord [rather than writing],

That they be content with the food they have,
That they be pleased with the clothes they have,
Satisfied with their dwellings and enjoying their customs.
The neighboring settlements may be so close
That one can hear the cocks crow and the dogs bark,
But the people may grow old and die
Without ever going back and forth.

This does not seem to be the description of a utopia of the primeval past. Clearly we are in a period when "advanced technology" is available. The sage-ruler, however, sees to it (lit. "causes") that it is rejected. The sage realizes that the complexity of civilization is to some extent the function of size; therefore, he prescribes a "small community." What the language suggests is not a spontaneously emerging "anarchist" state of affairs, but a state of affairs brought about by a sage-ruler. Presumably, the sage is able to inaugurate his policies because he has won the hearts of the people, but however negative the policies are, they nevertheless seem to require some kind of intervention.

The whole idea is to reduce to a minimum all the projects of civilization, making it possible for the people to sink back into the simple life, in which they remain so self-sufficiently contented with their essential daily nonaction routines that they require no outside stimulation. It is, in a sense, pointless to discuss the nature of the system here envisaged. If it is anarchism, it is anarchism completely lacking in dreams of individual freedom and "creativity" and not incompatible with the idea of sage-rulers. If it is collectivism, it is a collectivism that reduces dynamic collective undertaking to the vanishing point. If it is laissez-faire, it is a laissez-faire that has nothing to do with economic enterprise. Contrary to Needham's assertion that technology is only disapproved of in Taoism because it is exploited by feudalism, there seems to be the assertion here that precisely the same calculating consciousness which produces technology also produces sharp social differentiation and hence oppression. The two are indivisible. They spring out of the same contriving consciousness of deliberate action.

It is true that the behavior of the sage-ruler seems to involve unresolved contradictions. He seems quite deliberately to create a utopia that will turn the world back to the simplicity of the Tao. The restoration of the primitive must be a conscious project. Here again, we have the problem of the moralistic torque, which introduces a basic inconsistency into the entire vision of the *Tao-te-ching*. There can be no human morality without preference, without rejection, and without deliberate choice. The civilization-negating "policies" of the sage-ruler seem themselves to be an example of deliberate action. The contradiction remains unresolved.

There is, however, another interpretation of the text's sociopolitical orientation, which would dismiss the entire interpretation proposed above as naive and literal. The compiler of the *Tao-te-ching*, in this view, is a cunning and canny would-be statesman who wraps his Machiavellian political advice in mystical verbiage. Just as Lau insists that the book centers on a down-to-earth concern with individual survival as a supreme value, others insist that it is mainly an esoteric handbook of wily statecraft. And indeed the text was—up to a point—treated in this "instrumental" way by the entire stream known as Huang-Lao Taoism. The contention here is that the soft is really stronger than the hard, that the feminine is ultimately more potent than the masculine, and that water will wear down a stone. Might this not really represent a strategy of "stooping to conquer," something like the spiritual antecedents of judo, literally the "way of softness"? The practitioner of judo is obviously "out to win." Viewed in this light, the sage of the *Tao-te-ching* empties the people's minds in order to make them instruments of the ruler's policies, which are themselves aimed at maximizing his goals of wealth and power. The large state's policy of winning over small states by kindness and humility is nothing more than a more subtle brand of imperialism. An observation which seems particularly wily is that

> In order to shrink it, one must purposely allow it to expand;
> In order to weaken it, one must purposely allow it to grow
>   strong.
> In order to do away with it, one must purposely allow it
>   to establish itself firmly;
> In order to take away, one must first give.
> This is called subtle illumination.
> The soft and weak can overcome the hard and strong. (ch. 36)

Here, indeed, one finds the cunning of judo strategy. It is designed to bring about the fall of the proud and mighty, in the apt words of Lau, "giving the strong enough rope to hang themselves" (1958, 359). It is quite legitimate for the sage-rulers or Taoist adepts to encourage the strong to overreach themselves. This by no means necessarily implies, however, that the soft and weak are simply bent on inheriting the place of the strong and the powerful or that they have been converted to their delusive goals.

Similarly, the contention that the *Tao-te-ching* is basically concerned with military strategy rests on one or two passages. While the drift of the entire book is overwhelmingly pacifist, there does seem to be recognition that even the sage-ruler may become involved in war, given the actualities of the times. In that case,

> He aims only to achieve results.
> He does not dare to intimidate.
> He achieves results and does not boast,
> Does not brag, is not arrogant.
> He carries out war only when there is no other way. (ch. 30)

In carrying out war, the true "Taoist" general does not seek a battle, knows when to retreat, does not become angry, does not lord it over his men, and knows how to use them. He never underestimates his enemies. All of this may be sound military advice, and the knowledge of how to use others was to become a centerpiece of Huang-Lao Taoism. Yet it is also quite compatible with the general vision of the entire text and does not in any way prove that the *Tao-te-ching* is mainly or centrally interested in military science.

Seen in the context of the entire work, these passages do not indicate that the *Tao-te-ching* harbors "esoteric" aims for individuals or for the sage-ruler defined as power, wealth, and honor. The man of true gnosis, who is the only fit ruler, is by the very nature of his mystical insight not ensnared by these goals; he sees through them. The primitivist critique of the civilization that produces these deluding and fictitious goals is maintained throughout. One need not deny that isolated passages in the text will later lend themselves to be used to support such "instrumentalist" interpretations, just as other passages will be used to support the Yang Chu doctrine of survival and longevity as the supreme goal. Indeed, the same passages will later be used to support the entire cult of immortality. When viewed within the context of the mystical and primitivist core of the book, however, it becomes difficult to take such interpretations seriously as interpretations of the vision of the text as a coherent whole.

Conclusion

The *Tao-te-ching*, a complex and problematic text, much discussed and even more translated, is therefore controversial in much of its interpretation. Is it a coherent whole? Or is it an assembly of sayings only loosely strung together that anyone can make of whatever he wants?

If we analyze the text using conventional and familiar categories, it might easily seem the latter, a compendium rife with contradictory tendencies. The most comprehensive vision makes it appear as a mystical text centered on an otherworldly reality, and yet—unlike other mysticisms, it is world-affirming, and the ultimate otherworldly reality is nothing other than the natural and organic order of the world itself. It seems to attack all value judgments, but on the other hand is clearly "biased" in favor of yin qualities as opposed to yang ones. It seems to advocate a natural or "uncivilized," even primitive social anarchism devoid of intentional action, and yet thinks that this society needs to be brought about by the deliberate activity of that most "unnatural" of civilized institutions, a king or emperor. It seems to advocate humility and softness but also appears to promise the rewards of high status and victory to the humble and soft.

Taken together, the *Tao-te-ching* might seem prime material, then, for a modern deconstructionist reading, a paradigm text to illustrate the deconstructionist view that the apparent unity of classic texts masks numerous internal contradictions that undermine their authority. Nevertheless, in my reading I venture rather in the opposite direction, finding a coherence in multivalence, a unity in multiplicity, and still suggesting that the very uniqueness of the *Tao-te-ching* consists in the way it has of challenging the conventional categorizations that produce its apparent contradictions, and bringing together into a unified whole tendencies that otherwise might seem to be in conflict. In the words of Arthur Waley, "All these conflicting elements the author of the *Tao-te-ching* . . . adapts, subtly weaving them into a pattern perfectly harmonious and consistent, yet capable of absorbing the most refractory elements" (1934, 97). In this sense, the *Tao-te-ching* in its thought is both coherent and contradictory, universally relevant as a form of mysticism and culturally based as an expression of the uniqueness of ancient China.

Notes

1. Editors' note: This article is a slightly abbreviated reprint of Schwartz 1985, 194–215; copyright Harvard University Press. Used by permission.

To maintain the formal coherence of this volume, some editorial changes have been made, including the replacement of *Lao-tzu* with *Tao-te-ching* and the integration of footnotes as reference notes in the text of the contribution. In addition, a new conclusion was supplied by the author.

2. Editors' note: Translations from the *Tao-te-ching* are referred to by chapter. They are based on the rendition in Lau 1963.

3. Editors' note: This refers to Schwartz's earlier discussion of Yang Chu as a thinker who emphasized the "inborn" predispositions inherent in human nature to "pursue natural desires for health, long life, and freedom from anxiety" (1985, 175).

References

Lau, D. C. 1958. "The Treatment of Opposites in Lao-tzu." *Bulletin of the School of Oriental and African Studies* 21: 344–60.

———. 1963. *Lao Tzu: Tao te ching*. London: Penguin Classics.

Needham, Joseph, et al. 1956. *Science and Civilisation in China*. Vol. II: *History of Scientific Thought*. Cambridge: Cambridge University Press.

Schwartz, Benjamin. 1985. *The World of Thought in Ancient China*. Cambridge, Mass: Harvard University Press.

Waley, Arthur. 1934. *The Way and Its Power*. London: Allen and Unwin.

Watson, Burton. 1968. *The Complete Works of Chuang-tzu*. New York: Columbia University Press.

9

Naturalness (Tzu-jan), the Core Value in Taoism: Its Ancient Meaning and Its Significance Today

Liu Xiaogan

What is the core value of Taoism? This issue has not been sufficiently investigated. It is common knowledge that the Tao or Way is the highest and the central concept in Taoist philosophy and that this philosophy is expressed above all in the *Tao-te-ching*, the first and most representative Taoist text, written by Lao-tzu, an elder contemporary of Confucius in the sixth century B.C.E.[1] This identification of the Tao as the key concept in the *Tao-te-ching* may be true from the viewpoint of conventional studies of traditional or metaphysical philosophy. However, does it still hold true if we study Lao-tzu's philosophy from the perspective of human life and the theory of value? Did Lao-tzu really want to establish a metaphysical structure and speculative philosophy like his Western counterparts Plato and Aristotle?

It has also been a prevalent understanding that spontaneity or *tzu-jan* and nonaction or *wu-wei* are two essential notions in Taoism, whose meanings are often thought to be identical. There has, therefore, been hardly any serious attempt to analyze the two concepts and the relation between them. Did Lao-tzu hold *tzu-jan* and *wu-wei* to be the same and interchangeable, or did he conceive significant differences between them? To examine these questions, this essay focuses on the core value in Lao-tzu's philosophy and the relation between *tzu-jan* and *wu-wei*, arguing that *tzu-jan* is the cardinal and central value of Taoism while *wu-wei* is the essential method to realize it in social life. The Tao in this context is understood as a metaphysical concept that works dialectically as an experiential doctrine that supports both the core value and its method. On the basis of this understanding, I will offer an experimental reinterpretation of *tzu-jan* and *wu-wei*, with special reference to their significance in the contemporary world.

The Word *Tzu-jan*

The word *tzu-jan* in the *Tao-te-ching*, as in classical Chinese in general, is commonly used as an adjective, as for example in "always being *tzu-jan* [spontaneous] without anyone's command" (ch. 51), or "the people all say that I am *tzu-jan* [natural]" (ch. 17). *Tzu-jan* here essentially means "spontaneous" or "natural," "so of itself," the word being a subject-predicate compound, namely self-such, literally meaning it is what it is by itself. However, as a philosophical concept, *tzu-jan* has been used as a noun, as for example in "helping the *tzu-jan* [naturalness] of the ten thousand things" (ch. 64), and "the Tao models itself after *tzu-jan* [spontaneity]" (ch. 25). In general, usage of words as nouns can be seen as a sign that a term is becoming a philosophical concept (Liu 1988, 138), so this reading of *tzu-jan* in the *Tao-te-ching* indicates that it is a philosophical term.

Tzu-jan thus means either natural or naturalness, spontaneous or spontaneity. In spite of the syntactical difference in its use, the meaning of the term is still the same. However, by no means does *tzu-jan* mean "nature" in our sense as the natural world. Even when *tzu-jan* is used as a noun, the meaning of the word is still primarily adjectival, indicating "natural" instead of "nature," and it is thus far better to translate the noun *tzu-jan* as "naturalness" or "spontaneity." To render *tzu-jan* as "nature" and imply conclusions about the intent of early Taoist thought is a common mistake in Taoist studies. For example, both Lin Yutang (1948, 196, 248) and Wing-tsit Chan (1963, 148, 153) translate *tzu-jan* as "nature," and thereby imply a modern naturalistic view of the world quite alien to the *Tao-te-ching*. They make this mistake because *tzu-jan* does in fact mean "nature" or "the natural world" in modern Chinese,[2] and they follow the common tendency to read a classical word in its modern sense. In this case, the attribution could not be more erroneous. Nature in the modern Western sense—if there is such a concept in ancient China—would be expressed in classical Chinese not by *tzu-jan* but more likely by descriptive, cosmological terms such as *t'ien* (heaven), *t'ien-ti* (heaven and earth), or *wan-wu* (the ten thousand things).

Still, *tzu-jan* is also translated as "nature" in the sense of the essential quality or fundamental character of something or someone. For example, R. B. Blakney renders chapter 25 as "The Way conforms to its own nature" (1970, 50) and chapter 23 as "sparing indeed is nature of its talk" (1970, 46). However, rather than the inherent characteristics of things, *tzu-jan* indicates their natural or spontaneous origination, a development free from prompting and interruption. The Chinese word *tzu-jan*, therefore, typically does not mean the own-nature of things in this context, although it could later indicate one's own nature.

Most certainly, one should translate a classical Chinese term with different English words or phrases, depending on the context. However, the purpose of varying translations of the same word is to get as close as possible to its original meaning as determined by the context in which it occurs. The translations ideally should not diverge from the essential meaning of the word or attach a new sense or definition to it, although that is somtimes unavoidable. To approach the original intent of *tzu-jan* in the *Tao-te-ching*, one should therefore translate it as "to be natural," as proposed by D. C. Lau (1963, 80, 112, 126), but even here there is not a perfect match between the Chinese word and the English expression. Keeping this in mind, one might use the words *natural* or *naturalness*, *spontaneous* or *spontaneity* equally well as English renditions of *tzu-jan*—or one can, as this chapter does, leave the original in Chinese transliteration. However, when we use *naturalness* or *spontaneity* in this chapter as renditions of *tzu-jan* for the sake of variation or fluency, we just take them as tokens of the Chinese term without implying any specific meaning the terms may have in their Western context.

Tzu-jan in the *Tao-te-ching*

Tzu-jan appears in five chapters in the *Lao-tzu*, four of which show relevant aspects of the term's meaning. First, in chapter 17, it describes the high quality of the ideal ruler:

> The best rulers are those whose existence is merely
>   known by the people,
> The next best are loved and praised.
> The next are feared.
> And the next are reviled.
>
> [The great ruler] prizes his words highly.
> He accomplishes his task; he completes his work.
> Thus his people all say that he is *tzu-jan* [natural].[3]

This passage describes a gradation of the quality of rulership. Best of all is the ideal king of Taoism, who just reigns without ruling. People know of his existence but do not feel his interference, so they praise him for being "natural." Obviously, "being natural" is highly valued.

Second comes the perfect ruler of the Confucian tradition, who bestows favors upon people and receives love and praise from them. He is optimal in the light of the common political standard, but not in the perspective of Taoism because even good rulers interrupt the people's natural activities. Rulers of the third group are crude, thus the people dread to meet or mention them. Needless to say, they are bad sovereigns. The worst, finally, are the cruel tyrants who make people hate and insult them. This kind of monarch is often the cause of rebellion.

While the last three kinds of rulers are graded in the light of general standards or traditional views, Lao-tzu goes beyond these in his final evaluation. He does not reject the standards but places the ideal sovereign of Taoism above all, a sovereign who is, above all *tzu-jan*. Thereby Lao-tzu shows his concern with *tzu-jan* as a core value in his thought, especially in its social and political dimension. Obviously, the ideal ruler reigning without ruling is a Taoist sage who practices the principle of *wu-wei* and takes no intentional action.

In chapter 64, *tzu-jan* appears next as the principle of handling affairs between humans and the ten thousand things (*wan-wu*). *Wan-wu*, one of the classical terms for the natural world, includes animals, plants, rocks in the material universe, as well as all the features, forces, and processes that happen or exist independently of people, such as the weather, the sea, mountains, reproduction, and growth. Lao-tzu emphasizes the natural existence and development of all things in the world through his view of the sage:

> Therefore the sage desires to have no desires.
> He does not value rare goods.
> He learns to be unlearned, and returns to what the
>   multitude has missed.
> So he supports all things in their *tzu-jan* [natural
>   state] but dares not take any action.

Here the sage is Taoist as opposed to mainstream Chinese or Confucian since he has desires that go against the wishes of the ordinary people. He neither seeks to be rich nor fights for objects the multitude is fascinated with. Not preying on others or taking from them, he supports their *tzu-jan* and is, in fact, a protector of the environment, however little he may know about ecology. Still, the emphasis here is on naturalness, not the natural world and ecology; despite the continued Western stress on Taoist "naturalism," it is in fact not a topic in the text at all. Ancient Taoists never made environmentalist statements or discussed physical nature at any length because their primary focus was human life and personal perfection, not the exploitation or preservation of natural resources in the environment. In Lao-tzu's age, protection of the natural world was not an essential concern or issue, and if some texts mention that one should not catch young animals or fishes, they are more concerned with preserving the inherent naturalness of beings than with protecting the environment. That does not mean, however, that Taoists could not be the best possible companions of today's environmentalists. But what Lao-tzu really says in this passage is that the sage continues to support the natural and spontaneous existence of the ten thousand things without ever daring to flaunt his intelligence, capability, or power over them. He helps things be what they are, and thus defines himself as the sage.

While *tzu-jan* in chapter 64 is the natural way of being of all things, in chapter 51 it is the ultimate principles of the universe, on which even the Tao, the source of the universe, models itself:

> Tao produces them [the ten thousand things].
> Virtue fosters them.
> Matter gives them form.
> Circumstances and tendencies complete them.
> Therefore the ten thousand things prize Tao and
>   honor virtue.
> Tao is prized and virtue is honored without
>   anyone's order.
> They always come *tzu-jan* [spontaneously].
>
> Therefore Tao produces them, fosters them.
> Completes them, matures them.
> Nourishes them, and protects them.
> It produces them but does not take possession
>   of them.
> It acts, but does not rely on its own ability.
> It leads them but does not master them.
> This is called profound virtue.

This passage articulates the connection between two important points of the Tao: its great role and absolute naturalness. The nobility, respectability, majesty, and loftiness of the Tao come naturally without asking or pursuit, bestowal or offering. It is also easy, simple, casual, smooth, aimless, indifferent: it seems that the Tao is doing nothing (*wu-wei*) although it is a quasi-mother to the universe. In terms of its role and effect, the Tao is almost like God—but its main characteristic or feature is void and indefinitely open, where God is full and definite. The Tao, one might say, is God but without an active and defining consciousness to it. It is beyond reality and imagination, so there are no words suitable to describe it, words ultimately being anthropomorphic and therefore falling far short of the Tao. Beyond humanity or divinity, the Tao is greater and more powerful than any human or divine power, or even God. No word can describe this paradox or contradiction, except maybe *tzu-jan*, naturalness or spontaneity. Only *tzu-jan* has nothing to do with humankind or divinity but is infinite, creative, effectual, and powerful.

So far, therefore, *tzu-jan* in the *Tao-te-ching* is used to discuss issues of ruler and subjects, the effect and attitude of the sage as the ideal human being, and the quality of all things in the world as well as of the Tao itself. This breadth shows the wide and even universal applicability of the term, and indicates its importance and deep significance in Lao-tzu's philosophy.

The Cosmic Importance of *Tzu-jan*

The key passage on the position of *tzu-jan* in the text, however, is found in chapter 25, which contains a cosmology of the Tao:

> There was something undifferentiated and yet complete,
> It existed before heaven and earth.
> Soundless and formless, it depends on nothing and is
>   without change.
> It operates everywhere and is free from danger.
> It may be considered the mother of the world.
> I do not know its name; I call it Tao.
> If forced to give it a name, I shall call it the Great One.
>
> And so Tao is great.
> Heaven is great.
> Earth is great.
> The king is also great.
> There are four great things in the world, and the king
>   is one of them.
>
> Man models himself after Earth.
> Earth models itself after Heaven.
> Heaven models itself after Tao.
> And Tao models itself after *tzu-jan*.

There are three ways to read the last line, each with a different syntactical structure and interpretation. The first reads it as noun-verb-noun to mean "Tao models itself after nature." This, as mentioned before, is incorrect, not because of the syntax, which imitates the previous lines closely, but for its use of *tzu-jan* as a definite noun and linking it with modern ideas of the natural world and its corresponding divergence from the definition of *tzu-jan*.

The second reading interprets the syntax to be noun(possessive)-noun-adjective and renders: "The model of the Tao is natural," emphasizing that the Tao models itself after nothing. While there is no problem with the translation of *tzu-jan* in this version, it switches the pattern and loses the parallelism with the chapter's earlier lines. Nevertheless, a number of Chinese scholars read the sentence thus, following the ancient commentary of Ho-shang-kung, and understand the nature of the Tao as natural and its modeling itself after nothing whatsoever, being a complete end in itself. Following this, John Wu renders the line as: "Tao follows its own ways" (1961, 51), giving a reading in accordance with the ancient spirit of Taoism but not ultimately correct.

The third rendition matches both syntax and the correct meaning of *tzu-jan*, using the term as a nominal object and keeping its classical definition as naturalness or spontaneity. Relevant translations are by D. C. Lau: "And the way (models itself) on that which is naturally so" (1963, 82), and Robert Henricks: "And the Way models itself on that which is so on its own" (1989, 77, 236). Thus we prefer to read the sentence as the Tao models itself after the principle of spontaneity or *tzu-jan*.

Accepting the latter reading, then, we can see how Lao-tzu in this chapter presents a full portrait of the Tao as unique, eternal, eminent, and magnanimous. It is at the top of the ascending chain: man-earth-heaven-Tao. The Tao is the ultimate reality, the source of the universe— but even its greatness comes from *tzu-jan*, spontaneity or naturalness. Although this *tzu-jan* is not a concrete entity, a real actuality, although it is different from humanity, earth, heaven, and the Tao, it is yet the model of all. In other words, humanity, earth, heaven, and the Tao all follow the principle of *tzu-jan* and are fully spontaneous and natural. Omitting, furthermore, the intervening items of the chain, the ultimate message from Lao-tzu becomes clear: Ideally people, and especially rulers, should act in accordance with perfect naturalness. This naturalness is thus the cardinal value in the system of Lao-tzu's philosophy, and its significance is embodied by the Tao, the final metaphysical reality in the *Tao-te-ching*. In short "the Tao models itself after naturalness" articulates the key role *tzu-jan* plays in Lao-tzu's thought.

Wu-wei as the Method of Naturalness

Lao-tzu accentuates the core value *tzu-jan* yet discusses *wu-wei* at great length, for it is the principal method to actualize naturalness.[4] He highlights *wu-wei* because the way to achieve the goal, once it is clarified as the objective, requires more attention than the goal itself. *Tzu-jan* is the ideal overall condition of a society and even the world, while *wu-wei* directly concerns human behavior and action, and thus exerts a great influence on the situation and quality of human life.

Wu-wei, commonly rendered "nonaction," designates the way by which people and things can and should realize their own naturalness in the world. Here again the earlier caution applies, and "nonaction" is only a token representation of *wu-wei*, which like many other classical terms has no exact equivalent in modern languages, including even modern Chinese. The term appears twelve times in ten chapters of the *Tao-te-ching*,[5] literally meaning "no-action" or "no-behavior" but not intended in this meaning in the *Lao-tzu* text.

What, then, is the true meaning or best definition of *wu-wei* in the *Tao-te-ching*? This question is more difficult to answer than that about *tzu-jan* because *tzu-jan* is a positive term with identical literal and actual meanings. *Wu-wei*, on the contrary, is a negative compound with a vague and uncertain denotation, and its literal and theoretical meanings are widely divergent if not actually opposite. Taken literally, *wu-wei* seems to deny all human behavior and action, but in philosophical fact does nothing of the kind. Rather, the overall implication of *wu-wei* is to eradicate or reduce certain, not all, human actions, so that our task now is to find what actions exactly should be eliminated or lessened according to Lao-tzu's theory.

First, the primary agent of *wu-wei* in the *Tao-te-ching* is the sage and not the ruler or the people. Among the ten chapters that discuss or use the term, five (2, 3, 57, 63, 64) explicitly and four (38, 43, 48, 10) implicitly indicate that the sage is the subject of *wu-wei*. Only chapter 37 says that the Tao usually acts in nonaction but leaves nothing undone and that, if the kings keep it, the ten thousand things will transform themselves.[6] The sage, therefore, is the primary agent to exercise *wu-wei* to deal with society or the world in a nonactive manner, allowing the core value *tzu-jan* to be realized. The sage is different from the ruler in that he exerts personal and nonpolitical influence on the society and the people. His image reflects an ideal type of social leader who practices *wu-wei* to allow the achievement of natural harmony in human life. Contrasting this ideal with the ruler, Lao-tzu indirectly criticizes the rulers of the actual world and provides a behavioral suggestion for their government.

Chapter 57 clearly bears this out:

> The more taboos there are in the world,
> The poorer the people will be.

The more sharp weapons people have,
The more disordered the state will be.
The more skill people possess,
The more vicious things will appear.
The more laws and orders are made known,
The more thieves and robbers there will be.

Therefore the sage says:
I *wu-wei* [take no action], and the people of themselves are
    transformed.
I love quiet, and the people of themselves become
    correct.
I engage in no activity, and the people prosper of
    themselves
I have no desires, the people of themselves become simple.

The first half of this chapter introduces the experiential argument against conventional value and rulership, while the second specifies the way in which the Taoist sage deals with people, also emphasizing the advantages of *wu-wei* in influencing and educating them.

Here the realm of action is presented in terms of opposites, two different attitudes toward human life resulting in very different consequences. One side is the taking of action (*yu-wei*), the traditional or common way to govern a country and control people, such as making prohibitions, establishing law and order, making sharp weapons, learning cunning and skill, pursuing goals, and seeking to satisfy desires—all of which only lead to poverty, trouble, viciousness, and crime. The opposite side of this is *wu-wei*, the way of the Taoist sage, taking no action, living in nonaction: loving tranquillity, engaging in no activity, and having no desires—which leads to natural transformation, correctness, prosperity, and simplicity. Lao-tzu's first aspect of nonaction might thus be summed up as follows: the more the ruler acts, the worse the social situation becomes; the less the ruler does, the more peaceful the people become. Thus, Lao-tzu claims, the less manipulation there is, the less interference with the naturalness of people and things, the better.

Although *wu-wei* is essentially the ideal art of leadership, it is also a general way of life for ordinary people. In their lives too, it pays to go against the traditional way of doing things, by acknowledging the opposite of commonly accepted values of thinking and acting. Thus Lao-tzu states that *wu-wei* is the best way to fulfill the purpose of *yu-wei*, or taking action, for action can never realize its own aims. Accordingly, he says in chapter 36:

> Wishing to contract, it is necessary first to expand.
> Wishing to weaken, it is necessary first to strengthen.
> Wishing to destroy, it is necessary first to build up.
> Wishing to take, it is necessary first to give. . . .
> Thus the weak and soft overcome the hard and strong.

This paragraph represents Lao-tzu's methodology. In order to realize a purpose, such as contracting, weakening, and so on, it is better first to do the opposite. In order to overcome the hard and strong, he recommends adopting the manner of the weak and soft. The advantage of the weak and soft is that of *wu-wei*. As he points out in chapter 43:

> The softest things in the world overcome the hardest.
> Nonbeing penetrates where there is no space.
> Through this I recognize the advantage of *wu-wei* [taking
>   no action].
> Few in the world can understand this teaching without
>   words and the benefits of *wu-wei* [taking no action].

"Overcoming," "penetrating," and "teaching" are the usual means associated with advantage or purpose. "The softest things," "nonbeing", "without words", and *wu-wei* are the reverse of commonly accepted ways of life. Realizing this, one can reach the desired goal through the reverse approach—thus the advantage of being without action.

A similar argument is found also in chapter 63:

> Act without action,
> Do without doing,
> Taste without tasting. . . .
> Repay injury with virtue.
> Prepare for what is difficult while it is still easy,
> Deal with what is big while it is still small.
> Difficult projects always begin with what is easy,
> Great projects always begin with what is small.
> Thus the sage never strives for the great,
> And so the great is achieved.

Here "great," "big," and "difficult" describe one set of values while "small" and "easy" as well as "never striving" describe their opposites. To achieve success, great and difficult undertakings should begin with the small and easy, so the sage achieves the great without striving. Starting from one point in order to obtain the opposite is the key to Lao-tzu's way of life, the way to live in the midst of action while maintaining an approach of nonaction.

Here, as in earlier passages, the meaning of *wu-wei* remains vague. That is because it is not a simple word but a cluster of ideas formulated in the negative that describe the opposite of conventional or common values and methods. Thus people should have "no words," "no desire," "no business," and "no competition"; they should "not strive," but keep to the passive, to humility, to the black, and so on. Through this inverted way of acting, the natural harmony of the entire society can and should be realized.[7]

The Philosophy of Naturalness

Philosophically speaking, naturalness in the Taoist context primarily means "so on its own," just as the term consists of the subject *tzu* (self) and the adverbial suffix *jan* (such). It indicates the condition when a thing is what it is by itself without any external impulse or interruption. "Tao is esteemed and virtue is honored without anyone's order," Lao-tzu says. "They always come naturally." Naturalness thus clearly emphasizes that the esteem and honor of the Tao and its virtue come from nowhere and nobody, but that they are esteemed and honored because of themselves.

Similarly, if a farmer gets up to work in the field in the morning, and comes back for dinner and sleep in the evening without anyone's driving him, he can be considered to be leading a natural life. If he is compelled to do this, it is not natural. So, if the government drafts farmers into military service, the farmers' natural life is interrupted, and the way of rulership is not natural. This is why Lao-tzu says that "the best rulers are those whose existence is merely known by the people." A Taoist ruler does not do anything to push people or show off his existence, thus people only know he is there without feeling his existence, let alone his interference or threat. Vice versa, even the ruler is natural only as long as he is not pushed by his people or ministers to do something.

A thing is what it is due to itself—this is the primary meaning of naturalness. If one's existence is forced or interfered with, one is not in naturalness; on the other hand, if someone forces or interferes with the existence of another, he also ruins that other person's naturalness. The concept of naturalness thus postulates the independence and subjectivity of each individual although it claims also to foster harmony in general. Beyond that, the statement that a thing originates and exists by itself without external driving and interruption implies that the thing is what it is in itself now and will continue to be so in future.

Naturalness, therefore, comes with a continuity of its own. For example, if the farmer's son began to help his father in farming while very young and was expected to continue this later on, this would be perfectly natural. Natural life, life in naturalness, is predictable. On the contrary, if one day the farmer or his son suddenly decided to become a fisherman instead of farming for a living, he would no longer follow his naturalness. This is not because of the change in itself, but because of its suddenness, even if the decision was made entirely independently by the person himself. It thus becomes clear that naturalness excludes abrupt transformations, breaks in continuity. As Lao-tzu says, "[The sage] supports all things in their natural state but dares not take any action." The "natural state," whatever else it may be, is always steady, continuous, and predictable, and so the sage "dares not take any action" because he is afraid of any unexpected change, of causing a harmful break. The principle of naturalness thus requires a smooth curve in movement and conversion.

In addition, it is now clear that naturalness means a balanced and harmonious situation without conflict and strife. If the farmer had to fight for his livelihood, his life would no longer be one of naturalness, despite the fact that there was no drastic change. Vice versa, if he discovered an improved way of making a living because of certain transformations in the society and pursued it without getting into conflict with others, the change would be conceived of as natural, despite the radical transition in his life. For this reason, the principle of naturalness is not necessarily opposed to any kind of transformation or reformation, but in all cases excludes conflict and strife. As Lao-tzu says, "The sage accomplishes his task and completes his work; thus the people all say that he is natural." This is praiseworthy because the sage reaches a successful end without breaking the balanced and harmonious atmosphere of the world.

Tzu-jan or naturalness in the *Tao-te-ching* therefore indicates the way a thing or living being is by itself and on its own, how it exists and develops smoothly without conflict or strife. It is manifest mostly in predictable and harmonious situations, those devoid of sudden change or abrupt transformations. Obviously, to realize or maintain a natural life for individuals and a harmonious condition of the world, people have to cancel or control certain actions, such as external enforcement, sudden internal whims, abrupt discontinuity, drastic divergences, strife, and conflict. This is exactly the meaning and significance of *wu-wei*. The best social management should have a good effect yet feel as if nothing were happening at all.

While this holds true for the classical context, how can it be suitable or applicable in the contemporary world today?

Naturalness Today?

Lao-tzu's philosophy is the product of a primarily agricultural society, and there are thus obvious limits to its applicability in the industrialized and commercialized society we live in today. However, naturalness can still serve as a value in situations of modern life. For example, people still say that something is natural or unnatural, and in many cases prefer the natural to the unnatural. Why? Because naturalness is a constant value, even if only a subconscious one, and peace and harmony are lasting ideals of humanity. How, then, can and should one redefine the concept of naturalness to clarify its possible significance in the contemporary world?

Lao-tzu's age and ours differ massively in terms of the rapidity and intensity of development and transformation, competition and stress. Obviously, classical Taoist naturalness had no need to deal with radical social change or severe competition, while we today cannot deny or avoid them. Nevertheless, even with these significant differences, naturalness can still be relevant as a value. But this is a different naturalness, one that needs a new definition. The new concept of naturalness, or modernized naturalness, must take into account rapid transformation and stressful competition.

The primary focus of the concept of naturalness, its emphasis on inner causes, is still central even today. "Inner causes" means voluntary decision-making, internal impulsion, personal motivation, and a continuous dynamism. If the farmer, to return to our example, realized by himself the advantages of modern agricultural methods and decided to initiate a reform on his farm, this would be a natural development. If someone or something, on the contrary, forced him to buy and drive a tractor and combine harvester, this would not be a natural change, however much it actually might benefit him. External influence here is not excluded—there must be modernization, after all, for the farmer to realize its advantages—but it is clearly secondary to the voluntary acceptance of the transformation by the person in question. The principle of naturalness, therefore, prefers inner dynamism to external force. It no longer merely means that something is so on its own, but that something develops and transforms because of its own free will.

Another important aspect of naturalness also still applies today—the emphasis on smooth transformation. If the farmer erected some buildings to lease as guest houses, from which he received rental income, then, inspired by his success, built a motel, a hotel, or even a resort, and eventually gave up farming altogether to become a hotel manager, it would be a perfectly natural transition because it came gradually and on his own initiative. If, on the contrary, he was forced to change his livelihood by war or natural disaster, because of a sudden inheritance or a surprise whim, it would not be in line with naturalness. Thus naturalness does not exclude reformation or progress, but implies a smooth development without sudden discontinuity, an easy progress without sharp turns from the direction of continuous movement.

Naturalness, therefore, means a balanced and harmonious state even within complicated movement and competition. This state, however, is not easily attained in modern industrialized and commercialized societies, where competition is inevitable. This competition provides high efficiency and good production quality, but also causes tension, stress, and conflict. Thus it is best to keep competition within limits and regulate it with the help of laws, to maintain an overall peace in society. So, if our farmer provided better products and services and thus beat his competition without causing trouble to others, this would be acceptable as natural and would not break social harmony. If he fought and strove with other companies to win in competition, it would not be a natural success and thus go against the principle of *wu-wei*. Yet again, if he ventured to break the law for extra profit, he would be a criminal and not only go against the principle of naturalness but also harm his fellow men.

In this context, then, do laws and regulations necessarily oppose *tzu-jan* and *wu-wei*? Yes, Lao-tzu says, "the more laws and orders are made known, the more thieves and robbers there will be." That, however, does not mean that he denies the need for laws in general. While *tzu-jan* prefers the internal course, natural motivation, and spontaneous dynamism, it does not negate external influences. As long as the external influence does not take the form of direct interference or massive disruption, it is acceptable. For this reason there is room for laws to exercise their function. Laws, in fact, are necessary to maintain the natural order and social harmony of the modern world.

Traffic regulations, to take an easy example, as much as the complex codes of civil and criminal law, are there to allow competition among individuals while at the same time maintaining the social order and general harmony. Both the policeman regulating traffic in the center of an intersection and the intricate system of highways with its many signs are forms of *yu-wei* or taking action and thus interfere with the natural state. Nevertheless, they are necessary to make traffic flow smoothly, thus enabling a state of *wu-wei* or natural order. On the other hand, there are also laws that bring oppression to societies and provoke rebellion, which is neither natural nor nonactive. Therefore, laws and lawmakers, authorities, governments, and leaders have the important responsibility to keep the natural order with the spirit of *wu-wei*, lest they ruin natural harmony by overdoing their lawmaking.

Although Lao-tzu promotes *tzu-jan* and *wu-wei* essentially for the sake of society and human beings, the spirit of these concepts is also useful to individuals. Let us take a college student as an example. If she chose to go to medical school of her own free will because of her family background and a desire to help the sick, she is following the natural way and acting in nonaction. If, on the other hand, she has no strong personal aspiration to be a physician and just chooses medicine because of the high future income, she does not act naturally. Even worse, if her family or friends force her to go to medical school, she is aggressivly hurting both herself and the principle of naturalness. In all these cases, the key definition of naturalness is the first criterion of *tzu-jan*, the inner impulse or cause. The more an action comes from internal sources, the more natural it is.

Another important criterion of *tzu-jan* is the smooth development of events. If the student loves to perform on stage but gradually recognizes that she will never make a great actress and then finds herself drawn to a medical career, that is natural, no matter whether or not she will ultimately succeed in her goal. If she loves art but is deserted by her artist boyfriend and chooses medicine out of spite, the degree of naturalness is significantly reduced. Any sudden discontinuity or sharp turn in development lessens the quality of *tzu-jan*.

In addition, the principle of naturalness also rejects strife, fights, and conflicts. If the student's parents wish for her to pursue a legal career and she ends up fighting with them rather than persuading them of her superior suitability as a physician, it means a major breach in the spontaneous harmony of life and thus destruction of naturalness—however much the decision may be her own and may have grown gradually. Also, if the student ends up going to medical school but has to overwork herself for financial support, thus adding a great deal of strife to an already difficult curriculum, naturalness suffers.

This, however, by no means implies that she is doing anything wrong. To be natural and follow the inherent course of oneself and of circumstances is better and more worthy of pursuit than to force things, but that does not mean that an unnatural act or situation is morally or even personally wrong. Sometimes people feel that a narrow win is so much more exciting than an easy run, that a hard-won success is all the more laudable. Still, pragmatically, in the course of day-to-day life, people tend to prefer a natural achievement to an unnatural one, a steady growth to a superhuman effort. Obviously, in this context, practical, social, or historical perspectives must remain clearly separate from moral or emotional

considerations, but in all cases peace, harmony, and ease are concomi-
tants of a natural process.

Lao-tzu does not give specific opposites of *tzu-jan*, but he mentions
a number of things by implication: artificiality, forced effort, falseness,
affectation, reluctance, abruptness, and competition. Generally speaking, people do not like any behavior of these kinds, which goes to show
that naturalness is still a value acceptable today. People do not like unnatural things or actions, although sometimes they have to accept them—
still, as Lao-tzu teaches us, one can be more conscious of one's nature
and try to improve the value of *tzu-jan*.

Tzu-jan then applies both in general social situations and in individual conditions. For anyone, be s/he a farmer, student, or whatever,
an action of internal impulse, peaceful movement, and freedom from
struggle is natural or close to natural. A society, independent of its
individual competition, with a smooth development and harmonious
atmosphere, free from conflicts and external disruptions, is natural or
close to naturalness. Otherwise, it is not very natural or even unnatural.
Tzu-jan, it becomes evident, can be graded: very natural, natural, almost
natural, close to the natural, not natural, unnatural, and antinatural. In
addition, it can be analyzed: some elements of a course or process may
be natural, while other elements are not. For example, an action may be
natural as it is initiated by inner causes, but it is not so natural because it
involves a serious conflict. *Tzu-jan*, therefore, can be described as a
general and universal value, but it is certainly not an absolute one. Few
values, in fact, are absolute. *Tzu-jan*, as a result, should be joined with
other values and used in balance with them. Even the value of naturalness should be accepted naturally, maintaining the spirit of naturalness
itself.

Understanding the value correctly and applying it with these modi-
fications and cautions, *tzu-jan* can serve as a valid concept to guide human
beings in the contemporary world. It stands for the smooth development
and easy transformation that issue from a genuine inner motivation, for
the spontaneous dynamism that allows competition among individuals
but insists on an overall balance and social peace. It may not be easy to
realize, but may well be worth the try.

Notes

1. This dating and evaluation of Lao-tzu follows recent Chinese
views (Liu 1994a, 172–186; Liu 1994b) that are different from the prevailing Western hypothesis, which places Lao-tzu in the fourth or third

century B.C.E. even after the creation of the *Chuang-tzu*. See Graham 1981, 5; Graham 1989, 216; Henricks 1989, ix; Seidel 1990, 229; and Zürcher 1992, 285.

2. Zhang Dainian (Chang Tai-nien) says that the poet Juan Chi (210–263) was the first to use *tzu-jan* to indicate the natural world (1989, 81), thus contradicting the later interpretation of Tai Lian-chang, who read Juan Chi differently (1993, 310–11).

3. Translations of the *Tao-te-ching* are adapted from Chan 1963. The traditional interpretation of the last line is "Nevertheless their people say that they simply follow Nature" (Chan 1963); or "The people all say, 'It happened to us naturally'" (Lau 1963).

4. An earlier version of this section appeared in Liu 1991, 42–44, where it formed part of a discussion of nonaction in early Taoist thinkers.

5. In the silk manuscripts, it appears nine times in seven chapters: 2, 38, 43, 48, 57, 63, and 64. In the traditional version, it is also found in chs. 3, 10, and 37.

6. Although the first sentence in the silk manuscript is that the Tao is constantly nameless, the basic idea in the chapter is still the same.

7. Recently the character *wu* has been found to indicate not the absence of something or absolute nothing, but the gods or ghosts that are invisible and inaudible yet exist somewhere else (P'ang 1986, 62–74, "Shuo-wu"). In accordance with the classical meaning of *wu*, a new definition of *wu-wei* becomes possible as a way of social management that seems like nothing but has good effects. Nonaction would then mean a way that keeps the society in overall harmony and individuals in fruitful interchange by providing a spontaneous order for the community at large.

References

Blakney, R. B. 1970. *The Sayings of Lao Tzu*. Taipei: Confucius Publishing.

Chan, Wing-tsit. 1963. *A Source Book in Chinese Philosophy*. Princeton, N.J.: Princeton University Press.

Graham, A. C. 1981. *Chuang-tzu: The Seven Inner Chapters and Other Writings from the Book of Chuang-tzu*. London: Allen & Unwin.

———. 1989. *Disputers of the Tao: Philosophical Argument in Ancient China*. La Salle, Ill.: Open Court.

Henricks, Robert. 1989. *Lao-Tzu: Te-Tao ching*. New York: Ballantine.

Lau, D. C. 1963. *Lao Tzu Tao Te Ching*. Harmondsworth, England: Penguin Books.

Lin Yutang. 1948. *The Wisdom of Laotse*. New York: Random House.

Liu, Xiaogan. 1988. *Chuang-tzu che-hsueh chi-ch'i yen-p'ien*. Peking: Academy of Social Sciences.

———. 1991. "Wuwei (Non-Action): From *Laozi* to *Huainanzi*." *Taoist Resources* 3.1: 41–56.

———. 1994a. *Classifying the Zhuangzi Chapters*. Ann Arbor: University of Michigan, Center for Chinese Studies Monographs, no. 65.

———. 1994b. "Lao-tzu tsao-ch'i shuo-shih hsin-ch'eng." *Tao-chia wen-hua yen-chiu* 4: 419–37.

P'ang P'u. 1986. *Chung-kuo wen-hua yü Chung-kuo che-hsueh*. Shen-chen, PRC: Tung-fang ch'u-pan-she.

Seidel, Anna. 1990. "Chronicle of Taoist Studies in the West 1950–1990." *Cahiers d'Extreme-Asie* 5: 223–347.

Tai Lian-chang. 1933. "Juan Chi's Concept of Nature." *Bulletin of the Institute of Chinese Literature and Philosophy of the Academia Sinica* 3: 305–33.

Wu, John, C. H. and Paul K. T. Sih. 1961. *Lao Tzu, Tao Teh Ching*. Asian Institute Translations, no. 1. New York: St. John's University Press.

Zhang Dainian. 1989. *Chung-kuo ku-tien che-hsueh kai-nien fan-ch'ou yao-lun*. Peking: Academy of Social Sciences.

Zürcher, Erik. 1992. "Lao Tzu in East and West." In *Proceedings of the International Conference on Values in Chinese Societies*, 281–316. Taipei: Center for Chinese Studies.

Part IV

Critical Methods

10

Situating the Language of the *Lao-tzu*:
The Probable Date of the *Tao-te-ching*

William H. Baxter

Locating the origins of the *Lao-tzu* in time and space has proved an especially thorny problem. The historical techniques which have been successful in clarifying the origins of some other early Chinese texts have not succeeded in producing a consensus among modern scholars in this case. In the present essay, I will attempt to clarify the origins of the *Lao-tzu* not from the biographical details of its supposed author or from its place in the development of early Chinese philosophical thought, but from the linguistic characteristics of the text itself.

Two major types of linguistic features will be addressed: (1) the rhetorical characteristics of the text, including the units of which it is composed and their formal features; and (2) the pronunciations implied by the numerous rhymed passages. In the latter case, we will find that recent research on early Chinese pronunciation helps to clarify the problem.

We are fortunate in having at least some hard evidence about the date of the *Lao-tzu*, for in 1973 two almost complete manuscript versions of the text, written on silk, were discovered when Chinese archeologists excavated a tomb at Ma-wang-tui, in Hu-nan Province; they are referred to as Ma-wang-tui manuscripts A and B. Since the tomb is known to have been closed in 168 B.C.E., the *Lao-tzu* must at least have been composed by that time.

In fact, the contents of these manuscripts themselves allow us to push the date back a little further, because of the traditional Chinese taboo on using an emperor's personal name after his death. The first emperor of the Han dynasty (206 B.C.E. to 220 C.E.) was Liu Pang, who died in 195 B.C.E.; his personal name "Pang" is a word meaning "country." One of the Ma-wang-tui manuscripts of the *Lao-tzu* (manuscript A) still freely uses the word *pang*; this shows that it must have been written

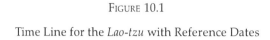

Figure 10.1

Time Line for the *Lao-tzu* with Reference Dates

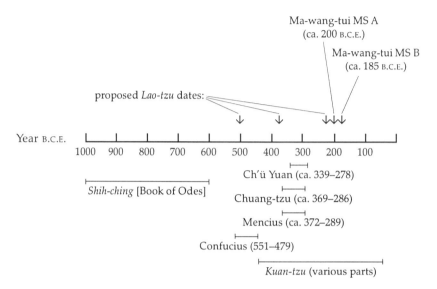

down before his death in 195 B.C.E. In manuscript B, on the other hand, *pang* has been replaced by *kuo*, another word for "country," out of respect for the recently deceased emperor (Boltz 1984, 214n).

So the Ma-wang-tui discoveries have now clearly established that the *Lao-tzu* must have been composed no later than 195 B.C.E. But whether it was composed several centuries before, or only a few years before, is still the subject of much debate.

The most common approach to dating the composition of the *Lao-tzu* text has been to try to date the lifetime of Lao-tzu the person, its supposed author, relative to the dates of better-known persons or of more easily datable texts. There have been three main theories, briefly discussed below. Here and later through our discussion, in may be useful to refer to the timeline given in figure 10.1.

1. One traditional view attributes the *Lao-tzu* text to a certain person called Lao-tzu who is recorded as having had conversations with Confucius. Since Confucius's dates are 551–479 B.C.E. or thereabouts, this theory dates the *Lao-tzu* at somewhere around 500 B.C.E.

2. A second traditional view dates *Lao-tzu* considerably after the time of Confucius, but before the philosopher Chuang-tzu, whose dates

are approximately 365–285 B.C.E. In this view, the *Lao-tzu* is generally attributed to a figure named Lao Tan who is said to have been
the Grand Historiographer of Chou, and to have visited the state
of Ch'in during the reign of Duke Hsien in 374 B.C.E. This theory,
then, dates the *Lao-tzu* in the early fourth century B.C.E.—let us
say, at about 375 B.C.E.

3. In the twentieth century, there has been considerable support for
    dating the *Lao-tzu* text (at least in its final version) much later, well
    after the lifetime of Chuang-tzu: probably in the late third cen-
    tury, say, about 225 B.C.E. (Boltz 1993, 270–71).

Modern scholarship is still divided among these theories. It is tempt-
ing to dismiss the first traditional theory as an attempt by Taoist propa-
gandists to give their founder priority over Confucius. As D. C. Lau points
out, there is a whole genre of such anti-Confucian stories in which
Confucius meets, and is somehow bested by, a Taoist-like hermit or sage
(1963, 158–60). But Liu Xiaogan has argued on the basis of literary form
and vocabulary that such an early date is, if not required, at least "plausible" (1994, 32).

The second theory, according to which Lao-tzu the person (and
therefore *Lao-tzu* the text) are later than Confucius but earlier than
Chuang-tzu, also has considerable support in Chinese tradition. By the
Han dynasty, Lao-tzu was regarded as the founder of the Taoist philosophical school, and Chuang-tzu as his follower. This is consistent with
the fact that the *Chuang-tzu* mentions Lao-tzu or Lao Tan by name, and
includes quotations from the *Lao-tzu*.

The theory that the *Lao-tzu* actually postdates the *Chuang-tzu*, although at odds with traditional views, has received support from some
twentieth-century scholars. Ch'ien Mu, for example, pointed out that
although the *Lao-tzu* is quoted in some chapters of the *Chuang-tzu*, it is
not quoted in the "Inner Chapters," that part of the *Chuang-tzu* which is
generally attributed to Chuang-tzu himself. From this and from rather
vague considerations of style and content, Ch'ien therefore dates the
Lao-tzu after Chuang-tzu (1935, 44).

In the present study, rather than focusing on the dates of the person
or persons called Lao-tzu (about whom virtually nothing is known with
certainty), we will focus on the *Lao-tzu* text itself—specifically, first, its
rhetorical patterns and then secondly the pronunciations implied by its
rhymes. Comparing these with the characteristics of other texts, we will
conclude that the *Lao-tzu* was probably composed around 400 B.C.E.—
that is, after Confucius but before Chuang-tzu, a view consistent with
the second traditional view above.

Before we proceed, a few words about notation are in order. Chinese words are usually given in the Wade-Giles romanization; but when it is necessary to discuss early pronunciation, we will cite reconstructions of Old Chinese pronunciation—the Chinese pronunciation at the time the classical texts were written. Old Chinese pronunciations are reconstructed according to the system of Baxter 1992; they are always preceded by an asterisk ("*"), and they include a few phonetic symbols: (1) "ʔ" (glottal stop): a catch at the back of the mouth, such as some Cockney speakers of English substitute for the t-sound in "bottle"; (2) "ɨ" (barred "i"): a vowel similar to the short "u" of "cut"; and (3) "ɦ" (hooktop "h"), a murmured, "h"-like sound. A few other notations are explained as they occur. Translations are by me unless otherwise specified.

The Rhetorical Characteristics of the *Lao-tzu*

By rhetorical characteristics I mean primarily those features that mark a text as belonging to one genre or another. A genre is just a particular type of literary production; modern examples of genres include the novel, the book review, the scientific research report, the country-western song, the gossip column, and the jump-rope rhyme. Genres differ in organization, subject matter, style, length, and physical form: a scientific research report, for example, normally contains an abstract, a text, and references, and sometimes illustrations; it generally describes the results of a scientific experiment, is written in rather impersonal language, and is printed in small type in a scientific journal. A country-western song usually has none of these features, but it has others: it usually rhymes, is sung with a certain conventional accent, and is short enough to be played between commercials on the radio. Moreover, genres are social products of particular times and places; it is safe to say that none of the genres just listed existed in ancient China (with the possible exception of the jump-rope rhyme). Because genres differ over time and space, identifying the genre of a text can help to place it in historical and geographical context.

An example of text-dating based on genre is the attempt of Liu Xiao-gan to date the *Lao-tzu* by examining its poetic form (1994, 172–86). Liu takes as his starting point the fact that much of the *Lao-tzu* is rhymed poetry, and he attempts to place it in time relative to the *Shih-ching* (the Book of Songs) and the *Ch'u-tz'u* (the Songs of Ch'u), taken as two milestones in the development of Chinese verse. The *Shih-ching* is an anthology of poems composed between 1000 and 600 B.C.E.; the *Ch'u-tz'u* is a later anthology, the earliest parts of which are attributed to the poet Ch'ü Yuan (ca. 339–278 B.C.E.). Liu concludes that the *Lao-tzu* is more similar

in form to the *Shih-ching* than to the *Ch'u-tz'u*, and argues that this supports the first traditional theory mentioned above, dating the *Lao-tzu* to
500 B.C.E. or earlier:

> My point is that it is more plausible that the *Lao-tzu* was produced
> under the influence of the *Shih-ching* than that it was written in
> the middle of the Warring States, when the *Ch'u-tz'u* represented
> the main trend of verse. I conclude that it is plausible that the main
> part of *Lao-tzu* was written during the sixth century B.C. (p. 173)

As a starting-point to our own discussion of genre, let us examine
Liu's argument in somewhat more detail. Liu identifies three structural
similarities between the *Lao-tzu* and the *Shih-ching*:

1. Rhythm. The rhymed parts of the *Lao-tzu* often show the four-
   character line which is typical of the *Shih-ching*; by contrast, the
   Ch'u-tz'u typically has longer, two-part lines, with the word *hsī*
   ("ah!") inserted after the first part (see quotation below).
2. Repetition. The *Lao-tzu* shows "the intensive repetition of words
   or sentences within or among stanzas" found also in the *Shih-ching*;
   but there is little repetition in the *Ch'u-tz'u*.
3. Rhyme. As in the *Shih-ching*, rhymes in the *Lao-tzu* are frequent,
   and there is no single dominant pattern. By contrast, the *Ch'u-tz'u*
   has rhymes only at the end of its rather long lines.[1]

These characteristics of the *Ch'u-tz'u*—the long, two-part lines, with
hsī ("ah!") between the parts, and a rhyme at the end—are illustrated by
first two lines of Ch'ü Yuan's poem "Li-sao" (Encountering Sorrow), the
first and most famous poem of the *Ch'u-tz'u*. (In this and subsequent
examples, the words which rhyme in Chinese are printed in small capitals; reconstructed Old Chinese pronunciations of the rhyme words are
given in parentheses, preceded by an asterisk.)

> Ti Kao Yuan chih miao yi hsi,
>   chen huang k'ao yueh Po YUNG (*ljong)
> She-t'i chen yü Meng-tsou hsi,
>   wei keng-yin wu yi CHIANG (*krong(s))

> Scion of the High Lord Kao Yang,
>   My father's name was Po YUNG.
> When She-t'i pointed to the first month of the year,
>   On the day *keng-yin*, I PASSED FROM THE WOMB.
>   (See Hawkes 1959, 51)

To Liu's arguments we must add some qualifications. The style of the *Lao-tzu* is indeed quite distinct from that of the *Ch'u-tz'u*; but this in itself does not prove that the *Lao-tzu* preceded the *Ch'u-tz'u*. Even if the *Ch'u-tz'u* had been around when the *Lao-tzu* was composed, the author of the *Lao-tzu* would not necessarily have imitated it. In fact, the *Lao-tzu* is quite distinct in genre from both the *Shih-ching* and the *Ch'u-tz'u*. Identifying its major structural features can help clarify its origins, but will not align it clearly with either the *Shih-ching* or the *Ch'u-tz'u*. In the remainder of this section, we will examine three kinds of rhetorical features of the *Lao-tzu*: (1) its patterns of rhyme and semantic parallelism, (2) its patterns of repetition, and (3) characteristics of its content.

Rhyme and Semantic Parallelism

First, it is true that a considerable proportion of the *Lao-tzu* is rhymed; but unlike the *Shih-ching*, the rhymed passages of the *Lao-tzu* are often closely integrated with the unrhymed portions of the text. Consider, for example, chapter 81 of the *Lao-tzu*, quoted below in its entirety. As above, rhyme words are in small capitals, and reconstructed Old Chinese pronunciations are given in parentheses, preceded by an asterisk. (The notation "*pien* < *bjen?*" means that the modern pronunciation *pien* developed from the Old Chinese pronunciation *bjen?*.) In addition, words in italics participate in relations of semantic parallelism or antithesis with corresponding words in adjacent lines, marked also by rounded boxes. I have also inserted line breaks and indentations to make the structure of the chapter clearer:

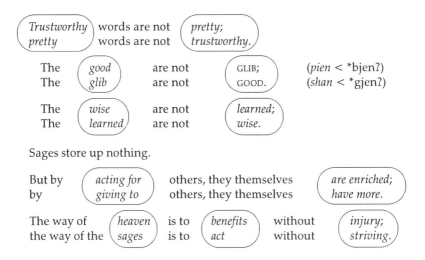

Although there is only one rhyme in this chapter, the semantic alternations within and between the lines (trustworthy/pretty, good/glib, wise/learned, etc.) are clearly used as a poetic device also; it is not a question of a short verse passage surrounded by prose. The entire chapter is in tightly structured verse whose main organizing principle is semantic parallelism and antithesis rather than rhyme—much like the verse of the Hebrew Bible, for example, Psalm 19:1–2 (Revised Standard Version):

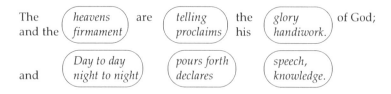

Clearly, the *Lao-tzu* is not simply a collection of rhyming poems with prose sprinkled around them; it represents a genre in its own right, quite different from the traditions found in either the *Shih-ching* or the *Ch'u-tz'u*, in which semantic parallelism plays a major role. The first characteristic feature of this genre is, as we have seen, that both rhyme and semantic patterning are used as poetic devices; the vast majority of the *Lao-tzu* text shows either one or the other or both. Passages containing either device should be considered verse, not just those in which there is rhyme. A few passages, as Lau has pointed out already (1963, 51), show no such devices and can be considered prose; in some of these cases, what was originally commentary may have crept into the text.

These devices tie some chunks of the text together as rhetorical units; in chapter 81, for example, the pattern of paired sentences makes the first three sentences a single unit, the last two sentences also form a unit, and the part in between is a third unit. The boundaries of units are often marked by transitional phrases such as *ku*, "thus, truly," or *shih-yi*, "hence," or there may be an introductory sentence at the beginning (such as, "Sages store up nothing"), or a summing up at the end. The chapter divisions, by contrast, are often artificial.

Patterns of Repetition

A second major structural characteristic is repetition. Although there is, as Liu Xiaogan points out, a good deal of repetition in the *Lao-tzu*, it is often of a rather different nature from that found in the *Shih-ching*. Consider one of the passages cited by Liu, chapter 59:

For ruling men and serving Heaven
    nothing surpasses CAREFUL HUSBANDRY (*sè* < *srjɨk).

Now *careful husbandry*
    is called *beginning* WORK (*fú* < *bjɨk)[2] *early.*
To *begin work early*
    is to *heap virtue upon* VIRTUE (*té* < *tɨk).
If one *heaps virtue upon virtue,*
    nothing is beyond one's ABILITY. (*k'ò* < *khɨk);
If *nothing is beyond one's ability,*
    one's LIMITS (*chí* < *k(r)jɨk) *are unknown.*
If *one's limits are unknown,*
    one can *possess a* STATE (*kuó* < *kʷɨk)
By *possessing* the MOTHER (*mǔ* < mɨʔ) of a *state,*
    one can *long* ENDURE (*chiǔ* < kʷjɨʔ).

This is called the way of deep roots and firm foundations,
long life and far sight.

This passage shows what we might call a chain repetition pattern: the end of each line is repeated in the beginning of the next. A glance at part of the Chinese version of the text will perhaps make the structure clearer. A literal gloss is supplied under each syllable; repeated elements are in square boxes, linked by lines; the rounded box surrounds the syllables which rhyme:

chìh	jén	shìh	t'iēn,	mò	jò	sè (*srjɨk);
rule	people	serve	heaven	nothing	like	frugal
fú	wéi	*sè,*	shìh	wèi	*tsǎo*	fú (*bjɨk);
now	as-for	*frugal*	this	called	early	work
tsǎo	*fú*	wèi	chīh	*ch'úng*	chī	tè (*tɨk);
early	work	call	it	repeat	amass	virtue

[etc.]

The patterns of repetition in the *Shih-ching*, on the other hand, are quite different: in one typical pattern, the same words are repeated in each stanza, providing a framework for the rhyming words, which change from stanza to stanza. Consider, for example, Ode 72:

						pǐ there	ts'ǎi pick	kó (*kat) KUDZU	hsī, ah,
yí one	jìh day	pú not	chièn, see	jú like	sān three			yuèh (*ngʷjat) months	hsī. ah.

						pǐ there	ts'ǎi pick	hsiāo (*siw) ARTEMISIA	hsī, ah,
yí one	jìh day	pú not	chièn, see	jú like	sān three			ch'iū (*tshjiw) AUTUMNS	hsī. ah.

						pǐ there	ts'ǎi pick	ài (*ngats) MUGWORT	hsī, ah,
yí one	jìh day	pú not	chièn, see,	jú like	sān three			suì (*swjats) YEARS	hsī. ah.

Picking KUDZU *there:*
one day without meeting—
it's like three MONTHS!

Picking ARTEMISIA *there:*
one day without meeting—
it's like three AUTUMNS!

Picking MUGWORT *there:*
one day without meeting—
it's like three YEARS!

To be sure, not all repetition in the *Lao-tzu* is of the chain type described above. We also find, as in the *Shih-ching* passage just quoted, repetition of the same words over several lines, providing a framework into which varying material is inserted. The following passage from chapter 19 (Lau 1963, 75) is an example:

> *Cut away* the sage,
> *throw away* wisdom,
> and the *people* will benefit a hundredFOLD (*pèi* < *bɨʔ).
>
> *Cut away* 'humanity',
> *throw away* 'wisdom',
> and the *people* will again be filial and LOVING (*tz'ú* < *ɦtsjɨ(ʔ))
>
> *Cut away* cleverness,
> *throw away* 'benefit',
> and there WILL BE (*yǔ* < *wjɨʔ) no more robbers and bandits.

Content: Paradox and Absence of Narration

Another characteristic of the *Lao-tzu*, central to the style of Taoist discourse, is the use of paradoxical statements—statements which are jarring because they seem to fly in the face of common sense. Consider chapter 45, whose phonology we will examine later:

> The greatest perfection seems deficient,
>   but in use it is without flaw.
> The greatest fullness seems empty,
>   but in use it is inexhaustible;
>
> The greatest straightness seems crooked;
> The greatest cleverness seems stupid;
> The greatest eloquence seems to stammer.

Still another characteristic, finally, which separates the *Lao-tzu* from much of early Chinese philosophical discourse, is that it is entirely free of narration, in the sense that its statements are general and not anchored to any particular persons, times, or places. There is no indication of who is speaking, no direct reference to historical events. This contrasts strikingly with typical Confucian discourse. The *Meng-tzu* (Works of Mencius), for example, purports to record conversations of actual persons:

> Mencius had an audience with King Hui of Liang. The king said: 'Venerable sir, you did not think a thousand *li* too far to come; I suppose you must have brought something that will be of benefit to my state?' (Mencius, chapter 1)

Temporal and spatial anchors are not, of course, confined to Confucian texts such as the *Mencius*; we find similar passages in the *Chuang-tzu* as well. Their absence from the *Lao-tzu* is a distinctive characteristic of the genre of philosophical discourse which it represents.

The Lao-tzu *Compared to the* Kuan-tzu

Many of the rhetorical characteristics just discussed are present, to one degree or another, in early Chinese texts of various types and periods; a full study of their distribution is beyond the scope of this study. But these features suffice to distinguish the genre of the *Lao-tzu* from both the *Shih-ching* and the *Ch'u-tz'u*, and from the "Inner Chapters" of the *Chuang-tzu* as well. On the other hand, we do find parallels in other philosophical texts.

Some similar texts are found in the *Kuan-tzu*, a lengthy and diverse anthology of writings named for a famous minister named Kuan Chung, who died in 645 B.C.E. Actually, much of the *Kuan-tzu* has little to do with

Kuan Chung; the texts in it are probably no earlier than 450 B.C.E., and some may be as late as 50 B.C.E. (Rickett 1993, 246–49). Certain sections of the *Kuan-tzu* show a structure very similar to that of the *Lao-tzu*; such as the following passage from *Kuan-tzu* 38:

Tào chě,

Tz'ŭ wèi tào yĭ.

> The Way—
>> If *one person uses it*,
>>> one does not hear of *a surplus*.
>> But if it is *applied everywhere under Heaven*,
>>> one does not hear of *an insufficiency*.
>> This is what is called the Way.

Notice the use of semantic patterning, the framing of the passage with introductory and concluding elements, and the use of paradox. Indeed, parts of the *Kuan-tzu* contain passages which are quite similar to the *Lao-tzu* in content as well as in form. For instance, the following passage occurs in *Lao-tzu* 35 (Lau 1963, 94):

> When the Way comes out of the mouth, it is insipid
>> and has no taste.
>> Looking at it, there's nothing to *see*,
>> listening to it, there's nothing to *hear*,
>> but using it, it is never *used up*.

This is quite similar to the following passage from *Kuan-tzu* 49 (Endō 1989–92, 827):

>> The way—
>>> the *mouth* cannot *speak* it,
>>> the *eye* cannot *look* at it,
>>> the *ear* cannot *listen* to it.

Another good example is *Lao-tzu* 2:

> Therefore the sage
>> *keeps* to the *business* of *doing nothing*
>> and *implements* the *doctrine* of *saying nothing*.

This is quite close to *Kuan-tzu* 36 (Endō 1989–92, 680), where the expressions "saying nothing" and "the business of doing nothing" also figure prominently. It says,

> Therefore
>> one must know *the* BUSINESS *of saying nothing and doing nothing;*[3]
>> only then does one know the LEADING THREAD of the Tao.

Finally, in chapter 74 of the *Lao-tzu*, we find:

> It is the Eternal Executioner who kills.
> Killing in the place of the Executioner
>> is like hewing wood in place of the master woodworker.
> Hewing wood in place of the master woodworker,
>> there are few that do not injure their hand!

This idea—that one should not attempt to act in place of a specialist—is also found in *Kuan-tzu* 36 (Endō 1989–92, 679):

> Do not run in place of the horse;
>> you will exhaust its strength.
> Do not fly in place of the bird;
>> you will cause its feathers and wings to collapse.
> Do not move in anticipation of things,
>> but observe their principles.

The fact that there are sections of the *Kuan-tzu* (especially chapters 36, 37, 38, and 49) which express ideas similar to those of the *Lao-tzu* has been recognized for a long time; moreover, these chapters are also generally considered to be among the oldest parts of the *Kuan-tzu* (Lo 1958, 469–71, 479–81; Endō 1989–92, 769; Yanaka 1992). As Rickett points out, these *Kuan-tzu* chapters also show similarities in form and content to the four texts which precede the *Lao-tzu* in Manuscript B from the early Han tomb at Ma-wang-tui (1993, 248–49). For our purposes, the similarities in form among these texts are as important as the similarities in ideas, for they show that the *Lao-tzu* is not a text in a vacuum; rather, it represents a genre of which there are other examples.

Of course, these *Kuan-tzu* chapters, and the manuscripts from Ma-wang-tui, failed to reach the status of "classic" (*chīng*), and from a modern point of view, they may seem far less important than the *Lao-tzu*. The *Lao-tzu* is one of the most translated books in the world (and the subject of many books such as this one), whereas the other texts have received relatively little attention. But the compilers of these texts cannot have known in advance that the *Lao-tzu* would win out in such spectacular fashion. If we wish to clarify the early history of the genre which the *Lao-tzu* represents, these other texts could turn out to be as useful as the *Lao-tzu* itself.

Phonological Characteristics of the *Lao-tzu*

The sounds of any language change over time, slowly but continuously; and they do not necessarily change the same way in different parts of a speech community. Since many of the devices used in poetry—such as rhyme, meter, and assonance—are based on sound, changes in sound also tend to change the way these devices are used. Consider the following stanza from Shakespeare (*As You Like It* II.7):

> Freeze, freeze, thou bitter sky,
> That dost not bite so nigh
> >As benefits forgot:
> Though thou the waters WARP,
> Thy sting is not so SHARP
> >As friend remembered not.

Although *warp* (in phonetic transcription, [wɔrp]) and *sharp* ([ʃɑrp]) are not a good rhyme today (at least for speakers who distinguish between the vowels [ɔ] and [ɑ]), we can tell from this rhyme, and from much other evidence, that they did rhyme in Shakespeare's time; the rhyme was later spoiled by a regular sound change of [wɑ] to [wɔ] (compare also "war" vs. "far", "ward" vs. "hard", "wart" vs. "smart", etc.).

Rhyme and other sound-based poetic devices can therefore provide clues about pronunciation. To take another example from English, the rhymes of Chaucer give us evidence that in his variety of Middle English there were two different long "e" vowels, phonetically [e:] and [ɛ:], and two parallel long "o" vowels, [o:] and [ɔ:], even though his spelling does not distinguish them.

Just as rhymes in poetry of known origin can help us study the pronunciation of its time and place, known changes in pronunciation can help us date and place texts in which rhymes appear. This is what we will attempt to do with the *Lao-tzu*. We will see that the rhymes of *Lao-tzu* show some differences from those of the *Shih-ching* (ca. 1000–600 B.C.E.); but that the *Lao-tzu* also preserves other distinctions which are found in the *Shih-ching*, yet appear to be lost by the time of the *Chuang-tzu* and the *Ch'u-tz'u* (roughly 300 B.C.E.). This suggests that substantial parts, at least, of the *Lao-tzu* are probably earlier than the *Chuang-tzu* and the *Ch'u-tz'u*. We will also find traces of this same pattern in those early parts of the *Kuan-tzu* which are similar to the *Lao-tzu* in form and content.

First, a word about research on the Old Chinese pronunciations implied by the rhymes of the *Shih-ching*. Chinese scholars of the Ch'ing dynasty (1644–1911 C.E.) did considerable careful research to determine which words regularly rhymed with which in the *Shih-ching* and other early Chinese poetry. The culmination of their research was the system of rhyme categories for Old Chinese set up by Wang Nien-sun (1744–1832) and Chiang Yu-kao (died 1851). In their systems—which, though developed separately, are almost identical—each rhyme category is identified by a character which rhymes in that category; for example, the *Tūng* ("East") category includes all the words which they believed could rhyme with *tūng*. This analysis is recognized as a major scientific achievement, and it forms the basis of the research on Old Chinese pronunciation by Bernhard Karlgren and other twentieth-century scholars (Baxter 1992, 139–74).

However, research in recent decades has indicated that, brilliant as it was, the Ch'ing scholars' analysis can be improved upon. Although the distinctions it identifies are generally correct, it overlooks other distinctions: in some cases, words which actually do not rhyme in Old Chinese are assigned to the same rhyme category.[4] Moving to an improved reconstruction of Old Chinese pronunciation, and to a finer-grained analysis of Old Chinese rhyming, makes it possible to characterize the rhyming of particular early texts more precisely.

With respect to the *Lao-tzu* and its origins in both time and space, we will examine two kinds of rhyme evidence:

1. Cases where the *Lao-tzu* preserves distinctions found in the *Shih-ching* which are lost in other texts (such as the *Chuang-tzu* and the *Ch'u-tz'u*)
2. Cases where the *Lao-tzu* diverges from the *Shih-ching* in ways which may clarify the dialect it represents, and thus its geographical origins

An exhaustive discussion of each relevant case is beyond the scope of this study; we will instead focus on representative examples.

Shih-ching *Distinctions Preserved in the* Lao-tzu

Old Chinese *-at ≠ *-et ≠ *-ot. The Ch'ing scholars set up a category *Chì* ("Sacrifice"), reconstructed by Karlgren (1954) as *-ât or *-âd, by Li

(1980) as *-at or *-adh. But recent research has shown that this category can be further divided into an *-at(s) category, an *-et(s) category, and an *-ot(s) category which are normally kept distinct in the *Shih-ching* (Baxter 1992, 389–413).

The distinctions among *-at(s), *-et(s) *-ot(s) appear to be well pre-served in the *Lao-tzu*. Indeed, the distinction between *-et(s), on the one hand, and *-at(s) and *-ot(s), on the other, is clearer in the *Lao-tzu* than in the *Shih-ching* itself, where the examples are few and complicated by textual problems. A good instance is found in chapter 45:

> The greatest perfection seems DEFICEIENT,   (*ch'uēh* < *kh^W(j)et)
> But in use it is without FLAW.   (*pì* < *bjet(s))

Both *ch'uēh* < *k^{w}h(j)et, "deficient," and *pì* < *bjet(s), "flaw," can only be reconstructed with *-et; their later pronunciations rule out *-at or *-ot. Thus this rhyme sequence is independent evidence of the distinction. Other cases of rhymes with *-et(s) are found in chapters 58, 79, and possibly 76.[5]

An example of a rhyme in *-ot(s) is found in chapter 54:

> What is set up well
>   will not be UPROOTED.   (*pá* < *brot or *ɦprot)
> What is well embraced
>   will not COME LOOSE.   (*t'ō* < *hlot)
> By the offering of sacrifices,
>   the line of descendants
>   continues UNBROKEN.   (*ch'uò* < *trjot)

Another *-ot(s) rhyme is found in chapter 56 (*tuì* < *lots, "openings," and *juì* < *ljots, "sharpness".

There are numerous rhymes in *-at(s), which is generally kept quite separate from *-et(s) and *-ot(s).[6] The one apparent exception, a passage in chapter 39 turns out to be quite interesting. The Wang Pi version reads as follows:

> Without what makes it clear,
>   Heaven might TEAR APART.   (*lièh* < *C-rjat)
> Without what makes it stable,
>   Earth might be STIRRED UP.   (*fā* < *pjat)
> Without what makes them powerful,
>   the spirits might EXHAUST themselves. (*hsiēh* < *xjat)

Without what fills them,
    valleys might DRY UP;   *(chiéh* < *ɦkjat)
Without what gives them life,
    the myriad things might DIE OUT.   (*mièh* < *mjet))
Without what gives them nobility
    lords and kings might TOPPLE.   *(chuéh* < *kʷjat)

All these words are reconstructible with *-at except for *mièh*, "die out," in the next to last line, which must be reconstructed with *-et.[7] But as it happens, the irregular line with *mièh* can be shown, on quite independent grounds, to be a late insertion. It is not found in either of the Ma-wang-tui manuscripts, and William Boltz has shown that although the line is included in the version of the text which now accompanies the late Han commentary by Ho-shang-kung, it was probably inserted later there as well, after the commentary itself was written (1984, 220–24; 1985). It would appear, then, that the *Shih-ching*'s three-way distinction among *-at, *-et, and *-ot is preserved in the *Lao-tzu*.

    In the "Inner Chapters" of the *Chuang-tzu*, however, there are several examples where original *-et rhymes with *-at; perhaps *-et had changed to something like *-iat by this time. An example is the following sequence in chapter 4, other examples being also found in chapters 3 and 6:[8]

If in your actions, you follow along
    and are being pulled in,
you will be overthrown and DESTROYED   (*mièh* < *mjet)
    wiped out and HUMILIATED   (*chuèh* < *kʷjat)
If in your mind, you harmonize
    and are being drawn out,
you will be talked about and named,
    blamed and CONDEMNED.   (*nièh* < *ng(r)jat)
                    (See Watson 1968, 62)

Parallel to the distinction among *-at, *-et, and *-ot, there was a distinction in *Shih-ching* rhyming among *-an, *-en, and *-on (Baxter 1992, 370–89). This distinction, too, is preserved in the *Lao-tzu* as far as we can tell, as in the following passage from chapter 81:

The good are not GLIB   (*pièn* < *bjenʔ)
The glib are not GOOD.   (*shàn* < *gjenʔ)[9]

There is also an unmixed *-en rhyme in chapter 38 of the *Kuan-tzu*.[10] But as there do not seem to be clear examples of *-en rhyming with *-an in the *Ch'u-tz'u* or the *Chuang-tzu*, these examples tell us nothing about relative chronology.

Old Chinese *-aj ≠ *-oj. In the traditional Kō ("Song") rhyme category, there is a distinction between *-aj and *-oj which is parallel to the *-at ≠ *-ot and *-an ≠ *-on distinctions (Baxter 1992, 418). This distinction is consistently observed in the *Shih-ching*, though there are only a few examples of *-oj (Baxter 1992, 420–21). The distinction is quite clear in the *Lao-tzu*, as in the following four-word *-oj sequence in chapter 29:

Thus some things go forth, some FOLLOW;	(*suí* < *zljoj)
Some breathe, some BLOW;	(*ch'uī* < *thjoj)
Some are strong, some DEPLETED;	(*léi* < *C-rjoj)
Some build, some DESTROY.	(*huī* < *hljoj)

Another *-oj rhyme is found in chapter 2 (*hó* < *goj and *suí* < *zljoj; Lau 1963, 58). There are also some six unmixed *-aj sequences (Baxter 1992, 421).[11] As far as we can tell, the *-aj ≠ *-oj distinction is also preserved in the four *Kuan-tzu* chapters mentioned above, though examples are few.[12] But in the *Ch'u-tz'u* ("Li-sao"; Hawkes 1959, 24), we find *-oj rhyming with *-aj:[13]

I pulled up roots to bind the valerian	
And thread the castor plant's fallen	
CLUSTERS with;	(*juĭ* < *njoj?)
I trimmed sprays of cassia for plaiting melilotus,	
And knotted the	
LITHE, LIGHT TRAILS of ivy.	(*shĭh* < *srjaj?)

It seems plausible that rhymes like this reflect a change of *-oj to *-waj which had not yet occurred when the *Lao-tzu* was first composed.[14]

Shih-ching *Distinctions Lost in the* Lao-tzu

Although conservative in some respects, the *Lao-tzu* also shows some pronunciation changes not found in the *Shih-ching*. Tung T'ung-ho (1938) identified several characteristics of *Lao-tzu* rhyming which he described as dialect features of the Ch'u region (roughly, modern Hu-nan Province). The most important are the following:[15]

1. Confusion of the traditional *Tūng* ("East") and *Yáng* ("Yang") rhyme categories (i.e., of Old Chinese *-ong and *-ang).

2. Confusion of the traditional *Chih* ("It") and *Yū* ("Dark") rhyme categories (i.e., of Old Chinese *-ɨ and *-u).

3. Confusion of the traditional *Yü* ("Fish") and *Hóu* ("Marquis") rhyme categories (i.e., of Old Chinese *-a and *-o).

These characteristics are also found in the *Ch'u-tz'u* and the *Chuang-tzu*. Since they have been ably discussed by Tung T'ung-ho, I will only cite a few examples from the *Lao-tzu*.

1. A typical example of *-ang rhyming with *-ong is found in chapter 12 of the *Lao-tzu*; several other examples might be cited:

The five colors make man's eyes BLIND.	(*máng* < *mrang)
The five tones make man's ears DEAF.	(*lúng* < *C-rong)
The five tastes DAMAGE man's mouth.	(*shuǎng* < *srjang(ʔ))

2. The confusion of Old Chinese *-ɨ and *-u seems to affect mostly words in the rising tone (those reconstructed with final glottal stop *-ʔ in Old Chinese). A typical example is found in chapter 30. Here we have:

Once thing is vigorous,	
it then becomes OLD;	(*lǎo* < *C-ruʔ)
This is what is called	
'not following the WAY'.	(*tào* < *luʔ)
Those who do not follow the Way	
are soon FINISHED.	(*yǐ* < *ljɨʔ)

3. The confusion of Old Chinese *-a and *-o is not so common in the *Lao-tzu*; it also typically occurs in rising-tone words. It probably reflects a change of *a to *o in certain phonetic environments. A typical example is found in chapter 26:

What good are the ten thousand	
chariots of a RULER	(*chǔ* < *tjoʔ)
if he takes himself too lightly	
before the whole WORLD?	((*t'iēn*) *hsià* < *graʔ)

Though these features of pronunciation may have been characteristic of a certain place as well as a certain time (being associated with the Ch'u dialect), the *Shih-ching* pronunciation is more conservative in each case; it is probably safe to conclude that the pronunciation implied by the *Lao-tzu* developed out of the system we find in the *Shih-ching*, and that the pronunciations found in the *Chuang-tzu* and the *Ch'u-tz'u* are later developments still.

Conclusion

Our linguistic examination of the *Lao-tzu* has focused on structural features on the one hand and phonological characteristics on the other. From a structural point of view, the *Lao-tzu* represents a specific genre which is different both from the poetry of the *Shih-ching* and the *Ch'u-tz'u* and from the narrative prose we find in many other early works of Chinese philosophy. The text is structured phonologically and semantically so as to form a succession of short, paragraph-like units of verse, sometimes loosely framed by elements which function as introductions, transitions, or summaries. Unlike many early philosophical texts, the *Lao-tzu* is almost entirely free of reference to specific individuals and events.

The existence of other texts with similar characteristics, such as certain chapters of the *Kuan-tzu*, has been recognized for some time; but the canonical status of the *Lao-tzu* may have tended to hide the importance of these similarities. Study of these sometimes obscure texts may clarify the history of the *Lao-tzu* more than comparison with other texts which happen to have been recognized as classics. Certainly, the development of the genre which the *Lao-tzu* represents cannot be studied from the *Lao-tzu* alone. A reasonable conjecture would be that the *Lao-tzu* and similar texts emerged from a distinctive tradition of philosophical verse with strong oral elements and little concept of individual authorship.

From a phonological point of view, improvements in Old Chinese reconstruction make it possible to see that the *Lao-tzu* preserves a number of distinctions in pronunciation which the *Ch'u-tz'u* and the "Inner Chapters" of the *Chuang-tzu* have lost, and this suggests that it may be earlier than they are, and closer to the time of the *Shih-ching*. Given that these texts are generally dated to the late fourth or early third century B.C.E., it is linguistically quite plausible to date the bulk of the *Lao-tzu* to the mid or early fourth century, a view that agrees with much of the traditional scholarship.

Notes

1. Notice that Liu's arguments on rhyme are structural rather than phonological; he is concerned with the frequency and position of rhyme words in the text. Our phonological discussion, on the other hand, will be concerned with the pronunciations implied by the choice of rhyme words, whatever their position in the text.

2. Since Chinese and English word orders are different, the rhyme words in the English translation do not always appear at the end of the line.

3. Some scholars have emended the text to make the speech and action aspects more parallel: Wang Nien-sun reads, "The words that say nothing, the business of doing nothing"; Kuo Mo-jo has, "The idea that says nothing, the business of doing nothing." See Endō 1989–92, 682.

4. See, for example, Cheng-Chang Shang-fang 1987; Starostin 1989; and Baxter 1992. To a large extent, these studies pursue ideas originally proposed by S. E. Jaxontov (1959 and later works). The existence of these distinctions is confirmed by a probabilistic analysis in Baxter 1992.

5. Ch. 58 (Lau 1963, 199): *ch'á* < *tshr(j)et, "alert"/*ch'uē* < *kʷh(j)et, "cunning"; ch. 79 (Lau 1963, 141): *ch'ì* < *khets, "tally" / *ch'è* < *thrjet, "exaction." As for ch. 76, some versions have a rhyme *mièh* < *mjet, "destroy" / *ché* < *tjet, "cut, chop down" (Lau 1963, 192), which would be an additional *-et rhyme. There might be some question about whether to reconstruct ché, "cut, chop down," as *tjet or *tjat, but it seems to rhyme as *-et in texts that distinguish *-at from *-et. Also, I believe it is cognate to Written Tibetan *gcod-pa*, "to cut; to cut off, chop off; to cut down, to fell" (perfect *bcad*, future *gcad*, imperative *chod*). The root of this form can be reconstructed as pre-Tibetan *tyat, where the sequence -ya- regularly corresponds to Old Chinese *-e-. Moreover, Chinese also has an intransitive/passive reading *shé* < Middle Chinese *dzyet* < Old Chinese *fitjet, "to be cut," which corresponds regularly to Tibetan *fichad-pa* (perfect *chad*) < *fityat, "to be cut (off)."

6. The regular *-at(s) rhymes are as follows: ch. 25 (Lau 1963, 82): *tà* < *lats, "great" / *shìh* < *djats, "recede"; ch. 35 (Lau 1963, 94): *hài* < *fikats, "harm" / *t'ài* < *hlats, "excessive"; ch. 73 (Lau 1963, 135): *shā* < *srjat, "kill" / *huó* < *gʷat, "live" / *hài* < *fikats, "harm."

7. Actually the word *lièh*, here translated as "split," could be reconstructed as either *C-rjat or *C-rjet (see Baxter 1992, 403–5). If it should turn out that the correct reconstruction for "split" is *C-rjet, then this passage would show an irregular rhyme between *-et and *-at. In that case, there are three possibilities. First, as the "a" in Lau's section number (85a) indicates, this passage appears to be a commentary on the preceding section 85; it might thus represent a later stratum of the *Lao-tzu* text, written at a time when *-et and *-at already rhymed as they do in the *Chuang-tzu* and the *Ch'u-tz'u*. Second, the word here might mean something besides "split"; other possibilities are "burn" or "disaster," which

are unrelated to "split" and regularly rhyme as *-at. Third, perhaps *-at really does rhyme with *-et here, and our generalization about *Lao-tzu* rhyming is incorrect. The first and second possibilities seem most likely to me.

8. The *Ch'u-tz'u* offers little evidence either way on the rhyming of *-at, *-et, and *-ot. There seem to be no clear examples of *-at rhyming with *-et, for example. We do find *-at rhyming with *-ot in the poem "The Princess of the Hsiang" (Hawkes 1959, 37), where *yì* < *ljat(s) ("rudder") rhymes with hsuĕh < *sjot ("snow"), suggesting that *-ot may have changed to something like *- wat. But this poem may be too late to be relevant; there is no agreement on its origin, and it is not necessarily by the poet Ch'ü Yuan.

9. The word *shàn*, "good," which I reconstruct as Old Chinese *gjenʔ, could also theoretically be reconstructed as *djanʔ or *djenʔ; but the choice of *gjenʔ is supported by two "sound glosses" by the Han-dynasty scholar Cheng Hsuan (127–200 C.E.). Sound glosses were a traditional way of explaining one word in a classical text by giving another word of similar pronunciation. In his commentary to the *Chou-li* (Rites of Chou), Cheng Hsuan twice glosses the related word *shàn* ("repair, make good") with the word *chìn(g)* < *kjengs, "strength" (Coblin 1983, 206, #210, and 212, #389). Only by reconstructing "good" as *gjenʔ can we explain why a word like *kjengs ("strength") would have sounded similar enough to be used as a sound gloss here.

10. The rhyme words are *pièn* < *bjenʔ (or perhaps *bjen(ʔ)s), "debate" / *hsièn* < *ɦikens, "appear".

11. Note, however, that Old Chinese *-jaj sometimes rhymes with *-e in the *Lao-tzu*, something which does not happen in the *Shih-ching*.

12. In *Kuan-tzu* 38, for example, we find a rhyme *hó* < *goj ("harmonize") / *suí* < *zljoj ("follow"), as in ch. 2 of the *Lao-tzu*. There is also a rhyme *huī* < *hljoj ("destroy") / *k'uēi* < *kh(r)joj ("deficient")—though conceivably the latter could also be reconstructed as *kʷh(r)jaj. There is an *-aj rhyme in ch. 37: *huà* < *hngʷraj(s) ("transform") / *yí* < *ljaj ("move"). See Endō 1989–92, 710, 700.

13. Since *-jaj and *-je are sometimes confused in texts of this period, it is difficult to tell whether *shǐh* ("long, trailing") should be reconstructed as *srjajʔ or as *srjeʔ, especially since the meaning is uncertain. The phonetic element of the character would normally imply *-e, but we cannot assume that this character is the original one. So actually, this rhyme in "Li-sao" might have been either *njwajʔ with *srjajʔ, or *njweʔ

(from earlier *njwaj?) with *srje?. In either case, the *-aj ≠ *-oj distinction has been lost.

14. If we are correct in reconstructing *k'uēi* ("diminish") as *kh(r)joj (see note 12 above), then we have other examples of *-oj rhyming with *-aj in lines 60–61 of the "Li-sao" and in the last stanza of the "Ta-ssu-ming" (The Great Master of Fate), both in *Ch'u-tz'u*. In the former *k'uēi* rhymes with (*lù*)-*lí* < *-(C)-rjaj, ("scattered"), in the latter with *hó* < *gaj ("what") and *wéi* < *w(r)jaj ("do").

15. Tung also mentions a fourth characteristic, occasional confusion of the traditional *Chēn* ("True") and *Kēng* ("Plow") rhyme categories (i.e., of Old Chinese *-in and *-eng). Actually, I find that this confusion is not very common in the *Lao-tzu*. A possible example is found in ch. 13: *chīng* < *krjeng ("startle") rhyming with *shēn* >*hljin ("body"). But many of the possible examples of this confusion (including this one) might not have been intended as rhymes at all.

References

Baxter, William H. 1992. *A Handbook of Old Chinese Phonology. Trends in Linguistics: Studies and Monographs*. Berlin: Mouton de Gruyter.

Boltz, William G. 1984. "Textual Criticism and the Ma-wang-tui *Lao tzu*." *Harvard Journal of Asiatic Studies* 44: 185–224.

———. 1985. "The *Lao tzu* Text That Wang Pi and Ho-shang Kung Never Saw." *Bulletin of the School of Oriental and African Studies* 48.3: 493–501.

———. 1993. "Lao tzu Tao te ching." In *Early Chinese Texts: A Bibliographical Guide*, ed. Michael Loewe, 269–92. Berkeley, Calif.: Society for the Study of Early China.

Cheng-Chang Shang-fang. 1987. "Shang-ku yun-mu hsi-t'ung ho ssu-teng, chieh-yin, sheng-tiao te fa-yuan wen-t'i." *Wen-chou shih-yuan hsueh-pao, she-hui k'o-hsueh pan* 1987.4: 67–90.

Ch'ien Mu. 1935. *Hsien-Ch'in chu-tzu hsi-nien k'ao*. Hong Kong: Hong Kong University Press.

Coblin, W. South. 1983. *A Handbook of Eastern Han Sound Glosses*. Hong Kong: Chinese University Press.

Endō Tetsuo. 1991. *Kanshi*. 3 vols. Shinyaku kanbun taikei, vols. 42, 43, and 52. Tokyo: Meiji Shoin.

Hawkes, David. 1959. *Ch'u Tz'u: The Songs of the South: An Ancient Chinese Anthology*. Oxford: Clarendon Press.

Jaxontov, Sergej Evgen'evič. 1959. "Fonetika kitajskogo jazyka 1 tysjačeletija do n. e. (sistema finalej)" [The phonology of the Chinese language of the 1st millennium B.C.E.]. *Problemy Vostokovedenija* 1959.2: 137–47.

Karlgren, Bernhard. 1954. "Compendium of Phonetics in Ancient and Archaic Chinese." *Bulletin of the Museum of Far Eastern Antiquities* 26: 211–367.

Lau, D. C. 1963. *Lao Tzu Tao Te Ching*. Harmondsworth, England: Penguin Classics.

———. 1970. *Mencius*. Harmondsworth, England: Penguin Classics.

Li, Fang-kuei. 1980. *Shang-ku-yin yen-chiu*. Peking: Shang-wu yin-shu-kuan.

Liu Xiaogan. 1994. *Classifying the Zhuangzi Chapters*. Translated by William E. Savage. Ann Arbor: University of Michigan, Center for Chinese Studies Monographs, no. 65.

Lo Ken-tse. 1958. *Chu-tzu k'ao so*. Peking: Jen-min ch'u-pan-she.

Loewe, Michael, ed. 1993. *Early Chinese Texts: A Bibliographical Guide*. Berkeley, Calif.: Society for the Study of Early China.

Rickett, W. Allyn. 1985. *Guanzi: Political, Economic, and Philosophical Essays from Early China: A Study and Translation*, vol. 1. Princeton, N.J.: Princeton University Press.

———. 1993. "Guanzi." In *Early Chinese Texts: A Bibliographical Guide*, ed. Michael Loewe, 244–51. Berkeley, Calif.: Society for the Study of Early China.

Starostin, Sergej Anatol'evic. 1989. *Rekonstrukcija drevnekitajskoj fonologiceskoj sistemy* [Reconstruction of the Old Chinese phonological system]. Moscow: "Nauka," Glavnaja Redakcija Vostocnoj Literatury.

Tung T'ung-ho. 1938. "Yü Kao Pen-han hsien-sheng shang-ch'ueh 'tzu-yu ya-yun' shuo chien lun Shang-ku Ch'u fang-yin." *Bulletin of the Institute of History and Philology, Academia Sinica* 7: 533–43.

Watson, Burton. 1968. *The Complete Works of Chuang-tzu*. New York: Columbia University Press.

Yanaka Shin'ichi. 1992. "*Rōshi* to *Kanshi*: Sono seiritsu shiteki haikei no ichi kōsatsu." *Tōhōgaku* 83: 34–48.

11

Recovering the *Tao-te-ching's* Original Meaning: Some Remarks on Historical Hermeneutics

Michael LaFargue

The *Tao-te-ching* has been subject to a rather bewildering variety of interpretations. Much of this variety is due to the fact that, as in the case of all "canonical" texts, different interpreters throughout the centuries have tried to draw from it lessons relevant to a wide variety of contexts and concerns, an issue I deal with in the first pages of the present essay. Some variety, however, is also due to the rather undeveloped state of theory and methodology applied to the project of recovering the original meaning of the *Tao-te-ching*—the bulk of this essay is thus devoted to some specific proposals about theory and methodology relevant to this project.

General Interpretation Theory

I suggest, to begin with, that some confusion about interpretations can be cleared up if we distinguish two different goals one can have in studying the *Tao-te-ching*:[1] one goal is to draw from it some ideas of interest and value to a contemporary reader; the other is to try to understand the meaning this text had for its original authors[2] and audience. These goals are not by any means exclusive, and it is possible to combine them, but it is important to recognize that they are different goals, and each implies a different criterion for deciding what a good interpretation is.

Reading for Contemporary Relevance

The first goal has been and probably continues to be by far the dominant one among the majority of readers. This accords with the status of the *Tao-te-ching* as a classic, or a scripture. Here the reader approaches the text assuming that it has something important to say to her. The main problem to be overcome is the apparent cultural distance between the contemporary reader and the ancient writing. The text must be brought into the world of the modern reader, who wants to find some way she can read the text as though it were written for her, addressing the questions that are of most interest to her. A given interpretation is most successful if it allows her to find in the text something stimulating, moving, or inspiring.

This becomes the main criterion by which readers decide what a good interpretation is: The best interpretation is the one felt to have the most meaning for one's life, or something significant to say on questions one regards as important. Often also readers want an interpretation compatible with the key elements of their own worldview. Different Chinese commentators throughout history each interpreted the *Tao-te-ching* in accord with their own worldview, and this approach continues among modern Western interpreters. Heideggerians want a Heideggerian interpretation (Chang 1975; Fu 1976, 115–17, 136–37; Parkes 1987, 47–144); analytic philosophers prefer an interpretation in accord with that tradition (Hansen 1981; 1992, 210–30); and Zen devotees want a Zen interpretation (Mitchell 1988). Those who like mysticism want to interpret it as mysticism, while those who dislike mysticism want to interpret it in a nonmystical way. Readers who come with some already formed notion of Taoism want what they can regard as a "truly Taoist" interpretation.

Exposure to so many interpretations has led many modern readers to favor a laissez-faire approach to interpretation: each reader should judge for herself what a good interpretation is, based on what she feels is most interesting, has most meaning for her own life, and is congruent with her own values and assumptions. I think there is merit to this latter attitude. It seems true to say that, *taken as a classic*, the *Tao-te-ching* does in fact have many meanings; it is indeed "polysemic" as Isabelle Robinet asserts in her work here. And the source of this polysemy seems also obvious. To take a book as a classic is to take it as a work disassociated from any particular context, and from the concerns and assumptions of any particular person or group. Each reader is free, then, to read the text in her own context in the light of her own concerns and assumptions. Reading the text from a multitude of perspectives will of course generate a multitude of different interpretations.

The problem that might arise here, however, is that some readers taking a basically scriptural approach also think of themselves as intuitively divining the essential core of the *Tao-te-ching*'s original meaning. For example, Stephen Mitchell cites his own Zen training as the basis for his claim that his translation conveys the mind of Lao-tzu. In his words, "I had personal experience of the inner tradition of Lao-tze. . . . [Lao-tze's] true descendants were the Zen masters . . . and I underwent many years of intensive training with a Zen master in the U.S. . . . I felt this experience allowed me a kind of insight into the mind of Lao-tze, rather than just the words of Lao-tze."[3]

The implicit argument here is one often associated with scriptural interpretation: Since (a) the *Tao-te-ching* teaches the truth, and (b) in Mitchell's mind Zen Buddhism teaches the truth, then (c) the true meaning of the *Tao-te-ching* is identical with the truths he discovered through Zen training. The mistake here is that, even if one were to grant that Zen Buddhism represents the truth about life, this is no *historical* evidence that the *Tao-te-ching*'s authors had arrived at this truth. And, logically speaking, we can't know whether Zen Buddhists are the true descendants of the *Tao-te-ching*'s authors without knowing what their views were. This again requires historical evidence. Anyone who claims that they can divine a text's original meaning because they belong to the true descendants of its authors begs the question at issue.

This example highlights the crucial difference between the two goals mentioned above, the goal of drawing from the text some ideas that will stimulate or edify the contemporary reader, and the goal of understanding what it meant to its original authors and audience. It may well be argued that Mitchell's translation accomplishes the first goal, at least for Zen-inclined readers, better than any scholarly and historically accurate translation could do.[4] But pursuing the second goal is an historical task, that must be done using historical methods and historical evidence.

Historical Hermeneutics

On the other side, I would argue that, for the sake of neutrality, the historical interpreter must drop the *a priori* assumption traditionally accompanying classic texts, that the *Tao-te-ching* surely has special value and relevance for all readers everywhere. Historical research must allow itself to be led wherever historical evidence leads. And this means one must be initially open to discovering that the original meaning of the *Tao-te-ching* is one that has little or no plausible relevance or value for people today.

For those approaching the *Tao-te-ching* as a classic, then, the fact that it has become a text floating free of specific historical context represents an opportunity: Each reader is free to read into it whatever message she finds most meaningful. For those trying to reconstruct what the *Tao-te-ching* meant to its original authors and audience, on the contrary, the fact that the *Tao-te-ching* has become detached from its original context is not an opportunity but a problem and a challenge. For this project, the task is to reconnect it with this original context with the aid of whatever historical evidence is available. Here I think one must initially assume that, for its original authors and audience, the *Tao-te-ching* had some relatively circumscribed meaning, not the endless variety of meanings that it has come to have as a classic.

Some will raise here the common objection that the *Tao-te-ching*'s author intentionally wrote an ambiguous text so that people could draw many different meanings from it. My reply is that this represents an historical hypothesis, and on the face of it an unlikely one. It needs to be supported by historical evidence. To the other common objection—that the *Tao-te-ching* itself says that its message cannot be put into words, and therefore lacks definiteness and specificity—I would reply that this objection confuses depth with vagueness. There are many feelings and perceptions difficult to put into words, such as wordless joy and the indescribable beauty of a sunset. This is due to the limitations of language, not to the fact that the feelings and perceptions in themselves are vague and have no definite character.

I would argue that interpreting the *Tao-te-ching* as a classic and interpreting it as an expression of the views of some particular historical group are both valid and worthwhile activities. Many conflicts and confusions would be eliminated if these were recognized as different kinds of interpretation and if the limitations of each were more strictly adhered to. Mainly, edifying or inspirational interpretations should drop the claim that they are divining the original "mind of Lao-tzu." On the other side, historical interpretations should give up the implicit claim that the original meaning they strive to uncover is also the one that has most importance for modern readers simply because it is original.

To summarize the argument thus far: Is it wrong for any given reader to ignore the historical question about the *Tao-te-ching*'s original meaning, and draw from it whatever inspiration she can for her life today? No. If one does take such an approach, are there such things as correct and mistaken interpretations? No. Is it also possible and useful to try to recover the *Tao-te-ching*'s original meaning? Yes. If one does attempt this project, are there such things as correct and mistaken interpretations? Yes. Can we be absolutely certain which interpretations are accurate and which are mistaken? No—but we can do the best we can with the evidence available.

Competence as the Key to Historical Interpretation

One who attempts to uncover the original meaning of an ancient text needs to proceed on the assumption that she is trying to discover something that is—or was once—in some sense objectively there in the text. But herein lies the key problem for interpretive theory, "hermeneutics" as it is now called (see Palmer 1969; Müller-Vollmer 1988). In what sense is meaning ever objectively there in a set of written or spoken words?

It is helpful to begin on the most basic level of written text or spoken sounds. Meaning is never something completely objective, completely there in the text or sounds independent of any subjective involvement of a reader or listener. Strictly speaking, what is objectively there is simply a series of marks on a paper, or sounds made by vocal cords. These marks or sounds would be meaningless if there were no human beings with subjective associations, associating these marks or sounds with words and meanings. The important thing to note, however, is that "subjective" here does not imply that the associations are arbitrary or indeterminate, or that they vary unpredictably from subject to subject. Speech can only communicate meanings in a community of people all of whom associate a given set of ink marks or sounds with the same words having roughly the same meaning. These shared associations are part of what the linguistic theorist Noam Chomsky calls "competence" (Culler 1975, 9). Shared competence is the necessary mental, subjective component of meaning, necessary in order that the external component—sounds or ink marks—actually convey some definite meaning to some particular community of people.

Jonathan Culler has suggested that we extend the notion of competence beyond vocabulary and grammar, to include such things as those shared assumptions operative when we read a poem *as a poem*, or a scientific treatise *as a scientific treatise* (1975, 113–30). I have argued elsewhere that it is very useful when doing historical interpretation to extend the notion even further and include in it all those aspects of the mindset of the original authors and audience of a given text that implicitly determined how they understood the words of that text (LaFargue, 1985, 4–9; 1988, 354; 1994, 36–40, 145–49). This potentially might include many and complex factors, such as word associations, shared concerns and questions related to contemporary social and political conditions, assumptions about the genre of verbal compositions, and even possibly special spiritual experiences shared by the original authors and audience.

One advantage of the notion of competence is that it avoids the problems surrounding the more common notion that, if a text has a definite meaning, that meaning lies in "the author's intention" (see Hirsch 1967; Iseminger 1992). It explains how words can have definite meanings, without appealing to the questionable notion of an author's intention. For example, if I say, "One small black" to a cashier in a donut shop, he knows that I want a small cup of coffee with no cream, for which I am ready to pay him. He does not know this because he has some access to some ideas in my mind independent of my words, but because he hears my words in the context of certain assumptions which we both share. He is "competent" to understand my words because we share the same set of assumptions.

The notion of competence also solves some problems that arise if one assumes that the meaning of a given set of words is something that can be extracted from these words and conveyed more directly and straightforwardly using a different set of words (a "paraphrase"). Such a notion makes for problems especially when dealing with such things as jokes, poems, and some religious literature. Everyone knows, for example, that the point of a given joke cannot adequately be stated in a simple declarative sentence. This might lead one to conclude that the point of a joke is something vague and open to indefinite interpretations. But this goes against the common experience in which someone fails to "get" the joke, which implies that there is something quite definite to get or not to get. The notion of competence obviates this difficulty: For the competent listener—the listener who involves herself with the joke as a joke, and who shares certain key assumptions with the joke teller—*the words of the joke themselves* convey its point. This suggests also a possible answer also to the age-old problem as to how the words of the *Tao-te-ching* can describe a Way that is "nameless" (chs. 1, 14, 32, 37, 41), and is properly conveyed only by a "teaching without words" (chs. 2, 43). That is, the meaning is not *literally* in the words, in the sense that anyone with a literal understanding of the words would get it. The words of the text only convey their intended meaning for someone who engages with them in a certain spirit—as an answer to certain specific personal concerns, and against the background of certain specific personal experiences. For such a person, the words of the text are "easy to understand," but for others they are not (ch. 70).

I therefore suggest that we approach the *Tao-te-ching*, or any other text, with the initial assumption that it had some relatively definite meaning for its original authors and originally intended audience. This meaning was at one time objectively there, in the only sense that meaning is ever there in language: the words conveyed a single definite meaning for a group of people with a shared competence. Reconstructing the elements and character of this shared competence ought to be the central organizing focus for historical research into the *Tao-te-ching*'s original meaning. Such reconstruction can make use of many traditional methods, such as studies of ancient Chinese word-meanings, of historical events and ancient social structure, and of other ancient Chinese thinkers, insofar as there is some evidence that these influenced the concerns and assumptions of the *Tao-te-ching*'s original authors and audience. There is also much to be learned from indirect indications in the text itself as to the assumptions and concerns of the original authors and audience.

The ideal would be for the modern reader to vicariously internalize this competence and let it implicitly inform her reading. Insofar as a modern reader is able to approximate and internalize the competence of the original readers, the words of the text will have approximately the same meaning for her as they did for them. This is what I mean by "recovering the *Tao-te-ching*'s original meaning." Proposing this as an ideal goal does not of course say anything about how successful we can be in achieving it. Rather, success is determined by the amount and quality of the historical evidence available to us. Besides historiographical difficulties due to dearth of evidence, there are also psychological difficulties that will prevent a modern reader from ever fully internalizing the concerns and assumptions of an ancient Chinese audience. These difficulties—sometimes cited as reasons to abandon the attempt to recover original meanings entirely (Gadamer 1982, 253)—should make us modest about the claims we make for any given reconstruction of the *Tao-te-ching*'s original meaning. They are not necessarily grounds for abandoning the project or lowering our ambitions, for not doing the best we can with the evidence and abilities available.

Reconstructing the Competence Appropriate to the Tao-te-ching:
Genre and Coherence as Key Historical Problems

I have elsewhere tried to deal comprehensively with the complex elements of competence relevant to *Tao-te-ching* interpretation (LaFargue 1994). Here I would like to explain the results of my research and analysis on only one issue, related to the question of genre and coherence. I offer this as an illustration of how the proposed competence-based hermeneutics outlined above looks in practice.

The views I arrived at on this subject can be contrasted with those interpretations that construe the message of the *Tao-te-ching* on the model of a philosophical system. Such interpretations assume that the statements in it belong to the typical genres associated with systematic philosophy, and we should expect it to have that particular kind of coherence we have come to expect of philosophical systems. Specifically, philosophical systems should consist of some statements that state doctrines of extremely general import, which serve as the foundational first principles of the system. The remainder of the system ought to consist of other doctrines, or rules for conduct, that can be logically deduced from these first principles. A system is consistent if all the logical implications of its first principles are adhered to; it is self-contradictory if they are not.

A common view, for instance, is that the *Tao-te-ching* teaches the general theory that all value judgments are invalid (see Schwartz 1985; Hansen 1992, 212–24). Since first principles are understood to be absolute and universal in scope, any other statements in the *Tao-te-ching* that in fact express value judgments must represent an internal contradiction, an incoherence in its message. There are of course many apparent indications that the *Tao-te-ching* does make value judgments (see Lau 1958): it seems to prefer femininity over masculinity, softness over hardness, stillness over excitement, and the traditional culture of small agrarian villages over the "progress" of civilization. Benjamin Schwartz takes these indications seriously, and thinks that this does indeed represent an internal contradiction in the *Tao-te-ching*. Chad Hansen chooses the other alternative. In treating the *Tao-te-ching*'s apparent idealization of simple agrarian life, for example, he concludes that this apparent value judgment must be only apparent. It cannot be seriously intended, because this would make the text incoherent (1992, 229–30). Such philosophical interpretations, however, make certain assumptions about what constitutes competence in understanding the *Tao-te-ching*. If we think that a statement belongs to the genre "general theory," or "first principle," we understand it in a much different fashion than we would if we thought it belonged to the genre of poetry or proverb. Similarly, if we assume that some body of writing outlines a "philosophical system," we look for a kind of coherence in it different from the kind we look for in a body of poetry or collection of proverbs. Assumptions about genre and coherence fall in the area of "competence" because they belong to those assumptions some readers bring to their reading which implicitly shape the way they understand the words they read.

The question about the genre-related competence appropriate to the *Tao-te-ching* is not only a literary, but also an historical question. To use a contemporary analogy: A future historian who took "When it rains it pours" as a general theory—expressing the belief that drizzles never exist, only downpours—would not only be making a literary mistake about genre, but would also commit an *historical* error, a mistake about the beliefs of twentieth-century Americans who used this proverb. What we need then is some kind of evidence that would help us decide whether the *Tao-te-ching*'s original authors and audience probably understood some particular statements in the *Tao-te-ching* as philosophical doctrines. Our own opinions about the importance or superior status of philosophical writing over against other kinds of writing are irrelevant as historical evidence.

An Example of Competence-Based Historical Hermeneutics: Understanding Polemic Aphorisms in the *Tao-te-ching*

We should not begin by asking, "What philosophical doctrines does the *Tao-te-ching* teach?" but rather, "Does it mean to teach philosophical doctrines?" I have argued elsewhere that the answer to the latter question is more likely no (LaFargue 1994, 47–48, 112–118, 196–98). Instead, from the viewpoint of genre and life setting, statements or sayings in the *Tao-te-ching* fall into two major groups. One consists of proverb-like sayings that I call "polemic aphorisms," sayings such as "sincere words are not elegant" and "one who speaks does not know," which are directed against some common human assumptions or tendencies that they try to correct (LaFargue 1994, 133–74). The other consists of sayings belonging to several different genres, all of which have self-cultivation as their life setting, for example, some that recommend cultivating femininity (chs. 10, 28), and others that celebrate the cosmic importance of femininity (ch. 6) and the benefits that come from its cultivation (ch. 61; LaFargue 1994, 175–266). Because of space limitations, I will deal here only with some aspects of polemic aphorisms (LaFargue 1990; 1992, 201–5).

The Semantic Structure of Aphorisms in General

My general thesis here depends on the argument that in their original setting the proverb-like aphorisms in the *Tao-te-ching* were implicitly understood to have the same *formal* structure as aphorisms generally, including aphorisms in our own culture, and so we can use aphorisms familiar to us as a starting point of understanding them. This follows Culler's argument that we can only build reliable models of formal linguistic structure by reflectively making explicit the structure of sentences whose formal structure we are sure that we already implicitly understand (1975, 22–26).

"Aphorism" here is a technical term of convenience to refer to several kinds of statements that have a common semantic structure. These include most prominently many folk sayings ("Haste makes waste," "It ain't over 'til it's over") as well as

1. What we might call "quips" (Yogi Berra's "The future isn't what it used to be," Leo Durocher's "Nice guys finish last")
2. Short sayings one might find on bumper stickers, posters, graffiti, or on greeting cards ("The one who dies with the most toys wins," "The more I see, the less I smile," "Love is when you don't have to be with somebody")
3. Slogans used in public campaigns ("Safety is no accident," "Love

it or leave it," "Legal Seafoods—where the customer comes second")
4. Pithy statements made by philosophers in a nonsystematic mode (Nietzsche's "God is dead," Derrida's "There is nothing outside of text," Wittgenstein's "Whereof one cannot speak, one must keep silence")

It might at first seem that aphorisms are simple to understand, and this is true in the case of familiar aphorisms. When reflecting not on *what* familiar proverbs mean, but on *how* they mean—the competence we *implicitly* bring to bear in understanding this genre—one discovers that they have a structure that is considerably complex, especially when compared to the relatively simple structure of factual reports and philosophical first principles. In what follows, I will first give the main results of my reflections on the semantic structure of aphorisms familiar in modern American culture. After discussing this in some detail, I will give several examples showing the relevance of this analysis to the interpretation of polemic aphorisms in the *Tao-te-ching*.

The meaning-structure of aphorisms in general can be described in terms of three essential elements:

1. A "target" that the aphorism means to criticize and correct
2. An "image" which the aphorism evokes
3. An "attitude" expressed in the aphorism, and the value-orientation underlying this attitude

The Target of Aphorisms

Aphorisms are essentially compensatory wisdom. They are directed against some opposing human tendency that they mean to correct or compensate for. "Slow and steady wins the race," is a common proverb, although it is not reliable as a general law about who wins races. "The race usually goes to the swift" is more true, but is not a proverb. Why? People have a tendency to assume that being swift is always the only way to win races, and "Slow and steady wins the race" compensates for this tendency, to wake people up to an alternative possibility they tend to neglect. This is its "point." But there is no tendency to think that fast people won't win. "The race goes to the swift" has nothing to compensate for. Although it is true, it has no useful point in everyday life. I call this opposing human tendency the target of a given aphorism. Aphorisms usually do not directly mention their specific target, but the target of any given aphorism is nonetheless an essential part of its meaning.

Most Americans will recognize immediately the usual target of "It takes two to tango" (the tendency to blame one person where two are at fault). If a foreigner does not understand its usual target, he would not be able to understand its meaning.

Further, the meaning of any given aphorism seems to be exhausted in making a point against its particular target. This restricts aphorisms in their intended scope, and this in turn constitutes a crucial difference between aphorisms and general laws and philosophical principles. The latter are intended to be universal and unrestricted; there should be no exceptions to general laws, like Newton's law of the conservation of energy, or to first principles like Kant's "treat others as ends not as means." But it is obvious that haste does not always make waste, that sometimes you can in fact tell a book by its cover, and certainly less is not always more. The meaning of "less is more" is not a general theory in any sense; rather, it is restricted to drawing a person's attention to an important but overlooked consideration relevant only to a very limited range of circumstances.

The restricted scope of aphorisms also means that they are not necessarily related to any further body of principles and ideas. "You can't teach an old dog new tricks" is not based on any first principle. It is capable of standing alone, evoking by itself a persuasive basis on which it hopes to win acceptance; that is, it appeals to a familiar insight derived from life-experience, that sometimes old age is connected to decreased ability for new learning. The restricted scope of aphorisms also affects the way we understand apparent conflicts between aphorisms. On one occasion I might think it appropriate to say, "You can't teach an old dog new tricks," and on a different occasion, "It's never too late to learn." Since neither of these sayings expresses a general theory or doctrine about whether older people can or cannot learn, I am not necessarily contradicting myself if I use them on different occasions.

The Image in Aphorisms

Aphorisms typically suggest a connection between two things, such as the connection between "being a nice guy" and "finishing last." But, again unlike general laws, they do not mean to say that these two things are always connected, or even that they are most often connected. "A watched pot never boils" does not state a natural law about what always or even most often happens when one watches a pot. It means to suggest to us an image, that of a person anxiously watching a pot and *feeling* as if it will "never boil." The image evokes a sensed connection, which does not always occur but sometimes occurs, between anxious waiting and the feeling that what is waited for will never come.

This feature of aphorisms is important because it often considerably narrows the meaning of the terms used. In the proverb just quoted, not just any *watching* is intended, but anxious watching. And "never boiling" has a psychological rather than a physical reference—it *seems* to the anxious watcher that the pot will "never boil." This kind of connection and the consequent narrowing of meanings is an aspect of aphorisms that is implied and suggested rather than directly stated—but this does not mean that the suggested connections and meanings are vague or indeterminate, or that the given aphorism has many possible meanings.[5] If, for some given person, "A watched pot never boils" fails to evoke the experience just described, we would say that that person did not understand a crucial aspect of this proverb as it is normally understood. This means that aphorisms are not dogmatic, but mean to evoke an image in which the basis for connecting two ideas is clear to our minds. "Haste makes waste" does not mean to assert dogmatically that all instances of haste necessarily lead to waste, and ask the listener to take this on blind faith. It asks the listener to imagine and fill in some rational connection, some reason why some instances of haste do lead to waste.

The image offered by an aphorism is typically a *counterimage*, intended to correct some common opposing view, to wake someone up to some consideration they are in danger of overlooking. This explains the fact that aphoristic images are often cast in absolute terms, and also sometimes in terms that are highly exaggerated and paradoxical. "Never believe anything you hear, and only half of what you see" is clearly hyperbole, an exaggerated expression of the insight that one cannot always trust appearances or hearsay. The hyperbole aids the aphorism in countering its target, the human tendency toward gullibility. Similarly, paradox heightens and dramatizes the contrast between the image offered by an aphorism and the target mentality that it opposes. The paradoxical saying "Less is more," for example, is phrased in a way that evokes its seemingly more commonensical opposite, the idea that "more is more." In this way it dramatizes the contrast with its target, the tendency in some situations—say the writing of an essay—to ignore the disadvantages of adding more.

Paradox is sometimes celebrated as somehow an attack on rationality. It does of course undermine some common thought habits. But if the above argument is correct, "Less is more" does not advocate irrational thinking. Nor does it assert dogmatically that whenever a person has less of something they always have more, asking the listener simply to take this dogmatic assertion on blind faith. Rather, it invites the listener to stretch her imagination to fill in some rational connection, some plausible way in which some kinds of "having less" in some situations amount to "having more." Filling in such a rational connection is crucial to an intelligent understanding and use of the saying, which does not advocate all kinds of "having less" in whatever situation, but means to draw attention to those certain kinds of having less that do in fact give one some advantage.

The Attitude Expressed in Aphorisms

Suppose a person is considering a somewhat risky stock investment. In such a situation a friend might choose to bring up the saying, "Better safe than sorry." Or she might choose to give opposite advice by bringing up the saying, "Nothing ventured, nothing gained." Both sayings evoke some rational insight into possible connections, so both are to some degree true. But, following my present argument, it is irrelevant to ask whether either saying is really true, because the point of proverbs is not to assert the necessity or probability of such connections. It is to assert that some particular complex has some special *relevance and significance* in the situation addressed.

We implicitly perceive the speaker as having made a choice about what particular image to bring up in the present situation. In making such a choice she has "taken a stand" about what is important in the situation. She says either that this is a situation is one in which the image of being-sorry-for-not-having-played-it-safe is the crucial image to keep in mind. Or she says that it is a situation in which it is better to bring up the image of losing-an-opportunity-for-profit-by-playing-it-safe. In making these choices one expresses an attitude toward the situation; a "conservative" attitude is expressed in the former case, an "adventurous" attitude in the latter case. The speaker of either proverb is essentially inviting the listener to take either a conservative or an adventurous attitude toward the situation. The listener will perceive either saying as "good advice" in this situation insofar as she finds either of these attitudes appropriate to the situation.

Choosing to bring up one image rather than another in any given situation expresses an attitude toward that situation. And very often such attitudes are motivated by specific value orientations. "Nice guys finish last" is not an objective and neutral report about which people usually lose. It expresses a certain value orientation, that of a person who takes a hard-bitten attitude toward competition and looks down on the naiveté of so-called nice guys. As normally understood, the saying really suggests that nice guys *deserve* to lose. This is especially evident if we consider a saying that expresses the opposite attitude, such as the somewhat moralistic "Cheaters never prosper"—suggesting that cheaters deserve not to prosper.

Although on the surface many aphorisms might appear to be simply neutral and objective observations about what usually happens, this is deceptive. When a person uses an aphorism, they are implicitly asserting the relevance of the image evoked to some given situation, and this assertion frequently implies some kind of judgment as to what kind of values are to be given prime consideration in this situation. What this suggests about *Tao-te-ching* interpretation is that we do not look for coherence or unity in it by comparing the explicit content of different sayings, looking for some logically articulated system of doctrines. Rather, we ought to ask, about each saying, what value priorities would be implied in choosing to present this particular image as a corrective to this particular target mentality. Then we ought to compare different sayings in the *Tao-te-ching* on the basis of the value priorities implicitly expressed in such choices.

Understanding Polemic Aphorisms in the Tao-te-ching

Now to some illustrations of the relevance of the above observations to *Tao-te-ching* interpretation, beginning with an interpretation of the famous line: "One who speaks does not know" (ch. 56). If this line has the aphoristic semantic structure outlined above, it does not mean that literally anyone who ever says anything must lack understanding.[6] An attempt to make its meaning fully explicit might go as follows:

1. You might be easily impressed by skillful speech, and so assume that the eloquent speaker is a person of great understanding. (This is the saying's target.)
2. To counter this, I call your attention to the image of empty-headed eloquence, so you can see a connection between skillful speech and lack of real knowledge. (This is its image).
3. As a reason for accepting this point, I invite you to adopt a value orientation, in which substance is all-important even when it is not impressive, while outward show is of little import. (This is the attitude behind the saying).

Further, as earlier mentioned, aphorisms do not dogmatically ask for blind assent, but mean to evoke some rational connection between two terms. So in considering the saying, "Wishing to be high above the people, you must in your speech put yourself below them" (ch. 66), we ought to ask, What kind of "putting yourself below the people in your speech" could be rationally connected to some result plausibly described as "being above them"? The connection here seems rather easy to imagine: A leader who addresses his subordinates in a deferential way will frequently gain their respect in this way, and so become higher in their esteem. Here also we get some help from other passages referring to an ancient Chinese custom whereby rulers sometimes referred to themselves in self-deprecating ways, as "the orphan," "the friendless," or "the destitute" (chs. 39, 42). Chapter 39 says, "what is noble [the king] takes what is lowly [these lowly titles] as a foundation", meaning that kings gain more respect, become higher in their subjects' eyes by self-deprecation. Since self-deprecation and deference are clearly not the only, or the most effective, means for a leader to gain respect, we can suspect that this saying implicitly expresses a particular value preference. The suggested connection is probably not only a practical, but a moral one:[7] Deferential leaders *deserve* more respect than overbearing ones. Filling in these kinds of rational connections also limits the meaning of the terms of these sayings. First, they seem to assume a leader who is already admirable on some other grounds, who becomes all the more admirable because of his deferential manner—otherwise we would have the extremely implausible idea that a person could gain respect simply by being deferential, with no other claim to respect whatsoever. Second, if the saying suggests that the deferential leader *deserves* admiration, it clearly does not have in mind the hypocritical leader who merely puts on an appearance of deference in order to manipulate the people under him, an objection raised by later Confucians (Lau 1958, 359).

Finally, it is important to note that the meaning of terms in an aphorism are heavily influenced by the suggested connection between terms within a given aphorism. This is unlike the case in modern academic and philosophical writing, for example, where authors frequently try to define key terms in their vocabulary and then consistently adhere to these defined meanings throughout their writing. Interpreters often assume this about the *Tao-te-ching*. But this is clearly not the case, for example, with the terms "low" and "high." In some passages, "being low" refers to a deferential manner, but other lines assume that it is also desirable to "be high" in the people's estimation (chs. 61, 66). In yet other chapters, "low" is used straightforwardly to mean "inferior" and contrasted with "high" as superior (chs. 38, 41). If aphorisms are a predominant genre in the *Tao-te-ching*, one must be extremely sensitive to context in thinking about the meaning of terms.

Implied Generalizations in Aphorisms

The suggested connection evoked by an aphorism often implies a kind of generalization. Whereas the saying quoted above speaks more specifically of "becoming high" by "putting oneself low," there is a general insight suggested, namely that deference gains respect. This might apply to deference of other kinds, as well as other kinds of gaining respect.

This is relevant in *Tao-te-ching* interpretation because it draws attention to the fact that its aphorisms cluster around specific insights of general import. For example, another saying (ch. 61) advises again to "be low" but this time as a means of "winning out" in interstate diplomacy. This saying refers to a different area of human life than the one about becoming high in the eyes of one's subordinates. Still it is probably based on the same general insight: "Being low" refers to a deferential manner in conducting diplomacy, and thus plausibly leads to "winning out" because it wins the respect and cooperation of the other leaders. Both sayings seem built on the same generalizable insight, and in fact belong to a somewhat larger cluster of six sayings all built on this insight (found in chs. 7, 39, 42, 61, 66, 68).

Similar observations can be made about several other clusters of sayings built around other generalizable insights (see LaFargue 1992; 1994, "Topical Glossary"). This clustering gives us valuable indications of the structure and contours of the original worldview expressed in the *Tao-te-ching*—the ways in which sayings were probably originally related to each other—and thus enables us to follow the contours inherent in it rather than imposing our assumptions on it.

If one regards the implied generalizations, rather than the specific applications, as the core of the *Tao-te-ching*'s thought, this also can be the basis for applying the thought of the *Tao-te-ching* to situations other than its authors intended. For example, one might think of many situations in modern life—the situation of parents, policemen, teachers, supervisors, and so on—where it is important that people in positions of authority gain and maintain the respect of those in their charge. Applying the *Tao-te-ching*'s advice about "becoming high by being low" to these situations would be in perfect accord with its historical meaning.

Dealing with Apparent Contradictions

The body of aphorisms in the *Tao-te-ching* contains apparent contradictions; there are conflicts between passages that advise "doing nothing" and others which encourage specific forms of intervention. Some of these passages seem to advise against working to change the world, saying that "working ruins" (ch. 29) and insist on "not doing, so that nothing will remain not done" (ch. 48). Then again there are some passages that give advice specifically about how to intervene, assuming that on occasion one must act in opposition to the natural tendencies of things, to "nip things in the bud," break them when they are fragile, or scatter them when they are small (ch. 64, also ch. 36).

To address these apparent contradictions, one should note first that on the above aphoristic analysis, the saying "do not doing and nothing will remain not done" is not a dogmatic assertion of an implausible general principle that "doing nothing will always cause everything to get done." One should rather imagine and fill in some rational connection and thereby narrow the meaning of the terms. The question is then, what mode of taking care of things that could be described in a some fashion as "not doing" could plausibly be expected to "get things done"? Second, a plausible analysis of the two apparently conflicting groups of sayings is that they are in fact directed against two different targets.

The first group is directed against the tendency of rulers to look upon society as a passive field for their own accomplishments, presenting instead the image of the world as a "spirit-thing," something demanding extreme respect, rather than something to be controlled (ch. 29). Again, they suggest not just any kind of literal "not doing," but an attitude of self-effacement that encourages the people to develop along their own lines (chs. 17, 49, 57). The intent of these images is exhausted in making their point against their target, and expressing a particular kind of value-motivated stance. There is no general theory involved about whether one should or should not ever intervene, nor any general theory about whether society is or is not always spontaneously good.

The other group of sayings has a different target: the tendency of those in charge to use confrontational tactics when intervening. One saying (ch. 36) urges people to take an indirect approach, analogous to our "Give him enough rope and he'll hang himself." Another advises one to destroy or redirect tendencies before they get big enough to require forceful and disruptive confrontation (ch. 64). While the various sayings in this set have different targets and offer different images, there is a plausible unity to their stance and its motivation. All favor a "low-profile" in the ruler as opposed to a political philosophy that emphasizes a striking show of force to dramatize the fact of superior control.

Conclusion

This essay does not pretend to solve all the problems in *Tao-te-ching* interpretation, or even all the problems in interpreting its polemical aphorisms. Its attempt to formulate and apply a model of *how* aphorisms mean does not settle all questions as to *what* any given *Tao-te-ching* aphorism means, a question that can only be answered through further linguisting and historical research. If it is appropriate, this model warns against some mistaken directions interpretations can take—such as interpreting some given aphorism as a "general law" or as a philosophical first principle. And it suggests some general directions that historical research should take—as, for example, an inquiry into the historically most likely targets of *Tao-te-ching* aphorisms.

This essay is part of a larger project to work out a controlled analytic methodology for the interpretation of difficult texts like the *Tao-te-ching*. Even the mention of "analysis" and "method" will probably provoke objections from many general readers, as well as from some current hermeneutic theorists. General readers of the *Tao-te-ching* will prefer to rely on personal intuition; influential hermeneutic thinkers, persuaded by Hans-Georg Gadamer's *Truth and Method*, will find that, in interpretation, "method" is if anything an obstacle to "truth." My central argument here is, to the contrary, that it *is* possible to make the interpretation of works like the *Tao-te-ching* a *historical* endeavor, an attempt to understand the particular meanings some historical group of people were trying to get across when they composed the words that have come down to us in the book. Historical research has to rely on historical evidence and on careful rational analysis of this evidence—however "un-Taoist" this may be. It requires not less analysis, but more careful and more subtle analysis.

Such analysis is of course not the same thing as understanding. It is only a first step toward reconstructing those elements constituting the "competence" of the *Tao-te-ching*'s original readers, which made them understand its words they way they did. Our ultimate goal should be to vicariously *internalize* these elements of competence that our analytical method has reconstructed and read the words of the *Tao-te-ching* from this point of view. Only such *disciplined* intuition can enable us to engage with the *Tao-te-ching* in something like the way its original authors and audience engaged with it, and thereby understand in a feelingful way the very Tao they were trying to embody in the artful and extremely careful way they chose their words.

Notes

1. Arthur Waley makes a similar distinction between what he calls traditional scriptural interpretations of the *Tao-te-ching*, and his own attempt at an historical interpretation (1934, 12–13). This also corresponds roughly to the distinction E. D. Hirsch draws between the meaning that a text had for its original author, and the significance it has for later people (1967, 8). It is unfortunate that Hirsch associates this distinction with his idea that the original meaning of a text should be identified with the author's conscious intention (LaFargue 1994, 7–12).

2. In this essay I speak of "authors" in the plural, following the opinion of modern critical scholars that the *Tao-te-ching* was not written by a single author but consists of sayings that ciculated in the oral tradition. See Lau 1963, 163–74; Kimura in Hurvitz 1961; Mair 1990, 119–26; Waley 1934, 97; Karlgren 1932, 25n1; Kaltenmark 1969, 13; Creel 1970, 6. My own development of the implications of this understanding for *Tao-te-ching* interpretation employs the form critical method first developed in biblical studies (see MacKnight 1969; LaFargue 1994, 126, 129–31).

3. "Translation of Ancient Tao Text Brings $130,000;" *New York Times*, March 16, 1988, 18. Mitchell makes a similar claim in the introduction to his translation: "A fourteen-years-long course of Zen training . . . brought me face to face with Lao Tzu" (Mitchell, 1989, x). He studied with the Korean Zen Master Seung Sahn, who arrived in the United States in 1972. For a selection of Seung's teachings, see Mitchell 1976.

4. Huston Smith, author of a popular textbook on world religions, declares Mitchell's translation to be "as close to being definitive for our time as any I can imagine" (quoted on the cover of Mitchell 1988, paperback edition).

5. Aphorisms of course need to be *general* truths, applicable to many situations. One might say that in this sense a given aphorism "has many meanings." But this is the same sense in which "2 + 2 = 4" also has many meanings.

6. Such a literal understanding underlies the poet Po Chü-yi's (772–846) famous comment on this line: "If we are to believe that Lao-tzu was one who knew/ how comes it that he wrote a book of five thousand words" (Waley 1919, 269).

7. The use of the term "moral" in relation to the *Tao-te-ching* will probably strike many as extremely un-Taoist, and in fact the text severely criticizes conventional morality. I have argued for a broader theory of the good permitting the plausible claim that the vision of the *Tao-te-ching* is based on some judgments about what is truly good (LaFargue 1994, 270–77).

References

Chang, Chung-yuan. 1975. *Tao: A New Way of Thinking*. New York: Harper & Row.

Creel, Herrlee G. 1970. *What is Taoism?* Chicago: University of Chicago Press

Culler, Jonathan. 1975. *Structuralist Poetics: Structuralism, Linguistics, and the Study of Literature*. Ithaca, N.Y.: Cornell University Press.

Fu, Charles Wei-hsün. 1976. "Creative Hermenutics: Taoist Metaphysics and Heidegger." *Journal of Chinese Philosophy* 3: 115–43.

Hansen, Chad. 1981. "Linguistic Skepticism in the Lao Tzu." *Philosophy East and West* 31: 231–46.

———. 1992. *A Daoist Theory of Chinese Thought: A Philosophical Interpretation*. New York: Oxford University Press.

Hirsch, E. D. 1967. *Validity in Interpretation*. New Haven, Conn: Yale University Press.

Hurvitz, Leon. 1961. "A Recent Japanese Study of *Lao-tzu*." *Monumenta Serica* 20: 311–67.

Iseminger, Gary. 1992. *Intention and Interpretation*. Philadelphia: Temple University Press.

Kaltenmark, Max. 1969. *Lao Tzu and Taoism*. Transated by Roger Greaves. Stanford, Calif.: Stanford University Press.

Karlgren, Bernhard. 1932. *On the Poetical Parts of Lao-tsi*. Göteborg, Sweden: Elanders Boktryckeri Aktiebolag.

LaFargue, Michael. 1985. *Language and Gnosis: The Opening Scenes in the Acts of Thomas*. Philadelphia: Fortress Press.

———. 1988. "Are Texts Determinate? Derrida, Barth, and the Role of the Biblical Scholar." *Harvard Theological Review* 81: 341–57.

———. 1990. "Interpreting the Aphorisms in the *Tao-te-ching*." *Journal of Chinese Religions* 18: 25–43.

———. 1994. *Tao and Method: A Reasoned Approach to the Tao Te Ching*. Albany: State University of New York Press.

Lau, D. C. 1958. "The Treatment of Opposites in *Lao-tzu*." *Bulletin of the School of Oriental and African Studies* 21: 344–60.

———. 1963. *Lao Tzu Tao Te Ching*. Baltimore: Penguin.

Mair, Victor H. 1990. *Tao Te Ching: The Classic Book of Integrity and the Way*. New York: Bantam.

MacKnight, Edgar. 1969. *What is Form Criticism?* Philadelphia: Fortress Press.

Mitchell, Stephen. 1976. *Dropping Ashes on the Buddha: The Teaching of Zen Master Seung Sahn*. New York: Grove Press.

———. 1988. *Tao Te Ching*. New York: Harper & Row.

Müller-Vollmer, Kurt, ed. 1988. *The Hermeneutics Reader*. New York: Continuum.

Palmer, Richard E. 1969. *Hermeneutics: Interpretation Theory in Schleiermacher, Dilthey, Heidegger, and Gadamer*. Evanston, Ill.: Northwestern University Press.

Parkes, Graham. 1987. *Heidegger and Asian Thought*. Honolulu: University of Hawaii Press.

Waley, Arthur. 1919. *170 Chinese Poems*. New York: Knopf.

———. 1934. *The Way and Its Power: A Study of the Tao Te Ching and Its Place in Chinese Thought*. London: Allen and Unwin.

Wimsatt, C. K. 1954. *The Verbal Icon: Studies in the Meaning of Poetry*. Lexington: University of Kentucky Press.

12

On Translating the Tao-te-ching

Michael LaFargue and Julian Pas

As an old wine of exquisite and mysterious vintage attracts sophisticated enjoyers of life, so likewise has the *Tao-te-ching* over the centuries and till the present put a magic spell on sophisticated readers, searching for the meaning of life. Both sinologists and amateurs, fascinated by the intoxicating qualities of this little book, have tried to capture its flavor and have devised ever new bottles for it, ever new translations. In China, hundreds of commentaries have been written. In the West, the *Tao-te-ching* was only discovered in the nineteenth century after, and also because, Confucianism had lost its earlier position of prestige (Zürcher 1992, 290). In this climate of change, the discovery of the *Tao-te-ching* was not just a surprise, it was seen as a welcome message. And the West's "love affair" with the text has not ended yet. New translations keep forthcoming. So far about 250 translations into Western languages have been made, most of them in English, German, or French (see Appendix).[1]

We cannot hope in this brief essay to review all of these translations, or to settle all the problems about how the *Tao-te-ching* should be translated. Instead, we concentrate on sample passages taken from seventeen of the more popular and influential translations:

1. Eight older translations (1930s–1960s): Waley (1934), Ch'u (1937), Lin (1944), Bynner (1944), Duyvendak (1954), Wu (1961), Chan (1963a), and Lau (1963).
2. Nine recent translations (1970s–1990s): Feng and English (1977), Wilhelm (1985), Mitchell (1988), Chen (1989), LaFargue (1992), and Addiss and Lombardo (1993)—including three translations of the Ma-wang-tui manuscripts: Lau (1982), Henricks (1989), and Mair (1990).

The bulk of this contribution explains the main reasons for variations among these translations. It is supplemented by a detailed discussion of two lines from the *Tao-te-ching* (chs. 4 and 13) that illustrate what kind of problems translators face, and how the different ways of solving these problems have resulted in varying translations.

Some variations in translations are, of course, due to variations in the competence of translators. Some have great talent, and some have a solid background understanding of the historic milieu and the world of thought in ancient China. Others again are weak in one or even both of these areas. But aside from this translations also differ because different translators work out different solutions to some basic problems that all translators face. These can be divided into three main categories:

- Problems concerning the text itself
- Problems in understanding the meaning of the text
- Problems in the transition from Chinese to English

We will address these one by one.

Problems Concerning the Text: Which Chinese Text Are Translators Translating?

One task facing the translator is to try to determine what the original of the *Tao-te-ching* looked like—what Chinese characters actually made it up? There are two potential problems here:

1. The oldest manuscripts sometimes differ from each other,[2] and the translator must choose which manuscript to follow.
2. Sometimes, for various reasons, a particular scholar-translator thinks that all of the manuscripts we possess have been corrupted in some way, so our only choice is to emend the text—alter or insert characters based on some educated conjecture as to what the scholar thinks the original most probably looked like.

Until recently, the first problem was not a major source of differences between *Tao-te-ching* translations. Manuscript variants were not numerous or of serious consequence. Most translators simply accepted the Chinese text of the *Tao-te-ching* as printed together with Wang Pi's commentary, occasionally borrowing readings from the Ho-shang-kung commentary or a few other manuscripts.[3] This situation changed with the discovery of the Ma-wang-tui manuscripts (dated to before 168 B.C.E.) in 1973, because they contain more variations when compared to previously known manuscripts.[4] We now have several translations based completely on these texts (Lau 1982; Mair 1990; Lin 1977; Henricks 1989); and the translations of Chen (1989), Addiss and Lombardo (1993), and LaFargue (1992) also occasionally borrow readings from those manuscripts.

The second issue, suspected corruptions casting doubt on all extant manuscripts, is a more important source of variations, especially prominent in the translations by Duyvendak (1954) and Ch'u (1937). Both follow the lead of radical modern Chinese text-critics,[5] who were convinced that, during the process of its transmission, all manuscripts of the *Tao-te-ching* were severely corrupted, both as to the wording of the text and its arrangement. This view is based on the fact that, in all existing manuscripts, many lines are difficult to make sense of, it is often difficult to see any connection between adjacent sayings in the same chapter, and some sayings are repeated verbatim in two or more different chapters.[6] These Chinese text critics thus suppose that the original was more plain in its meaning, was arranged in a much more logical way, and did not contain duplicate sayings (see Duyvendak 1954, 3). Consequently wherever possible they eliminate duplicate sayings, move some individual sayings from one chapter to another to produce a more logical order, and emend the text so that it makes clearer sense.[7] D. C. Lau has specifically argued against the project of rearrangement, because he thinks that the text was no more than a loosely arranged collection of sayings from the beginning (1963, 163–74). On the other hand, he often emends the text when he thinks specific lines do not make sense (see 1963, 189–92). However, most recent translations seem to show a general trend away from emendations that have no manuscript support.

Problems in Understanding the Meaning of the Chinese Text

It might at first seem that the problem of how to *understand* the *Tao-te-ching* should not enter into the process of translation. The job of the translator is simply to translate Chinese words into English words, and her own opinions as to how to understand the words should not influence this process. Indeed, in some passages in the *Tao-te-ching* this is a possible option—the problems of a literal word-for-word translation will be discussed below. However, none of the translations under consideration have attempted a strict word for word translation. At a minimum, each at various times paraphrases the Chinese text, and also adds words, which we will call "clarifying expansions," better to convey to the reader what the translator thinks the text means. This is probably due to the desire of translators to produce an English text that makes more sense than a word-for-word translation would. And there are also a variety of reasons why, for many specific passages in the *Tao-te-ching*, a word-for-word translation is not really feasible and sometimes the Chinese text presents the translator with uncertainties and/or ambiguities that simply cannot be carried over into English. The translator then has to decide on what he or she thinks the text probably means, and translate accordingly. This is why, very often, problems about what a given passage means must be addressed in the act of translating.

There are three principal sources of such problems in understanding:

1. The use of "loan characters" in ancient Chinese
2. The wide range of meaning of some words
3. Uncertainties about syntax due to the fact that ancient Chinese is uninflected.

Loan characters. Ancient Chinese writing was not entirely standardized, so that sometimes different scribes used different characters to represent the same word. This happened especially in cases involving homophones, two words having the same sound but different meanings. For example, in English, "one" and "won" are homophones, pronounced the same, but written differently and having different meanings. Similarly, there are two words in Chinese, both now transliterated as *te*, that are pronounced the same but usually written differently and have different meanings. One word *te* means "virtue" (or "power, charisma"), the other *te* is usually a verb, "to obtain." Sometimes a scribe might use the character normally meaning "virtue," to represent the word "to obtain"— equivalent in English to saying: "We one the game." This is relevant, for example, to our understanding of *te shan*, a phrase in ch. 49. The character for *te* here is the one that usually means "virtue," and accordingly the normal reading would be "virtue [is] good." But some translators find it puzzling why anyone would say such a thing, so they suppose that this character is being used as a loan character for the homophone "to obtain," resulting in the meaning "[he] obtains goodness." There is no way of telling for sure what the original author of this line meant to say. There is also no way to leave this matter uncertain in an English translation. Each translator must decide which understanding of the line is probably the one originally intended, and translate accordingly.

Words with a wide range of meanings. This is a problem not unique to Chinese, but present in all languages. For example, "draw" in English has a rather wide range of meanings, illustrated in the phrases, "draw a picture," "draw some water," "the game ended in a draw," "it was a long drawn-out affair," and so on. Similarly, in chapter 51 of the *Tao-te-ching* we have a word *shih* that has different meanings ranging from "energy" (Addiss/Lombardo) to "circumstances" (Lau). Again, at the end of chapter

5, there is a character for *chung* that Addiss takes to mean "centered," Duyvendak takes to mean "middle course" (between two extremes), and Waley renders as "what is within." Each of these is a plausible rendition of *chung*.

Uncertainties of syntax. English words are capable of being inflected—undergoing internal changes—to indicate things such as tense, number, and part of speech: "Thing," singular, changes to "things" plural; "run" present tense, changes to "ran," past tense; "good" as an adjective changes to "goodness" as a noun, and so on. Ancient Chinese allows no such inflections. The Chinese word *shan*, morally "good" or "skilled," for example, is written and spoken the same whether it is used as an adjective "good," an abstract noun "goodness," a concrete noun "[a] good [person]," a stative verb "to be good," a transitive verb "to consider something good," "to be good to someone," or "to be good at something."

Lack of inflection frequently makes for uncertainties about how words are related to each other. This problem is exacerbated by the fact that written Chinese permits the omission of such things as pronoun subjects ("gets goodness" instead of "he gets goodness"), connectives and conjunctions ("all recognize" instead of "when all recognize"), and copulas ("this ugly" instead of "this is ugly"). The *Tao-te-ching* generally favors a succinct style in which such omissions are frequent.

To illustrate how this affects translations, consider the three-word phrase in chapter 8, *hsin shan yuan*, literally "heart good depth."

- Mair translates, "the quality of the heart lies in its depths." He apparently construes the syntax as follows: *hsin shan* is a phrase meaning "[the] heart's good [quality]"; this phrase is the subject of a sentence with an implied copula. He construes this sentence: "[the] heart['s] good [quality] [is] depth."
- Chan translates, "in his heart he loves what is profound." His syntax has *hsin* as adverbial, "[as to his] heart," *shan* as a verb, "to consider good," that is, to love, and *yuan* meaning "depth" as the object of the verb, with an implied subject "he." The sentence is thus construed as "[as to his] heart [he] considers depth good."
- Chen translates, "her heart is in the good deep water." Her construal of the syntax: *hsin*, "heart," is the subject of an implied verbal phrase, "is in"; *yuan* is a concrete noun, "deep water," modified by the adjective *shan*, "good." She construes the sentence as "[her] heart [is in the] good deep-water."

A helpful analogy here, I believe, is the style of modern newspaper headlines. Here too, succinctness is important, the relations between words are often suggested rather than stated, and the writer depends on a reader attuned to certain issues and vocabulary to construe the words correctly. For example,[8]

- "THE DOCTOR IS ON LINE," taken by itself, could mean either that a doctor is standing in a line to get something, or that a doctor is making use of the Internet.
- "REBELS BURN TANKER, TRAIN IN SRI LANKA," could mean that rebels in Sri Lanka burned a tanker and a train, or that rebels burned a tanker and also underwent military training in Sri Lanka.
- "AFTER TWO YEAR DELAY TUNNEL VISION IS A REALITY," could mean that someone developed narrow-mindedness ("tunnel vision") because something they wanted was delayed for two years, or that plans for a tunnel were finally finished after a two-year delay.

One can see that dictionaries by themselves would be of little help to foreigners trying to decide between possible meanings these headlines might have. What helps most is a knowledge of specific circumstances, of certain ways of speaking, and of the kinds of things one can expect in a newspaper in a given city on a given day. For example, reading the first example, it helps greatly to know that being on line on the Internet is currently a hot topic of conversation, and there seems little reason to have a newspaper article about a doctor standing on line. Such uncertainties are the most important reason behind variations among scholarly *Tao-te-ching* translations. No matter what Chinese text one chooses to translate, there are in fact many sentences in the work that could theoretically be construed in a number of different ways. It seems most likely that, like our modern headline reader, the *Tao-te-ching*'s original readers had the background knowledge necessary to construe these sentences the way their authors intended them. But we do not always have good sources for reconstructing this background knowledge. Every translator thus begins by looking at some passages in the *Tao-te-ching*, makes the best guess he or she can about how to construe these passages, gradually builds up some impression of the themes and views expressed in the whole, and then uses this overall impression as a guide to choosing from various possible meanings of each given passage.

Every translator is thus caught in something like the well-known "hermeneutic circle." She must use some understanding of the whole as a context that will clear up ambiguities about the meaning of individual passages. But she can only build up such a knowledge of the whole by trying to understand individual passages, many of which are not unambiguously conveyed in the wording. Translations differ because different translators have built up different understandings of the overall message of the book, and this in turn has guided the choices they make between different possible understandings of ambiguous passages.

Translators vary greatly, both as to their overall views of the *Tao-te-ching*, and also in the degree to which they let their overall views influence their translation of individual lines. Still, one can speak of three general sources they rely on to help them reconstruct this message. First, there are traditional Chinese commentators, from Han Fei, Wang Pi, and Ho-shang-kung up until the eighteenth century. These commentators gave explanations of obscure passages that have passed into the common understanding of what the *Tao-te-ching* means, so that all translators in one way or another are under their influence.

Second, there is modern critical historical scholarship. As Waley notes, most traditional Chinese commentaries are primarily scriptural rather than historical (1934, 12). Even though, of course, all claim to be conveying the original mind of Lao-tzu, they are primarily choosing meanings that are most in accord with the assumptions of their own cultural milieux and respond to problems they consider most pressing. *Systematic critical* historical scholarship—the attempt to set aside one's own concerns and assumptions and to reconstruct the mind of ancient authors using only objective historical evidence—only began around the eighteenth century. Using these methods, some scholars like Waley have come to see a strong contrast between the way we would understand the *Tao-te-ching* if we relied on traditional commentaries, on the one hand, and the way we would understand it based strictly on what we could discover through independent historical research. This is comparable to the situation in current biblical studies, where modern critical scholars typically ignore the traditional commentaries written by later famous Christian teachers like Augustine and Aquinas. Most English translations of the *Tao-te-ching* are based at least in part on a critical attitude toward the commentators and a greater trust in modern historical scholarship, although one will still find many views of traditional Chinese commentators mentioned in the notes of Chan (1963a) and Chen (1989), for example. It is also worth mentioning that critical historical scholarship on pre-Han China is still in its infancy, so that there are few reconstructions of ancient culture that have drawn widespread agreement. As a result, even those translators like Waley (1934) and Mair (1990) who have done original research on ancient China often disagree on details.

Third, most translators have undertaken their work because they have discovered in reading the *Tao-te-ching* some views that have moved them personally, or at least that they think have considerable intrinsic merit. Given the suggestive character of the text, this means that many translators tend to intuitively feel some "deeper meaning" underlying the literal words of the text, which then influences the way they understand and translate individual lines. Granted, as most readers and scholars seem to agree, that the meaning of the *Tao-te-ching* does not lie completely on the surface, even the most objective historian, after his or her technical historical and philological research has been done, must to some degree follow his or her intuitive feeling about what the words are trying to convey. This is true whether one is dealing with the *Tao-te-ching*, the prophet Amos, the *Bhagavad Gita*, or Aeschylus's *Agamemnon*. But this also encourages the personal proclivities of the translator to come into play. For example, scholars who personally favor clear rationality and distrust mysticism will try to see clear rational meanings wherever they can, while those who believe in the importance of ineffable mystical realities will feel these evoked by the text wherever this seems plausible.

This third factor also opens the door to what Waley calls "scriptural" as opposed to "historical" interpretations: translators to varying degrees trust their own personal sense of what is most edifying, inspirational, or true, as guides to the "deeper" or "inner" meaning underlying the words of the text, and use this instead of historical research as a guide to understanding what the text means. This is most clearly exemplified in the case of Bynner (1944) and Mitchell (1988). Neither has any knowledge of classical Chinese, neither pays much attention to historical scholarship about ancient China, and both freely insert interesting and inspirational lines in their translations that correspond to nothing in the Chinese text.

On the other hand, this is a matter of degree. One must keep in mind that all translations are bound to be influenced to some extent by each translator's intuitive feelings about the deeper meanings of the text, but that there is no plain and simple way of discovering what this deeper meaning is. This is perhaps the principal source of variations among translations, and it is due to a problem that does not admit of any easy solution. That is, readers tend to favor those translators whose sense of what a "deeper" or "truer" meaning might be matches their own. But one's own feeling about what is true, even if it is correct, cannot serve as *historical* evidence that the *Tao-te-ching's* authors meant to teach this truth. On the other hand, intuitive sympathy with the worldview of the *Tao-te-ching's* authors—if indeed it is a historically accurate sympathy with their actual worldview—is undoubtedly a great help in understanding the deeper meanings of the text.

The Transition from Chinese to English

The third issue translators have to make decisions on concerns how to make the transition from a Chinese text to an English text, another important source of differences among *Tao-te-ching* translations. There seem to be three principal problems:

1. Whether to stick as closely as possible to a word-for-word translation, or to use paraphrases or clarifying expansions to make the meaning of the text clearer
2. Whether to give translations that require readers to understand details about ancient Chinese culture, or to play these down to make it easier for the reader to apply the text to her own life
3. Whether to focus on conveying substantive thought, or to try also to capture the style and feeling of the original Chinese text

Word-for-word translation. Some modern readers may be under the impression that it would be possible, perhaps even easy, to do a completely transparent translation of the *Tao-te-ching*. The translator could simply translate every Chinese character into an exactly equivalent English word, and the resultant English sentences would bring every reader into clear, unmediated contact with the thought of the *Tao-te-ching*'s author(s), without interference from the mind of the translator. We have argued in the previous section that this is a mistaken impression. No one has immediate access to the mind of the *Tao-te-ching*'s authors, and every translation is to some extent based on conjectural understandings of what the translator thinks the text probably means.

Nonetheless, a translator can choose to stick as close as possible to a word-for-word translation,[9] and it will be useful here to discuss the possibility of this, and the extent to which translators have generally adhered to or departed from this ideal. First, it is true that the syntax of classical literary Chinese is in many respects similar to English syntax, apart from the fact that Chinese lacks articles, inflections, and tenses, and allows the omission of many implied connectives, such as personal and demonstrative pronouns. This means that many passages of the *Tao-te-ching* in fact allow something like a word-for-word Chinese-to-English translation that makes good sense. An example of this is the first two lines of chapter 44 in Mair's translation (1990):

> Name or person, which is nearer?
> Person or property, which is dearer?

All Mair has added here, which is not in the Chinese text, is an implied copula ("is"), and some punctuation marks. Otherwise he has just substituted English words for Chinese words, leaving the word order unchanged. ("Dearer" perhaps stretches the meaning of a Chinese word normally meaning "close," "nearby," but this meaning seems clearly implied here.)

Such word-for-word translation is not always possible, however. Sometimes, for example, a word-for-word translation would be hard to make sense of or read very awkwardly in English. For example, a word-for-word translation of a line in chapter 63 would go something like: "Plan difficult in its easiness." Addiss and Lombardo (1993) attempt something like a literal translation, "Map[10] difficult through easy." This would probably be somewhat difficult to make sense of for most English readers, and this is probably why Mair (like most other translators) abandons literal translation here and gives a longer English sentence that reads more smoothly and conveys well what seems the most probable meaning: "Undertake difficult tasks by approaching what is easy in them." In chapter 64, there is a line that would read in a word-for-word translation: "Do it in not-yet being." Addiss and Lombardo translate this, "Create before it exists," departing from the syntax of the Chinese and using the word "create," which stretches the normal meaning of *wei chih* ("do it") and opens up the line to many interpretations that are probably counter-indicated by the context. The context, in fact, suggests that the line means something like Mair's, "Act before there is a problem," although this translation is even further from a word-for-word rendering of the line.

For the sake of clarity, all translators at one time or another depart from literal translation and offer paraphrases or add clarifying expansions. Mair is giving a paraphrase, for example, when in chapter 48 he translates *wu-wei*, "nonaction" or "not doing," as "free of involvements." Translators typically add such clarifying expansions when they supply English words that have no correspondence in the Chinese in order to bring out more clearly what the translator thinks the text means. Many such expansions are relatively innocent—they merely make more clear and explicit what almost everyone agrees is implied. For example, Chan (1963a) translates the first line of chapter 18, "When the great Tao declined, the doctrine of humanity and righteousness arose." The words "the doctrine of" have no match in the Chinese. But this clarifying expansion does not seem to express any personal or controversial ideas that one could accuse Chan of reading into the text. It only makes explicit what almost all scholars agree is the meaning of the Chinese text—the line refers to the arising of the Confucian teaching about humanity and righteousness.

Not all clarifying expansions are as innocent and non-controversial as this one, however. Sometimes the text is unclear or ambiguous, and clarifying the text means also clearing up the uncertainties or ambiguities in a certain way favored by the translator. Among the scholarly translations considered here, Waley (1934) is perhaps the author who adds most to the text in the way of clarifying expansions. For example, in chapter 28, where the Chinese text has "he . . . becomes the ravine of [all] under heaven," he has "he . . . becomes like a ravine, accepting all things under heaven." The meaning of the ravine image is unclear when left by itself; Waley's translation, based on a parallel passage in the *Chuang-tzu*, clears it up by pointing to the way that things tend to fall down toward the bottom of ravines. But, of course, we cannot be sure that this is actually the main intent of the image. Similarly, Chen (1989) adds the word "like" to a line in chapter 16, in order to avoid what she considers an unlikely idea, that a person might become Heaven and Tao—she thinks that the text means that a person might become *like* Heaven and Tao, so she departs from her usual literal translation here and writes, "like Heaven . . . like Tao." Again, she may be right, but we cannot be sure—the author may mean to say that a person might become Heaven and Tao.

It is important here to note the fundamental difference between clarifying expansions by historian-scholars like Waley and Chan, on the one hand, and expansions by nonscholars like Bynner and Mitchell. Waley's clarifications are based on his extensive historical research and familiarity with ancient Chinese literature and thought. Bynner and Mitchell, on the other hand, add phrases and lines that correspond to nothing in the Chinese text, following their own intuitive feeling for truths they think the text hints at. For example, where the Chinese text of chapter 8 says literally "not competing so no blame," Mitchell has, "When you are content to be simply yourself and do not compare or compete, everybody will respect you." Where the text has "achieve success, withdraw self, Tao of Heaven" (ch. 9), Bynner has, "Do enough, without vying, be living not dying." Some of the added ideas here—be yourself rather than comparing yourself to others, devote yourself to "living"—are distinctively modern, and are not found elsewhere in the *Tao-te-ching*, or in ancient Chinese literature generally.

Historical versus modernizing rendition. A related issue is whether the translator will try to bring the reader back into the world of ancient China, or will try to bring the *Tao-te-ching* into the world of the modern reader. To illustrate, the Chinese text of chapter 46 of the *Tao-te-ching* describes a good, peace-loving country that gives saddle horses the more mundane but useful task of hauling manure, and contrasts it with a bad, war-loving country where people "raise war horses outside the towns." Understanding the imagery here requires projecting oneself back to a time when wars were fought on horseback, and in which most people valued saddle horses too much to wear them out hauling manure. Stephen Mitchell obviously wants to do all he can to make it easy for the reader to apply the text to modern conditions, so he substitutes here equivalent modern images: When a country is good "factories make trucks and tractors," and when a country is bad "warheads are stockpiled outside the cities."

Addiss and Lombardo also often strip the text of historically specific references to make it easier to relate to modern life. For example, in chapter 3, "not promoting the worthy" echoes a phrase found in contemporary Mohist and Confucian writings, "promote the worthy." This is advice that rulers should appoint officials on the basis of competence and merit rather than because of family connections or personal favoritism. Addiss and Lombardo translate, "do not glorify heroes"—a related thought, and one easier for modern readers to identify with.

Substance and style. Most writing not only expresses some substantive ideas, but through its style also conveys a certain feeling or flavor. Sometimes it is difficult for a translator to compose English sentences that both convey accurately the substantive ideas in the Chinese text of the *Tao-te-ching*, and also reflect the style and flavor of the original. So sometimes there is a choice between these two goals. The extremes here seem well represented by the contrast between Waley and Addiss and Lombardo. Waley explicitly says that he is abandoning any attempt to give a literary translation, providing instead a philological one, focused on "reproducing what the original says, with detailed accuracy" (1934, 14). His translation is indeed rather prosaic and inelegant in places.

Addiss and Lombardo, on the other hand, declare that they wish to "recreate much of the terse diction and staccato rhythm of the ancient Chinese" (1993, 16). Of course, there are some places at which, in order to make a flowing English sentence, one has to add words not in the Chinese. But this team offsets this in that very often they manage to use fewer English words than are contained in the Chinese. For example, in the opening line of chapter 2, they use three English words to render eight characters in Chinese. Because of this, their translation is probably better than most others in conveying in English something of the style and feeling of the original. Mair and Mitchell also have obviously taken care to present their translation in succinct but graceful English.

It is difficult to generalize about translations. General tendencies can be described, but no translator follows any given tendency with absolute consistency.[11] One way of characterizing translations, therefore, is by speaking of three general aims of translators, corresponding to three general desires on the part of readers.

1. A translator can stick as closely as possible to a literal translation. This will often produce English sentences that are unclear, ambiguous, and/or somewhat difficult to make sense of. This has the advantage of inviting the reader to participate in the act of making sense of the text, which after all remains uncertain in many parts. At the same time it may also encourage a scriptural rather than historical reading in that a reader unfamiliar with ancient China will tend to make sense of ambiguous sentences by reading ideas more familiar in modern culture into them. But, of course, many readers may prefer this to a more historically accurate understanding. The translations of Mair, Chen, Wu, and Wilhelm seem the most literal of the translations being considered here. Addiss and Lombardo also tend toward literal translation, although sometimes they use paraphrases that give the text a more modern ring, and sometimes omit Chinese words to make their translation more terse.

2. A scholar can compose a translation that offers the reader the results of his or her own research into ancient Chinese thought—that is, a translation like Waley's that generally aims to clear up potential ambiguities and uncertainties—and convey clearly to the reader what he or she thinks the text meant in its original context. The disadvantage here is that the reader becomes dependent on the translator's opinions and is accorded a more limited role in the process of making sense of the text. The advantage, for the reader unfamiliar with ancient Chinese culture, is that the translator's opinion about what the text meant to its original authors and audience is better informed, and probably on the whole more likely to be historically accurate, than that of a reader untrained in this field. The translations of Waley, Duyvendak, and LaFargue are examples of renditions that convey the translator's historical research into original meanings.

3. A translator can do his or her best to offer the reader intellectual stimulation or spiritual inspiration, presenting a translation that conveys the results of his or her own personal reflections or meditations on the text. The disadvantage of this is that the historical and cultural context of the original is largely lost and that the reader is presented with a highly personalized and modernized vision. On the other hand, it has the advantage of bringing an ancient document to the contemporary age, making its wisdom relevant today. Bynner and Mitchell are the best examples of this, frequently departing from literal translation, and from any historically plausible reconstruction of original meanings, to offer the reader what may well be genuinely good advice and inspiring thoughts.

Two Selected Passages

The following serves to illustrate the points made earlier, providing a detailed discussion of two short sections from the *Tao-te-ching* to show how different translators have chosen to deal with them. In each case, we give first the Chinese text, with alphabetical transliteration and a rough English equivalent underneath each character. Then various translations are presented, followed by explanatory notes on specific parts of the passage. The lines in question were not selected for their crucial role in understanding the text or its ideas, but because they serve well to illustrate some typical translation problems and strategies.

Chapter 4:1

道	沖	而	用	之	或	不	盈
tao	*ch'ung*	*erh*	*yung*	*chih*	*huo*	*pu*	*ying*
Tao	empty	and	use	it	seem	not	fill

Addiss   Tao is empty/ Its use never exhausted.
Bynner   Existence, by nothing bred,/ Breeds everything.
Chen   Tao is a whirling emptiness/ Yet in use is inexhaustible.
Ch'u   Tao, when put in use for its hollowness, is not likely to be filled
Duyvendak   The Way is like an empty vessel which, in spite of being used, is never filled.
Lau ('63)   The way is empty, yet use will not drain it.
Lau ('82)   The way is empty, yet when used there is something that does not make it full.
LaFargue   Tao being Empty,/ it seems one who uses it will lack solidity.
Lin   Tao is a hollow vessel,/ And its use is inexhaustible!
Mair   The Way is empty,/ Yet never refills with use.
Mitchell   The Tao is like a well:/ used but never used up.
Waley   The Way is like an empty vessel/ That yet may be drawn forever.

It seems impossible to offer a word-for-word translation of this line that would make sense in English. Following the understanding most translators prefer, the closest one might come would be something like, "Tao [is] empty but using it, [it would] seem not filled." Mair's and Chu's translations are maybe the most literal, but they are also the hardest to make sense of. Mair gives, "The Way is empty yet never refills with use." "Yet" suggests a contrast, but why would one expect something empty to be refilled with use? Ch'u's translation is open to the same objection: "Tao, when put into use for its hollowness, is not likely to be filled."

Waley, Lau, Chen, and Lin depart rather far from literal translation, and typically add the word "vessel," in order to convey the sense that they think this line has. They take it to mean that, although Tao appears empty, it is a kind of magical vessel from which one can keep on drawing without ever refilling it. Waley also adds "never *needs to be* filled," to give the statement this sense. Lin, Chen, and Addiss and Lombardo abandon literal translation entirely and convey the same basic idea by saying that Tao is "inexhaustible." Lau does the same by saying that "use will not *drain* it."

However, there is nothing in the Chinese text that says directly that the Tao is full or inexhaustible, or that it never *needs* filling. Chen justifies the inference by appealing to other passages in the text which do suggest that the Tao is inexhaustible (chs. 5, 45, 6, 35). She also justifies her addition of "*whirling* emptiness" on grounds first suggested by the modern Chinese commentator Kao Heng, that *ch'ung* can also mean "to agitate." She finds it attractive to draw on this alternate meaning of *ch'ung* because she thinks it is better to conceive of Tao as a dynamic emptiness.

Duyvendak's translation is similar to those above, but in his notes he explains that he arrived at this translation by a different route—he chose a different manuscript tradition, contained in a stone inscription made during the T'ang dynasty, which has *chiu* ("long," "lasting") instead of *huo* ("perhaps"). The last three words in this text would read literally "long-time not filled," which Duyvendak translates as "is never filled."

The Ma-wang-tui manuscripts also have a variation in the first line, *yu fu ying yeh*. Henricks comments on this by saying that the character *yu*, normally meaning "there is," is a known variant for *huo*, so that the two major editions do not substantially differ here. Lau, however, in his Ma-wang-tui translation (1982), takes the character *yu* in its common meaning. Taking *ying* as a transitive verb, "to make full," he translates the phrase as "there is something which it [Tao] does not make full." Pas, moreover, suggests that all extant texts are corrupt here and need emending, and that the Ma-wang-tui version gives the best clue from which to reconstruct the original. Instead of *yu fu ying*, "there is something that it does not fill," the original read *wu fu ying*, "there is nothing that it does not fill" (1990, 136).

LaFargue has a different solution to these problems. He suggests taking "seems not full" to refer not to Tao, but to people who "use" (internalize) Tao (as in ch. 35). A literal translation following this understanding would be, "Tao [being] empty, [one who] uses it seems not full." His translation is based partly also on his view that the word *ying* in the *Tao-te-ching* designates a quality of people, better translated as "solid," and is opposite to the quality "empty," which the *Tao-te-ching* wants people to cultivate (1992, 69). Hence LaFargue reads this line as a version of the saying in chapter 15, "One who keeps this Tao does not desire [to be] full."

One can see that Bynner and Mitchell are not struggling with difficulties in the Chinese here, but are trying to divine some meaning that attracts them, suggested by the other translators they are relying on. Bynner understands the first line to be about the origin of things, and understands "Tao" to be equivalent to "Existence" (understood as a metaphysical principle). The image of something not needing to be filled suggests to him the idea of an Existence-as-origin that does not itself have a prior origin: "Existence, by nothing bred,/ Breeds everything." Mitchell transforms Waley and Duyvendak's vessel-image into a well-image: "The Tao is like a well, used but not used up." Then characteristically he adds two lines that expand on this image to suggest an idea that (aside from picking up the word "empty" in the first line) corresponds to nothing in the Chinese: "It is like the eternal void: filled with infinite possibilities."

Chapter 13:1

寵	褥	若	驚	貴	大	患	若	身
ch'ung	ju	jo	ching	kuei	ta	huan	jo	shen
favor	disgrace	like	disturb	honor	great	trouble	like	body

Addiss	Favor and disgrace are like fear/ Honor and distress are like the self.
Bynner	Favor and disfavor have been called equal worries,/ Success and failure have been called equal ailments.
Chen	Accept honours and disgraces as surprises,/ Treasure great misfortunes as the body.
Lau ('82)	Favor is disgrace and is like being startled;/ Honor is a great trouble like your body.
Lin	Favor and disgrace cause one dismay;/ What we value and what we fear are within our Self.
Ch'u	Favor and disgrace are like fear;/ fortune and disaster are like our body.
Duyvendak	Favor and disgrace are both like goads;/ Value great disasters as your body.

Feng	Accept disgrace willingly./ Accept misfortune as the human condition.
Henricks	Regard favor and disgrace with alarm/ "Respect great distress as you do your own person."
LaFargue	Favor and disgrace: this means being upset/ high rank does great damage to your self.
Mair	Being favored is so disgraceful that it startles,/ Being honoured is an affliction as great as one's body.
Waley	Favor and disgrace goad as it were to madness;/ high rank hurts keenly as our bodies hurt
Wilhelm	Grace is as shameful as a fright./ Honour is a great evil like the persona.
Wu	Welcome disgrace as a pleasant surprise./ Prize calamities as your own body.

From a translator's point of view, this is one of the most difficult lines in the *Tao-te-ching*. The words themselves can be construed in various ways, and it is difficult to make sense of them in almost any construal. Duyvendak declares simply, "The text of this chapter is certainly corrupt. The first two sentences . . . cannot be construed in a satisfactory manner (1954, 43).[12]

The fact that the words can be construed in a number of different ways stems largely from two features of Chinese usage mentioned above: Conjunctions like "and" and auxiliary verbs like "is" are often implied but unexpressed, and Chinese lacks word-inflections so that the same word can serve either as a verb, adverb, adjective, or noun, depending on the context. Hence grammatically the first two words *ch'ung ju*, "favor disgrace," can plausibly be construed as

- Favor and disgrace (Waley, Lin, Chen, Ch'u, LaFargue, Duyvendak, Addiss and Lombardo)
- Favor is [a] disgrace (Lau, Wilhelm, Mair)
- [One should] favor (welcome) disgrace (Wu, Feng and English)

Similarly, in the second phrase, *kuei ta huan*, "honor great trouble," can be read:

- Honor and great trouble (Lin, Ch'u, Addiss and Lombardo)
- Honor is a great trouble (Waley, Lau, LaFargue, Mair, Wilhelm)
- [One should] honor (prize) great trouble (Wu, Chen, Feng and English, Henricks, Pas)

Another cause of variation is that *ching* in the first line has a wide range of meanings: "dismay, startled, surprise, fright, upset, alarm, worry, madness"—all plausible construals. Most translators give it a negative sense,[13] except for Wu, who translates: "Welcome disgrace as a pleasant surprise." (This understanding perhaps underlies Feng and English's otherwise puzzling "accept disgrace willingly.")

Perhaps the most difficult thing to make sense of in this line is the phrase *jo shen*, "like the self/body" (*shen* can refer either to the physical body or to the person as a whole). Waley, Lau, Wilhelm, and Mair understand this phrase to evoke the way in which having a body is troublesome (being honored is as troublesome as having a body). Alert to possible parallels in ancient India, Mair cites here in his notes a passage from the early Buddhist *Questions of King Milinda*, "The body . . . is like a wound" (1990, 115).[14] Wu, Chen, Duyvendak, and Henricks understand the phrase to evoke the fact that people prize their bodies (prize great troubles as you do your body). Ch'u and Addiss and Lombardo just leave the phrase ambiguous: honor and distress are like the body/self. Lin's "What we value and what we fear are *within our Self*," strays far from any plausible literal construal. The same can be said of Feng and English's "Accept misfortune as the human condition," and even more so Bynner's "success and failure [are] equal ailments." Mitchell apparently gave up entirely on this line, substituting for it the nice phrase, "hope is as hollow as fear," which bears no relation whatsoever to the Chinese text.

In his notes, Waley suggests a different solution to the puzzle about *jo shen*. He thinks that this passage is actually a quotation from a Yangist source, that is, from a group associated with the philosopher Yang Chu, who was noted for his view that one should not enter public service since public life was too anxiety-producing and thus damaging to one's health. Waley thinks that, in its original Yangist understanding, the character *jo* did not indicate "like" but replaced its homophone "your" (Karlgren 1957, 205). As a result, the phrase meant, "High rank is greatly detrimental to your body [health]." Waley thinks that the *Tao-te-ching*'s authors disagreed with this meaning and so rewrote *jo* as "like." But Waley's suggestion about the original Yangist understanding is the source of LaFargue's "high rank does great damage to your self."

Conclusion

The two passages discussed in detail here were chosen partly because they are unusually problematic and so illustrate some of the main problems translators face, as described in the earlier part of this essay. This ought not to leave the reader with the mistaken impression that such problems are characteristic of the entire *Tao-te-ching*. The vast majority of passages in the book, in fact, do not present anything like the difficulties and ambiguities that these two do. If one were to consider only fairly recent translations by linguistically and historically competent scholars— say those of Chan, Wu, Lau, Chen, Mair, LaFargue, and Henricks—one would probably find considerable consensus among them as to the basic meaning of some 80 percent of the book. We might hope that someday a team of scholars will come together to produce an annotated edition of the *Tao-te-ching* that at least points out those passages in which the basic meaning of the words and the fundamental syntax seem relatively clear and above controversy, while at the same time listing the most plausible alternatives for construing all those passages where word meanings and syntax are more problematic.

Notes

1. Knut Walf (1989) lists 83 English, 64 German, and 33 French translations.

2. Ho (1936) conveniently lists in parallel columns variant readings from about twenty of the principal manuscripts and stone inscriptions.

3. For example, many translators include a line in chapter 46— [Of] calamities none [is] greater than the desirable—contained in Ho-shang-kung and some other texts, but not in Wang Pi (see Chan 1963a, 181).

4. Even these numerous variants are seldom of much substantive significance. As Henricks notes, the Ma-wang-tui manuscripts "do not differ in any radical way from later versions of the text. . . . [T]here is nothing in [them] that would lead us to understand the philosophy of the text in a radically new way" (1989, xv). Mair, on the other hand, claims that the Ma-wang-tui manuscripts allowed him to "strip away the distortions and obfuscations of tradition" and "produce a totally new translation of the *Tao-te-ching* far more accurate and reliable than any published previously" (1990, xii). But he mentions no specific examples, so it is difficult to evaluate the basis for this claim.

5. Ma Hsü-lun is perhaps the most radical and influential of these. Duyvendak (1954, 3–4) has also drawn on the work of Kao Heng, and

Ch'u (1937, 9) has used a collation by Ch'en Chu of all the major text-critical studies of the *Tao-te-ching*.

6. A complete listing of duplicate sayings is given in LaFargue 1994, 594n25 (verbatim repetitions) and n. 26 (slightly different versions of the same saying).

7. Mitchell also shows occasional influence from these scholars, as for example in his omission of the middle section of chapter 4. Note also that the Chinese text of the *Tao-te-ching* currently available on the Internet at cnd.org. contains many emendations and rearrangements.

8. The following headlines examples were selected from a random look through the *Boston Sunday Globe* for November 5, 1995.

9. For readers desiring a word-for-word translation, the translations of Paul Carus and D. T. Suzuki (1913) and by Yi Wu (1989) contain the Chinese text with an English word next to each Chinese character. Unfortunately, the latter is already out of print, and the former often works with an unreliable Chinese text.

10. *T'u* as a verb usually means "to plan, scheme"; Addiss and Lombardo are drawing on its noun meaning, "map, diagram."

11. For example, Chen (1989) tends toward a highly literal translation, using her extensive notes to make the meaning clear. Sometimes, however, she departs from the literal translation when there is some important philosophical issue at stake for her. A case in point the phrase "recover life" in chapter 16: "Life" here is an unlikely translation of *ming*, which usually means "command," "commission," "destiny."

12. Lau similarly thinks that the text is corrupt and that *kuei* in the second sentence has crept in by mistake. He gives as one reason for this suspicion the fact that, without *kuei*, the two sentences would be more parallel, having four characters each. The line then would mean "great trouble is like one's body."

13. Waley cites a passage in *Kuo-yü* (Record of the States) 18, where the phrase *jo ching* seems to mean "beside oneself" with excitement: "Hearing of even one good deed, he was so excited that he was *jo ching*." Waley accordingly understands the first sentence to mean, "favor and disgrace (make a person) beside himself," although he understands "beside himself" in a negative sense as "madness."

14. A distinctive feature of Mair's approach to the *Tao-te-ching* is his idea that its authors were actually influenced by Indian thought, espe-

cially of the kind expressed in the *Bhagavad Gita* (1990, 140–61). He brings out the parallels most clearly in the foot notes. The present passage is one of the few places where these ideas obviously influence his translation.

References

Addiss, Stephen, and Stanley Lombardo. 1993. *Lao-tzu, Tao Te Ching*. Indianapolis: Hacket Publishing.

Bynner, Witter. 1944. *The Way of Life According to Lao tsu*. New York: Perigree.

Carus, Paul, and D. T. Suzuki, 1913. *The Canon of Reason and Virtue: Lao Tzu's Tao Teh King*. La Salle, Ill.: Open Court Publications.

Chan, Wing-tsit. 1963a. *The Way of Lao Tzu*. New York: Bobbs-Merrill.

———. 1963b. "The Natural Way of Lao Tzu." In *A Source Book in Chinese Philosophy*, ed. Wing-tsit Chan, 136–76. Princeton, N.J.: Princeton University Press.

Chen, Ellen Marie. 1989. *The Tao Te Ching: A New Translation with Commentary*. New York: Paragon House.

Ch'u Ta Kao. 1937. *Tao Te Ching*. London: Mandala Books. Reprinted Unwin Paperbacks, 1976.

Duyvendak, J. J. L. 1954. *Tao te ching: The Book of the Way and Its Virtue*. London: John Murray. Published in French in 1953.

Feng, Gia-Fu, and Jane English. 1977. *Lao Tsu Tao Te Ching*. New York: Vintage Books.

Graham, A. C. 1959. "Being in Western Philosophy Compared with Shih/Fei and Yu/Wu in Chinese Philosophy." *Asia Major* 7: 79–112.

Henricks, Robert. 1989. *Lao-Tzu Te-Tao Ching: A New Translation Based on the Recently Discovered Ma-Wang-tui Texts*. New York: Ballantine.

Ho Shih-chi. 1936. *Ku-pen Tao-te-ching hsiao-k'an*. Peking: National Peiping Academy.

Karlgren, Bernard. 1974. *Analytical Dictionary of Chinese and Sino-Japanese*. New York: Dover.

———. 1975. "Notes on Lao Tze." *Bulletin of the Museum of Far Eastern Antiquities*. 47: 1–13

LaFargue, Michael. 1992. *The Tao of the Tao Te Ching: A Translation and Commentary*. Albany: State University of New York Press.

———. 1994. *Tao and Method: A Reasoned Approach to the Tao Te Ching*. Albany: State University of New York Press.

Lattimore, David. 1978. "Introduction to The Way of Life according to Laotzu." In *The Works of Witter Bynner: The Chinese Translations*, 307–27. New York: Farrar, Straus, and Giroux.

Lau, D. C. 1963. *Lao Tzu Tao Te Ching*. Harmondsworth, England: Penguin Books.

———. 1982. *Chinese Classics: Tao Te Ching*. Hong Kong: Chinese University Press.

Lin, Paul J. 1977. *A Translation of Lao Tzu's Tao-te-ching and Wang Pi's Commentary*. Ann Arbor, Mich.: Center for Chinese Studies.

Lin Yutang. 1944. *The Wisdom of Laotse*. London: Michael Joseph.

Mair, Victor. 1990. *Tao Te Ching, the Classic Book of Integrity and the Way, Lao Tzu: An Entirely New Translation Based on the Recently Discovered Ma-Wang-Tui Manuscripts*. New York: Bantam.

Miles, Thomas H. 1992. *Tao Te Ching: About the Way of Nature and its Powers*. Garden City Park, N.Y.: Avery Publishing Group.

Mitchell, Stephen. 1988. *Tao Te Ching: A New English Version*. New York: Harper & Row.

Pas, Julian. 1990. "Recent Translations of the Tao-te ching," *Journal of Chinese Religions* 18: 127–41.

Robinet, Isabelle. 1977. *Les commentaires du Tao to king jusqu'au VIIe siècle*. Paris: Collège de France, Institut des Hautes Études Chinoises.

Schwartz, Benjamin. 1985. *The World of Thought in Ancient China*. Cambridge, Mass.: Harvard University Press.

Waley, Arthur. 1934. *The Way and Its Power: A Study of the Tao Te Ching and Its Place in Chinese Thought*. London: Allen & Unwin, 1934. Reprinted, New York: Grove Press, 1958.

Walf, Knut. 1989. *Westliche Taoismus-Bibliographie/Western Bibliography of Taoism*. Essen, Germany: Verlag die blaue Eule.

Welch, Holmes. 1957. *The Parting of the Way: Lao Tzu and the Taoist Movement*. Boston: Beacon Press.

Wilhelm, Richard. 1985. *Lao Tzu Tao Te Ching: The Book of Meaning and Life*. Translated by H. G. Ostwald. London: Routledge and Kegan Paul. First published in German in 1926.

Wu, John C. H. and Paul K. T. Sih. 1961. *Lao Tzu, Tao Teh Ching*. Asian Institute Translations, no. 1. New York: St. John's University Press.

Wu, Yi. 1989. *The Book of Lao Tzu (Tao Te Ching)*. San Francisco: Great Learning Publishing Company.

Zürcher, Erik. 1992. "Lao Tzu in East and West." In *Proceedings of the International Conference on Values in Chinese Societies*, 281–316. Taipei: Centre for Chinese Studies.

Appendix: Chronological List
of Major English *Tao-Te-Ching* Translations

1868   John Chalmers, *The Speculation on Metaphysics, Polity and Morality of "The Old Philosopher,"* Lao-tsze (London: Trubner).

1884   F. Henry Balfour, *Taoist Texts, Ethical, Political, and Speculative* (Shanghai: Kelly and Walsh).

1886   Herbert A. Giles, *The Remains of Lao Tzu* (London: John Murray).

1891   James Legge, *The Texts of Taoism* (London: Trubner & Co.).

1895   G. G. Alexander, *Lao-tsze: The Great Thinker with A Translation of His Thoughts on the Nature and Manifestation of God* (London: K. Paul, Trench, Trubner & Co.).

1898   Paul Carus, *Lao-tze's Tao-teh-king: Chinese and English with Introduction* (Chicago: Open Court Publications).

1904   Walter Gorn Old, *The Simple Way: Laotzu (The 'Old Boy')* (Madras: Theosophical Society).

1904   Lionel Giles, *The Sayings of Lao Tzu* (London: John Murray).

1905   C. Spurgeon Medhurst, *Tao Teh King: Sayings of Lao Tzu* (Wheaton, Ill.: Theosophical Press).

1913   Paul Carus and D. T. Suzuki, *The Canon of Reason and Virtue: Lao Tzu's Tao Teh King* (Chicago: Open Court Publications).

1919   Dwight Goddard, *Lao Tsu's Tao and Wu Wei* (New York: Brentano's.

1922   Isabella Mears, *Tao Teh King: By Lao Tzu* (New York: Theosophical Publication House).

1934   Arthur Waley, *The Way and Its Power: A Study of the Tao Te Ching and Its Place in Chinese Thought* (London: Allen and Unwin).

1937   Ch'u Ta-kao, *Tao Te Ching* (New York: Routledge Chapman & Hall).

1942   Lin Yutang, *The Wisdom of Laotse* (New York: Random House).

1944   Witter Bynner, *The Way of Life According to Laotzu* (New York: Perigree).

1946   Hermon Ould, *The Way of Acceptance: A New Version of Lao Tse's Tao Te Ching* (London: Andrew Dakers).

1954   J. J. L. Duyvendak, *Tao Te Ching: The Book of the Way and Its Virtue* (London: John Murray).

1955   R. B. Blakney, *The Way of Life: Lao Tsu* (New York: New American Library).

1958   Archie J. Bahm, *Tao Teh King: By Lao Tzu, Interpreted as Nature and Intelligence* (New York: F. Ungar).

1958   Eduard Erkes, *Ho-Shang-Kung's Commentary of Lao Tse* (Ascona: Artibus Asiae).

1961   John C. H. Wu, *Lao Tzu: Tao Teh Ching* (New York: St. John's University Press).

1961   Leon Hurvitz, "A Recent Japanese Study of Lao-tzu: Kimura Eiichi's *Roshi no shin kenkyu*" (*Monumenta Serica* 20: 311–67).

1963   Wing-tsit Chan, *The Way of Lao Tzu: Tao-te ching* (Indianapolis: Bobbs-Merrill).

1963   D. C. Lau, *Lao-tzu: Tao Te Ching* (New York: Penguin Books).

1975   Chang Chung-yuan, *Tao: A New Way of Thinking* (New York: Harper & Row).

1975   Bernard Karlgren, "Notes on Lao Tze." *Bulletin of the Museum of Far Eastern Antiquities* 47: 1–18.

1976   Stephen Skinner, *Alister Crowley's Tao Te King* (London: Askin Publishers).

1977   Ch'en Ku-ying, Rhett Y. W. Young, and Roger T. Ames, *Lao-tzu: Text, Notes and Comments* (San Francisco: Chinese Materials Center).

1977   Paul J. Lin, *A Translation of Lao-tzu's Tao-te-ching and Wang Pi's Commentary* (Ann Arbor: University of Michigan, Center for Chinese Studies Publications).

1977   Gia-fu Feng and Jane English, *Lao Tsu* (New York: Random House).

1979   Ariane Rump and Wing-tsit Chan, *Commentary on the Lao-tzu by Wang Pi* (Honolulu: University of Hawaii Press).

1982   D. C. Lau, *Chinese Classics: Tao Te Ching* (Hong Kong: Hong Kong University Press).

1985   Herrymon Maurer, *Tao, the Way of the Ways: Tao Te Ching* (New York: Schocken Books).

1988   Stephen Mitchell, *Tao Te Ching: A New English Version* (New York: Harper & Row).

1989   Robert Henricks, *Lao-Tzu: Te-Tao ching* (New York: Ballantine).

1989   Ellen Marie Chen, *Tao-te-ching: A New Translation* (New York: Paragon Books).

1989   Tsai-Chih Chung, Koh-Kok Kiang, and Wong-Lit Khiong, *The Sayings of Lao Zi* (Singapore: Asiapak Comic Series).

1990   Victor H. Mair, *Tao Te Ching: The Classic Book of Integrity and the Way* (New York: Bantam).

1990   Waldo Japussy, *The Tao of Meow* (Columbus, Ohio: Enthea Press).

1991   Thomas Cleary, *The Essential Tao: An Initiation into the Heart of Taoism through the Authentic Tao Te ching and the Inner Teachings of Chuang Tzu* (San Francisco: Harper SanFrancisco).

1991   Shi F. Huang, *Tao Teh Ching: The Taoists' New Library* (Taoism Publications).

1992   Michael LaFargue, *The Tao of the Tao-te-ching* (Albany: State University of New York Press).

1993   Ren Jiyu, *The Book of Laozi* (Beijing: Foreign Languages Press).

1993   Stephen Addiss and Stanley Lombardo, *Lao Tzu. Tao Te Ching* (Indianapolis: Hackett Publishing Company).

Appendix: Index to Citations from *Tao-te-ching* Chapters

Glossary

Ai T'ai-t'o (Ai Taituo)　哀駘佗
An-ch'i Sheng (Anqi Sheng)　安期生

ch'ang (chang)　常
chang-chü (zhangju)　章句
Chang Chung-ying (Zhang Zhongying)　張中英
Chang Liang (Zhang Liang)　張良
Chang Lu (Zhang Lu)　張路
Chang Tao-ling (Zhang Daoling)　張道陵
Chao Chih-chien (Zhao Zhijian)　超志堅
Chao Ping-wen (Zhao Bingwen)　趙秉文
Chao Shih-an (Zhao Shi'an)　趙實庵
Chen (Zhen)　眞
Ch'en Ching-yuan (Chen Jingyuan)　陳景元
Ch'eng Hsuan-ying (Cheng Xuanying)　成玄英
Cheng-yi (Zhengyi)　正一
Ch'en Hsiang-ku (Chen Xianggu)　陳象古
Chen-kao (*Zhengao*)　眞誥
Chen Luan (Zhen Luan)　甄鸞
ch'i (qi)　氣
Chiang Mu (Jiang Mu)　姜慕
chieh (jie)　介
Chieh-chieh (*Jiejie*)　節解
Chieh Yü (Jie Yu)　接輿
Chien-k'ang (Jiankang)　建康
Chih (Zhi)　之
Chih Ch'ien (Zhi Qian)　支謙
chih-kuo chih-shen (zhiguo zhishen)　治國治身
Ch'ih-sung-tzu (Chisongzi)　赤松子
Ch'ih-yu (Chiyou)　蚩尤
ching (jing)　經
Ch'ing-ching-ching (*Qingjing jing*)　清靜經
Ching-miao (Jingmiao)　靜妙
ch'ing-tan (qingtan)　清談

305

Ch'ing-yang-kung (Qingyang gong)   青羊宮
Ch'in Shih (Qin Shi)   秦失
Chin-shu (*Jinshu*)   晉書
chiu (jiu)   久
Ch'iu (Qiu)   丘
ch'iung-ch'i (qiongqi)   窮奇
Chou-yi lüeh-li (*Zhouyi lueli*)   周易略理
Ch'üan-chen (Quanzhen)   全眞
Chuang Chou (Zhuang Zhou)   莊周
Chuang-tzu (*Zhuangzi*)   莊子
Chu-jung (Zhurong)   祝融
Ch'un-ch'eng-tzu (Chunchengzi)   春成子
chung (zhong)   中
Ch'ung-hsuan (Chongxuan)   重玄
Chung-kuo wen-wu pao (*Zhongguo wenwu bao*)   中國文物報
Chung-yung (*Zhongyong*)   中庸
Chu Po-hsiu (Zhu Boxiu)   諸伯休
Ch'ü Po-yü (Qu Boyu)   蘧伯玉
Ch'u-tz'u (Chuci)   楚辭
Chü Yuan (Qu Yuan)   屈原

fan (fan)   反
fang-shih (fangshi)   方士
fa tzu-jan (fa ziran)   法自然
fo-hsiang (foxiang)   佛像
Fo-tao lun-heng (*Fodao lunheng*)   佛道論衡
Fu Hsi (Fu Xi)   伏羲
fu-ming (fuming)   復命

Han-fei-tzu (*Hanfeizi*)   韓非子
Han-shih wai-chuan (*Hanshi waizhuan*)   韓詩外傳
Han-shu (*Hanshu*)   漢書
heng (heng)   恆
Ho-ming-shan (Heming shan)   鶴鳴山
Ho-shang-kung (Heshang gong)   河上公
Hou (Hou)   候
Hou Han-shu (*Hou Hanshu*)   後漢書
Hsiang-erh (*Xianger*)   想爾
Hsiang Hsiu (Xiang Xiu)   向秀
Hsiao-ching (*Xiaojing*)   孝經
Hsiao-tao-lun (*Xiaodao lun*)   笑道論
hsing (xing)   性

hsin-shan-yuan (xin shan yuan)　心善淵
Hsi-sheng-ching (*Xisheng jing*)　西昇經
Hsi-tz'u (*Xici*)　繫辭
Hsiu Hsiu-an (Xiu Xiu'an)　休休庵
hsü (xu)　虛
Hsuan-hsueh (Xuanxue)　玄學
Hsuan-miao nei-p'ien (*Xuanmiao neipian*)　玄妙內篇
Hsuan-miao yü-nü (Xuanmiao yunü)　玄妙玉女
hsuan-p'in (Xuanpin)　玄牝
Hsuan-tsung (Xuanzong)　玄宗
Hsü Chia (Xu Jia)　徐甲
Hsün-tzu (Xunzi)　荀子
hua-hu (huahu)　化胡
Hua-hu-ching (*Huahu jing*)　化胡經
Huang-Lao (Huang-Lao)　黃老
Huang-ti (Huangdi)　黃帝
Hui Shih (Hui Shi)　惠施
Hui-tsung (Huizong)　徽宗
hun (hun)　魂
Hun-yuan chen-lu (*Hunyuan zhenlu*)　混元眞錄

jen (ren)　仁

K'ai-t'ien-ching (*Kaitian jing*)　開天經
K'an (Kan)　坎
Kao-shang lao-tzu nei-chuan (*Gaoshang laozi neizhuan*)　高上老子
　內傳
Keng (Geng)　耕
Keng-sang-ch'u (Gengsang Chu)　庚桑楚
Ko Ch'ao-fu (Ge Chaofu)　葛巢甫
Ko Hung (Ge Hong)　葛洪
K'ou Ch'ien-chih (Kou Qianzhi)　寇謙之
Kuang-ch'eng-tzu (Guangchengzi)　廣成子
Kuan-tzu (Guanzi)　管子
Kuan-yin-tzu (*Guanyinzi*)　關尹子
K'uei Ching-shu (Kui Jingshu)　夔靖叔
Ku Huan (Gu Huan)　顧歡
K'ung-tzu chia-yü (Kongzi jiayu)　孔子家語
K'un-lun (Kunlun)　崑崙
kuo (guo)　國
Kuo Hsiang (Guo Xiang)　郭象
ku-shen (gushen)　谷神

Lao-chün chieh-ching (*Laojun jiejing*)　老君戒經
Lao-chün ching-lü (*Laojun jinglü*)　老君經律
Lao-chün pa-shih-yi hua t'u-shuo (*Laojun bashiyi hua tushuo*)　老君
　八十一化圖說
Lao-chün ts'un-ssu-t'u (*Laojun cunsi tu*)　老君存思圖
Lao-chün yin-sung chieh-ching (*Laojun yinsong jiejing*)　老君音誦戒
　經
Lao-lai-tzu (Laolaizi)　老萊子
Lao Tan (Lao Dan)　老聃
Lao-tzu (Laozi)　老子
Lao-tzu chang-chü (*Laozi zhangju*)　老子章句
Lao-tzu chih-lüeh (*Laozi zhilue*)　老子旨略
Lao-tzu chung-ching (*Laozi zhongjing*)　老子中經
Lao-tzu hua-hu-ching (*Laozi huahu jing*)　老子化胡經
Lao-tzu k'ao-yi (*Laozi kaoyi*)　老子考異
Lao-tzu-ming (*Laozi ming*)　老子銘
Lao-tzu nei-chieh (*Laozi neijie*)　老子內解
Lao-tzu pien-hua ching (*Laozi bianhua jing*)　老子變化經
li (li, principle)　理
li (li, ritual)　禮
Li (Li, name)　李
Li Ao (Li Ao)　李翱
Li-chi (*Liji*)　禮記
Li Chieh (Li Jie)　李解
lieh (Lie, split)　裂
lieh (Lie, burn)　烈
Lieh-hsien-chuan (*Liexian zhuan*)　列仙傳
Li Erh (Li Er)　李耳
Li Jung (Li Rong)　李榮
Ling-pao (*Lingbao*)　靈寶
Lin Hsi-yi (Lin Xiyi)　林希逸
Li-sao (Lisao)　離騷
Li T'an-hsin (Li Tanxin)　李曇信
Liu Hsiang (Liu Xiang)　劉向
Liu Pang (Liu Bang)　劉邦
Liu-t'ao (*Liutao*)　六韜
Liu Wei-yung (Liu Weiyong)　劉惟永
Li Yueh (Li Yue)　李約
Lou-kuan (Louguan)　樓觀
Lu Chiu-yuan (Lu Jiuyuan)　陸九淵
Lu Hsi-sheng (Lu Xisheng)　陸希聲
Lu Hsiu-ching (Lu Xiujing)　陸修靜

Lü Hui-ch'ing (Lü Huiqing)　呂惠卿
Lun-yü (Lunyu)　論語
Lü-shih ch'un-ch'iu (Lüshi chunqiu)　呂氏春秋
Lu Te-ming (Lu Deming)　陸德明

Ma-wang-tui (Mawangdui)　馬王堆
Meng Su (Meng Su)　盟蘇
Meng-tzu (Mengzi)　孟子
Miao-chen-ching (Miaozhen jing)　妙眞經
mieh (mie)　滅
ming (ming, name)　名
ming (ming, mandate)　命
ming (ming, understand)　明
Mo-tzu (Mozi)　墨子

Nan-jung Ch'u (Nanrong Chu)　南榮趎
nan-kuan (nanguan)　男官
Nan-shih (Nanshi)　南史
nei-tan (neidan)　內丹
Niu Miao-ch'uan (Niu Miaochuan)　牛妙傳
Ni-wan (Niwan)　泥丸
nü-kuan (nüguan)　女官

Pai Yü-ch'an (Bai Yuchan)　白玉蟾
pang (bang)　邦
Pao-p'u-tzu (Baopuzi)　抱樸子
P'eng Ssu (Peng Si)　彭耜
Pien-cheng-lun (Bianzheng lun)　辨正論
Pien Shao (Bian Shao)　邊韶
pi-hsieh (bixie)　辟邪
p'o (po)　魄
Po-yang (Boyang)　伯陽

San-chiao-lun (Sanjiao lun)　三敎論
San-huang (Sanhuang)　三皇
San-t'ai-ching (Santai jing)　三台經
San-t'ien nei-chieh ching (Santian neijie jing)　三天內解經
San-tung chu-nang (Sandong zhunang)　三洞珠囊
Seng-chao (Sengzhao)　僧肇
Seng-shun (Sengshun)　僧順
Shan (Shan, good)　善
Shan (Shan, repair)　繕

Shang-ch'ing (Shangqing)　上清
Shao Jo-yü (Shao Ruoyu)　紹若愚
shen (shen, body)　身
shen (shen, spirit)　神
Shen-hsien-chuan (Shenxian zhuan)　神仙傳
Shen-nung (Shennong)　神農
shih (shi)　勢
Shih-ch'eng Ch'i (Shicheng Qi)　士成綺
Shih-chi (Shiji)　史記
Shih-chieh-ching (Shijie jing)　十戒經
Shih-ching (Shijing)　詩經
Shih Fa-lin (Shi Falin)　釋法琳
shih-san (shisan)　十三
Shih san-p'o-lun (Shi sanpo lun)　釋三破論
Shih-tsu (Shizu)　始祖
Shih Yung (Shi Yong)　石雍
shou (shou)　壽
Shu-hsueh pu-yi (Shuxue buyi)　述學補遺
Shuo-kua (Shuogua)　說卦
Shuo-yuan (Shuoyuan)　說苑
Ssu-ma Ch'eng-chen (Sima Chengzhen)　司馬承禎
Ssu-ma Ch'ien (Sima Qian)　司馬遷
Ssu-ma Kuang (Sima Guang)　司馬光
Su Ch'e (Su Che)　蘇撤
Sui-jen (Suiren)　燧人
Sui-shu (Suishu)　隨書
Sun Teng (Sun Deng)　孫登
Su Tung-p'o (Su Dongpo)　蘇東坡

Ta-hsueh (Daxue)　大學
T'ai-p'ing (Taiping)　太平
T'ai-p'ing kuang-chi (Taiping guangji)　太平廣記
T'ai-shang hsuan-yuan tao-te-ching (Taishang xuanyuan daode jing)
　太上玄元道德經
T'ai-shang lao-chün (Taishang laojun)　太上老君
T'ai-tsu (Taizu)　太祖
T'ai-tzu jui-ying pen-ch'i ching (Taizi ruiying benqi jing)　太子瑞應本
　起經
T'ai-wei-ching (Taiwei jing)　太微經
Tan (Dan, Astrologer)　儋
Tan (Dan, Lao-tzu)　耽
Tang-jan (Dangran)　當染
Tao (Dao)　道

T'ao-chai tsang shih-chi (Taozhai zang shiji)　陶齋藏石記

tao-hsiang (daoxiang)　道像

T'ao Hung-ching (Tao Hongjing)　陶弘景

Tao-lun (Daolun)　道論

tao-min (daomin)　道民

tao-shih (daoshi)　道士

Tao-te chen-ching hsü-chueh (Daode zhenjing xujue)　道德眞經序訣

Tao-te-ching (Daode jing)　道德經

T'ao yin-chü nei-chuan (Tao yinju neizhuan)　陶隱居內傳

Ta-ssu-ming (Da siming)　大司命

te (de, virtue)　德

te (de, attain)　得

Teng Yi (Deng Yi)　鄧錡

te-shan (deshan)　得善

te-shan (deshan)　德善

T'ien-shih (Tianshi)　天師

T'ien-t'ai (Tiantai)　天台

T'ien-yin-tzu (Tianyinzi)　天隱子

tsai (zai)　載

Tseng-tzu-wen (Zengzi wen)　曾子問

Ts'ui Hao (Cui Hao)　催浩

Tsung-mi (Zongmi)　宗密

Ts'ung-shu chi-ch'eng (Congshu jicheng)　叢書集成

t'u (tu)　圖

Tu Ch'ung-? (Du Chong?)　杜崇？

Tu Kuang-t'ing (Du Guangting)　杜光庭

Tung (dong)　東

Tung Ssu-ching (Dong Sijing)　董思靖

Tu Tao-chien (Du Daojian)　杜道堅

tzu (zi, self)　自

tzu (zi, master)　子

Tzu-hsia (Zixia)　子夏

tzu-jan (ziran)　自然

Tzu-kung (Zigong)　子貢

Tzu-lu (Zilu)　子路

Tz'u-yi wu-lao pao-ching (Ciyi wulao baojing)　雌一五老寶經

Wang An-shih (Wang Anshi)　王安石

Wang Ch'un (Wang Chun)　王淳

Wang Chung (Wang Zhong)　王中

Wang Nien-sun (Wang Niansun)　王念孫

Wang P'ang (Wang Pang)　王雱

Wang Pi (Wang Bi)　王弼

Wang Tao-yi (Wang Daoyi)　王道義
Wei-shu (Weishu)　魏書
Wei Wen-lang (Wei Wenlang)　魏文朗
Wen-hsin tiao-lung (Wenxin diaolong)　文心調龍
Wen-shih nei-chuan (Wenshi neizhuan)　文始內傳
Wen-shuang-tzu (Wenshuangzi)　溫爽子
wu (wu)　無
Wu Ch'eng (Wu Cheng)　吳澄
Wu-ch'ien-wen (Wuqian wen)　五千文
Wu-ch'ien-wen ch'ao-yi (Wuqian wen chaoyi)　五千文朝儀
Wu-shang pi-yao (Wushang biyao)　無上秘要
wu-ssu (wusi)　無私
wu-wei (wuwei)　無爲

Yang (Yang)　陽
Yang Chih-jen (Yang Zhiren)　楊智仁
Yang Chu (Yang Zhu)　楊朱
Yang Hsi (Yang Xi)　楊羲
Yang Tzu-chü (Yang Ziju)　陽子居
Yao Ch'ang (Yao Chang)　姚萇
Yao Po-to (Yao Boduo)　姚伯多
Yao Yi-chung (Yao Yizhong)　姚弋仲
Yen Tsun (Yan Zun)　嚴遵
yi (yi)　義
Yi-ching (Yijing)　易經
Yi-hsia-lun (Yixia lun)　夷夏論
ying (ying)　營
Yin Hsi (Yin Xi)　尹喜
Yin T'ung (Yin Tong)　尹通
yu (you)　有
Yu (You)　幽
Yü (Yu)　魚
Yuan-shih t'ien-tsun (Yuanshi tianzun)　元始天尊
Yuan-yang-ching (Yuanyang jing)　元陽經
Yü Ch'ing-chung (Yu Qingzhong)　喻清中
yu-ch'iu (youqiu)　幽求
Yü-lan-p'en ching (Yulanpen jing)　盂蘭盆經
Yu-lung-chuan (Youlong zhuan)　猶龍傳
Yün-chi ch'i-ch'ien (Yunji qiqian)　雲笈七籤
Yung-ch'eng-tzu (Yongchengzi)　容成子
Yung-lo ta-tz'u-tien (Yongle da cidian)　永樂大辭典
yu-wei (youwei)　有爲

Contributors

William H. Baxter is associate professor at the University of Michigan, Ann Arbor. His specialization is the linguistic study of ancient Chinese and he has published widely in this area. His major work to date is *A Handbook of Old Chinese Phonology, Trends in Linguistics: Studies and Monographs* (Berlin: Mouton de Gruyter, 1992).

Alan K. L. Chan, a graduate of the University of Toronto, is senior lecturer of Philosophy at the National University of Singapore. He specializes in the philosophical study of medieval Taoism and has published prominently on Lao-tzu commentaries. He has written *Two Visions of the Way: A Study of the Wang Pi and the Ho-shang-kung Commentaries on the Laozi* (SUNY Press, 1991), and is the co-author of *Taoism: Outlines of a Chinese Religious Tradition* (Singapore, 1994).

A. C. Graham, at the time of his untimely death in 1991, was professor emeritus of Classical Chinese at the School of Oriental and African Studies, University of London, and a fellow of the British Academy. A world-renowned specialist of early Chinese thought, he translated and edited numerous classical works, including the *Chuang-tzu, Lieh-tzu, Mo-tzu*, and many others more. Among his major publications are *Chuang-tzu: Textual Notes to a Partial Translation* (London: School of Oriental and African Studies, University of London, 1982), and *Disputers of the Tao: Philosophical Argument in Ancient China* (La Salle, Ill.: Open Court Publishing, 1989).

Julia M. Hardy is former assistant professor at Hobart and William Smith College in Geneva, N.Y., now pursuing her research in Kobe, Japan. Her research concerns the reception of Eastern religious traditions in America, especially Taoism and Chinese religions. Her dissertation, from Duke University, is entitled "Archaic Utopias in the Modern Imagination."

Livia Kohn received her doctorate from the University of Bonn, Germany, in 1980, and completed a Habilitation degree at the University of Goettingen in 1990. She was an overseas student at the University of

California at Berkeley and spent many years as a research fellow at the Institute for Research in Humanities of Kyoto University, Japan. She is currently serving as asssociate professor of Religious Studies at Boston University and visiting professor at the Kyoto Center for Japanese Studies of Stanford University. Her major works include *Early Chinese Mysticism: Philosophy and Soteriology in the Taoist Tradition* (Princeton, 1992), *The Taoist Experience: An Anthology* (SUNY Press, 1993), and *Laughing at the Tao: Debates Among Buddhists and Taoists in Medieval China* (Princeton, 1995).

Yoshiko Kamitsuka, a graduate of Tokyo University, is associate professor at Nagoya University. She specializes in the study of medieval Taoist scriptures and thought, focusing especially on the texts of Highest Clarity, both from the Six Dynasties and T'ang. She has published many works, among which articles on Wu Yun, Ssu-ma Ch'eng-chen, the *Chen-kao*, and the Taoist vision of demon kings are most prominent. Her most recent work is a Japanese translation of the *Agamas* (Tokyo: Hirakawa, 1995).

Michael LaFargue is Lecturer in Religion and Philosophy, and Director of East Asian Studies at the University of Massachusetts, Boston. He was trained in biblical hermeneutics at Harvard Divinity School, and specializes in the application of methods developed in biblical studies to the study of pre-Han Taoist and Confucian texts. Ha has published a book on methodology in *Tao-te-ching* interpretation (*Tao and Method: A reasoned apporach to the Tao Te Ching*. SUNY Press, 1994), and his results are summarized in his translation and systematic commentary (*The Tao of the Tao Te Ching*. SUNY Press, 1992).

Liu Xiaogan, a graduate and former associate professor of Beijing University, is senior lecturer of Chinese at the National University of Singapore. He specializes in the philological and philosophical study of early Taoism and has published mainly on the *Chuang-tzu*, including his prominent *Classifying the Zhuangzi Chapters* (University of Michigan Press, 1994).

Julian Pas is professor emeritus of religion at the University of Sasketchewan, Saskatoon. He was trained in Christian theology in Belgium and in Chinese studies in Taiwan and at McMaster University, Ontario. His areas of specialization include medieval Chinese Buddhism and contemporary popular religion, and he served for many years as the editor of the *Journal of Chinese Religions*. His most recent book is *Visions of Sukhavati: Shan-tao's Commentary on the Kuan wu-liang-shou fo-ching* (SUNY Press, 1995).

Isabelle Robinet, professor of ancient and medieval Chinese history at the Universite de Provence in Aix-en-Provence, is a renowned specialist of Taoism and Chinese thought and cosmology. Her major work on the meditative practices of Taoism was published in English under the title *Taoist Meditation* (SUNY Press, 1993). Her two most recent books are *Histoire du Taoisme: Des origins au XIVe siècle* (1991) and *Introduction à l'alchimie intérieure taoiste: De l'unité et de la multiplicité* (1995), both from Editions Cerf, Paris.

Benjamin Schwartz recently retired as Leroy B. Williams Professor of History and Political Science at Harvard University. A world-renowned specialist in his field, he has covered Chinese intellectual history from the beginnings to the twentieth century. His works are numerous, but outstanding among them is *The World of Thought in Ancient China* (Harvard University Press, 1985).

Index